D1297948

COMPUTERS
&
INFORMATION PROCESSING

Gerald A. Silver
Los Angeles City College

Myrna L. Silver

1817

HARPER & ROW, PUBLISHERS, New York
Cambridge, Philadelphia, San Francisco,
London, Mexico City, São Paulo, Singapore, Sydney

Sponsoring Editor: Fred Henry
Development Editor: Mary Lou Mosher
Project Editor: David Nickol
Text Design: Edward A. Butler
Cover Design: Edward A. Butler
Cover Illustration: Roy Wiemann
Text Art: Vantage Art, Inc.
Photo Research: Linda Lilienfeld/Kevin A. Wayne
Production: Willie Lane
Compositor: Black Dot, Inc.
Printer and Binder: Kingsport Press

Computers & Information Processing

Library of Congress Cataloging-in-Publication Data

Silver, Gerald A.
    Computers & information processing.

    Includes index.
    1. Computers.   2. Electronic data processing.
I. Silver, Myrna.   II. Title.
QA76.S5175   1986   004   85-17625
ISBN 0-06-046159-4

85 86 87 88 9 8 7 6 5 4 3 2 1

Contents in Brief

Contents in Detail

José A Colón

PART TWO   COMPUTER HARDWARE

2

PART THREE   MICROCOMPUTER SYSTEMS

PART FOUR   COMMUNICATIONS AND INFORMATION SYSTEMS

PART FIVE   SOFTWARE AND PROGRAM DESIGN

5

PART SIX   INFORMATION SYSTEMS IN ACTION

7 PART SEVEN COMPUTERS AND THE FUTURE

To the Instructor

Computers & Information Processing is designed for the introduction to computers course that is offered in almost every college in the country. It is a one-semester course, open to majors and nonmajors alike, without prerequisites. Students with an enormous diversity of backgrounds and from all disciplines—business, liberal arts, science, you name it—enroll in the course.

How do you go about selecting the right text for this course, and for the students who will be taking it? What do you look for? Here are just some of the significant and distinctive features of *Computers & Information Processing* that we believe will make it the clear first choice for your introductory students. The sound and practical reasons why you should adopt it include:

1. *State of the art topical coverage*. The material presented is current and represents state of the art information. Included are discussions of robotics, artificial intelligence, expert computers, decision support systems, local area networks, voice synthesis, and voice recognition output. These are only a few of the topics that will help your students stay on top of this rapidly changing discipline.

2. *Extensive microcomputer coverage*. This book presents two complete chapters devoted exclusively to microcomputer hardware and software. They explain to students the fundamentals of word processing, data base, spread sheet, graphics, and communications software. Microcomputers are also integrated throughout the text. In spite of the microcomputer's significance, many other texts do not give as much space to this material, and some do not include full chapters on it.

3. *Developed with the comments and suggestions of many instructors*. The original manuscript was thoroughly reviewed by dozens of instructors and written comments from hundreds of others were carefully considered in assembling the material for this book. In addition, focus sessions were held with instructors, and their comments and suggestions were also integrated in the developmental process.

4. *Visual and graphic treatment of subject matter*. All photographs, drawings, and figures have been carefully conceived to complement the text and are integrated into the text discussions, unlike many other books, where often pictures have been added to serve merely a decorative purpose.

5. *A direct, interesting, and easy-to-understand writing style.* As an instructor, you understand the need for a book that is well written and stands on its own. We have written numerous successful textbooks. When you adopt this book you will find that it answers many of the students' questions. This reduces the need to spend precious classroom time going over material that should be learned by simply reading the text.

6. *Information directly from industry and primary research sources.* Since the facts and figures in this book were acquired from leading data research organizations, all tables and statistics are the most current available. You are thus assured of current and accurate information for the classroom.

7. *A most extensive support package.* Many instructors stressed to us the importance of having the complete support package with the text. We have listened! When you adopt this book, you will find that the support package arrives with the book and contains two language supplements, a computerized test bank, an applications software package, full-color transparencies, and an author-written instructor's manual, as well as a useful study guide for the student in both printed and computer interactive form.

ORGANIZATION OF THE TEXT

Part One introduces the computer age, describes the expanding use of computers and their general characteristics, and covers something of their history.

Part Two discusses computer hardware and the technology behind these electronic marvels. The discussion moves from a survey of fundamental concepts in Chapter 3 to principles of data input, the central processing unit, secondary storage, and output.

Part Three explores the rapidly expanding world of microcomputers. Two complete chapters are devoted to microcomputer hardware and software. These treat some of the latest software now on the market and discuss operating systems in a form that is understandable to the average student. The rapidly growing technologies of data communications and information systems are discussed in Part Four, with coverage of distributed data processing networks, data communications principles, data base usage, and management information systems.

Part Five presents a systematic discussion of software and program design. It shows the student how programs are planned and designed. The principles of flowcharting and programming logic are covered, with emphasis on structured programming concepts. Chapter 14 reviews the major programming languages, giving examples and comparative information to help the student assess language applications.

Part Six discusses the automated office and systems analysis and design.

Part Seven speaks directly to the student about careers and job opportunities in the computer industry. In the final chapter a balanced view of major social issues is presented to help the student grasp the changes computers are bringing to society. The topics of artificial intelligence, robotics, voice recognition, voice synthesis, CAD/CAM, and color graphics are explained with liberal illustrations.

Appendix A introduces BASIC language programming. It is included for students who will be exposed to BASIC in a computer laboratory. BASIC language statements are explored with examples and illustrations. The appendix is based on Microsoft BASIC, one of the most prevalent versions of the language. Alternate versions of Appendix A in Pascal and in COBOL are available separately.

Appendix B describes data representation and computer arithmetic for students who wish to acquire a grasp of this material.

An extensive glossary of key terms is included. The glossary defines the terms used throughout this book in an accurate, easy-to-understand manner.

SUPPLEMENTS PACKAGE

A full support package of supplements is available. The items include:

- STUDY GUIDE. Each chapter of the *Study Guide* lists the chapter learning objectives, and restates the chapter summary and key terms sections. Student self-tests include matching questions (key terms and their definitions), 15 multiple-choice questions, 20 true-false questions, and 10 completion questions. Answers are given at the end of each chapter. The *Study Guide* was written by the Silvers.

- STUDY AID. *Study-Aid* is a fully interactive computerized version of the *Study Guide*. An order card is inserted at the end of this book.

- INSTRUCTOR'S KIT. The Instructor's Resource Manual is a hardback, three-hole-punched folder that can be customized to include, depending on the needs and preference of the instructor, any or all of the following:

  - INSTRUCTOR'S MANUAL. In the *Instructor's Manual*, for each chapter there are learning objectives, a chapter overview, lecture guidelines, answers to the chapter-end text exercises with the questions restated, notes on how to use the boxed feature material as lecture launchers, suggested teaching resources, and a list of key terms with definitions from the text glossary. The *Instructor's Manual* was written by the Silvers.

  - TEST BANK. The *Test Bank* consists of upwards of 2,500 objective questions in a printed form. It was prepared by Herbert Bomzer and Frank Shu of Fordham University.

  - OVERHEAD TRANSPARENCIES. A package of 72 transparencies, 64 in full-color, contains key line illustrations and tables from the text.

  - COBOL SUPPLEMENT. The *COBOL Supplement* supplies the COBOL equivalent of the BASIC appendix in the text for those whose language of choice in this course is COBOL. It was prepared by Roger Lamprey of Valdosta State College.

  - PASCAL SUPPLEMENT. The *Pascal Supplement* supplies the Pascal equivalent of the BASIC appendix in the text for those whose language of choice is Pascal. It was prepared by Roger Lamprey of Valdosta State College.

- MICROTEST. *Microtest* is Harper & Row's computerized testing system. The questions in the test bank are available on floppy disks for use in an IBM PC, IBM XT, and most IBM compatible computers, or the Apple II family of computers. The Microtest system allows the instructor to add, delete, or alter questions at will, as desired.

- APPLICATIONS SOFTWARE. Developed especially for this text, the applications software consists of a survey of the four major families of applications software: word processing, graphics, spreadsheets, and data base management. It, too, is available in Apple or IBM versions.

ACKNOWLEDGMENTS

The authors wish to thank the following reviewers who have provided valuable input for the text. Their suggestions, comments, and critiques of the text and illustrations have been of immeasurable aid in preparing this book.

John C. Beers
Rockland Community College

Herbert W. Bomzer
Fordham University

William L. Bonney
Hudson Valley Community College

Larry Buch
Milwaukee Area Technical College

Laura Cooper
College of the Mainland

Jerry Elam
St. Petersburg Junior College

Enid Erwin
Santa Monica College

Clinton P. Fuelling
Ball State University

Jean Longhurst
William Rainey Harper Community College

W. Leon Pearce
Drake University

Robert Ralph
Fayetteville Technical Institute

Maria S. Rynn
Northern Virginia Community College

Alice Schamber
North Iowa Area Community College

Alfred St. Onge
Springfield Technical Community College

Timothy Stebbings
Barrington College

Ronald Teichman
Pennsylvania State University

Richard Westfall
Cabrillo College

Charles Williams
Georgia State University

Wayne M. Zage
Purdue University

A major undertaking such as this involves the skills, talents, and energies of many people. The staff at Harper & Row has been a pleasure to work with. We would particularly like to thank Fred Henry, Mary Lou Mosher, and David Nickol for their valued assistance. Credit must also be shared with Lauren Bahr, Judy Rothman, John Greenman, and Neale Sweet for their important input, Ed Butler for his creative design efforts, and Linda Lilienfeld for her excellent photo research efforts.

Gerald A. Silver
Myrna L. Silver

Part 1 Introduction to the Computer Age

Learning Objectives

After studying this chapter, you should be able to
1. Define key terms related to computers and data processing
2. Contrast digital and analog data
3. List characteristics of computers
4. Describe the data processing cycle
5. Contrast three major methods of data processing
6. List demands on business which create the need for computers

Chapter Outline

Expanded Use of Computers
What Is a Computer?
  Size of Computer Systems
  Digital and Analog Computers
Characteristics of Computers
  Self-direction
  High Speed
  High Accuracy
  Reliability
  Low Cost Per Unit of Data Processed
What the Computer Can Do
Definition of Data Processing
Methods of Processing Data
  The Data Processing Cycle
  Manual Information System
  Unit Record Information System
  Computer Information System
How Computers Meet Business Needs
  Time Factor
  Cost Factor
  Accuracy Factor
  Better Control of Data
  Better Utilization of Resources
  Improved Service
  Mechanization
How Computers are Used in Business
  Sales and Marketing
  Accounting
  Order Point Calculations
  Word Processing
  Personnel Management
  Manufacturing Information Control
  Banking and Credit
  Modeling and Planning
  Design

Computers: An Introduction

Once in a while in history events occur that are so explosive and significant that society is shaken to its foundations. In the eighteenth century the world was transformed and our lives changed forever by the Industrial Revolution, which created the factory system. The dawn of the machine age relieved men and women of much arduous physical labor. Many cottage industries, which had been the mainstay of society, were abandoned as people flocked to the cities. No one was left untouched by the Industrial Revolution.

Now another revolution, even more far reaching in its implications, is under way. The computer age is upon us and once again our lives are being irrevocably changed. The computer and information technology are transforming the way people live, think, conduct business, and communicate with one another. The computer has the potential to free the human mind from tedious mental tasks, in much the same way that machines freed the human body from much physical drudgery.

Four decades ago the computer was an expensive scientific wonder, understood by only a handful of researchers and mathematicians. Today the computer is very nearly indispensable in scientific research and in business and is within the financial reach and understanding of almost everyone. In the early 1950s a computer cost millions of dollars and was so large that all its necessary parts and equipment filled several rooms. Today a computer costing $100 and small enough to be held in one hand may be faster, more accurate, and able to handle more data than its million dollar ancestor. Modern computers have become so small that they can be incorporated inside business machines, automobiles, and home appliances or kept available for immediate use on a desktop (Figure 1-1).

The computer age has dawned, and the implications for civilization stagger the imagination.

You are about to begin the study of this fascinating age. You will learn about machines that fit on a piece of silicon smaller than the head of a pin. You will study devices that can store every word and number in a major metropolitan telephone book on a thin plastic disk that weighs only a few ounces. You will read about

Figure 1-1   Changes in Computer Size. New technology has enabled manufacturers to produce machines smaller in size, lower in cost, and greater in speed, accuracy, and reliability.

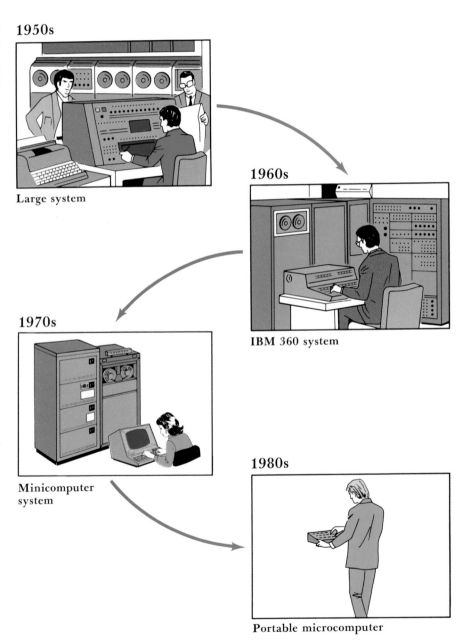

1950s

Large system

1960s

IBM 360 system

1970s

Minicomputer system

1980s

Portable microcomputer

electronic marvels that can perform millions of calculations in a second. You will begin to comprehend how one of the world's most complicated and sophisticated devices can compose music, draw pictures, play games, write poems, and even carry on a conversation. You will learn about the languages that enable human beings to communicate with a computer and direct its efforts. In short, you are about to begin the study of the computer.

EXPANDED USE OF COMPUTERS

There has been an enormous increase in the number of computers used in business, industry, education, home, and recreation. According to International Data Corporation, a leading market research organization, about $17 billion worth of mainframe computers (large-scale machines) were shipped in 1980. By 1985 this figure had risen to almost $25 billion. It is projected that by 1990 over $34 billion of mainframe computers will be shipped (Figure 1-2). As impressive as these figures are, they take into consideration only large computers.

In addition, there has been an even more spectacular increase in the number of small computers shipped. In 1980 a little under $1 billion of personal computers were shipped. By 1985 the figure had jumped to $15 billion, and it is expected that by 1990 $50 billion will be shipped. It is expected that by the year 1987 the shipment of personal computers will exceed mainframes. Personal computers cost from $100 to perhaps $3000, and are becoming commonplace. Low-cost computers are used in large and small businesses, homes, offices, schools, colleges, and laboratories (Figure 1-3). They are also found in game rooms, arcades, and family entertainment centers (Figure 1-4). The computer industry is one of the few that have an annual growth rate of almost 10 percent.

WHAT IS A COMPUTER?

In general terms a computer is any instrument that computes, calculates, or reckons. Thus, the abacus, adding machine, and hand-held calculator are all forms of computers. However, for our purposes we

Figure 1-2   Computer Sales. Sales of large computer systems have increased dramatically during the 1980s, but sales of small systems and personal computers for individual use show an even more spectacular increase, rising from under $1 billion in 1980 to overtake projected large-system sales before the end of the decade. (*Source:* International Data Corporation.)

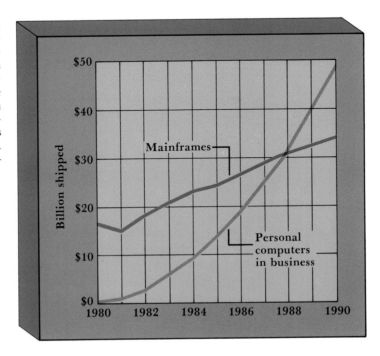

Figure 1-3   Computers Used in Research. A laboratory technician can process, analyze, and report hundreds of tests that would not have been possible without computer capabilities.

Figure 1-4 Computers in the Home. Before the late 1970s only a few electronic hobbyists had "home computers." The mass production of electronic games introduced the general public to the microcomputer, and it is now rapidly becoming an essential tool for studying, managing personal finances, acquiring information, and even monitoring household appliances, as well as entertainment.

need a more precise definition of a computer. We will define a **computer** as an electronic data processing device capable of receiving input, storing instructions for solving problems, and generating output with high speed and accuracy (Figure 1-5).

Computers are electronic machines composed of switches, wires, and printed circuit boards, transistors, or integrated circuits. They may include screen displays, keyboards, line printers, card readers, card punches, magnetic tape drives, and other devices. These components are wired together into a network called a computing system. The entire system is often called, simply, a computer.

SIZE OF COMPUTER SYSTEMS

The size of computer systems ranges from small hand-held devices to huge machines occupying several large rooms. A system may be constructed as a single device or as many separate pieces of equipment that function as a unit. The individual parts may be located within the same building or scattered across the country, connected by telephone lines or microwave circuits.

Figure 1-5 Computer Systems. Computer systems receive input, follow a program or set of instructions for processing the input, and produce output in the form of printed material or visual display.

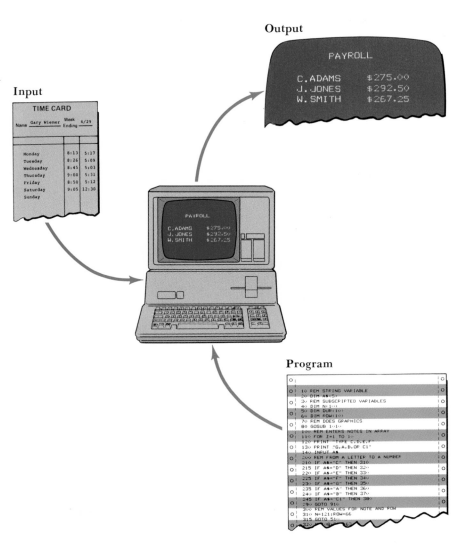

A fully functioning computer may be small enough to place on a desktop or in a briefcase (Figure 1-6). Slightly larger versions may be found in offices, laboratories, or classrooms (Figure 1-7). These smaller systems are generally referred to as **microcomputers**.

Where larger volumes of data must be processed, medium-size computers are used, such as shown in Figure 1-8. These machines may consist of a central processing unit and several input and output

Figure 1-6 Briefcase-size Computer. Newly introduced systems can outperform the large systems of a few years ago. Microcomputers may be self-contained units with a keyboard for input, tape or disk for storage, and a printer or display screen for output. They are light enough and small enough to be carried easily.

Figure 1-7 Desktop Computer. The capability of a small computer can be expanded with additional pieces of equipment to give greater storage and more diverse printed and display output. Even with these additional components, the system remains compact enough to fit on a desktop and so is suitable for the small office or the home.

Figure 1-8 Medium-size Computer System. As the size of computer systems increase, they can provide faster processing speeds, larger storage capacity, and a greater variety of output devices. Medium-size systems are designed to handle heavy volume and complex data processing in such business and industrial applications as payroll, inventory control, production scheduling, general ledger, and process automation.

Figure 1-9 Large Computer System. Machines such as these are used by government agencies, universities, and large corporations. Their ability to accept and deliver vast amounts of information, as well as their modeling and design capabilities make them invaluable in scientific and engineering research. Shown here are the radio telescopes and the computer of the astronomy research program at Socorro, New Mexico.

devices. They can process and store the information needed for small- and medium-size businesses.

Large computer systems, illustrated in Figure 1-9, are designed to receive input from many sources, store vast amounts of information, and output data in many forms. The term **mainframe** refers to these larger systems. (It is also sometimes applied to the central processing unit, as distinct from input or output devices, in a medium or large system.) Such systems are used by large business organizations and government agencies.

DIGITAL AND ANALOG COMPUTERS

Computers may be characterized by the way in which they receive and process data. Some systems process letters and numbers represented by electrical voltages of fixed values; others process data represented by voltages that are not fixed, but rise and fall continuously.

We sometimes describe information as being represented by an analog. For example, the amount of fuel in the tank of your automobile rises and falls throughout any period of time during which you drive. The needle on the gas gauge gives an analog representation of the changes occurring. The movement of the needle is analogous to the amount of gas remaining in the tank.

Analog computers process data input in a continuous form. Data, such as voltage, resistance, temperature, and pressure, are represented in the computer as a continuous, unbroken flow of information. In engineering applications—where quantities to be processed exist as waveforms or continually rising and falling voltages, pressures, and so on—analog computers are very useful. For example, they are used to control processes in the food and petroleum industries. However, they are not suitable for processing business data.

Digital computers process data in the form of discrete letters or numbers and are therefore more useful in business applications. The analog-digital distinction can be illustrated by comparing how an increase in temperature is noted by an engineer and an increase in inventory is noted by a businessperson (Figure 1-10). The increase in temperature, say from 60 to 90 degrees, is not abrupt and may be represented as a continuum. The best way to input this information is by using an increasing electrical voltage, analogous to the rise in

Figure 1-10 Digital and Analog Data. The list of inventory items is a digital representation of discrete amounts. The graph showing an increase in temperature is an analog representation of a data continuum.

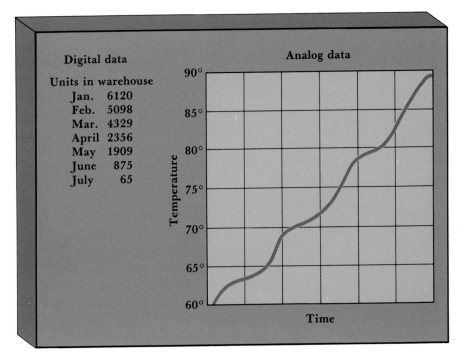

temperature. An increase in the number of units of an item in stock, on the other hand, is represented by a discrete number. An inventory total may increase from 105 to 106 units, but not from 105 to 105½ units. Similarly, employees increase in units of one, a paycheck is a discrete amount, and a sales price is quoted as a specific number.

Since this book deals primarily with business data processing, we mean a digital computer when we say computer. However, the distinction between digital and analog computers is rapidly diminishing. Most modern computers are capable of processing both digital and analog input once the data have been converted into a form suitable to the computer. Nevertheless, it is useful to know that there is a distinction between the two.

CHARACTERISTICS OF COMPUTERS

Computers possess qualities that make them highly suitable for processing information. They are largely **self-directing**, that is, they are

Figure 1-11 Computer Programs. Programs direct the computer to input information, process it according to predetermined formulas or manipulations, and print out results in a specified format. The computer is called a self-directing machine because by following a program it can be said to direct its own activities. Human intervention is not necessary for it to proceed through the set of instructions.

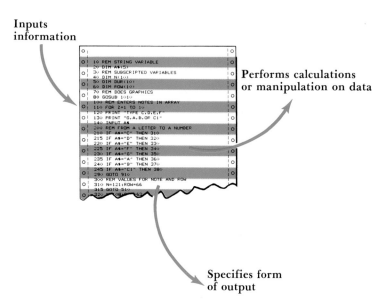

Inputs information

Performs calculations or manipulation on data

Specifies form of output

able to follow sets of instructions without human intervention. Computers are capable of processing data with greater speed and accuracy than any computational device ever invented. They are reliable. They can process large volumes of data at low cost. It is these qualities that have made the computer the most significant means of processing data today. Let's look at each of these characteristics in more detail.

SELF-DIRECTION

A computer is self-directing, that is, it is able to direct its own activities, because it can follow a program (Figure 1-11). A **program** is a series of instructions or statements recorded in a form that can be understood by a computer. These instructions direct the computer through a series of steps that are designed to solve a problem. Programs may be written by professionals, called **programmers**, or by users of the computer who have a specific problem to solve. They lay out each step in sequence and enter the instructions into the computer.

Once the program is in the computer, the machine carries out each step in sequence, performing actions and making comparisons

Figure 1-12   Computation Speed. The average human operator can perform roughly three or four mental computations in one second. In the same period a computer can perform many millions of computations involving far more complex numbers and data.

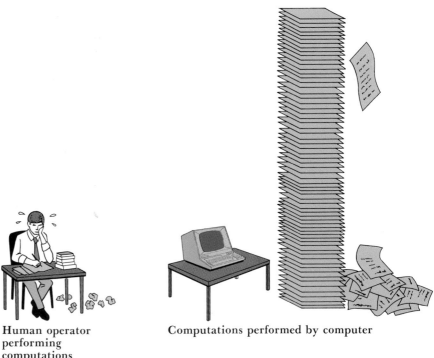

Human operator performing computations

Computations performed by computer

or calculations. Human intervention is not needed during the program run. After a successful program has been written and tested, the computer can process many different sets of data with that same program, greatly increasing its usefulness.

HIGH SPEED

The modern electronic computer can execute tens of thousands of instructions in only a fraction of a second (Figure 1-12). A program containing millions of instructions can be processed in a second.

Computers can be compared on the basis of their speed. One means is to compare the number of instructions each machine can process per second. Computers are rated in **millions of instructions per second** or **MIPS**.

Another means of comparing computers is based upon their

Figure 1-13 Speed Differences. Computers can process data at high speed because information is moved about in the form of electronic pulses traveling at the speed of light.

How far can an electronic pulse travel in one billionth of a second?

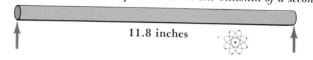

11.8 inches

How far can the fastest human runner travel in one second?

On July 3, 1983, Calvin Smith ran 100 meters in 9.93 seconds, breaking the world's record. In one second he can run 28 feet.

TABLE 1-1   Relative Speeds

METHOD	APPROXIMATE SPEED	
	Measured in	
Manual methods	Seconds	
Unit record systems	Milliseconds	
Early computer systems	Microseconds	
Modern computer systems	Nanoseconds	
MULTIPLES AND SUBMULTIPLES	PREFIXES	SYMBOLS
1 000 000 000 000 $= 10^{12}$	tera (ter'a)	T
1 000 000 000 $= 10^{9}$	giga (ji'ga)	G
1 000 000 $= 10^{6}$	mega (meg'a)	M
1 000 $= 10^{3}$	kilo (kil'o)	k
100 $= 10^{2}$	hecto (hek'to)	h
10 $= 10^{1}$	deka (dek'a)	d
1 $= 10^{0}$		
0.1 $= 10^{-1}$	deci (des'i)	d
0.01 $= 10^{-2}$	centi (sen'ti)	c
0.001 $= 10^{-3}$	milli (mil'i)	m
0.000 001 $= 10^{-6}$	micro (mi'kro)	μ
0.000 000 001 $= 10^{-9}$	nano (nan'o)	n
0.000 000 000 001 $= 10^{-12}$	pico (pe'ko)	p

internal electronic speed (Figure 1-13). Modern computers are rated in **nanoseconds**. One nanosecond (ns) is equal to one-billionth of a second. (Table 1-1). Earlier computers processed data at microsecond speeds. One **microsecond** (μs) is equal to one-millionth of a second.

The machines which use punched cards process information in **milliseconds**. One millisecond (ms) is equal to one-thousandth of a second.

The speed of a computer is truly appreciated when it is compared to manual methods of processing data. Manual methods, using the human hand or eye, are measured in seconds. Obviously, machines which can move data about in billionths of a second are vastly superior when high speed is important.

HIGH ACCURACY

A computer can add millions of figures without error. Modern computers are **solid state** electronic devices with few moving parts. Solid state electronic equipment is manufactured on chips of silicon and does not have filaments which are prone to burn out. They have built-in error checking systems to detect malfunctions. No other device yet invented possesses this high degree of accuracy.

Of course, the accuracy of the results can be no higher than the accuracy of the information supplied and the accuracy of the processing instructions. The common saying **Garbage In–Garbage Out (GIGO)** expresses the fact that the quality of the result can be no better than the quality of the information input. Many errors blamed on the computer are really caused by wrong data entered by a human operator.

RELIABILITY

Electronic computers are highly reliable. Since they involve almost no moving parts, computers do not have mechanical failures nearly as often as other machines. They can function year in and year out with long periods between failures or breakdowns. However, mechanical devices, such as tape drives or line printers, may malfunction, causing the failure of the entire system. A computer system is no more reliable than its weakest link.

LOW COST PER UNIT OF DATA PROCESSED

Because computers move data in the form of electronic pulses, they

Figure 1-14 Cost Differences. The cost per unit of data is a major factor in using computers for processing data. The economic advantage of electronic over manual data processing increases as the amount of data to be processed increases and becomes extreme when large amounts must be handled.

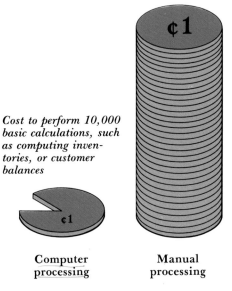

Cost to perform 10,000 basic calculations, such as computing inventories, or customer balances

¢1

Computer processing

Manual processing

are able to handle vast amounts of information at an extremely low cost (Figure 1-14). While large computers are expensive to install, once they are in operation the cost to process a given unit of data is very low.

WHAT THE COMPUTER CAN DO

Computers are able to store, structure, and manipulate vast files of information. Some of the most important uses of the computer involve **data base management systems (DBMS)**. Data base management systems, discussed in more detail in Chapter 11, allow government agencies, businesses, and other institutions to maintain and manage files containing millions of records quickly and easily.

The telephone, the telegraph, satellite relay stations, microwave circuits, and other forms of **data communications** are important parts of computers and data processing. Through data communications, one computer can exchange data with another thousands of miles away; it can send and receive data to and from hundreds of terminals located at distant points. We will study computer networks and data communications in more detail in Chapter 10.

Computers can scan hundreds of records in a minute or less. They can store millions of names, addresses, telephone numbers, or other information and keep it ready for immediate retrieval. Computers can solve all sorts of mathematical problems, ranging from the simple addition of a column of numbers to working out complex equations involving thousands of steps. Computers print out digital information, such as numbers, or text material, such as words or phrases. They can also draw pictures and plot curves or graphs. High-level activities such as these are actually accomplished in the computer with elementary mathematics, simple logic, and basic comparisons. Complicated programs are built up using these elementary tools.

Computers are not able to reason or think in the same sense as human beings do. Computers cannot set long-range goals or exhibit creativity and imagination. They are not capable of emotion and feelings, though their printouts may reflect the feelings and emotions of their human programmers.

DEFINITION OF DATA PROCESSING

Data are items of information of value to an individual or an organization. They are factual material, such as measurements or statistics, that are used as a basis for discussion, decision, and calculation. Data are compiled to form reports, letters, facts, figures, records, or documents.

In a narrower sense data consist of numbers or letters that may be manipulated, processed, or reordered by people or machines to increase their value or utility. Some writers prefer to define *data* as factual material and *information* as knowledge derived from the manipulation of data. In this book the terms data and information are used interchangeably.

Data processing, then, is the restructuring, manipulating, or reordering of data by people or machines to increase the data's usefulness for a particular purpose. Processing includes classifying, sorting, merging, recording, retrieving, calculating, transmitting, summarizing, and reporting.

Word processing, sometimes considered to be a subset of data processing, is the restructuring or reordering by machine of words,

Figure 1-15   The Computer Used in Word Processing.   The computer can manipulate words and phrases and generate letters, memos, and reports.

phrases, and other copy (the data) to produce reports or documents. It involves capture of data, editing, revising, and printing of reports (Figure 1-15).

METHODS OF PROCESSING DATA

Three methods of processing data have been widely used in business, industry, and government. It may be done by hand (manual information system), by simple machines (unit record information system), or by electronic machines (computer information system). In all three systems the data being processed go through a data processing cycle.

THE DATA PROCESSING CYCLE
The data processing cycle consists of three steps: data input, data processing, and data output (Figure 1-16).

Figure 1-16   The Data Processing Cycle.

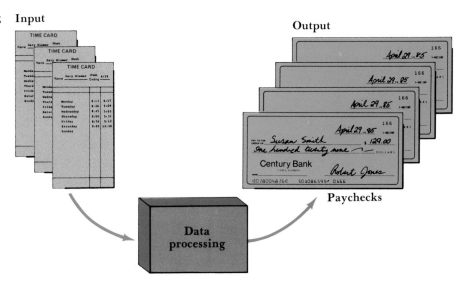

Input

Output

Paychecks

Data processing

1. Data input. Data input involves converting data from source documents into a form acceptable for processing by computer or other means. **Source documents** are the original records of a transaction (Figure 1-17). The data on these documents may be recorded by machine (such as employee time cards), handwritten (such as sales orders), or typewritten (such as memos). All such data must be translated into a form in which they can be entered into the system.

2. Data processing. During data processing the data are changed in form, order, or structure to increase their value or utility. Sales orders for the week may be totaled. A list of employees may be classified by department. A sales commission may be calculated. Data may also be stored for later use.

3. Data output. It is not enough that data be input and processed. The results of the processing must be communicated to the user (Figure 1-18). In the data output step the results of the two previous steps are made available in a form most suited for use by the organization. Output may consist of statements, lists, reports, tables, or graphs. It may be in printed form or be displayed on a cathode ray tube (CRT). Data output in one cycle may also be recorded on a storage device such as a magnetic disk to be used later in further processing, perhaps in a different physical location.

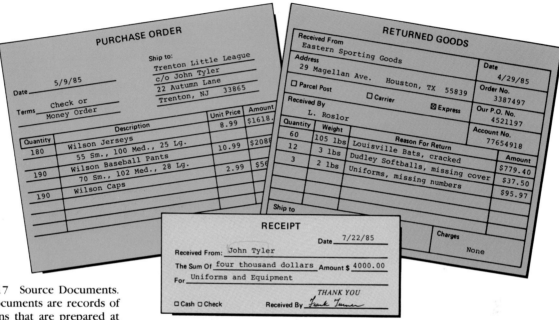

PURCHASE ORDER

Ship to:
Trenton Little League
c/o John Tyler
22 Autumn Lane
Trenton, NJ   33865

Date_____5/9/85_____

Terms___Check or_____
      Money Order

Quantity	Description	Unit Price	Amount
		8.99	$1618.
180	Wilson Jerseys 55 Sm., 100 Med., 25 Lg.	10.99	$2088
190	Wilson Baseball Pants 70 Sm., 102 Med., 28 Lg.	2.99	$56
190	Wilson Caps		

RETURNED GOODS

Received From
Eastern Sporting Goods

Address
29 Magellan Ave.   Houston, TX   55839

☐ Parcel Post   ☐ Carrier   ☒ Express

Received By
   L. Roslor

Date   4/29/85

Order No.   3387497

Our P.O. No.   4521197

Account No.   77654918

Quantity	Weight	Reason For Return	Amount
60	105 lbs	Louisville Bats, cracked	$779.40
12	3 lbs	Dudley Softballs, missing cover	$37.50
3	2 lbs	Uniforms, missing numbers	$95.97

Ship to

Charges   None

RECEIPT

Date___7/22/85___

Received From: John Tyler

The Sum Of four thousand dollars Amount $ 4000.00

For Uniforms and Equipment

THANK YOU

☐ Cash ☐ Check   Received By *Frank Turner*

Figure 1-17 Source Documents.
Source documents are records of
transactions that are prepared at
the time the transactions take
place. These original records are a
source of data for computer
input.

MANUAL INFORMATION SYSTEM

Manual information systems were the first means of processing data
(Figure 1-19). Many small business firms still use manual methods.
Input is done by writing data on forms by hand or on a typewriter.
Processing operations are done mentally or with paper and pencil,
adding machine, or desk calculator. Sorting, merging, and classifying
are performed by hand. Data are output by writing or typing, for example, writing a receipt or paycheck longhand or typing a balance
sheet, ledger card, or report. Running up totals to figure gross pay,
calculating account balances or credits due a firm, placing employee
time cards in sequence by department, and sorting orders by sales
personnel are examples of business processes that can all be done by
manual methods.

Manual methods are simple, easy to use, flexible, and inexpensive if the amount of data to be processed is low. Because complicated equipment and systems are not involved, changes can be made
easily. But, a manual system may prove to be slow, prone to error,
and costly when a moderate or large volume of data is involved. It is

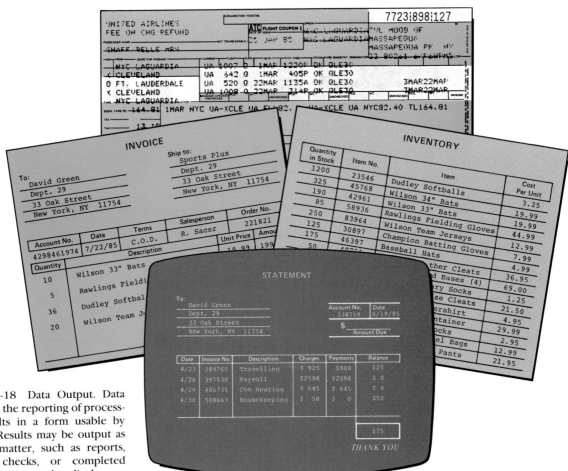

Figure 1-18 Data Output. Data output is the reporting of processing results in a form usable by people. Results may be output as printed matter, such as reports, graphs, checks, or completed forms, or generated as displays on a video screen.

difficult to standardize procedures and reporting. Manual data processing is limited by the speed of the human hand and eye.

UNIT RECORD INFORMATION SYSTEM

The **unit record information system** relies on human operators and electromechanical devices to process data. (An electromechanical device contains moving parts actuated by electric coils.) The system is sometimes called electrical accounting machine processing.

Figure 1-19 Manual Information System. Manual data processing involves mental operations and data in written form done by hand or by simple mechanical devices such as the typewriter or adding machine. Computation and recording of information are limited by the speed of the human hand and eye.

In the unit record system, data are translated into a pattern of holes and stored in that coded form on punched cards. Data from each transaction are punched on a separate card, hence the term *unit record*. The information from the punched cards is then entered in the system by card-reading machines.

The manipulation of data involves the use of machines that sort, collate, match, or merge decks of punched cards or calculate figures from the data input on the cards.

Results can be communicated in the form of the manipulated stacks of cards, a punched card, or a form printed from the punched cards.

These operations are done by machines that physically move the cards about. Human intervention is required in moving trays of cards and in starting and stopping the several machines involved. Unit record information processing has become largely outmoded because of computers.

COMPUTER INFORMATION SYSTEM

Electronic computers have become the major means of processing data in all businesses.

Several different types of **input media** can be used for the computer. A medium refers to the type of data storage system used. (The plural of *medium* is *media*.) Data can be processed or stored on magnetic tape or magnetic disks. Source documents may even serve directly as an input medium. Data printed in magnetic ink are input by magnetic ink character recognition devices, and handwritten or printed data are read and input by optical character recognition devices.

Once the data are entered in the computer, they are processed by electronic means. Data within computers are represented by electric signals, called **pulses**. These pulses are moved about within the computer in microscopically small circuits, and calculations are performed in billionths of a second. Output can be accomplished on high-speed line printers, video devices such as cathode ray tubes, or audio devices such as voice synthesizing units.

For most firms the computer is the most practical of the three means for processing data, because of its reliability, speed, accuracy, and low cost per unit of data processed. The initial price of computers has come down drastically. They are now within reach of almost all business firms.

One limitation of computers is that a program must be written before a problem can be solved. Inexpensive ready-made programs are available. But is is unfortunately quite possible to spend thousands of dollars writing a computer program to solve a relatively minor problem.

HOW COMPUTERS MEET BUSINESS NEEDS

Electronic data processing was originally developed for scientific and mathematical applications and is still widely used in these disciplines. Because of the specialized nature of early computers, they were impractical for business use. However, the introduction of low-cost computers and the development of more versatile programming languages have greatly increased their practical value to the ordinary

PRODUCING A REPORT AGAINST A DEADLINE: PAST, PRESENT, AND FUTURE

Source: Arthur D. Little, Inc.

THE PREINDUSTRIAL APPROACH

"I've lined up my secretary, Sandy, to work with George and me and his secretary through the weekend. We'll probably have to work night and day to get it out. I hope they will leave the office air conditioning system on—it can be terrible in July without it. My wife and kids are going up to the lake for the period since I can't see much of them until I get out from under the report."

TECHNOLOGY: Typewriters, copying machines, some dictating, handwritten corrections. Material is retyped four or five times.

THE INDUSTRIAL-AGE APPROACH

"I've arranged with the supervisor of the word processing center to line up a skeleton crew to work through the weekend. Our department will have to pay overtime charges. We can work in the word processing center, which is always air-conditioned. The word processing supervisor and I have agreed to a schedule for turning around drafts, and we'll have to stick to it. I expect we'll be free evenings."

TECHNOLOGY: Word processors and copying machines. Retyping is minimized but editing and correcting text is still a separate function performed by keyboarding specialists. The creative and mechanical functions are done by different people, and handling them requires negotiation across a formal organizational interface.

THE INFORMATION-AGE APPROACH

"I'm driving up to the lake tonight with my family to spend a four day telework-vacation weekend at the cottage. The job won't be very hard because 75% of the necessary material is already in our computer data bases. I can easily reorganize these materials, add whatever else is needed, and revise and edit the manuscript in the course of five or six early-morning and evening sessions—with George's help, of course. While he is visiting his sister in Toronto, we will stay in close touch and exchange materials via our terminal systems. Beside the calm, I will enjoy the sailing, swimming, and fishing between work sessions, as well as the time I will be able to spend with my family."

TECHNOLOGY: Portable terminals communicating with an office automation system and with each other. The system provides remote access to files, word processing power, personal computing resources, electronic mail, and public data bases. The final report, generated and completely edited remotely, is printed out by a secretary in the office. There is no need for the principal to be there or to review it further. The use of pre-existing materials reduces typing, and the computer can correct spelling errors. Composition, review, editing, and correction are integral functions, with no division of labor.

business. Electronic data processing owes much of its success to its ability to meet many of the demands placed on businesses operating in a highly competitive marketplace.

TIME FACTOR

To be of greatest value to an enterprise, data must be available at specific times in the business cycle. The accuracy and thoroughness of data processing are of little value to a firm unless the results are ready when they are needed. The success or failure of many businesses depends on this time factor. For example, credit data delivered after a transaction is completed is of little use to the sales manager who has already extended credit to a customer who turns out to be a bad risk.

The pace of modern business often requires the almost instantaneous processing of large volumes of data. Important decisions may have to be made on short notice. A big sale may hinge on a salesperson having current inventory or price of goods at his or her fingertips. Because the computer is capable of immediate record processing, such up-to-the-minute information is available (Figure 1-20).

COST FACTOR

Cost savings have led many firms to shift their data processing to computers. In the past sales could be written up and orders filled, with the bills and records of the transactions all prepared by hand. However, manual methods are now too expensive for many firms. The computer provides an inexpensive means of processing transactions.

ACCURACY FACTOR

Large investments in equipment, inventory, and other assets and the need to manipulate large sums of money require accurate data processing. In business decisions that involve millions of dollars a mistake in one calculation can be disastrous. Computers are a valuable business tool because of their high accuracy and low rate of error. Banks, for example, can post hundreds of thousands of deposits and

Figure 1-20 Real Time Processing. In real time processing the transaction is processed at the moment it takes place. When instant information is not required a delayed or batch processing system may be used. Transactions are gathered together and processed hours or days later. These customers' accounts will be brought up to date for the bank's records at the end of the day, and a statement of the status of the accounts will be generated and sent to the customers at the end of the month.

withdrawals to customer accounts and make all figures balance at the end of the day because of the computer's accuracy.

BETTER CONTROL OF DATA

Many organizations have experienced increases in the number of transactions that must be processed. Computers enable businesses and government agencies to handle a large volume of data and to structure the data in many forms. Without the computer it would be virtually impossible for stock exchanges to process the millions of buy and sell orders placed each week. Consider the dilemma the IRS and the Social Security Administration would face if they had to handle the staggering number of tax returns, checks, and reports without the use of computers.

Business people need precise control of the volumes of information processed. The computer can restructure a list of data in many different forms. For example, it can print out a list of the previous day's sales in chronological order. It can then reorganize the list by type of merchandise sold, by salesperson or by department.

This added flexibility gives the business manager more information and so more control.

BETTER UTILIZATION OF RESOURCES

Business firms have millions of dollars invested in buildings, equipment, inventory, and personnel. The computer enables managers to control and allocate their resources much more efficiently.

IMPROVED SERVICE

Computers help businesses provide individualized attention and better service to customers. A department store with 25,000 accounts, for example, can process sales, returns, payments, and other charges and have the information immediately available at sales counters and credit offices.

MECHANIZATION

Someone said, "Machines should work and people should think." Many business people believe that human resources should be applied to those tasks for which humans are uniquely qualified. Routine transactions and calculations should be done by machines, thus freeing people for more creative activities. Electronic data processing makes such a division of labor more possible.

HOW COMPUTERS ARE USED IN BUSINESS

The computer can provide data on all aspects of business and industry, for example, inventory, sales analysis, credit analysis, cost accounting, operating ratios, manufacturing schedules. This information is the foundation for making sound business decisions. Below is a brief sampling of the business applications for which computers are now used. At this moment computer engineers are working on new ways to use the computer in almost every phase of business and industry.

Figure 1-21   Sales and Marketing Applications.

Reports

Projections

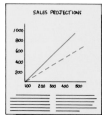

Order tracking

Real time order system

SALES AND MARKETING

The computer has found some of its most profitable applications in sales and marketing (Figure 1-21). Computers keep track of current sales, project future trends, and forecast changing demand. Using computers, marketing executives can plan advertising programs, project dealer inventories, and identify the best market for their product.

ACCOUNTING

Computers have become the mainstay of many accounting departments. They are used to prepare reports and maintain journals and ledgers. The computer prints out bills, tax reports, profit and loss statements, and balance sheets. It also computes ratios and indexes.

PERSONAL COMPUTERS MUST BE MANAGED

Source: Joseph E. Izzo, *Los Angeles Times*, May 29, 1983.

Personal computers are mushrooming in corporate offices these days, but, ironically, instead of improving the management of information, they are threatening to disrupt it.

This is not the fault of the computers, which can greatly enhance executive productivity and effectiveness. The problem is lack of corporate planning and control.

Business simply hasn't been prepared for the onslaught of personal computers and is not handling it well. This isn't surprising, considering how new these machines are. The personal computer industry is only 6 years old, and it has grown with amazing speed. . . .

Industry reports and evidence of our own and other consulting practices indicate that more and more companies are perplexed by the microcomputers in their midst. The headaches they're causing include deterioration in information quality; muddled communication; conflict between general management and data-processing management (never an altogether comfortable relationship), as the data-processing people see microcomputers diminishing their own importance to the organization, and rising costs, as companies pay for more and more personal computers.

The main problem with personal computers is that, although they simplify many business tasks, the information they generate frequently doesn't dovetail with overall corporate objectives. In that case, no matter how much it may be prized by its user, the computer becomes a hindrance to the corporation rather than the boon it can and should be.

Some illustrations:

—An engineering group of an aerospace manufacturer used a microcomputer's graphics capability to draw certain parts of an aircraft assembly for maintenance manuals. Putting together such computer-aided graphics is a precise and time-consuming task. In this case, however, it was unnecessary. The parts in question were already stored in graphics form in the company's mainframe computer. These engineers were, in effect, reinventing the wheel.

—A corporate planner used his computer to prepare a mathematical model that figured critically in the company's long-range business plan. Before the work was completed, the planner left the company. Because this executive developed the program for his model in unique, idiosyncratic fashion, and prepared no supporting documentation, no one else could use it. His former colleagues had to reconstruct the model. . . .

—In a large company, highly paid managers fascinated with their personal computers were spending many hours writing programs for their machines that an entry-level programmer could have produced in no time. Their use of computers was actually decreasing their productivity.

Larger companies are the most likely to be troubled with the rise in microcomputers, since, because of their relatively modest cost for a sizable organization, these units can readily find a home in many offices and go virtually unnoticed by top management until problems emerge. But small companies are not immune.

A main danger for smaller concerns is trying to make personal computers do too much, or to perform tasks for which they are not equipped. . . .

Personal computers were brought into corporations because executives perceived that they would help them do their jobs better and faster. They offer business a magnificent opportunity to increase the productivity not only of managers but of personnel at all levels. But, despite its small size, ease of handling and relatively low costs, the personal computer is still a computer. And computers must be managed, or they will manage us.

Payroll accounting is another productive application of the computer in business. Computers read payroll records, calculate earnings, withholding, and other deductions, figure commissions, and print out paychecks.

Cost accounting is a particularly useful area for computers. They analyze production costs and compute budgeted hourly costs for individual machines or entire departments. Computers are able to track jobs in production and determine their cost according to the amount of time and materials needed. They also calculate return on investment, calculate profit, and establish wholesale and retail selling prices.

ORDER POINT CALCULATIONS

The computer can monitor inventory. It can list the supply of goods on hand at any time and the date when replacements should be ordered to meet demand. It can compute the most economical and efficient quantity of goods to order at one time, giving minimum amounts that should be kept in stock and when reorders should be placed.

WORD PROCESSING

The computer can be used to generate reports, letters, correspondence, memos, and other material containing words and phrases. The computer as a word processing tool is an important part of many offices, aiding in the automation of paperwork for reports and documents.

Figure 1-22 Personnel Management Applications.

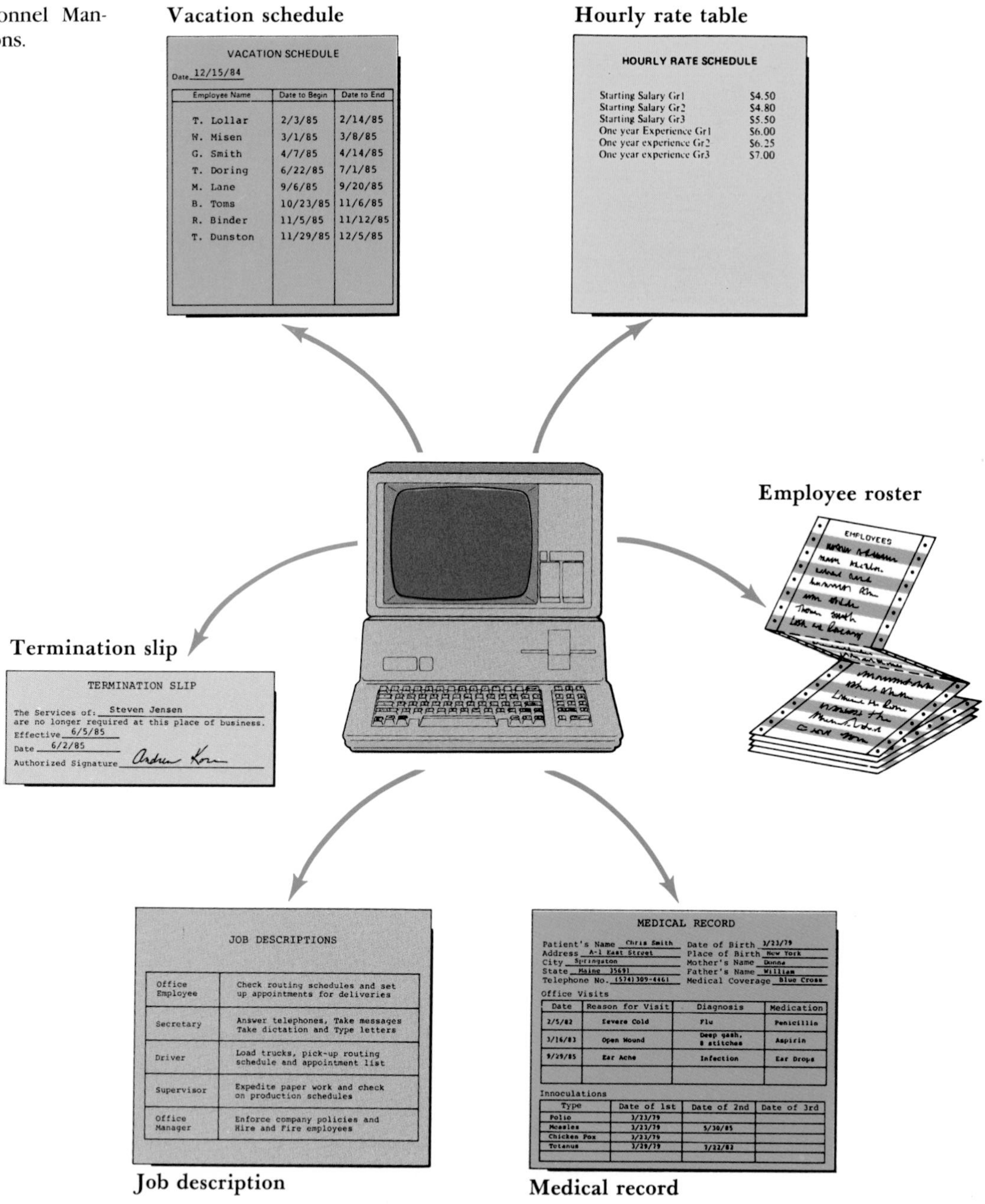

Vacation schedule

VACATION SCHEDULE

Date 12/15/84

Employee Name	Date to Begin	Date to End
T. Lollar	2/3/85	2/14/85
W. Misen	3/1/85	3/8/85
G. Smith	4/7/85	4/14/85
T. Doring	6/22/85	7/1/85
M. Lane	9/6/85	9/20/85
B. Toms	10/23/85	11/6/85
R. Binder	11/5/85	11/12/85
T. Dunston	11/29/85	12/5/85

Hourly rate table

HOURLY RATE SCHEDULE

Starting Salary Gr1	$4.50
Starting Salary Gr2	$4.80
Starting Salary Gr3	$5.50
One year Experience Gr1	$6.00
One year experience Gr2	$6.25
One year experience Gr3	$7.00

Employee roster

Termination slip

TERMINATION SLIP

The Services of: Steven Jensen
are no longer required at this place of business.
Effective 6/5/85
Date 6/2/85
Authorized Signature _Andrew Korn_

Job description

JOB DESCRIPTIONS

Office Employee	Check routing schedules and set up appointments for deliveries
Secretary	Answer telephones, Take messages Take dictation and Type letters
Driver	Load trucks, pick-up routing schedule and appointment list
Supervisor	Expedite paper work and check on production schedules
Office Manager	Enforce company policies and Hire and Fire employees

Medical record

MEDICAL RECORD

Patient's Name Chris Smith Date of Birth 3/23/79
Address A-1 East Street Place of Birth New York
City Springton Mother's Name Donna
State Maine 35691 Father's Name William
Telephone No. (574)309-4461 Medical Coverage Blue Cross

Office Visits

Date	Reason for Visit	Diagnosis	Medication
2/5/82	Severe Cold	Flu	Penicillin
3/16/83	Open Wound	Deep gash, 8 stitches	Aspirin
9/29/85	Ear Ache	Infection	Ear Drops

Innoculations

Type	Date of 1st	Date of 2nd	Date of 3rd
Polio	3/23/79		
Measles	3/23/79	5/30/85	
Chicken Pox	3/23/79		
Tetanus	3/29/79	5/22/82	

Figure 1-23 Manufacturing and Production Control Applications.

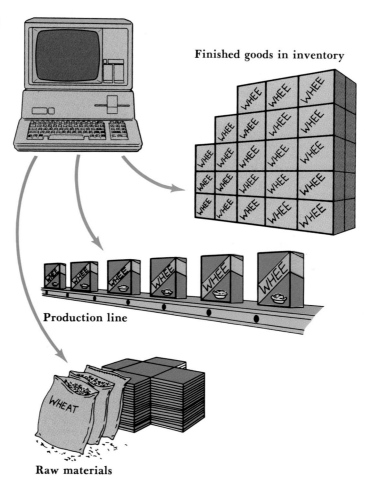

Finished goods in inventory

Production line

Raw materials

PERSONNEL MANAGEMENT
The computer provides management with data on the composition of its workforce (Figure 1-22). It can print out information on job classifications and personnel capabilities. It can list employees by department, salary schedule, or seniority. Computers prepare vacation schedules, overtime allotments, and health plan reports.

MANUFACTURING INFORMATION CONTROL
The computer is used in the manufacture and production of goods (Figure 1-23). It provides ordering, warehousing, and cost data, listed by part numbers or bills of lading.

The computer schedules work for an assembly line based on labor available by shift. It can print out a list of equipment and material needs for the assembly line for a given day. It can predict output, report the number of units produced, and provide follow-up cost data.

BANKING AND CREDIT

The computer is widely used in the finance, credit, and banking industries. It processes deposits, commercial and consumer loans, and revolving charge accounts for banks and department stores. It prepares credit card statements and maintains trust accounts. The computer is the heart of modern electronic banking. Without it, **electronic fund transfer systems (EFTS)**, such as Visa and MasterCard, would not be possible.

MODELING AND PLANNING

The computer has become an important planning tool. For example, business conditions can be analyzed and reduced to a mathematical model which is input to the computer. Then different sets of trial data can be fed in and the computer prints out results. Companies are spared the time and expense of actually testing in the marketplace.

As another example, a manufacturer may want to produce a food product of specific nutritive value, but not want to exceed a given cost or specific number of calories per ounce. The product must contain specified vitamins and a given amount of protein. It is difficult to decide on the proper formula since there are many ingredients that can be combined to make the product. The computer can quickly figure out all the possibilities and determine the best combination of components to produce the desired result at the lowest cost. The computer prints out a list of ingredients and quantities that most closely meet the desired specifications.

DESIGN

Computers have become important design tools in the automotive, aircraft, and electronic industries. They are used to design trademarks and to produce artwork for the print media. They generate action-oriented computer art for television titles and commercials.

In this chapter we have mentioned a few of the applications for which computers are used. We have also introduced you to a few unfamiliar terms. As you read on you will discover many more interesting applications for the computer. You will also learn many more terms that make up the rich vocabulary of computers and data processing. Becoming familiar with these new terms will be an asset in communicating with others.

SUMMARY AND KEY TERMS

• A **computer** is an electronic device composed of switches, wires, integrated circuits, and other parts capable of **input**, **storage**, the ability to follow a set of instructions called a **program**, and **output**.

• Large computer systems are composed of a **mainframe** and one or more input or output devices. Smaller personal computer systems, or **microcomputers**, have many applications in both the home and business.

• **Analog computers** process information in a continuous form. **Digital computers** process information in the form of discrete letters or numbers.

• A computer is **self-directing** because it can follow a series of instructions, containing the steps for the solution of a problem, without human intervention.

• The major characteristics of computers are high speed, high accuracy, reliability, and the ability to process large volumes of data at low cost.

• The speed of modern computers is measured in **millions of instructions per second (MIPS)**. Computers move data about in **nanoseconds (ns)**. A nanosecond is one-billionth of a second.

• **Data** are items of useful knowledge or **information** of value to an individual or business. Data and information are used synonymously in this text.

• **Data processing** is the restructuring, manipulation, or reordering of data to increase its usefulness and value. The major manipulations include classifying, sorting, merging, recording, retrieving, calculating, transmitting, summarizing, and reporting.

• **Word processing** is the manipulation of words and phrases to generate letters, memos, and reports.

• A **source document** is a record made at the time a transaction takes place.

• The **data processing cycle** consists of data input, data processing, and data output.

• In the **manual information system** input is performed by hand or typewriter. Processing is performed by the human mind, with the aid of simple machines such as adding machines or calculators. Output is handwritten or typed.

• In the **unit record system** data are input by being punched into cards. Processing involves machines that read and rearrange the cards to accomplish sorting, matching, and calculating data. Output is in the form of printed reports or punched cards.

• In a **computer information system** the input medium may be magnetic tapes or disks or source documents. The data are processed by electronic means. Output may be accomplished by printing devices, video devices, or audio devices.

• Computers are used in many aspects of business including sales, marketing, accounting, inventory control, word processing, and personnel management. They are also used in banking and credit, in the manufacture of goods, and for modeling and planning business systems and products.

EXERCISES

1. Define the term *computer*. How has the use of this term changed?

2. What is meant by the term *self-directing*?

3. What is the difference between an analog computer and a digital computer?

4. Compare the speeds of different methods of processing data.

5. Diagram the data processing cycle of a particular business firm or function. List source documents, processing requirements, and output.

6. What is a computer program? Write a set of approximately 10 instructions that tell, step by step, how to perform a task such as balancing a checkbook or determining monthly payments on a loan.

7. Why is the time factor important in data processing? Give several examples of the effect of the time factor on the value of data.

8. Describe how computers are used in modeling and planning.

9. Select a business firm with which you are familiar and give examples of the demands placed on it by operation in a highly competitive marketplace.

10. Only a few of the many applications of data processing have been mentioned in this chapter. Visit a business firm that does not have electronic data processing. List at least three applications of electronic data processing that would be of value to that firm.

11. Name four types of businesses that process data and might be able to use microcomputers.

12. Select a business firm to study. Interview its owners or employees. Draw a simplified diagram of the data flow to and from the firm. (Show the firm at the center, and indicate the names of the firms and organizations with which it interacts.)

2

Learning Objectives

After studying this chapter, you should be able to
1. Define the terms software and hardware
2. Trace the major developments in computer hardware
3. Trace the major developments in computer software
4. List some individuals who have made significant contributions to the field of computers and data processing
5. Describe the major computer generations
6. List the advantages of the internally stored program

Chapter Outline

The Manual Era
  Early Hardware
  Nineteenth-Century Hardware
The Unit Record Era
The Electronic Data Processing Era
  The Stored Program
  First Generation Computers
  First Generation Software
  Second Generation Computers
  Second Generation Software
  Third Generation Computers
  Third Generation Software
  Fourth Generation Computers
  Fourth Generation Software

The Evolution of Computers

Some inventions, such as the light bulb, sewing machine, and telephone, can be attributed to the genius of one person. But the modern electronic computer did not spring from the mind of a Thomas Edison or Alexander Graham Bell. It is the result of countless inventions, ideas, and developments made by many men and women throughout the last century. In this chapter, you will learn about the ideas, events, and inventions that led to the computer as we know it today.

A successful data processing center contains three elements: hardware, software, and personnel. Each must be present in order to perform meaningful data processing. A computer has no value without people and programs to direct its efforts.

Hardware consists of the physical equipment, that is, the machines and devices, used in the data processing cycle. Line printers, computers, and cathode ray tubes are examples of data processing hardware.

Software includes the programs, computer languages, procedures, and sets of instructions used in data processing. A computer program giving the steps to be taken in preparing and printing out payroll checks is an example of software. The language used to communicate with the computer and a diagram of the flow of information in a program are also software.

Computing requires skilled **personnel**. Modern computer installations employ hundreds of people as operators, programmers, librarians, systems analysts, and maintenance personnel.

Early efforts to develop data processing focused on hardware. But soon people realized that computers and other equipment could not be used effectively without adequate software. Early software was crude and limited. The first computer languages were difficult to learn and to use, and no systems were available to schedule jobs efficiently for the computer. The machines had to be made more versatile, efficient, and compatible with the skills of their human operators. New methods of instructing the computer and new programs to expand its range of applications were developed. Much of the growth and change in data processing in the last two decades has been in software and programming. At the same time it has become widely recognized that a skilled staff of trained

Figure 2-1 Major Eras in Data Processing.

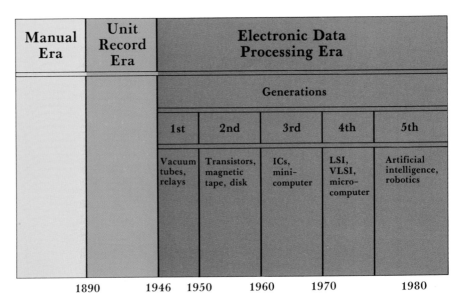

Manual Era	Unit Record Era	Electronic Data Processing Era				
		Generations				
		1st	2nd	3rd	4th	5th
		Vacuum tubes, relays	Transistors, magnetic tape, disk	ICs, mini-computer	LSI, VLSI, micro-computer	Artificial intelligence, robotics

1890   1946   1950   1960   1970   1980

computer personnel is just as important to an organization as its investments in hardware or software.

The rate at which new data processing inventions are finding their way into industry is increasing. As many new ideas and techniques have been introduced in the last decade or two as in the entire preceding history of data processing.

Data processing methods and technology have evolved through three major eras from primitive manual methods to modern electronic computers (Figures 2-1 and 2-2). The manual era began when people first started counting. The second major era started at the end of the nineteenth century when unit record processing became widely used. The invention of the computer in the 1940s ushered in the electronic data processing era.

THE MANUAL ERA

Throughout history human beings have used their creative powers to invent and develop devices and systems to help them in their tasks. The manipulation and recording of data are no exception.

Figure 2-2   Data Processing History

1980	Artificial intelligence, robotics, local area networks (LANs), microcomputers
1970	**FOURTH GENERATION** Monolithic circuits, cryogenics, integrated circuits, Pascal language
1960	**THIRD GENERATION** Multiprogramming, teleprocessing, OCR, MICR, BASIC language, minicomputer, audio response unit
1950	**SECOND GENERATION** Magnetic tape and disk, transistor, COBOL language, FORTRAN language
	FIRST GENERATION ENIAC, stored program, EDVAC, EDSAC, punched-card processing
1900	Monroe calculator Hollerith code Key-driven multipliers Felt's comptometer
	Babbage's Analytic Engine and Difference Engine
1800	Jacquard punched-card loom
1700	
	Leibnitz's calculator Pascal's numerical wheel calculator
1600	Slide rule (analog computer)
1500	
1400	
	Double-entry bookeeping system
1300	
PAST	Abacus Decimal system Finger counting

Figure 2-3 Roman Abacus. The abacus is a calculating device that has been in use for over 2,000 years. Operations are performed by manipulating the pebbles in the grooves.

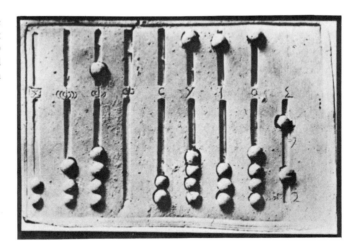

Human fingers were the first counting aids used to process data. Methods such as piling rocks or gathering sticks were used to help in figuring larger quantities. Mathematical systems advanced with written notation and the invention of Roman numerals. The Arab mathematicians took a giant leap forward with the introduction of Arabic numerals and the concept of the zero and the development of long division, logarithms, square roots, and trigonometric functions. It was the Italians who contributed double entry bookkeeping, still used today. Principles of higher mathematics were the software concepts that enabled humans to perform complex computations and to solve difficult problems.

EARLY HARDWARE

The **abacus** was one of the first mechanical devices developed to perform mathematical tasks. Although its origin is uncertain, the abacus has been used by many civilized peoples including the early Chinese and Romans. It is still common today in some parts of the world.

The abacus consists of a frame and beads strung along parallel rods. The beads are moved about to represent quantities. Addition and subtraction and other arithmetic operations are performed by manipulating the beads. The Romans moved pebbles, called *calculi*, in slots to perform computations (Figure 2-3).

Around 1617 John Napier, a Scottish mathematician, invented

Figure 2-4 Napier's Bones. John Napier invented a seventeenth-century version of the pocket calculator. By rotating a set of rods, engraved with numbers, the user can perform multiplication, division, and other operations.

Figure 2-5 Gunter's Scale. Edmund Gunter, a seventeenth century English mathematician and professor of astronomy, invented several calculating devices or aids, such as Gunter's chain (a 66-foot long chain used in land surveying), Gunter's quadrant, and Gunter's scale. The scale is a form of slide rule.

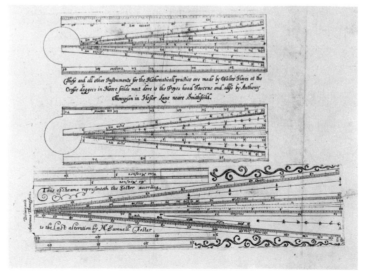

the device, later called **Napier's bones**, shown in Figure 2-4. Napier's bones are rods engraved with numbers. By rotating the rods, the user can perform multiplication, division, and square root problems.

The **slide rule** is an early example of an analog computer. This device appeared in several forms during the seventeenth century. Gunter's Scale, shown in Figure 2-5, was one form. It was ap-

Figure 2-6 Pascal's Numerical Wheel Calculator. Addition is performed by rotating index wheels that represent units, tens, hundreds, and so forth. The wheels move a series of interlocking gears that represent the numbers 0 through 9 for each place.

Figure 2-7 Leibnitz's Calculator. This mechanical device employs wheels, gears, and ratchets. It represents an improvement over Pascal's machine in that it can perform subtraction, multiplication, and extraction of roots as well as addition.

proximately two feet long and was used to perform multiplication.

In 1642 the French philosopher Blaise Pascal successfully built a **numerical wheel calculator**. This device, shown in Figure 2-6, performed calculations by means of wheels and cogs indexed to represent different quantities.

In 1671 the German mathematician Gottfried Leibnitz completed a machine that could add, subtract, multiply, and divide. The Leibnitz **calculator**, shown in Figure 2-7, operated by means of notched wheels and ratchets, features still found in some mechanical desk calculators.

Figure 2-8 Jacquard Loom. Joseph Marie Jacquard equipped his looms with a series of cards containing punched holes. The cards served as a means of process control in guiding threads to weave a patterned fabric. Eighty years after the weaver's invention, engineers recognized the possibilities of using the punched holes to represent items of data.

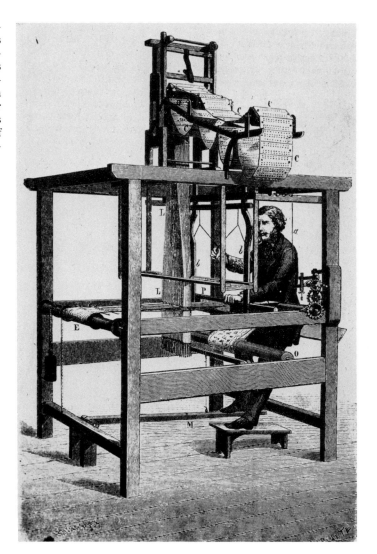

NINETEENTH-CENTURY HARDWARE

The next step in the evolution of data processing was the development of a device completely unrelated to early calculators and slide rules. In France in 1801, Joseph Marie Jacquard perfected an automatic system for weaving patterns into fabric. He used cards with punched holes to guide the warp threads on his loom (Figures 2-8

Figure 2-9 Jacquard Cards. The weaver could produce a specific pattern by selecting the proper card. Each fabric pattern was translated into a pattern of holes through which the warp threads were guided during weaving.

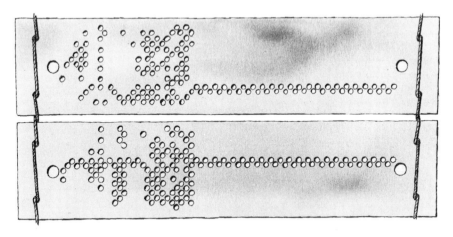

and 2-9). The holes in the card controlled the pattern that was woven into the fabric. The **Jacquard card**, was the forerunner of the punched cards used in unit record systems. Instead of the holes representing patterns or stitches, the holes in punched cards represent bits of data. A hole could represent the digit 1 and the absence of a hole the digit 0.

About ten years later in England, Charles Babbage, a visionary mathematician, began work on a calculator that would perform extremely complex arithmetic functions and calculations. Babbage spent part of his life and fortune attempting to build his **Difference Engine**. Figure 2-10 shows the portion that he completed in 1833. Later, he abandoned this machine in favor of a more complicated one, called the **Analytic Engine**, which would perform arithmetic functions on data read in from punched cards. Neither device was ever completed. The technology of the day was too limited. However, a prototype was built many years after Babbage's death which proved the validity of the device.

But Charles Babbage earned his place in the history of data processing as the man who attempted to construct the first complex computer. The hundreds of drawings and plans he left served as an inspiration and education to the inventors and mathematicians who came after him.

Although a century would go by before such a complex computer would finally be built, many small steps toward the goal were

Figure 2-11   Felt's Comptometer. This device was a functional calculator that was able to add multidigit numbers. It was one of several inventions before the turn of the century that led to the development of mechanical machines that could perform mathematical operations and print out the result.

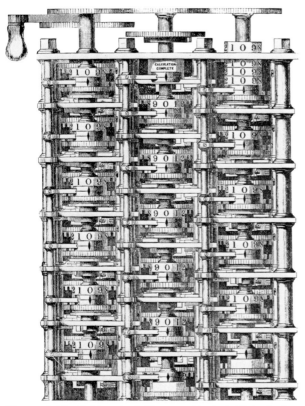

Figure 2-10   Babbage's Difference Engine. This device, while never actually completed until many years after Babbage's death, was designed to perform complex calculations.

taken during the next few decades. The era of industrialization and mechanization had begun. American inventors were actively pioneering new machines and devices.

Nineteenth-century inventors successfully developed machines that performed some of the operations Babbage had envisioned for his Analytic Engine. In 1872 Frank Stephen Baldwin built a calculator that performed all four basic mathematical functions. This marked the beginning of the calculating industry in the United States. In 1887 Dorr E. Felt patented a **comptometer** (Figure 2-11). This machine opened the way for adding multidigit numbers mechanically.

**PIONEERING PEOPLE:
CHARLES BABBAGE AND
ADA, COUNTESS
OF LOVELACE**

Source: Frank Rose, *In the Heart of the Mind*, Harper & Row, Publishers, 1984, pp. 29-31.

Computer hardware had its beginnings in the early 1800s with the work of an English mathematician, Charles Babbage. The son of a wealthy banker, Babbage was an eccentric and irascible individual, a man who hated street musicians and computational errors with equal intensity. He was also a polymath and a visionary. As an inventor, his contributions included both the cowcatcher and the speedometer. But his best-known invention is one to which he devoted both his life and his fortune without success: A steam-powered computer he called the "analytical engine."

Babbage was not yet thirty when, in 1821, he announced to the Royal Astronomical Society his intention to build an automatic calculating machine he called the Difference Engine. He'd been obsessed with the idea of mechanical calculation for nearly a decade, ever since his mind had wandered off one day as he was poring over a table of logarithms at Cambridge. These tables were filled with mistakes, as were the navigational tables and astronomical charts of the time—a fact that had dire consequences for the sailors who were shipwrecked as a result. Babbage designed his hand-cranked Difference Engine to compute them automatically. The British government supported him with grants that came to £17,000 over the next ten years, but the device was never built, partly because machinists couldn't meet the tolerances required. In 1833 the whole project was suspended with nothing to show but a pile of sprockets and cogwheels in a workshop on Babbage's estate.

Babbage, undeterred, came up with an even grander scheme: his Analytical Engine. Unlike the Difference Engine, which was to have been a special-purpose machine capable only of solving polynomial equations, this new concoction was intended to be a general-purpose computer—the first such device ever conceived. It was to include the three essential elements of any modern computer: a "store" (memory), a "mill" (central processor), and a means of initiating various "patterns of action" (programs). The store and the mill would consist of a clanking assemblage of rods and gears; for programming, Babbage would rely on the same kind of punched cards that were used to control the Jacquard loom, an automatic weaving device that had been invented in France some thirty years before. The resulting contraption, Babbage maintained, would be able to perform calculations at the rate of one per second.

Few people took him seriously. Virtually the only person who did, in fact, was the beautiful young Ada, Countess of Lovelace—Lord Byron's only legitimate daughter. Ada had been born in 1815, the year before Byron left for Switzerland with Shelley and his wife, and she had inherited not her father's poetic romanticism (possibly because she never saw him after her infancy) but her mother's head for mathematics. Taken as a girl to Babbage's workshop to see a model of his Difference Engine, she found herself entranced by its workings. Years later she became his partner in the attempt to bring the Analytical Engine to realization.

But it was not to be. Government funds weren't available this time—Babbage was offered a knighthood instead, but he snubbed it—and he and Lady Lovelace turned to other schemes to raise money: a tic-tac-toe machine, a chess-playing machine, and finally a foolproof system for playing the horses. This last proved quite disastrous, as it resulted in blackmail and twice necessitated the pawning of her husband's family jewels. (Both times her mother bought them back.) Ada died at thirty-six, and with her any chance of the project's completion. Babbage lived on another twenty years, an increasingly embittered old man; after his death his brain was pickled on the off-chance that someone, sometime, would be able to explain its peculiar workings.

THE UNIT RECORD ERA

In the 1880s Herman Hollerith, a special agent of the U.S. Census Bureau, successfully combined the concepts of Jacquard's cards with data recording and manipulation. He devised a coding system that could be punched into cards to represent data. This method is called the **unit record system**. Each punched card, according to Hollerith, should contain information on only one family or transaction and may not contain collective data, hence the term unit record. Figure 2-12 shows the machine Hollerith built to read and manipulate data read in from the cards.

The unit record system was used to process the 1890 census, and the job was done in one-fourth the time it took to do the 1880 census. This was possible because machines manipulated cards containing data and eliminated tedious manual tallying. The Hollerith coding system became the standard data representation method for the unit record system and for the modern computer.

Hollerith left the census department to manufacture and sell his data processing machine. Figure 2-13 shows an early data processing office. The company he founded eventually merged with two others to become the International Business Machines Corporation, or IBM—a leader in the production of electronic data processing machines.

The capability of the calculating machine was further expanded in 1892 when W. S. Burroughs developed a 90-key model that could process up to nine decimal digits and in 1914 when Jay R. Monroe and F. S. Baldwin designed and built the Monroe calculator.

About 1908 James Powers, a statistical engineer at the Census

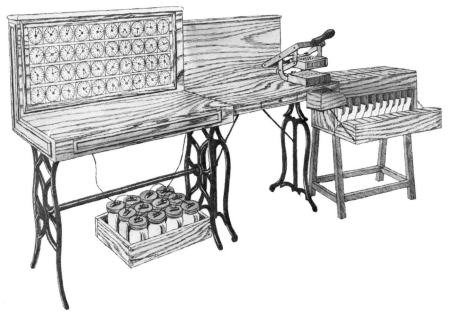

Figure 2-12 Herman Hollerith and the Hollerith Accounting Machine. In this early Hollerith machine, cards were placed under the hole-sensing device on the right side of the machine. Pins dropped through holes in the card completed an electrical circuit to index the counters on the left.

Figure 2-13 Data Processing Through the 1930s. Hollerith's unit record machines became an essential part of the equipment of any organization, business or government that had to handle large quantities of data. These operators were employed by the Census Bureau to tabulate data for census reports.

Figure 2-14 Wiring Board. Unit record machines were directed by electrical circuits formed by connecting hubs or terminals with a series of jumper wires.

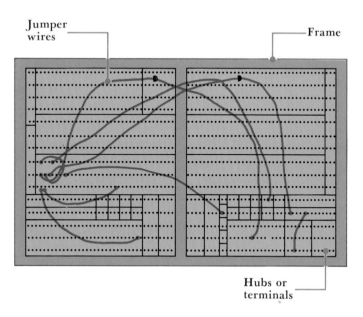

Bureau, developed a series of unit record machines that used round holes punched into cards. These machines were used to process the 1910 census. Powers left the Census Bureau and in 1911 founded his own company to manufacture unit record machines. The Powers Accounting Machine Company eventually merged with other companies to become part of the Sperry Rand Corporation. Then later they went on to produce and sell the UNIVAC computer.

The **wiring board**, consisting of a wiring panel with terminals and groups of jumper wires, was used to program unit record machines and was an early form of software (Figure 2-14). To program the system, the operator physically connected the appropriate terminals with the jumper wires to form electrical paths that direct the machine to carry out various functions. Errors in programming were hard to locate with this method, and programs were not easily transferred from one machine to another.

From 1930 to the 1960s the punched card and electrical accounting machines were the major means of processing data for large firms. While they are still used by some companies today, they have been largely replaced by computerized systems.

THE ELECTRONIC DATA PROCESSING ERA

Figure 2-15 John V. Atanasoff and Clifford Berry.

The first true computer was conceived by John Vincent Atanasoff, working at Iowa State College with Clifford Berry, a graduate assistant (Figure 2-15). They constructed a device in 1939 called the **Atanasoff-Berry computer** or just **ABC** (Figure 2-16). It used vacuum tubes and was capable of following a set of instructions.

For many years the Princeton mathematician John von Neumann was given credit for developing the concept of the first stored program computer which was built in 1946. But after years of litigation, in 1974 the courts recognized that it was actually Atanasoff and Berry who came up with the first true internally stored program computer.

In 1944 Howard G. Aiken, a physicist at Harvard University, perfected the **Automatic Sequence Control Calculator, Mark I**. The Mark I was an electromechanical calculator composed of numerous telephone relays and rotating mechanical wheels. Punched paper tape and punched cards were used to provide data input. While Aiken had the assistance of IBM in his venture, this machine is not considered a true computer because it lacked the ability to follow a set of instructions.

Shortly after the Mark I was introduced, two electrical engineers were working to solve ballistics problems for the Army. In the process John W. Mauchly and J. Presper Eckert of the University of Pennsylvania, along with their colleague Leslie Groves, developed a prototype device called the **ENIAC**, or **Electrical Numerical Integrator and Calculator** (Figure 2-17). It differed from Aiken's device in that it used 18,000 vacuum tubes instead of telephone relays and therefore operated much more rapidly than the Mark I. The ENIAC was fully electronic and had no moving parts.

The early computers were limited because they were programmed by an external set of instructions, usually a wiring board. What was needed was a device that would store a set of instructions internally, thereby greatly increasing its flexibility.

THE STORED PROGRAM

The ENIAC became obsolete when the **internally stored program**—a concept basic to all modern computers—was developed. John von

Figure 2-16 The Atanasoff-Berry Computer (ABC). Finding existing devices inadequate for his needs, Atanasoff pursued his own ideas and with Berry built the ABC. In 1942 he commented, "Many people told me I was a fool to use vacuum tubes in a digital manner."

Figure 2-17 The ENIAC Computer. This photograph of the ENIAC and its two inventors was taken at the Moore School of Electrical Engineering in Philadelphia in 1946 before the computer was moved to the Army Ordinance Ballistics Research Laboratory at Aberdeen, Maryland. John W. Mauchly is in the right foreground, and J. Presper Eckert, Jr., is at the left.

Figure 2-18 John von Neumann and the EDVAC. John von Neumann helped perfect the stored program concept used in virtually all modern computers. The EDVAC, built as a successor to ENIAC in 1947, is shown here being operated by T. Kite Sharpless, technical director of the research group responsible for its construction.

Neumann (Figure 2-18, *left*), who had developed a computer for the Institute for Advanced Studies, joined Eckert, Mauchly, and others in designing a machine, the **Electronic Discrete Variable Automatic Computer (EDVAC)** (Figure 2-18, *right*), that would accept and store a set of instructions (a program). While the EDVAC was being constructed, another device, the **Electronic Delay Storage Automatic Calculator (EDSAC)**, was completed at Cambridge University in England in 1949. EDSAC was a practical machine that operated following an internally stored program.

These machines took advantage of the fact that information could be stored electronically in a system of vacuum tubes and relays. Early programmers were able to write data into electronic storage (which came to be known as the machine's primary memory system) and replace it with new information as needed. Electronic memory quickly became much more efficient than unit record memory.

One method of storing information electronically makes use of binary numbers. The binary number system makes use of only two digits, 0 and 1, each called a *bit* (short for *b*inary dig*it*). Any number in the decimal system may be represented as a binary number. For example, 8 in the decimal system when converted to the binary system is 1000. (See Appendix B for a detailed description of binary numbers.) If a closed relay is thought of as representing a 1 and an open relay a 0, then one closed relay followed by three open ones represents the binary number 1000 or the decimal number 8. Since many electronic components have only two possible states (open/closed, conducting/nonconducting, on/off), binary numbers are most efficient for storage of numerical data in electronic memory. Various conventions have also been devised for representing letters of the alphabet and other symbols as patterns of 1s and 0s.

Von Neumann's internally stored program concept, with instructions read into the machine on punched cards, replaced the inconvenient wiring board. These instructions directed the machine to carry out a sequence of steps. The internally stored program gives the computer much of its power. Its advantages are:

1. The computer can be reprogrammed by entering instructions from another set of records, instead of rewiring or using wiring boards.
2. The program may be written and tested before the actual data are available.
3. The program makes the machine self-directing; a human operator does not have to guide each step.

Mauchly and Eckert were also involved in designing and building the first American commercial computer, the **Universal Automatic Computer (UNIVAC I)**. The company they formed eventually became the UNIVAC division of the Sperry Rand Corporation. The UNIVAC I was the first computer to be sold commercially. It was also one of the first machines to use magnetic tape as a means of data input and output. The UNIVAC received national attention in November 1952 when it predicted the victory of Eisenhower over Stevenson in the presidential election.

FIRST GENERATION COMPUTERS

The first generation of computers operated with vacuum tubes and relays and could store a program internally. They received their

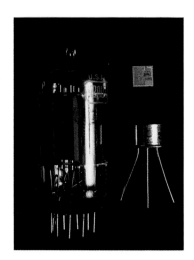

Figure 2-19   Four Generations of Computer Circuitry. Through its generations of development computer circuitry has greatly increased in reliability and decreased in size. The machines of the early 1950s employed vacuum tubes. By the 1960s the bulky tubes had been replaced by the transistor. The silicon chip appeared by the mid-1960s, and we are now into the more advanced microelectronics of the large-scale integrated circuit (LSI).

input data through paper tape or cards. The machines were large and often unreliable, because the many vacuum tubes overheated and burned out. First generation machines date from the late 1940s. They proliferated in the mid-1950s, until the introduction of the transistor made them obsolete. Figure 2-19 contrasts first generation circuitry with smaller and more reliable circuitry in present-day use.

FIRST GENERATION SOFTWARE

The development of the stored program meant a major change in the way computers could be directed to perform tasks. Instructions in a program could now be read into memory locations and stored inside the machine. At first storage was accomplished by a system of relays and switches. Later, magnetic core storage systems (discussed in Chapter 5) were developed.

Internal program storage eliminated physically wiring instructions in the computer. New programs could be input quickly to replace old ones, without the tedious task of rewiring. This improvement greatly increased the machine's general-purpose capabilities.

First generation computer programming was done in **machine language**. Machine language is the only language a computer can directly understand. The instructions are coded in the form of 0s and 1s to represent the two-state characteristic of the electronic components involved: off or on, low or high, right or left. Programming in machine language is time consuming and tedious. Each brand of computer had its own machine language, and so the exchange of program between computers was greatly limited.

The need for more efficient software led to the development of **assembler language**. In assembler language, instructions are given to the computer in symbols or abbreviations called **mnemonics**. These mnemonics, such as ADD, OR, and PACK, tell the machine to perform certain functions.

Assembler language is much easier than machine language for the programmer to use because it involves words or wordlike symbols rather than 0s and 1s. Because computers operate in machine language, assembler language has to be translated by a special program stored in the machine. This program converts the mnemonics into machine language. Most modern computers can still be programmed in assembler language, if desired.

PIONEERING PEOPLE: WILLIAM SHOCKLEY

Source: Reprinted with permission of *DATAMATION®* magazine, © Copyright by Technical Publishing Company, a Dun & Bradstreet Company, 1982—all rights reserved.

William Shockley, who shared in the 1956 Nobel prize for inventing the transistor, is one of the seminal figures of modern technology. He is the father not only of solid-state electronics, but the founder of the first Silicon Valley company. Had he withdrawn from public life [some years back], he would undoubtedly be revered as one of America's great contributors to the modern world. But in recent years, Shockley has gotten a great deal of adverse publicity for his ideas about eugenics and his participation in a California sperm bank that seems to be dedicated to the idea of breeding geniuses.

Despite such seemingly nonsensical notions, Shockley is a smart physicist, and the real immortality he has won comes from his work at Bell Labs and what followed from that.

In 1936, after earning a PhD from MIT in physics with a thesis dealing with the behavior of electronics in certain crystals, Shockley entered Bell Labs. At first, he did research on vacuum tubes, the electron valves of the day. He then moved on to work with semiconductors, which he believed could be made to exhibit the same effect. (Field-effect transistors do indeed act a bit like tubes; earlier current-controlled transistors behave in a comparable but distinct way.)

Shockley embedded a copper grid in an oxide and used it in an attempt to control the flow of electricity through the base device. Things didn't quite work out at first, however. In the midst of all this work, World War II broke out, during which time Shockley was in the hands of the Navy. After the war, work on the transistor resumed, and the first breakthrough came when the team Shockley led realized that certain surface effects were preventing the prototype transistor from working. In November 1947, the Bell team tried attaching electrodes to the surface of some germanium and using a stronger electric field to produce changes in conductivity of the material. By December, the first point-contact device—gold spikes were the electrodes—was a reality.

The invention was made public in June 1948; the world hardly seemed to notice. The vacuum tube was king, and it continued to reign. Shockley went on to develop the modern junction transistor, and after that others added the integrated circuit in its many forms as well as the many other semiconductor devices that have largely made the vacuum tube a thing of the past.

Within 10 years, there was a vast difference in electronics. Transistors were a real business; 30 million had been made and prices had fallen from about $20 a pop to $1.50. During that decade Shockley had gone west to take a job at Beckman Instruments, where he set up the company's semiconductor lab. The lab grew into a subsidiary, and was sold to Clevite Corp. and later to ITT. It was in that setting that Shockley's employees, including Robert Noyce, saw the way the world was going and left to start Fairchild Semiconductor, and, subsequently, many of the other companies that populate the high technology region of Northern California.

SECOND GENERATION COMPUTERS

The invention of the **transistor** in 1948 led to the development of smaller, more dependable second generation computers. These computers not only had greater speed and storage capacity than first generation machines, but they were more compact and cost less. Data were input by paper and magnetic tapes or, most often, by punched cards. By the late 1950s and early 1960s these machines were widely used.

Faster, more efficient, and larger-capacity means of data input, output, and storage were developed. **Magnetic disk storage** was introduced, giving the computer vastly improved storage characteristics.

SECOND GENERATION SOFTWARE

In the second generation **problem-oriented languages (POLs)** were developed. These languages stressed problem-solving features, were more like ordinary language than the symbolic assembler language and eliminated many of the programming details required in machine and assembler languages. Program languages that closely resemble spoken language are called **high-level languages**.

Instructions written in these problem-oriented languages still have to be translated into machine language before the computer can execute them. This is done by a **compiler**. A different compiler was developed to translate each problem-oriented language into machine language.

FORTRAN (**FORmula TRANslating system**), developed by John Backus, was one of the first problem-oriented languages. It became one of the major languages and still remains important for mathematics and science applications.

THIRD GENERATION COMPUTERS

The development of **microelectronics** led to the appearance of third generation computers in the mid-1960s. They were characterized by further reductions in size, lower cost, and improved methods of storing data. These machines used the **Integrated Circuit (IC)**, an electronic device in which hundreds of components are integrated onto a single, small **"chip"** (Figure 2-20).

Figure 2-20 Silicon Chip. Hundreds of transistors and other electrical components are manufactured on a chip of silicon small enough to fit through the eye of a needle. The components on a single chip form an integrated circuit (IC).

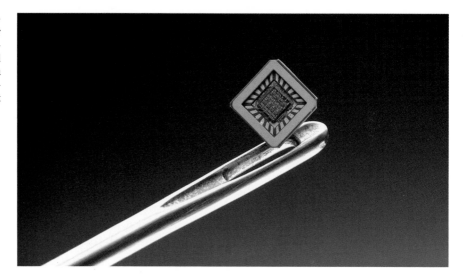

The minicomputer was a major development in the third generation. It appeared during the 1960s and spread in the early 1970s. Minicomputers are desktop computers possessing the major features of large machines, at a much lower cost. They are often used for small business and office applications and sometimes as part of a larger computer system. Minicomputers are now being widely replaced by microcomputers.

THIRD GENERATION SOFTWARE

Third generation computers called for new languages and better means of scheduling work. Early computer programs were set up and run one at at time, while an operator stood by to handle errors and problems. If an error appeared, the computer had to be stopped. This procedure was satisfactory as long as only a few programs had to be run. But as the volume of work increased, the need for a better method to schedule loads became imperative.

Special programs, called **operating systems**, were written to replace the human attendant in scheduling work. Operating systems start programs, stop them when they do not run properly, and deal with error conditions and interruptions efficiently without stopping the computer. Virtually all modern computers are equipped with operating system software.

COBOL (**CO**mmon **B**usiness **O**riented **L**anguage), another POL developed during the second generation of computers, became widely used during the third generation. Because COBOL closely resembles everyday business English, it brought programming within the reach of ordinary business people. It has become one of the major languages for large business computer systems.

Other languages developed or widely used during the third generation were **RPG (Report Program Generator)** and **PL/I (Programming Language I).** These languages, together with COBOL, are designed to run programs that handle data fed to the computer in batches and are referred to as **batch programming languages.**

In the 1960s new ways were being found to use the computer. Improvements in operating systems further expanded the computer's utility by allowing **multiprogramming**. Several programs could be processed at the same time by sharing the computer's available resources. Many computer terminals could be connected to one computer so that many programmers and devices could use the system at the same time. This concurrent use of one machine by several people or devices is called **time sharing**.

As the computer became more available through time sharing, programmers began to want to interact directly with the computer rather than having to wait for their job to be run in a batch. As a result, operating systems were improved to allow **interactive programming**. This led to the invention of languages suited to interactive programming. The most popular interactive languages developed during the third generation were **BASIC (Beginners All-Purpose Symbolic Instruction Code)** and **APL (A Programming Language).**

FOURTH GENERATION COMPUTERS

Fourth generation machines appeared in the 1970s, utilizing still newer electronic technology that made them even smaller and faster than computers of the third generation. Many new types of terminals and means of computer access were also developed in the 1970s.

One of the major inventions that led to the fourth generation was the **Large-Scale Integrated circuit (LSI)**. The LSI is a small chip containing thousands of small electronic components that function as a complete system. In effect, an entire computer can be manufac-

Figure 2-21 Large-Scale Integrated Circuit (LSI). In the LSI, thousands of components forming complete systems, such as a microcomputer, are manufactured on one chip. The pins mate with a socket so the device can be mounted on a printed circuit board.

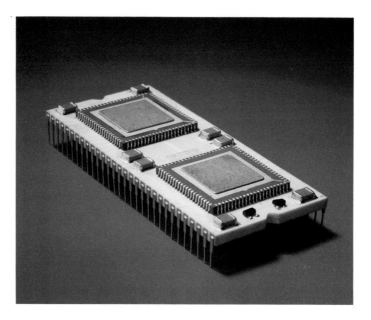

tured on a single chip no larger than a fifty-cent piece (Figure 2-21). One chip may perform the functions of an entire computer, calculator, or control device.

Another advance was the **Very Large-Scale Integrated circuit (VLSI)**. VLSIs contain thousands of electrical components and hundreds of complex functioning circuits which formerly would have required dozens of LSI chips.

This new microelectronic technology led to the development of the modern **microcomputer** and revolutionized the computer industry. It made it possible to manufacture computers of smaller size with greater speed, reliability, and capacity at lower cost (Figure 2-22). Some machines can be purchased for only a few hundred dollars; the actual processing chip may cost under $10.

The new computers spawned a need for more improved storage and output systems. During this period the **floppy disk** storage system was perfected. It allows hundreds of thousands of characters to be stored on a small plastic disk weighing only a few ounces. Faster and more efficient output devices, such as printers and screen displays, entered the market. **Color graphic computers** and **voice synthesizing machines** came into use.

Figure 2-22 Fourth Generation Computer. Microcomputers, machines of great speed and reliability, depend on the microelectronic technology of fourth generation computer hardware.

FOURTH GENERATION SOFTWARE

A major language to gain popularity during the fourth generation was **Pascal** (named for the French mathematician and philosopher, Blaise Pascal). This language was designed to make **structured programming** easier. Structured programming, discussed later, is an improved, more orderly means of designing and writing programs. Pascal and structured programming techniques have greatly simplified programming error detection.

New operating systems were developed, some specifically for microcomputer applications. One such operating system, **CP/M (Control Program for Microcomputers)**, is becoming a standard operating system of the home computer. Another, **MS-DOS** (Microsoft-Disk Operating System), is also gaining wide acceptance.

The next page is yet to be written on computer hardware and software. We are entering the fifth generation. Research is being conducted now on vastly improved memory systems that will allow millions of characters to be stored in a cube a fraction of an inch

ABACUS FINDS NEW POPULARITY AS LATEST COMPUTER CRAZE IN JAPAN

Source: Reprinted with permission of United Press International, Inc.

TOKYO (UPI)—The latest computer to catch on in Japan has no chips—and the only power it requires comes from the flicking fingers of its user. It is the age-old abacus or *soroban.*

Dozens of corporations are sending their employees to one of 30,000 *soroban jukus*—cram schools—for refresher courses. Abacus arithmetic involves shifting beads back and forth along a series of parallel wires. As for speed, experienced users can flick the beads far faster than they can push buttons. Recent winners of a national *soroban* championship whipped through 20 problems, each involving addition of 20 11-digit numbers, in less than five minutes.

Not that the Japanese have given up on electronics: At least one company is selling a hybrid math machine—an abacus with a calculator on the frame.

square. Computers that mimic human intelligence are being developed. These **artificial intelligence (AI)** machines will operate and reason much as human beings do without the structure required on earlier computers. Robots driven by "expert" computers will begin to act and think more like people. The field of robotics will come into its own. New computer network and communication programs and systems are being designed to link large and small computers into integrated national networks. Computers now on the drawing boards promise even greater breakthroughs in smaller size, higher speed, and lower cost.

SUMMARY AND KEY TERMS

• **Hardware** is the machines, devices, mechanisms, and other physical equipment used to process data, such as line printers, computers, and cathode ray tube displays.

• **Software** is the programs, computer languages, procedures and sets of instructions used to process data. The language used to communicate with the computer and a diagram of the flow of information in a program are also software.

• Data processing has evolved through three major eras. The **manual era** relied upon human calculation and problem solving aided by simple devices. Hardware of the manual era included the **abacus, Napier's bones, slide rules,** and **mechanical calculators.** Babbage's **Difference Engine** and **Analytic Engines** were the first plans for a complex computer but were never constructed.

• The **unit record era** relied upon punched cards. The unit record machine was designed by Herman Hollerith in the 1880s. It was based upon concepts used in the **Jacquard loom** and became the principal means of processing data from the 1930s through the 1960s.

• The **electronic data processing era** relies on the computer. The first electronic computer was designed and built by Atanasoff and Berry. Later machines were designed by Mauchly and Eckert. Early machines included the **EDVAC, EDSAC**, and **UNIVAC**. These machines relied upon the **stored program** to hold data and instructions.

• **First generation computers** were constructed from vacuum tubes and relays and were programmed in **machine language** or **assembler language**. A **compiler**, a program stored in the machine translates instructions into machine language.

• **Second generation computers** were constructed using **transistors** and were smaller and more reliable. They were programmed in **problem-oriented languages** (POL) such as **FORTRAN**. They utilized **magnetic tape** and **disk storage**.

• **Third generation computers** were constructed from **integrated circuits (ICs)**. **Minicomputers** were developed at the end of this era. **COBOL**, a POL, came into widespread use. Improved operating systems allowed **time sharing** and **interactive programming**. **BASIC** and **APL** are popular interactive programming languages.

• **Fourth generation computers** are based on **Large-Scale Integrated circuits (LSIs)** which allowed the introduction of the **microcomputer**. During this period **color graphics**, **voice synthesizers**, **structured programming**, and new operating systems came into use.

• Research is now under way on improved memory systems, **artificial intelligence**, **robotics**, and data communications.

EXERCISES

1. Define hardware and software.

2. What were the major developments in data processing techniques before 1900?

3. What is a stored program? What are the advantages of using one?

4. Outline the major developments in the first generation of hardware.

5. Outline the major developments in the second generation of hardware.

6. Outline the major developments in the third generation of hardware.

7. Outline the major developments in the fourth generation of hardware.

8. Describe the major changes in software from the first to the fourth generation.

9. What are microcomputers? Where are they used?

10. How does machine language differ from assembler language?

11. What are the advantages of problem-oriented languages?

Part 2

Computer Hardware

3

Learning Objectives

After studying this chapter, you should be able to
1. Define the term system
2. Describe input and output systems
3. Describe the function of the CPU
4. Describe the secondary storage system
5. Describe the function of the telecommunications system
6. Describe some typical modern computer systems and their physical characteristics

Chapter Outline

Definition of a System
The Computer System
Computer Subsystems
    Input System
    Central Processing Unit
    Secondary Storage System
    Output System
    Remote Terminals
    Telecommunications System
Classes of Modern Computer Systems
    Microcomputers
    Minicomputers
    Small Computers
    Medium Computers
    Large Computers

Fundamental Computer Concepts

Complicated devices are not difficult to understand if you take the time to learn how their components work. The most complex artifacts of the twentieth century, such as computers, spacecraft, and color television sets, are made up of simple parts. Each part, if viewed by itself, is relatively uncomplicated, but together the parts form a complex, useful machine. We see and hear an actor on television in lifelike color, we travel to the moon, or we compute millions of calculations in a fraction of a second, with machines that are built and conceived by the human hand and mind.

This chapter will give you an overview of the computer system and a survey of its major components. It lays out fundamental concepts and describes the relationship of important parts of the computer. In later chapters you will read in more detail how each individual component works.

DEFINITION OF A SYSTEM

A **system** is a collection of objects, procedures, or techniques that interact in a regulated manner to form an organized whole. All the elements in a system serve specific functions to accomplish the function of the system as a whole. Systems may be composed of smaller assemblages of parts known as **subsystems**. Each subsystem has its own function, but each is also one element in the larger system and acts to accomplish the function of the larger system. A change in one element in a system usually affects one or all of the other elements.

The human organism is one of nature's most perfect systems. Mental and physical attributes are elements of the total system. Working as a unit, they create an active, integrated, functioning person who is capable of sensing the environment, grasping a problem, structuring a solution, and, finally, affecting the environment. The components of this system could be called **input, processing, output,** and **memory** (Figure 3-1). Input is accomplished through the five senses. Processing and memory occur in the brain. Humans can remember hundreds of events,

Figure 3-1 The Human Data Processing System.

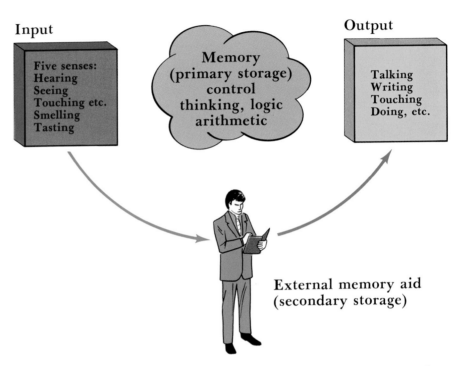

External memory aid
(secondary storage)

places, people, and facts. But memory is not an unlimited, totally dependable resource. Therefore, people take notes, write lists, look up facts, and keep records. These are external memory aids. Human beings achieve output by talking, writing, touching, or other actions. The results of input and processing must be exhibited in order for meaningful work to be accomplished.

People are capable of goal setting and self-direction. They can select a goal and coordinate all their resources to move toward it. Activities and actions are planned and performed, and behavior patterns are tested and adjusted, until the goal is reached. People are capable of feeding their own output back into the system for reprocessing. As a result, they can change, correct, and adjust their behavior so it leads more directly to their goal.

THE COMPUTER SYSTEM

Computers are systems that in some ways resemble the human system we have just described. As with people, input, processing, out-

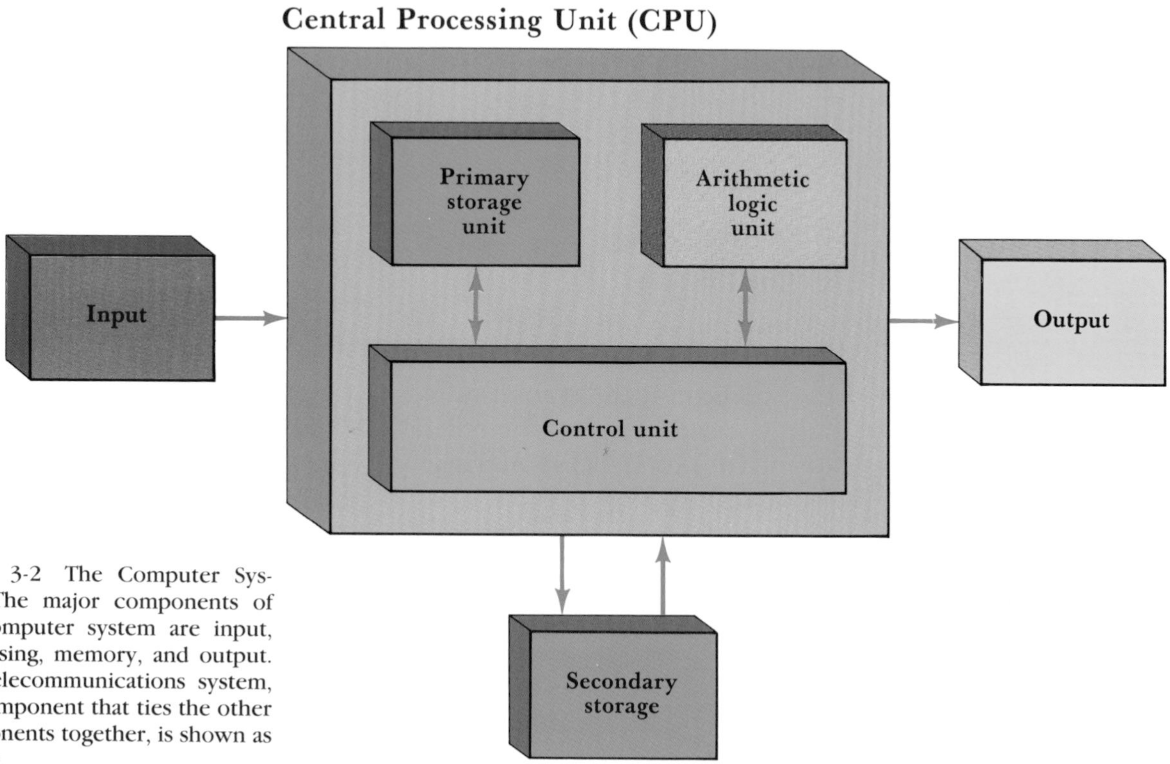

Central Processing Unit (CPU)

Figure 3-2 The Computer System. The major components of the computer system are input, processing, memory, and output. The telecommunications system, the component that ties the other components together, is shown as arrows.

put, and storage are major elements of the computer system (Figure 3-2). The computer receives data through a keyboard or other input device. It processes information in its central processing unit where it performs mathematical calculations and makes logical decisions. When it exceeds its internal storage capacity, it may call in external storage devices. The computer is self-directing to the extent that it can follow a set of instructions, process data, and output or store results without human intervention.

There are, of course, major differences between people and computers. Computers are incapable of long-range planning, generalizing from seemingly unrelated data, intellectualizing, or deep philosophical thinking. However, the computer's ability to function in data processing often surpasses what people can do. For example, computers can perform arithmetic computations much faster than humans and with much greater accuracy, and they can perform these

THE MAKING OF AN INTEGRATED CIRCUIT CHIP

The process of manufacturing chips is very complicated, and involves hundreds of steps. These photos show just a few of the steps in the manufacturing sequence to help you visualize the process.

Silicon is the second most abundant substance on earth. To start the chip-making process, it is extracted from rocks and sand. This photo shows the unrefined silicon raw material.

After the silicon is purified by heating, the molten silicon is doped, that is, a tiny amount of impurities are added to give it certain electrical characteristics. Then the silicon is crystalized into a cylindrical ingot . . . .

As a part of the etch and re-etch process, the etched wafer is washed to remove the photo-resisting coating . . . .

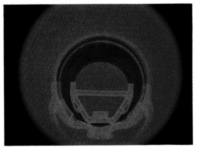

In a further step, the wafer is placed in a furnace filled with gases that add further doping impurities to the wafer to further change its electrical characteristics . . . .

After repeating the coating-etching-washing-heating cycle for as many as 18 times for complex chips, and after certain finishing steps, the final product looks like this. There are hundreds of chips on each wafer, and each chip—these are NS32032—is one-quarter inch square and has 60,000 transistors . . . .

The cylindrical ingots are sliced with a diamond saw to make thin, circular wafers. These wafers are polished to a glossy mirror finish . . . .

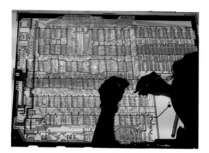

Meanwhile, the integrated circuit to be etched on the silicon wafer has been designed. A large-scale composite drawing might show 5 to as many as 18 overlays of circuitry. The drawing is 400 times larger than the finished size of the chip . . . .

Wafers are coated with a photo-resisting chemical, and then subjected to several processes, including this ion etching step, to etch the circuit pattern on the wafer . . . .

The individual chips are cut apart and mounted in metal or ceramic frames. Wires are connected so that electrical current can be carried into and out of the integrated circuits . . . .

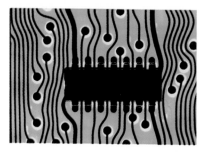

A greatly enlarged photo of a computer chip as it is wired into the circuit board of a microcomputer . . . .

And here is the end product: a microcomputer (in this case, a Radio Shack model) with a keyboard and video display. The circuit board with the chips is beneath the keyboard.

tasks over and over again without feeling or complaining about tedium.

COMPUTER SUBSYSTEMS

The computer is made up of several subsystems. Each subsystem is a functioning system in its own right, and each functions as part of the larger system. The major subsystems that make up a computer are:

Input

Central processing unit (CPU)

Secondary storage

Output

Telecommunications

The related input and output devices, such as optical character readers, cathode ray tubes, or line printers, are called **peripheral devices**. The exact function of these devices is explained more fully in Chapters 4 and 7. Peripherals are any input or output devices that are associated with a computer, but are not part of the central processing unit. The abbreviation **I/O** is often used to refer collectively to input and output devices.

INPUT SYSTEM

To send telegraph messages by Morse code, the telegraph operator converts words into a string of dots and dashes, which are electronically relayed over the line. Similarly, the **input system** of a computer reads data (in the form of printed characters on a page, holes in punched cards or paper tape, or magnetized areas on magnetic tapes or disks) and converts them into electronic pulses. It then transmits these pulses through wires to the central processing unit. In a computer each pulse is called a **bit** and represents one piece of data. The presence of a pulse can represent the digit 1 and the absence of the pulse, the digit 0. Groups of bits (pulses) are used to represent numbers, letters, or symbols. Such a group of bits is called a **byte.**

A computer may use one or several input devices, each handling a different form of input. The most common devices are:

1. Typewriter keyboard. Keystrokes on a typewriter cause electronic pulses to be sent to the central processing unit.

2. Laser beam scanner. Bar codes or symbols are scanned and translated into electronic pulses.

3. Optical character reader (OCR) and mark-sense reader. Handwritten, typewritten, or printed character forms or pencilled-in bubbles on a page are scanned and translated into electronic pulses.

4. Magnetic ink character reader (MICR). Magnetically coded characters on a page are scanned and translated into electronic pulses.

5. Card reader. Holes in a punched card are scanned and translated into electronic pulses.

6. Magnetic disk drive. Magnetized bits on a magnetic disk are scanned and translated into electronic pulses.

7. Magnetic tape drive. Magnetized bits on magnetic tape are scanned and translated into electronic pulses.

8. Paper tape reader. Holes punched into paper tape are scanned and translated into electronic pulses.

In the next chapter you will learn more about input devices and their functions.

CENTRAL PROCESSING UNIT

The most complex and powerful part of the computer is the **central processing unit (CPU)**, or processor. The CPU is the heart of the computer system. It integrates and coordinates overall operation. While the number and types of input or output devices may differ among computers, all must have a CPU. Keyboards, magnetic tape devices, line printers, and other system components are wired to the CPU (Figure 3-3).

The structure and operation of the CPU are described in some detail in Chapter 5. Here we list the main components of the processing subsystem.

The CPU may be small enough to hold in your hand (Figure 3-4) or as tall as a person (Figure 3-5). CPUs in large computers may

Figure 3-3 Parts of a Computer System. Most computers, regardless of size, contain at least one I/O device, a CPU which may be located beneath the keyboard, and secondary storage.

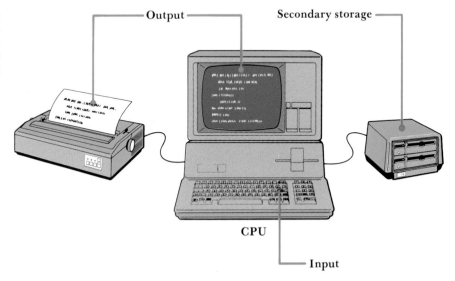

Figure 3-4 Pocket-size System. Even though this computer is battery powered and can be carried about, it still contains all the elements of a computer system—input device, CPU, and output device.

Figure 3-5 Large Computer System. A large IBM installation is the basis of this Weather Earth Command Station in Glenwood, New Jersey. The CPU of a system as large as this may occupy many cubic feet.

have control panels with many lights, buttons, and switches. They may also have a keyboard for entering instructions and a CRT to display information. On larger computers the CPU is called a **mainframe**. As we have mentioned, the term mainframe is sometimes used to mean an entire large computer with its I/O devices.

On smaller computers the CPU is a Large-Scale Integrated circuit (LSI) chip incorporated in the keyboard and not accessible or visible to the operator. All controls and directions to the CPU are made through the keyboard and no CPU lights or switches are present. On some computers the CPU is constructed from several chips that work together.

On a microcomputer the CPU is a solid state LSI chip, usually mounted on a printed circuit board with other chips (Figure 3-6). These chips may include memory control circuits which enable the CPU to communicate with peripheral devices. The circuitry is designed to move, store, and manipulate data electronically, but it has no moving parts—only electronic pulses move about inside the CPU. Its major parts are diagrammed in Figure 3-7.

Figure 3-6   Printed Circuit Board with Chips. Complex electronic circuits that function as the CPU and link the CPU to other components are manufactured on chips. The chips are then mounted on sockets that are soldered to a printed circuit board.

Basically, these circuits perform three major functions. They control the overall operation of the computer and coordinate its parts, perform arithmetic calculations and make logical decisions, and store the programs and data being processed.

CONTROL UNIT   The **control unit** supervises the operation of the entire computer. It is similar in function to the central switchboard of the telephone company which routes and directs calls from point to point. Control is achieved through the wires that connect all parts of the system to the central control board. The control unit monitors the line printer, tape drives, and other peripherals and provides a system for storing and remembering the instructions in programs. It opens and closes the circuits that feed data to and from storage.

For each particular application the CPU is directed by a program that has been written to solve that problem. This program is entered into the computer, usually along with the related data. It instructs the machine to perform mathematical calculations, read input, write information on the line printer, store data, and so on. The program is often called the **applications program**, and the collection of data to be processed is called the **data set**.

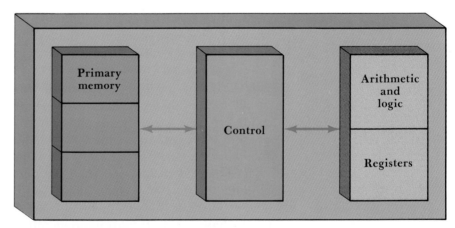

Figure 3-7   Parts of the Central Processing Unit. The three main sections of the CPU are primary memory, control, and arithmetic and logic unit (ALU). Primary memory has areas for input, working, output, and program storage. The registers of the ALU are used during processing.

ARITHMETIC AND LOGIC UNIT   Another section of the CPU, called the arithmetic and logic unit (ALU), performs mathematical calculations, compares numerical values, compares nonnumerical values (such as letters), and makes logical decisions. For example, the computer can be instructed to branch to one of three operations, depending on whether a value being tested is greater than, equal to, or less than another value.

When arithmetic calculations are to be performed, numbers are read into temporary holding stations. Numbers from several stations may be added, subtracted, or operated upon in some other way. After the calculations are completed, data are either output or returned to computer storage.

PRIMARY MEMORY   Primary memory, sometimes called primary storage, is another element of the CPU. In early computers this section of the CPU was composed of millions of magnetic storage cells. Newer computers use semiconductors, magnetic bubbles, flux rings, or charge coupled devices.

Primary memory is a reusable, fast storage medium, directly accessible by the control unit. Each storage cell is capable of storing one bit of data. A **bit** is the smallest unit of information that can be held in memory. Bits are stored in different forms, depending upon the type of primary memory.

Bits of data are generally stored in groups called bytes. A **byte** is a group of bits (pulses) that form a character—a digit, letter, or symbol. The number of bits that make up a byte depends on the coding system used. (These are discussed in more detail in Chapter 6.)

Primary memory capacity varies from one computer to another, ranging from a few thousand to over several million bytes. Storage capacity is one of the measures used to compare computer systems. The letter K (derived from the prefix *kilo*, meaning 1,000) is used to represent 2^{10} or 1,024 units. For example, 4K bytes means $4 \times 1,024 = 4,096$ bytes.

The student should be alert to the various forms that are used in the industry to refer to one thousand bytes. The letter K may stand for 1,024 (or more generally, 1000) as in 4K bytes to express 4,096 (four thousand) bytes. Kilobytes may be abbreviated to KB instead of K, as in 4KB. But it is never written 4KB bytes. Further, a

Figure 3-8 Magnetic Disk Devices. Disks coated with ferromagnetic material can store millions of characters. The disk pack, shown in use (*left*) and close up (*right*), consists of three or more disks mounted on a single shaft.

megabyte is one million bytes (or 1000 kilobytes, or 1000 × 1,024 bytes). Megabyte is abbreviated to M and MB (4M bytes, 4M, or 4MB).

    Primary memory is sometimes divided into parts, as shown in Figure 3-7. The control unit can allocate parts of its storage capacity to different tasks, and each part can function without interfering with the others.

SECONDARY STORAGE SYSTEM

The CPU uses its **secondary storage** system to store data that exceed its primary storage capacity. Secondary storage allows billions of numbers or characters to be stored until needed. (Secondary storage is discussed in detail in Chapter 6.)

    Data can be fed to and from primary storage in only a few billionths of a second, but it takes several thousandths of a second to retrieve a piece of data from secondary storage. Therefore, secondary storage is used for large files of data that need not be accessed con-

Figure 3-9 Floppy Disk Storage. Floppy disks, or diskettes, are small and lightweight and are easy to store and transport. The flexible disk is currently the most popular secondary storage medium for home and low-volume business use.

tinually, such as accounts receivable, accounts payable, inventory, and payroll records.

Most computer systems use a combination of primary and secondary storage media. The two most common forms of secondary storage currently in use are magnetic disk and magnetic tape.

MAGNETIC DISK   A **magnetic disk** is a metal or plastic disk, similar to a phonograph record without grooves, that is coated with a ferromagnetic material. Data are recorded on the disk for storage. They can be read out many times and will remain on the disk until they are erased. Once the data are erased, the disk can be reused.

There are several forms of disk storage. On large computer systems a **rigid disk** system, such as that shown in Figure 3-8, is most common. Several disks are assembled into an easily carried **disk pack**. A disk pack can store millions of characters in an arrangement called **random access storage**. This means data can be located on the disk without the computer having to search all the information stored in sequence. This feature gives disk storage great utility and access speed.

On microcomputers **floppy disk** storage systems are prevalent. A floppy disk, sometimes called a **diskette**, is a thin, flexible, plastic disk housed in an envelope (Figure 3-9). These inexpensive disks

Figure 3-10 Magnetic Tape Storage. Reels of magnetic tape can hold master files with hundreds of thousands of records. Tape is a popular medium for storing extremely large amounts of information that does not have to be accessed frequently or instantaneously. The tape library of a large research institution or government agency may fill warehouse rooms.

hold hundreds of thousands of bytes of data which can be accessed at random. An added feature of the floppy disk is that it can be easily filed, stored, or mailed, thereby greatly increasing its convenience and usefulness.

MAGNETIC TAPE **Magnetic tape** is a ½-inch-wide plastic ribbon, similar to the ¼-inch tape used on home tape recorders, that is coated with ferromagnetic material. It is wound on reels of varying length (Figure 3-10). Data are placed on tape by magnetizing small areas of the coating. These areas represent bits of data. It is a process similar to recording information on a home tape recorder except that digital data are encoded.

Magnetic tape allows large amounts of data to be stored in a comparatively small space. All data are stored in the sequence in which they were recorded, and the computer must search the data in sequence for the desired information. This arrangement is called **sequential access storage**.

OUTPUT SYSTEM

The computer's **output system** reports the results of processing by the CPU. Output is an essential step in the data processing cycle. Unless output is provided in some way, data processing has little value.

Figure 3-11   Cathode Ray Tube (CRT) Display. A CRT is an inexpensive means of making data immediately available to the user.

Reporting and outputting may be done on a variety of devices, such as line printer, card punch, cathode ray tube, or voice synthesizing unit. The output system converts electronic pulses from the CPU into documents, punched cards, visual display, or sounds to give the processed data in a usable form. The most common types of computer output are listed here. They are described in more detail in Chapter 7.

1. Cathode ray tube (CRT). Electronic pulses from the CPU are converted into a graphic display on a cathode ray tube. Drawings, illustrations, graphs, and tables can be displayed in black and white or color (Figure 3-11).

2. Console typewriter. Electronic pulses from the CPU are converted into readable characters by a typewriterlike printer.

3. Line printer. Electronic pulses from the CPU are converted into readable characters on a printed page. Line printers output large volumes of data such as multipage reports.

4. Plotter. Electronic pulses from the CPU are converted into graphic designs, plots, or line drawings on a sheet of paper.

Figure 3-12 Remote Computer Terminal. A terminal bring the power of a computer to locations far from the CPU such as homes, offices, and classrooms.

5. **Audio response unit** or **voice synthesizer.** Electronic pulses from the CPU are converted into sound. The devices are equipped with electrical circuits and amplifiers that can synthesize the human voice, musical tones, or other audible sounds.

6. **Card punch.** Electronic pulses from the CPU are translated into holes punched in a card.

7. **Paper tape punch.** Electronic pulses are converted into holes punched in a role of paper tape.

8. **Magnetic disk drive.** Electronic pulses from the CPU are stored as magnetized areas on a magnetic disk. The information on the disk may be stored and retrieved as necessary.

9. **Magnetic tape drive.** Electronic pulses from the CPU are recorded as magnetized areas on magnetic tape. The information may be stored and retrieved as necessary.

REMOTE TERMINALS

A **remote computer terminal** allows the user to gain access to a computer from a site different from that of the computer (Figure 3-12).

Data are transmitted from the terminal to the computer, and the results of processing return through the terminal. Long-range communication links, such as telephone or telegraph wires or microwave transmission, tie the terminal to the central computer.

Remote terminals make practical the processing of data that could not be done otherwise because it would be slow and expensive to send data physically to a central location. Terminals are used by large and small retailers to handle accounting, bookkeeping, and credit, by insurance companies to process claims, and by hospitals to process patients' records.

Many different types of terminals are available to meet different business needs. Some terminals print out typewriterlike copy, some display images on a CRT, others use punched cards or paper tape, and still others record on magnetic tape.

TELECOMMUNICATIONS SYSTEM

The **telecommunications system** is an integral part of all computers. It is the wires and circuits that tie all the input, output, and storage devices into a functioning whole (Figure 3-13). The telecommunications system is much like the human nervous system. It provides pathways over which signals, data, and instructions can be moved. The telecommunications system can also extend beyond a single computer to link several computers and remote terminals into a network.

Internal wiring integrates the computer's local devices. More elaborate and sophisticated external communication circuits, involving telephone lines, satellite links, or microwave transmission systems, enable data to be moved between computers and to and from remote terminals located thousands of miles apart.

CLASSES OF MODERN COMPUTER SYSTEMS

Computer systems are designed in a variety of sizes and prices. Small computer systems with limited input/output capacity may cost less than $100, while large, versatile systems with a variety of input/output devices can cost millions of dollars.

Table 3-1 lists some general classes of computers, showing

Figure 3-13 Telecommunications System. A series of CPUs and I/O devices within a local area can be linked together by coaxial cable.

their purchase price and their approximate monthly rental. The equipment configuration affects rental and selling price. A micro-computer with all possible peripherals may cost more than a less well-equipped small computer. Generally, the smaller systems, such as mi-

HOW TO TURN ON A COMPUTER

Source: Copyright © 1984 by The New York Times Company. Reprinted by permission.

How does one turn on a computer? Aside from whispering sweet nothings into its parallel port, the usual procedure is to flip the on-off switch. But even this simple act raises many questions for new users, many of whom may be afraid that hitting the wrong button will cause the machine, and perhaps Cleveland along with it, to blow up.

Does one turn the computer on before turning on the printer, modem, color monitor or other peripherals, or should the add-ons be powered first? Does it make any difference?

As usual, the answers from the experts are contradictory. The confusion appears to stem from the distant past of personal computing—that is, a couple of years ago—when some machines were not designed as well as they are today. When an electrical device is turned on, it sends a rush of voltage along the line. Such spikes may cause befuddlement among the ethereal data bits stored on floppies or hard disks.

Most computers are designed to withstand the tiny jolts that accompany the start-up or shut-down of common low-load computer peripherals, so the sequence in which these devices are turned on is of diminishing importance.

One school, which sounds the most sensible, holds that the proper sequence is to turn on the printer and other peripherals first and shut them off last, allowing them to vent their little outbursts when the computer is not on line. Naturally, the advice column in a leading magazine says this is madness, and recommends just the opposite.

The lesson is that if the sequence really made a big difference, half the experts would be sitting stupefied amid piles of smoking rubble.

TABLE 3-1   Computer Cost Comparison Table

	APPROXIMATE COST	APPROXIMATE MONTHLY RENTAL
Microcomputer	$100–5,000	$50–200*
Minicomputer	5,000–20,000	200–400*
Small computer	20,000–100,000	400-2,000
Medium computer	100,000–500,000	2,000–10,000
Large computer	500,000–10,000,000	10,000–200,000**

*Usually purchased, not leased.
**Usually leased, not purchased.

crocomputers, are purchased outright. Larger systems, on the other hand, are frequently leased rather than purchased.

The systems described below represent general classes of computer systems. Because improvements and changes in design occur frequently, they should be considered only as general illustrations, not as examples of specific models.

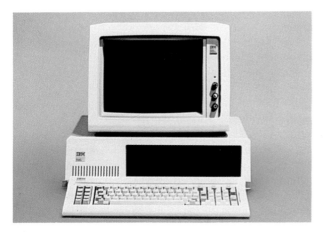

Figure 3-14   Microcomputer with 128K Memory. The first popular microcomputers had primary memory of 64K or under, but newer models have 128K, 256K, or in some cases even more.

Figure 3-15   Small Computer System. Small systems, with 64 kilobytes to 4 megabytes of storage capacity, may support from 2 to 20 or more secondary storage and I/O devices. They can handle batch input as well as immediate transactions. They may operate as stand alone units or accept data from or function as remote terminals.

MICROCOMPUTERS

Microcomputers are small, desktop systems that range in price from less than a hundred to several thousands of dollars. A typical system appears in Figure 3-14. Microcomputers usually have a limited number of input/output devices—perhaps only a keyboard for input, a floppy disk for storage, and a CRT display for output. These systems may have a primary memory of from 4K to 64K bytes or more.

Computers in this category are suitable for small business and domestic use. In the home they may be used for hobby and recreational activities; in business they are used in inventory, billing, payroll, and record-keeping applications.

MINICOMPUTERS

The next larger machine is classified as a minicomputer. A **minicomputer** is a general-purpose computing device, either rack mounted or small enough to fit on a desktop. These systems may have a minimum primary storage capacity of 32K or less bytes. Many include up to 128K bytes or more of memory. Minicomputers cost from under $5,000 to well over $20,000, fully equipped.

The category of minicomputer is becoming less widely recog-

Figure 3-16 Medium Computer System. The IBM 4300 Series, introduced in 1979, were the first IBM mainframes that could be used outside a central computing room.

nized, as microcomputers have gained acceptance. Many minicomputer systems in fact have microcomputer CPUs, and for all practical purposes there is little distinction between the two categories.

SMALL COMPUTERS

Figure 3-15 shows a typical **small computer system**. Such systems usually have a main memory system of 64K bytes or larger. The terminology may be a bit confusing because these machines are called *small* computers, but they are substantially larger than mini- or microcomputers. They include CRT displays, magnetic disk storage, and medium-speed printers capable of printing about 200 lines per minute. Small computer systems are used primarily by small business firms, manufacturing companies, schools, financial institutions, and government agencies.

MEDIUM COMPUTERS

Figure 3-16 illustrates a typical **medium computer system**. These systems usually include line printers, optical character readers, CRT dis-

Figure 3-17   Large Computer System. Machines such as this Burroughs 5930 may have millions of bytes of primary memory, hundreds of online secondary storage devices, and hundreds of online terminals allowing many users to input data or get information from the system. Primary storage may be organized to allow several simultaneous data transfers. A large system may involve one large computer with many I/O devices, or it may involve several large computers operating in complementary fashion.

plays, and disk and tape storage devices. Main memory may range from 96K bytes to 256K bytes or more.

Medium computers are used by retailing firms, factories, government agencies, and schools and universities. Common applications include order processing, payroll, inventory, and billing activities.

LARGE COMPUTERS

Figure 3-17 illustrates a **large computer system**. The primary storage capacity of large computers ranges from as little as 256K bytes to many millions. They are often equipped with magnetic tape and disk storage devices and specialized input and output devices. These large systems may support both remote terminals and local batch processing devices.

Such systems are used by large business firms, universities, government agencies, and the military. They are often linked with other computers to provide computing power in a large network of machines.

An outgrowth of these machines is a category sometimes called **supercomputers**, which are manufactured by Control Data Corporation, Cray, and others. These machines are even larger, cost millions of dollars, and provide enormous computing power.

In this chapter you have been introduced to the fundamentals of computer systems. Perhaps this overview has whetted your appetite and you want to know more about how computers read handwritten copy or perform calculations faster than the most brilliant mathematician in the world. In the next few chapters we will explore the fundamentals of computer systems. These chapters investigate input, processing, secondary storage, and output more thoroughly and will answer many questions. Together they will help you understand computer hardware.

SUMMARY AND KEY TERMS

- A **system** is a collection of objects, procedures, or techniques that interact in a regulated manner to form an organized whole. The major components of the computer system are its **input, central processing unit (CPU), secondary storage, output,** and **telecommunications systems.**

- A computer's input and output devices are known collectively as its **I/O** and may be referred to as **peripherals.**

- The **input system** converts data in the form of characters on a page, holes in tape, or areas magnetized on tape into electronic pulses which are sent to the CPU for processing. The presence of a pulse, or **bit,** may represent the digit 1 and its absence a 0.

- Major input devices include the **keyboard, laser beam scanner, optical character reader (OCR), mark-sense reader, magnetic ink character reader (MICR),** and **card, tape,** and **disk readers.**

- The **central processing unit (CPU)** integrates and coordinates the operation of the system. Its components are the **control unit,** the **arithmetic and logic unit,** and **primary memory.**

- Storage capacity is rated in **kilobytes (KB).** A kilobyte is 1,024 characters.

• The **secondary storage system** supplements a computer's **primary memory** capacity. Secondary storage may be provided by **magnetic disk** or **magnetic tape** systems.

• The computer's **output system** reports the results of processing. Output devices include **cathode ray tubes, console typewriters, line printers, plotters, audio response units** and **voice synthesizers, card** and **paper tape punches, magnetic tape drives,** and **magnetic disk drives.**

• A **remote computer terminal** allows a user at a site remote from the computer to gain access to it.

• The **telecommunications system** is composed of all the internal and external circuitry and communication links that tie all parts of a computer system into a functioning whole.

• **Microcomputers** are desktop devices with a limited number of input/output devices.

• **Minicomputers** are desktop or rack-mounted devices, usually containing approximately 64K bytes of memory.

• **Small computers** usually have at least a 64K byte main memory and include CRT displays, magnetic disk storage, and a medium-speed printer. They are designed for small-volume users such as small businesses, manufacturing companies, financial institutions, and government agencies.

• **Medium computers** contain memory up to 256K bytes or more and are used by medium-volume businesses and government institutions.

• **Large computers** may contain millions of bytes of memory and include a full range of input and output devices. Such systems are used by large businesses, schools, government agencies, and the military.

• **Super computers** are even larger and provide enormous computing power.

EXERCISES

1. What similarities and differences are there between the human system and the computer system?

2. List five common external memory aids that you use.

3. Explain what a system is and list several examples.

4. Draw a block diagram showing the related parts of the computer. Show input and output.

5. What do all computer input systems have in common?

6. Define peripheral device and CPU and explain how they differ in function.

7. Draw a schematic diagram showing the relationship of the parts of the CPU.

8. How does primary storage differ from secondary storage?

9. What kind of data are usually stored by a CPU in its primary memory?

10. What do all computer output systems have in common?

11. What is the function of the telecommunications system?

4

Learning Objectives

After studying this chapter, you should be able to
1. Define important terms relating to data input
2. Describe transaction-oriented processing
3. Describe batch data input systems
4. Describe various forms of optical input
5. List major forms of computer input
6. Contrast online and offline data input

Chapter Outline

Data Input Fundamentals
Input Modes
   Transaction-Oriented Processing
   Batch Processing
Data Input Requirements
   Accuracy
   Cost
   Speed
Online Data Input Devices
   Dumb Terminals
   Intelligent Terminals
   Voice Recognition Devices
   Touchtone Terminals
   Mice, Digitizers, and Other Devices
Source Data Input
   Point-of-Sale (POS) Terminals
   Laser Beam Scanners
   Optical Sense Readers
   Optical Character Readers
   Magnetic Ink Character Readers
Offline Data Input
   Key-to-Disk System
   Key-to-Tape System
   Key-to-Punched Card
Units of Input—from Bit to Data Base

Data Input

In this chapter you will learn about the first step in the data processing cycle—data input. All data, whether they be quantities or identifying numbers, names, or codes, must be converted into a form the computer can read before they can be processed. These data may originate from many sources. Payroll records, inventory reports, time cards, price tags, sales slips, shipping memos, telephone order forms—all create data which must be conveyed to the computer.

There have been many innovations in recent years in methods of collecting and entering data into the computer system. These new methods automate data input and reduce or eliminate the need for human operators.

You may wish to read this chapter in conjunction with Chapter 7, which discusses data output. There is a great similarity between input and output machines, and computer users sometimes refer to these devices collectively as I/O devices. Since input is the first step, we will look at it now and discuss output later.

DATA INPUT FUNDAMENTALS

A **source document** is created at the time of the original transaction. A source document may be a time card filled out by an employee, a list of parts prepared by an inventory clerk, an order taken over the phone by a salesperson. Sales, returns of goods, deliveries, shipments, goods on order, checks received, bills paid, or other transactions may generate source documents.

Regardless of the form of the source document, if the information it contains is to be processed by a computer, that information must be readable by the computer. A source document printed in machine-readable type, such as in Figure 4-1, is suitable for direct input to the computer. The handwritten information on the time card in Figure 4-2 is readable only by people and must be converted into machine-readable data by being punched into a card, keyboarded, or recorded on magnetic tape or disk for further processing.

Figure 4-1 Machine-Readable Source Document. This record of transaction can be optically scanned by a computer for input.

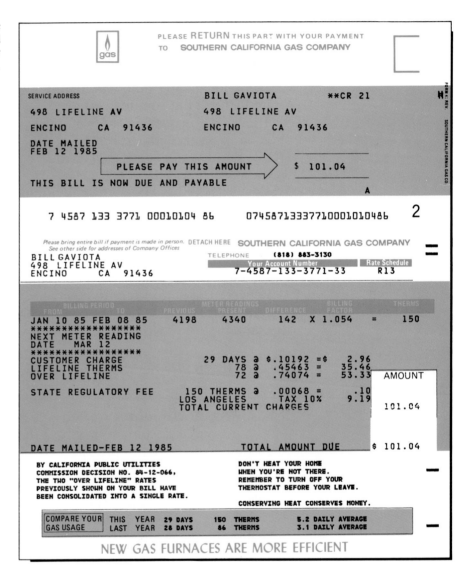

Data input machines translate the data on paper tape or cards, the magnetic areas on tape, or the optical images on forms into electronic pulses. The electronic pulses leave the input devices one at a time, forming a pulse train. A **pulse train** is a string of electronic pulses which transmit data (Figure 4-3).

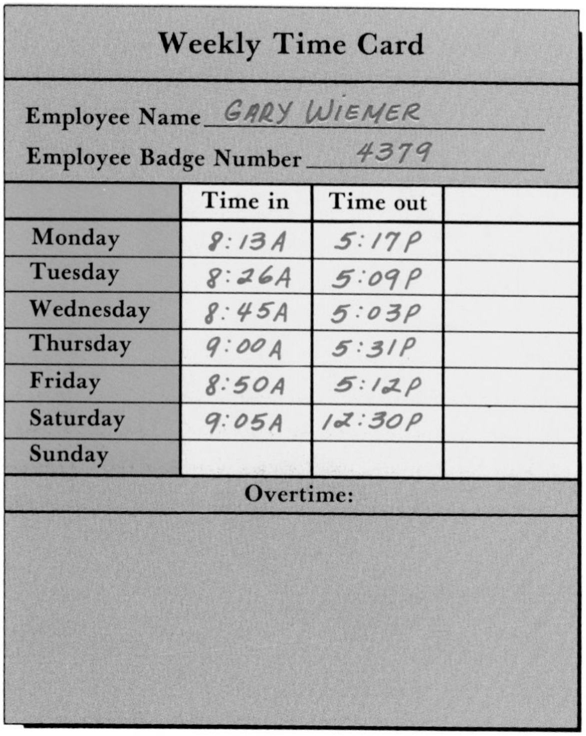

Figure 4-2 Handwritten Source
Document. In order to be input,
this type of transaction record
must be keyboarded or converted
into a form readable by the computer.

Weekly Time Card

Employee Name _GARY WIEMER_

Employee Badge Number ___4379___

	Time in	Time out	
Monday	8:13 A	5:17 P	
Tuesday	8:26 A	5:09 P	
Wednesday	8:45 A	5:03 P	
Thursday	9:00 A	5:31 P	
Friday	8:50 A	5:12 P	
Saturday	9:05 A	12:30 P	
Sunday			
Overtime:			

INPUT MODES

The two primary means of data input are transaction-oriented processing and batch processing. These two modes are described below.

TRANSACTION-ORIENTED PROCESSING

In **transaction-oriented processing** the computer receives information from a terminal at the time a transaction takes place (Figure
4-4). There is no delay between the time the information is entered
and its processing by the computer. This method is sometimes call
online processing or **real time processing**.

Information can be entered from automated devices which
read bar codes or scan optical or magnetic characters on a tag or
card. It may also be entered by a human operator who keyboards the
data.

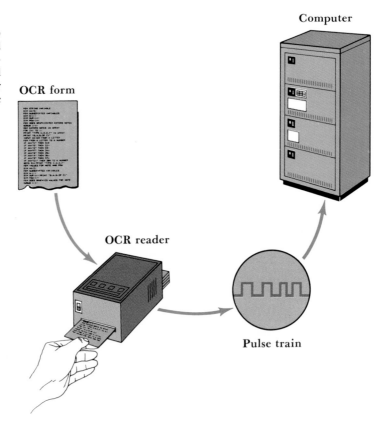

Figure 4-3 Data Converted to Electronic Pulses. Data recorded on an optical character recognition (OCR) form are read and translated by an optical character recognition reader into a pulse train for input.

One advantage of transaction-oriented processing is the speed with which data can be entered or retrieved. A clerk at an airline ticket counter may enter a request for a customer's seating preference or for a change in a ticket by keying data into a terminal. The computer will acknowledge the request immediately and process the information accordingly. A second advantage is that it eliminates the need for an intermediate storage step, such as punching data into cards.

BATCH PROCESSING

In **batch processing** data generated by a transaction are recorded on magnetic tape, floppy disks, or other media (Figure 4-5). At some

Figure 4-4 Transaction-Oriented (Online) Process. In this form of data input, information is entered into the computer directly from a terminal and processed immediately.

Terminal

Computer

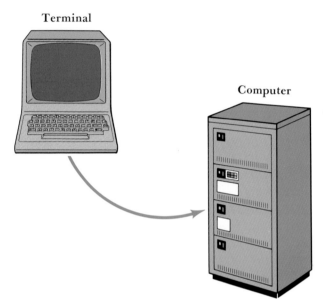

time after the data have been recorded, the computer processes them. Batch processing is sometimes referred to as **offline processing,** since the information is gathered away from the computer.

Batch processing was widely used before online systems were introduced. It is still used when information does not have to be acted on immediately or when stored data do not have to be kept up-to-date with every transaction. The information is relayed to a central point and processed at night when there is less load on the computer. Bank checking accounts are usually processed in a batch. The checks are honored as they are received at the bank, but then they are collected in a file and mailed to account holders in a batch with a statement at the end of the month.

DATA INPUT REQUIREMENTS

Whether transaction-oriented (online) or batch (offline) methods are used, three major factors are usually considered in judging the utility of a data input system.

Figure 4-5 Batch (Offline) Processing. In batch processing, information is stored on magnetic media and entered into the computer at some later time.

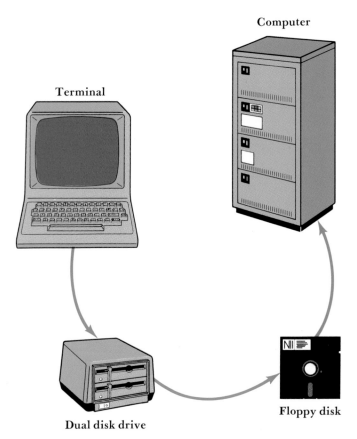

Computer

Terminal

Dual disk drive

Floppy disk

ACCURACY

The data input method must accurately reflect the details of the transaction and report information without error. Some methods, such as bar code scanners and punched card readers, are very accurate; they may read millions of pieces of information without an error. Other methods, such as keyboarding, involve human operators who can make mistakes. The operator must read and interpret handwritten or printed characters and then type the correct characters.

One means of improving the accuracy of data keyboarded by

GOODBYE TO QWERTY

Source: Reprinted from *Computer-Assisted Engineering,* copyright November 1984 by Penton/IPC, Inc., Cleveland, Ohio.

The days of the standard or Qwerty keyboard may be numbered. And good riddance say many workstation designers. The Qwerty keyboard was designed in 1872 specifically to slow the operator's typing speed. To minimize key jamming, a major problem in early mechanical typewriters, the developers of the Qwerty system positioned keys so that those letters most frequently used were spaced far apart necessitating long, speed-reducing reaches for the typist.

The introduction of the electric typewriter made this restriction unnecessary but Qwerty was so well established that none of the many more efficient keyboard designs offered were able to make any inroads. However, the need for greater data entry speed may finally be having an effect. In addition, two other factors are helping to pave the way for a change:

Computer keyboards are more complex than the old standard, usually containing many additional symbols. Because these new symbols must be learned anyway, it is not a great hardship to learn a totally new board.

Secondly, many engineers and managers who did not learn typing on a standard keyboard are now required to learn to enter data. They can, therefore, be more easily taught on a new keyboard.

The leading contender to replace the Qwerty seems to be the Dvorak, a keyboard designed by an American educator in 1932. Despite many attempts to introduce the Dvorak it has only recently been accepted by ANSI [American National Standards Institute] as an acceptable alternative to the standard keyboard.

The Dvorak keyboard is now available on the equipment of some major manufacturers such as Wang, IBM, and Apple, and is under consideration by many others. Advantages claimed for the Dvorak layout include:
• The usually stronger right hand does more work than the left (56% and 44% respectively). With the Qwerty its 57% left and 47% right.
• Work assigned to the different fingers is proportional to their strength.
• Key configuration is designed so that 70% of the typing is done on the home row, 22% on the third row and 8% on the first row. Therefore, finger motions from row to row are reduced 80%.

The end result is said to be a 40% increase in productivity.

Dvorak keyboard

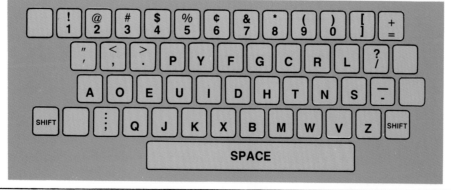

human operators is by **verifying**. In verifying a second operator reads the original source document and compares it to the entry made by the first operator. Information that has been entered by an operator is said to be verified if its accuracy has been checked by a second operator. Modern data input terminals are designed to reduce the need for verifying. For example, some systems display the entered line on a screen before transmitting it to the CPU. This allows the operator to check the accuracy of the key strokes.

COST

Cost is a major factor in data input. Automated input methods are designed to read bar codes and specially coded tags or to scan source documents such as checks without human operators. Such automation reduces labor costs.

SPEED

The amount of time required to input information into a computer is another important factor. In batch processing data is entered over a period of time and processing is delayed. Where immediate return of results is necessary, transaction-oriented systems are generally used. When a jumbo jet is sitting at a passenger gate, the ticket agent must be able to determine immediately how many seats are available. The delays inherent in a batch system would not serve the needs of the airline's ticketing process.

ONLINE DATA INPUT DEVICES

A variety of online data input processing methods have been developed. These include dumb terminals, intelligent terminals, voice recognition devices, Touchtone input, mice, and digitizers.

DUMB TERMINALS

Some computer terminals relay data directly to the computer. They have no memory or built-in logic. These devices are called **dumb ter-**

Figure 4-6 Dumb Terminal. The keyboard of a dumb terminal simply connects the user with the CPU. It has no processing capabilities.

Figure 4-7 Intelligent Terminal. Intelligent terminals combine terminal hardware with microcomputers, some of which may be programmed by the user. Online secondary storage units, such as floppy disk devices, may be used by the intelligent terminal to process small jobs without interacting with the CPU.

minals because they are unable to manipulate or process data. They rely upon the computer for formatting, error checking, and data storage. Dumb terminals serve only to collect data and forward them to the computer for processing (Figure 4-6).

INTELLIGENT TERMINALS

When inexpensive microprocessors were introduced, it became practical to construct terminals with their own built-in computers. These were called **intelligent** or **smart terminals** (Figure 4-7). Intelligent terminals can process data locally, reformat information, and check logic or accuracy before forwarding the information to the computer.

Intelligent terminals simplify data input because they can cue the operator by asking for information. Some have diskette storage devices attached. This enables the terminal to keep a record of data sent to the main computer. In the event of a loss of information at the main computer, the intelligent terminal can reconstruct the information.

Figure 4-8 Voice Recognition Input. This operator is speaking into a microphone. The equipment shown on the left will convert her voice into digital signals sent to the computer for processing.

VOICE RECOGNITION DEVICES

A good deal of research and development has been done on **voice recognition devices** (Figure 4-8). These input machines are capable of deciphering commands given by a human voice and converting them into pulses which are sent to the computer for processing or for display in digital form (Figure 4-9). This ability to interpret voice patterns eliminates the need for more direct data input methods such as keyboard or keypunch.

Voice recognition devices convert analog wave forms of human speech to digital form (Figure 4-10). The end point of each word is determined by silence and pauses. A computer then compares the resulting pattern to patterns of words stored in the machine. If a match is found, the word is displayed on a CRT or printed on a page. If a match cannot be found, the computer prompts the speaker to repeat the word or to use a synonym.

Several different forms of voice recognition equipment are

Figure 4-9 Marketable Applications of Voice Recognition. Data-entry, security, and telephone applications require improved recognition techniques to reach these projected market shares. Current technology is adequate to develop recognition machines for appliances, toys and video games, and other devices that need only simple commands such as "on," "off," "left," "right," "fire" and "kill."

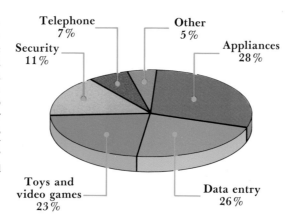

now on the market (Figure 4-11). The simplest is a machine that is programmed for a particular speaker and can recognize only that speaker's voice pattern using pitch and volume. Such a system is called **speaker-dependent**. A **speaker-independent** system is able to interpret the speech of many different people.

Voice recognition machines can decipher only a limited vocabulary of isolated words or short phrases. The ideal voice recognition equipment would be able to interpret continuous speech and be independent of the speaker. But to date no device has been built that can handle strings of sounds without pauses to identify words, words that sound alike, and the wide range of human voices. Perhaps soon machines will be able to recognize series of words spoken in different tones, inflections, accents, and dialects and so make communication between people and machines easier.

TOUCHTONE TERMINALS

The widespread use of the Touchtone telephone has led to the development of **Touchtone terminals** (Figure 4-12). Touchtone terminals are acoustic devices that emit sounds that are picked up by a telephone transmitter and sent over the line. Sound transmission eliminates the need for connecting wires between the telephone and the terminal.

Using a Touchtone input system, for example, a salesperson may dial his or her office computer and then enter order informa-

Figure 4-10 Voice Recognition Process. The voice recognition process consists of four basic steps:

(1) To convert voice input from analog to digital representation, the analog waveform is sampled thousands of times per second in various segments of the sound-frequency spectrum.

(2) In isolated word recognition, word endpoints are determined by the periods of silence. In continuous speech recognition, word endpoints may be ambiguous (for example, "porous" versus "pour us"), but endpoint determination can be aided by knowledge of the language syntax.

(3) Finding the best match between the input word and the admissible vocabulary involves extensive statistical analysis. Processing time in this step is proportional to the vocabulary size.

(4) After finding the best match, the system decides if the input word qualifies as a "recognition." If it is, confirmation is sent to the speaker by voice synthesis or CRT display. If the input word is not the best match, the system can prompt the speaker for more information to clarify the situation.

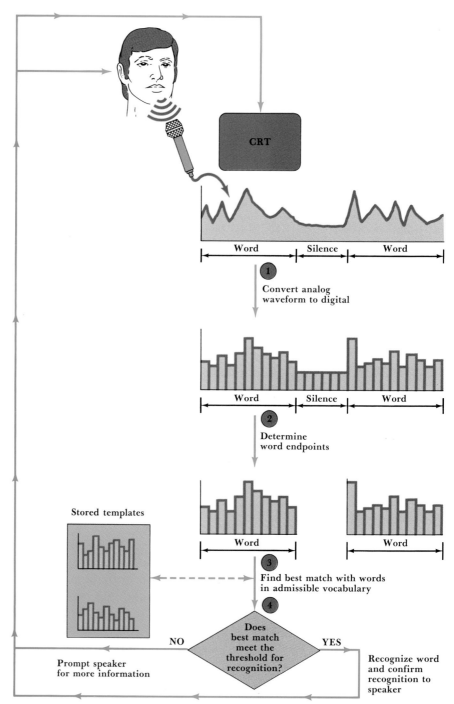

Figure 4-11 Voice Recognition Equipment. A variety of voice recognition equipment is on the market. Some devices are relatively inexpensive circuit boards that are plugged directly into the computer. More elaborate circuitry is able to recognize the voices of different speakers. Such equipment can be used, for example, for zip code sorting that requires recognition of different utterances which may be spoken without intervening pauses.

tion through a portable Touchtone terminal. As keys representing letters or numbers are pressed, the Touchtone terminal emits audible tones. There is no physical connection between the Touchtone terminal and the telephone line. In effect, every telephone becomes a point at which data can be entered. (Devices which input data acoustically are explained in more detail in Chapter 10.)

Figure 4-12 Touchtone Entry Device. Touchtone terminals emit tones that can be sent over ordinary telephone lines to a computer for processing.

MICE, DIGITIZERS, AND OTHER DEVICES

Another means of direct input is a device called a **mouse** (Figure 4-13). The mouse is moved about on a tabletop to direct a pointer on the screen of a CRT. The mouse is mounted on a rotating ball. When it is moved, optical sensors in the device detect the rotating motion, and the motion directs the pointer to various figures, or **icons**, displayed on the CRT. For example, the operator may wish to select a color from a list of colors displayed on the screen. The user moves the mouse to direct the pointer on the screen to a color on the

Figure 4-13 The Mouse. As the operator moves the mouse about, it positions a pointer on the screen, thereby eliminating the need for keyboarding instructions.

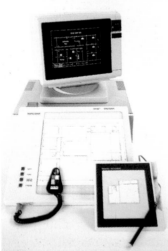

Figure 4-14 The Digitizer. The digitizing tablet holding a printed form is the work surface for this device. Digitizers such as these are frequently used in engineering and circuit design.

list and then presses a button on the mouse to input the desired color. This eliminates the need for a keyboard and therefore for typing skills.

Input can also be accomplished through the use of **digitizers**. The digitizer consists of a digitizing pad or tablet, a paper or pre-printed form to be used on the pad, and a conventional ball pen or other pointing device (Figure 4-14). The operator draws pictures or traces lines on the form which is placed on the digitizer pad. As lines are drawn, the pad generates x-y coordinates describing the lines and sends the coordinates to the computer. The information is processed and the lines are displayed on a screen or printer. No keyboarding is involved.

A variety of other devices are used to input data. A **joystick** enables data to be input by hand movements and does not require typing skills. A **light pen** is moved about on the face of a light-sensitive CRT and the computer responds to the movements of the pen. **Touch-sensitive screens** detect the touch of a human finger (Figure 4-15).

Figure 4-15 Touch-Sensitive Screen. Touch-sensitive screens enable operators to enter information by merely touching the screen. The elimination of keyboarding facilitates rapid and frequent manipulation of elements in solving design problems.

SOURCE DATA INPUT

Source data input, sometimes referred to as **point-of-sale (POS) input**, is the gathering of information at the time a transaction takes place. This type of input is widely used in retailing and banking. The most common source data input systems are bar code scanning, optical scanning, and magnetic ink recognition.

POINT-OF-SALE (POS) TERMINALS

The terminal illustrated in Figure 4-16 converts data entered from a sales clerk's keyboard into electronic pulses that are sent to a computer for processing. The **point-of-sale (POS) terminal** is now frequently seen in retail stores. It provides a convenient means of preparing invoices and receipts, updating inventory files, and checking credit at the time a sale is made.

Each terminal is provided with keys for entering information such as a product code or price. The computer locates the product code in an information file (often stored on magnetic disk or tape)

Figure 4-16 Point-of-Sale Terminal. Many retail establishments are equipped with POS terminals. They are used to enter sales data, check credit, and print receipts.

and processes the sale. It may adjust the inventory to reflect the purchase, post the sale to the customer's account or record the payment, and print out a receipt at the terminal showing the items purchased, price, and sales tax.

LASER BEAM SCANNERS

Laser scanning is a fast, accurate method of reading data from a product label for point-of-sale processing. The **laser beam scanner** uses a beam of coherent light to read bar codes or symbols on a product or package. Coherent light beams do not spread as ordinary light beams do. Instead they form a tightly focused, narrow ribbon of light. Items are moved across the scanner beam to input data to a computer (Figure 4-17).

Laser beam scanners are used in supermarkets for checking out goods (Figure 4-18). Most canned goods and articles sold in drugstores and supermarkets now carry the **Universal Product Code (UPC)** (Figure 4-19). Soft goods, such as vegetables or bulk goods, cannot be labeled with bar codes. For such items, the clerk inputs the data from a keyboard associated with the scanner.

Figure 4-17 Scanner Input Device. A laser beam is used to scan bar codes or symbols on products.

Figure 4-18 Supermarket Scanner. Supermarket checkers move products labeled with the universal product code across the beam. The scanner converts the bar code into electronic pulses and sends them to the CPU for processing.

Figure 4-19 Universal Product Code (UPC). A standard bar code has been adopted. The code uses vertical bars and spaces that are easily read by a scanner. Each product is identified by a different pattern consisting of 10 pairs of bars of varying thickness separated by spaces of varying thickness.

OPTICAL SENSE READERS

Optical sense readers are devices that are capable of interpreting pen or pencil marks from cards, tags, or packages (Figure 4-20). They do not decipher printed letters or numbers. The marks are converted into an electronic pulse that is sent to the computer for processing.

PUTTING DATA BEHIND BARS

Source: Mini-Micro Systems, June 1983, pp. 240-241.

There are three basic types of bar-code readers: wand, fixed beam and moving beam. Each works in the same way, bouncing a light beam off of a bar-code pattern and measuring the reflected light.

Pen-like wand readers, used primarily in inventory applications, are manually pressed against a bar code and pulled across the code at speeds as high as 30 in. per sec. MSI Data Corp. offers a completely self-contained wand reader, but most wands must be connected by cable to a signal-conditioning and -digitizing unit. Fixed-beam readers, popular in manufacturing work-in-progress tracking, use a laser source to scan code on objects passing on a conveyer belt at distances as far as 16 in. Supermarkets use moving-beam readers, incorporating a laser beam that sweeps across the code as many as 400 times per sec. The line of the sweep can be rotated automatically, so that objects to be scanned can be held at any orientation as long as the code is facing the reader. Intermec recently introduced a hand-held, moving-beam, laser scanner for inventory applications in which the contact required with wand readers is impractical.

There are about a dozen bar-code standards in use. The schemes vary in the number of characters represented, the number of bars and spaces required to specify a character, the relative width of thick bars to thin bars and error-detection provisions. The Universal Product Code used in retail applications, for example, is a fixed-length, numeric-only code in which each character is composed of two spaces and two bars. Code 39, popular for industrial applications, is a variable-

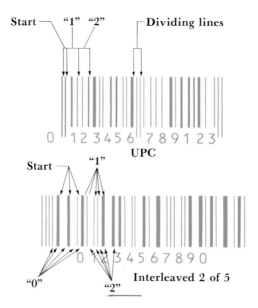

Start — "1" "2"   ┌Dividing lines

3 widths of bars and spaces
2 bars and 2 spaces per character
totaling 7 unit widths

0 1 2 3 4 5 6 7 8 9 1 2 3

UPC

Start — "1"

Two widths of bars and spaces

Five bars or five spaces per character, interleaved

Two wide bars or spaces per character

"0"   0 1 2 3 4 5 6 7 8 9 0
"2"   **Interleaved 2 of 5**

length, alphanumeric code using five bars and four spaces per character. Other codes include Interleaved 2 of 5, used in industry, and Codabar, popular for library-circulation and medical applications such as blood inventory.

Bar-code-reader reliability is limited more by bar-code print quality than by reader capabilities. With high-quality printing, most readers can correctly scan a code on the first try more than 99 percent of the time, with error rates of 1 in tens of million of characters. In actual applications, bar-code samples are made less readable by ink spreading, voids in bars, spots in spaces and uneven bar edges. The effects of low-quality code can sometimes be minimized by adjusting the size and shape of the scanning beam, but results can still be less than satisfactory: one western university library manually affixed 300,000 bar code labels to its books before discovering the code was unreadable.

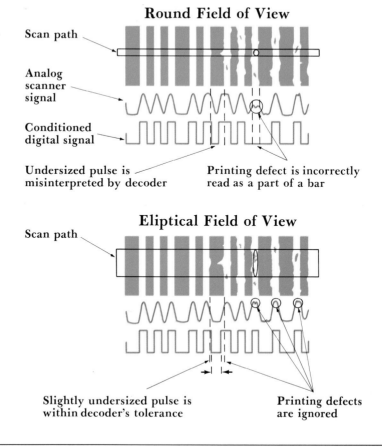

Round Field of View

Scan path

Analog scanner signal

Conditioned digital signal

Undersized pulse is misinterpreted by decoder

Printing defect is incorrectly read as a part of a bar

Eliptical Field of View

Scan path

Slightly undersized pulse is within decoder's tolerance

Printing defects are ignored

Figure 4-20 Optical Sense Reader. Devices such as these are able to read bar codes from tags and tickets in the field.

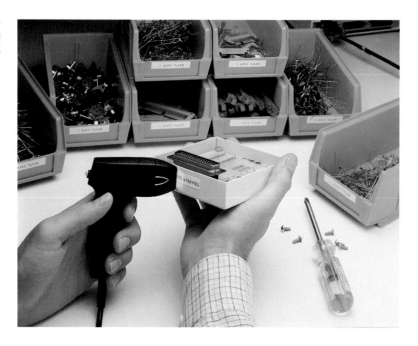

Figure 4-21 Optical Character Reader. OCR readers are capable of reading letters or numbers which are converted into electronic pulses sent to the computer for processing.

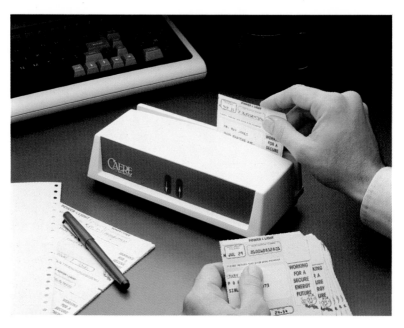

Figure 4-22 Optical Characters. Special type faces have been designed to be read by optical character readers.

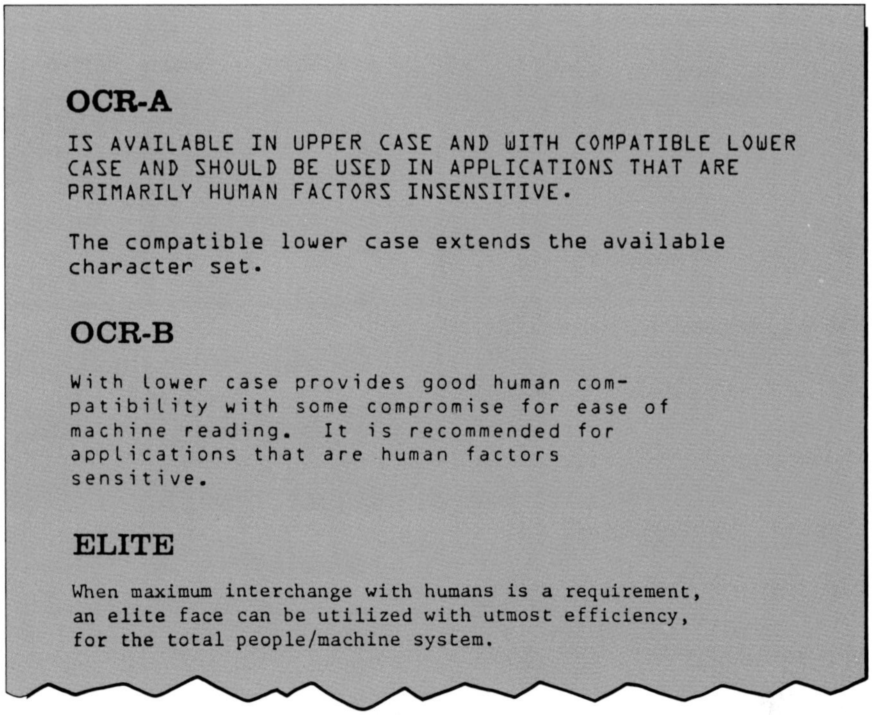

OCR-A

IS AVAILABLE IN UPPER CASE AND WITH COMPATIBLE LOWER CASE AND SHOULD BE USED IN APPLICATIONS THAT ARE PRIMARILY HUMAN FACTORS INSENSITIVE.

The compatible lower case extends the available character set.

OCR-B

With lower case provides good human compatibility with some compromise for ease of machine reading. It is recommended for applications that are human factors sensitive.

ELITE

When maximum interchange with humans is a requirement, an elite face can be utilized with utmost efficiency, for the total people/machine system.

Optical sense cards are used to record test scores, prices, order numbers, or stock inventory directly in the field. These source documents are then read by the optical sense reader directly and do not require verification. A card or other optical sense form and an ordinary pencil or pen become a convenient source of data input. However, accuracy does depend on the marks being made properly. Marks that are not solid or heavy enough may be misread.

OPTICAL CHARACTER READERS

The optical input device shown in Figure 4-21 is typical of **optical character recognition (OCR)** machines. It reads data optically and converts them to electronic pulses. **Optical character readers** are designed to read certain handwritten, typewritten, or printed numbers, letters, and special characters from orders, cash register tapes, adding machine tapes, utility bills, telephone bills, tickets, and similar source documents (Figure 4-22). They can be programmed to read

Figure 4-23 Handwritten Characters Read by OCR. Some OCR readers can interpret neatly printed and written characters.

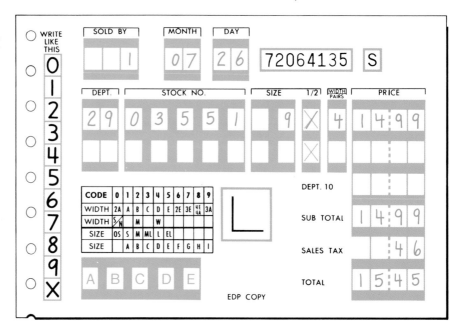

selected areas on a bill or order form. For example, they can read a price column, a total, a printed form number, or a handprinted message. Figure 4-23 illustrates handwritten numeric characters that can be read optically. The readers can decipher only precisely formed characters; they cannot yet interpret more casual handwriting.

OCR provides a convenient means of recording data in the field without keyboarding. The salesperson, secretary, or stock clerk can write each character in a separate block on specially printed forms, observing a few simple rules for letter shaping.

Devices that read cash register and adding machine tapes have input and take-up spindles to hold the rolls of tape. The tape is threaded from the input spindle, through the reading chamber, and onto the take-up spindle.

MAGNETIC INK CHARACTER READERS

Figure 4-24 illustrates a **magnetic ink character recognition (MICR)** device designed to read data printed in ink containing particles of

Figure 4-24 Magnetic Ink Character Reader. These machines read magnetically inscribed checks, deposit slips, or bills. The data can be processed immediately or transferred to magnetic tape for later processing. As the checks pass through, in addition to reading them and inputting their data, the machine sorts them into compartments according to their identification numbers.

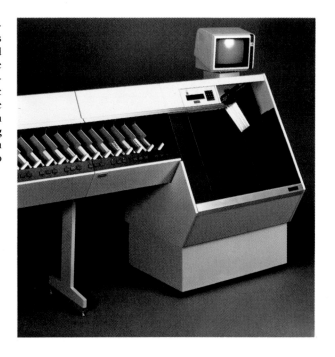

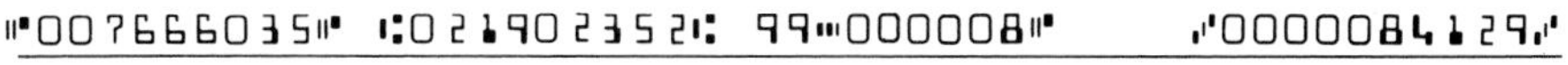

⑇"007666035"'⑆ ⑆021902352⑆ 99⑇000008"'⑆   ⑆"0000084129⑆

Figure 4-25 Magnetic Ink Characters. Magnetic ink characters are specially shaped characters printed in magnetic ink. They are readable by both humans and machines.

magnetic material. The most common magnetically inscribed documents in use today are checks, deposit slips, and bills. Specially shaped characters are printed on the documents in magnetic ink (Figure 4-25). Figure 4-26 shows the layout of the check form approved by the American Banking Association.

MICR readers include a document hopper, a read station, and a stacker. Hundreds of documents can be read and sorted in one minute. The machine can read documents of different sizes and thicknesses, such as a collection of checks from many different banks. As the documents move through the MICR device, they are scanned for the special ink images. The magnetic images on the page affect a magnetic field in the machine which sends electronic pulses to the computer for processing.

Figure 4-26 Approved Check Form with MICR Characters. The information encoded on blank checks is the account number and the number of the bank that handles the account. When the check is written out and first processed by a bank, personnel at that bank use a magnetic character inscriber to encode the amount for which the check was written on the check (as in the right hand lower corner of the example).

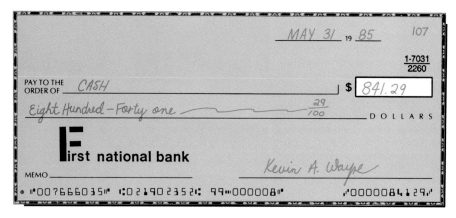

OFFLINE DATA INPUT

The major forms of batch or offline data entry include key-to-disk, key-to-tape, and key-to-punched card input.

KEY-TO-DISK-SYSTEM

The system shown in Figure 4-27 is a **key-to-disk** system. Data are keyboarded onto magnetic disks using a cathode ray tube terminal. A system may be designed to use either rigid or floppy disks. The disk is then placed on an online disk drive for input to the central processing unit.

Some systems prompt the operator by displaying formatted data on the screen. As the operator responds to the prompts, the data are stored on the disk. This type of system may include a verifier. If the verifier detects an error, it will interrupt the operator and ask for correct information to be inserted.

KEY-TO-TAPE SYSTEM

Data are recorded on magnetic tape using a machine that contains a keyboard and tape drive. As keys are struck, data are recorded on the tape. Then the information is sent to the CPU for processing. The cartridges are reusable. A **key-to-tape** system is shown in Figure 4-28.

Figure 4-27 Key-to-Disk System. Data are keyed onto magnetic disks from cathode ray tube terminals. A typical system has 8 to 64 work stations, each with a keyboard and display screen, that are linked to a minicomputer, sometimes referred to as the shared processor.

Figure 4-28 Key-to-Tape System. Data are stored on reusable tape and later entered into the computer. Single station or multistation devices may be used. There are also now key-to-disk-to-tape systems in which a computer program transfers data initially recorded on disks to tapes for later processing.

As keys are depressed, characters are recorded on magnetic tape. As each character is typed, it is displayed on a screen before the operator. A counter keeps track of the number of items or units of related items entered on each tape. To verify data, the tape is rewound to the beginning and the source document keyboarded a second time. An error is corrected by backspacing and rekeying.

Both key-to-tape and key-to-disk systems are more efficient than punched card entry. They allow millions of characters to be stored in a small amount of space, and tapes and disks are less expensive than punched cards.

Records on magnetic tapes are input by tape reading devices. **Magnetic tape readers** convert magnetized areas on a roll of magnetic tape into a string of electronic pulses which are sent to the CPU for processing. **Paper tape readers** translate holes in paper tape to pulses and relay them to the computer at speeds up to 300 characters per second. Both paper and magnetic tape are being replaced by floppy disks as input media because of the lower cost and higher reliability of disk storage systems.

Figure 4-29 Keypunch Machine. Each time a key is depressed, the proper Hollerith code representing the character is punched into the card. After the cards are punched, they are transferred to a verifier machine, on which an operator rekeys the data, and then they are ready to be fed into a card reader.

KEY-TO-PUNCHED CARD

In this system a keypunch operator punches data from a keyboard onto cards. Figure 4-29 illustrates a **keypunch machine**. As the operator presses a key, the appropriate code is punched into one column of the card and the character is printed at the top of the card at the same time. Some systems store the data in a buffer area until they are verified, and then the entire contents are punched onto a card.

Because a manual activity is involved in this system of converting source data into machine-readable form, a certain number of errors will occur. This makes verification of punched entries an essential step to ensure the accuracy of data input.

PUNCHED CARD   In referring to the **punched card**, several terms are used synonymously, such as IBM card, punched card, Hollerith card, tab card, unit record, and data card. The standard punched card is shown in Figure 4-30. Each card is $3\frac{1}{4} \times 7\frac{3}{8}$ inches, and sometimes a corner is cut. The card contains 80 vertical **columns**. Each column is composed of 12 punch positions for one alphabetic, one numeric,

Figure 4-30 Standard Punched Card. This card can hold up to 80 letters, special characters, or digits. The card reader does not read the characters we see on the card. It can read only punched holes.

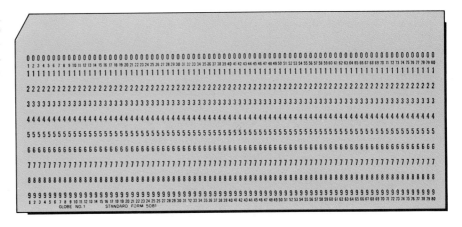

Figure 4-31 Standard Punched Card Code. A different set of punches is used to represent each letter, digit, or special character.

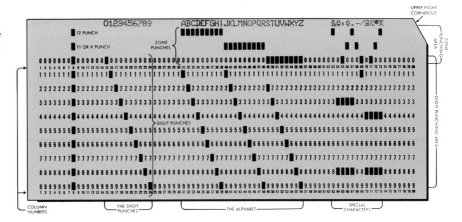

or one special character. Cards are available in a variety of colors, printed with special forms, or with a colored stripe for identification.

A punch position is sometimes called a **bit**. A group of bits (punch positions) are combined to form each character, or **byte**. One or more columns reserved for related information is called a **field**. Fields can range from 1 to 80 columns in width.

The standard coding system used to record data on a punched card is the **Hollerith code** (Figure 4-31). This coding system uses a combination of up to three bits to represent each digit, letter, or special character.

In 1971 IBM introduced a **96-column punched card** (Figure

Figure 4-32   96-Column Punched Card. Up to 96 columns of data can be punched onto a single card. The upper part of the card is a print area and can hold up to 128 printed characters.

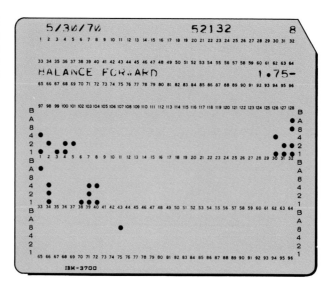

4-32) for use in their System 3 computers. Up to 96 columns of data can be punched onto a single card using a coding system in which a combination of six punch positions (bits) encodes each character. The card is relatively small ($2\frac{5}{8} \times 3\frac{1}{4}$ inches). The top portion, containing the printed information, is called the print area, and the lower portion is called the punch area.

Punched cards have been used for many years and are still found in some data processing operations, particularly in older installations that rely heavily upon mailing and processing cards to customers or clients. However, their use is rapidly diminishing. Punched cards are bulky to handle and store, they are subject to damage and mutilation, and manual encoding is less accurate and more expensive than more automated procedures.

UNITS OF INPUT—FROM BIT TO DATA BASE

Input can be broken down into units of different amounts of information. We will summarize the terms used for these units here, and then describe them in greater detail later as we discuss information management systems, especially in Chapter 11.

The smallest piece of information that can be entered into the computer is a *bit*. Bits used in combination make up bytes. A *byte* represents a letter, number, or special character. Bytes go together to make up a field. A *field* is a group of related characters that constitute an item of data (for example, a name, a rate of interest, an amount paid). Fields go together to make up a record. A *record* is a collection of related fields, that is, related data items, that are treated as a unit. In punched cards, columns holding related information constitute a field, and the whole card is a record. Records go together to make up a file. A *file* is a collection of related records that are treated as a unit. Files, in turn, make up a library. A *library* is a collection of various files. The sum total of all the libraries in an organization is called a *data base*. So, the smallest unit of input is a bit. At the other end of the scale is the data base containing all the information available for processing and retrieval by an organization.

In this chapter we have described many different input methods—from the early punched card machine to recent inventions such as the mouse, joystick, and digitizer. Improvements and innovations in input methods broaden the means by which data can be entered into the computer. Perhaps in the future you will be able to sit down before a computer and simply speak or point to objects on a screen in order to generate a neatly typed letter or report, properly spelled, punctuated, and formatted. But until this dream becomes a reality, you still need not only some keyboard and typing skills, but also a knowledge of how to use the devices now available.

SUMMARY AND KEY TERMS

- A **source document** is a record generated at the time a transaction takes place.
- Data input devices translate data on **input media** into a **pulse train** which is transmitted to the CPU for processing.
- In **transaction-oriented processing** there is no delay between the entry of information and its processing. This input mode is also called **online** or **real time processing**.

• In **batch processing** data are recorded on a storage medium and then processed at some time after the original transaction takes place. This input mode is called **offline processing**.

• The major factors to be considered in evaluating data entry systems are **accuracy**, **cost**, and **speed**.

• **Dumb terminals** have no built-in memory or logic. **Intelligent** or **smart terminals** can process data before they are transmitted to the CPU because they are equipped with microcomputers.

• **Voice recognition devices** are capable of deciphering commands given by the human voice and converting them into electronic pulses for processing.

• **Touchtone terminals** relay tones over a telephone line for processing and do not require hard wire connections.

• The **mouse**, **digitizer**, **joystick**, and **touch-sensitive screen** are input methods that increase the ways information can be entered into computers.

• **Point-of-sale (POS) input**, used in retail establishments, records a transaction at the time it takes place. POS devices include **point-of-sale terminals**, **bar code scanners**, and **optical scanners**.

• **Laser beam scanners** use a beam of coherent light to scan bar codes or symbols from products or goods. **Optical sense readers** sense pencil marks or bubbled in areas.

• **Optical character recognition (OCR) devices** convert letters or numbers into pulses for processing. **Magnetic ink character recognition (MICR) devices** convert magnetic ink characters into pulses for processing.

• **Key-to-disk**, **key-to-tape**, and **key-to-card** are forms of **offline** or **batch entry** systems. They store data on tape, disk, or punched cards for later entry into a computer.

• Keyboard to punched card input devices use **80-column** or **96-column punched cards** to hold data. Information punched into the cards is converted by a **card reader** into pulses sent to the CPU for processing.

EXERCISES

1. What are the advantages of transaction-oriented processing?

2. What is batch processing and what is its major limitation?

3. List the three major criteria for evaluating data input systems.

4. What is the difference between online and offline data input?

5. Describe the system used for reading magnetic ink characters.

6. How are characters converted from the printed page to electronic pulses by the optical character reader?

7. What is the difference between dumb and intelligent terminals?

8. Explain how key-to-tape data entry systems operate.

9. Visit the data center on your campus and list the input and output devices on the system. Categorize each according to whether it is fast or slow.

10. Visit a market or department store using point-of-sale terminals. Briefly describe what information is input, how it is input, and what information is output by the terminal.

5

Learning Objectives

After studying this chapter, you should be able to
1. Describe the advantages and limitations of primary memory
2. List the major components of the CPU
3. Describe how registers are used in the CPU
4. Contrast the instruction and execution cycles
5. Explain how the CPU executes an instruction
6. List some common primary memory media

Chapter Outline

Primary Memory Capacity
   Virtual Storage
Memory Access Systems
   Random Access Memory (RAM)
   Read Only Memory (ROM)
   Programmable Read Only Memory (PROM)
   Erasable Programmable Read Only Memory (EPROM)
Primary Memory Hardware
   Semiconductor Memory
   Bubble Memory
   Josephson Junction System
   Ferrite Core Memory
Memory Addresses
   Storage Locations
   Use of Addresses in Programs
Arithmetic and Logic Unit
   Registers
   Gates
Control Unit
   Cycle Clock
   Counters
   Decoders
How Computers Process Instructions
   Programming Instructions
   Machine Cycles
   Program Illustration

The Central Processing Unit: Functions and Components

The brain is without a doubt the most important organ in the human body. It is deep within the brain's convolutions that all works of art and scientific inventions are born. It is the brain that helps us distinguish right from wrong, hot from cold, and left from right. Just as the human brain controls our every activity and thought, so the **central processing unit (CPU)** controls the operation of the computer system.

The CPU is that portion of the computer that contains the control, primary memory, and logic units. It makes arithmetic calculations and logical decisions. It is capable of storing a program on how to process data and then executing the program, instruction by instruction. It controls and schedules the overall operation of the computing system.

The CPU is linked to the input and output (I/O) devices through circuits called I/O channels. Data from the input devices—terminals, magnetic storage devices, scanners, and so on—flow to the CPU through these channels. The data are processed in the CPU and results are fed back through the channels to the output devices.

The physical dimensions of the CPU vary greatly with the size and type of computer system. CPUs contain many complex electronic circuits. Figure 5-1 illustrates the circuitry for one computer system. The electrical components for a large system may occupy many large cabinets or racks (Figure 5-2). The CPU for a smaller system may be housed entirely in one large cabinet, about as tall as a person. The CPU for a microcomputer system may be mounted on a circuit board small enough to be held in the hand (Figure 5-3). The smaller the physical dimensions of the CPU, the more economical and portable is the complete computer system.

Regardless of their physical size, all CPUs perform the same principal functions of primary memory, arithmetic and logic, and control. This chapter is concerned with these three principal functions. It also includes a brief discussion of how the CPU executes programming instructions.

Figure 5-1 CPU Chip Layout. This enlarged view shows the complex circuitry manufactured on a CPU chip.

nROM

μROM

Control section

Address buffers

Address execution unit

Program counter execution unit

Tag cache

Bus controller

Clock generators

Interrupt

A2/A3 PLA

A1 PLA

Instruction pipe

Data buffers

A5/A6 PLA

Data execution unit

Data cache

Size logic

Function code logic

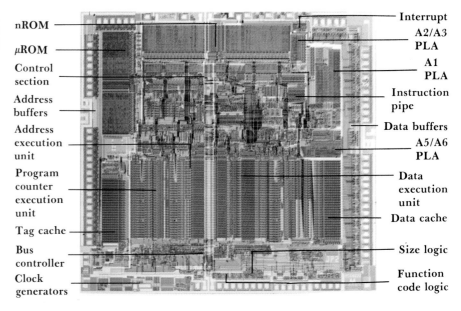

Figure 5-2 Large CPU. Large CPUs may occupy many feet of space and store millions of bytes of information.

Figure 5-3 Microcomputer CPU. This enlarged view shows a large chip mounted on a printed circuit board.

PRIMARY MEMORY CAPACITY

Primary memory, also called primary storage, main memory, or main storage, is the basic means of storing data and instructions within the CPU itself. It holds a special program called the operating system (discussed in Chapter 9), which controls the computer. It holds data files and frequently used programs. It provides a temporary work area for data produced by intermediate calculations and manipulation. Data ready for output are held in primary memory in the format required by the source program.

Primary memory is directly accessible within the CPU and therefore very fast. Millions of bits of data can be written into primary memory in less than a second, and data can be retrieved in millionths of a second. It is instantaneously available for saving directions, answers, and data. It is also a reusable storage medium. Data are easily erased by recording new data over old, a process called destructive read in.

A computer's primary memory capacity is rated in **kilobytes (KB)** or **megabytes (MB)**. As you will recall, a kilobyte is equal to

PIONEERING PEOPLE: JACK S. KILBY

Jack S. Kilby is the man behind the chip, an inventor par excellence with over 30 patents to his name. Among them is the silicon integrated circuit, which Kilby showed to his employer, Texas Instruments, back in September 1958.

Kilby worked hard to gain this high degree of self-confidence, starting as he did in 1947 by working for the only electronics company that would even offer him a job.

That company was the Centralab Div. of Globe-Union Inc., in Milwaukee. The division was selling components for radio and television, and one of their biggest concerns was trying to lower the cost of these components.

Kilby's first boss, we're told, was patient, and taught young Kilby how to break a complex problem into manageable pieces. It seemed to work for Kilby: he developed a technique of adjusting certain electronic circuits by sandblasting them. Kilby began to realize that he was a natural innovator.

In 1952, Bell Labs began to spread the word on the transistor that its scientists had developed. The company said it would sell licenses and set up a 10-day seminar to explain transistors. Centralab sent Kilby, and later put him in charge of a small project to make germanium alloy transistors. The project fascinated Kilby, who realized that the potential transistor market was huge. Nonetheless, Centralab was unwilling to invest much money. So he began to look around for a new job.

By this time Kilby had really begun to show his stuff. Plenty of companies were eager to have him on board. Kilby chose Texas Instruments. In the late '50s TI was a small company, but it had had a few dramatic successes, including the manufacture of the first silicon transistor.

Kilby was assigned to work on TI's Micro-Module project. The idea was to interconnect electrical components by making them all the same size and shape, stacking them vertically, and then running wires up and down the stack. Although Kilby's intuition told him it would be better to lay out the components horizontally, he developed the Micro-Module the way TI wanted him to. His prototype worked. But it was twice as expensive to build as he had expected.

Kilby then set to work doing what he had learned at Centralab—cutting costs. He realized this time that the answer lay in silicon, not germanium. TI was then one of the few companies that had invested heavily in expensive manufacturing equipment for silicon components. So why not make all of a circuit's components from silicon?, Kilby wondered.

With Kilby's notes and sketches, the company gave it a try. When all was said and done, TI spent about $100,000 to design and build a silicon IC. It worked. The company had a finished product in September 1958, applied for a patent in February 1959, and showed its invention to a skeptical world.

The rest is the history of the TI empire.

1,024 bytes, and a megabyte is 1 million bytes. Small computers provide only a limited amount of primary memory, generally from 64KB to 128KB, although some may have as much as 256KB ready for instantaneous access. Larger computers hold anywhere from 64KB to 64MB or more of primary memory. The greater the storage capacity, the greater the computer's ability to process and store data.

Ideally, computers would rely entirely upon primary memory, since it is fast and instantaneously available. However, the physical size required and the cost of manufacture place practical limits on primary memory capacity. It is, therefore, necessary for computers to rely upon cheaper and slower secondary storage systems (discussed in the next chapter).

Some computer systems with limited primary memory handle lengthy programs or large volumes of data by breaking them down into more manageable blocks or modules. These are entered into the CPU in sections, thus allowing large programs to be run on small computer systems.

VIRTUAL STORAGE

Some computer systems overcome the physical space limitations of primary memory by using an arrangement called **virtual storage** (Figure 5-4). This setup is composed of the computer's physical primary storage, called its **real memory**, and a disk or any direct access memory device, referred to as its **virtual** or **apparent memory**. In operation the virtual memory can be drawn upon as if it were part of the computer's primary memory.

When a job is run, all instructions and data in the program are assigned to a storage space on the virtual memory device. Then small parts of the program are transferred to primary memory, before they are needed, and executed, one by one, until the entire program has been processed. Each part is called a **page**. The transfer process is called **paging**. The process of swapping pages of information between the virtual storage device and the real memory is handled automatically by the computer.

This arrangement allows extremely large programs to be processed in a relatively small machine. A computer with only 256KB of

Figure 5-4 Virtual Storage Memory. Segments of programs or information, called pages, are brought from a storage device and held online in primary storage as they are needed. This greatly expands primary memory capacity.

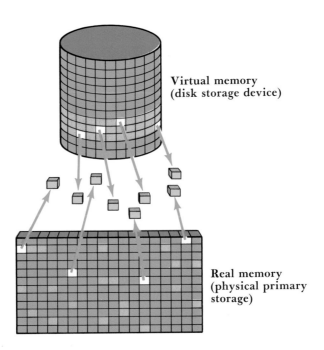

Virtual memory
(disk storage device)

Real memory
(physical primary
storage)

primary memory can appear to have many millions of bytes of storage. This process does not significantly slow down computations, since the system anticipates its memory needs and swaps in pages before they are actually needed.

MEMORY ACCESS SYSTEMS

Several different modes of memory access are used in central processing units. These include random access memory (RAM), read only memory (ROM) and programmable read only memory (PROM), and erasable programmable read only memory (EPROM). Together, these four systems make up the computer's primary memory capability. RAM enables data to be written in and changed at will. ROM has fixed contents and provides storage for frequently used blocks of information. PROMS and EPROMs provide a memory system somewhere in between RAMs and ROMs. They offer fixed blocks of storage that can occasionally be changed with the computer user's needs.

RANDOM ACCESS MEMORY (RAM)

Random access memory (RAM) is a type of computer memory chip on which program instructions and results can be stored, changed, and retrieved by the user. Data can be written into memory and selective pieces of information read out as needed. It is much like recording a whole album of songs on a tape recorder and then selecting pieces to be played back as desired. The contents of this memory can be changed at will. The RAM system is used in the computer's primary memory to hold data that will change, source programs, collections of data that are to be processed, and so on.

READ ONLY MEMORY (ROM)

Read only memory (ROM) is a memory chip that provides only readout (playback) capacity. Data can be read out as often as desired, but new data or programs cannot be recorded by the user. Important instructions that the computer needs in order to operate are permanently written into the memory device during manufacture. For example, a control program, a language compiler, or a mathematical formula may be implemented in ROM memory.

PROGRAMMABLE READ ONLY MEMORY (PROM)

A third type of storage system is called **programmable read only memory (PROM)**. It enables the user to add special information to the ROM supplied by the manufacturer as part of the system. Once on the PROM chip, the data can be read out many times, but they cannot be changed unless the chip is physically removed from the CPU and reprogrammed.

ERASABLE PROGRAMMABLE READ ONLY MEMORY (EPROM)

Some computers use a variation of the PROM chip called an **erasable programmable read only memory (EPROM)**. EPROMs can be removed from the computer and the contents erased by exposing the chip to ultraviolet light. Then new data can be programmed onto the chip. Once the chip is returned to the computer, it functions like a ROM chip in that it can be read out repeatedly as needed.

TABLE 5-1   Memory Systems
Compared

TECHNOLOGY	ADVANTAGE	LIMITATIONS
Ferrite core	Nonvolatile	High cost, power consumption
Cryogenic	Speed, high density, non-volatile	Refrigeration equipment required
Bubble	Nonvolatile, high density	Slow access
Charge coupled	High transfer rate	Volatile, slow serial access
Semiconductor	Low cost	Volatile
Photolaser	Speed	Equipment design

PRIMARY MEMORY HARDWARE

A variety of primary memory media have been employed in comput-ers. These include semiconductor, magnetic bubble, thin film, and ferrite core. Research is progressing on other methods, such as cryo-genic, photolaser, and charge coupled systems (Table 5-1). These new methods promise increased speed, greater capacity, or reduced size. Figure 5-5 illustrates how the physical size of computer memory systems has changed over the last 30 years.

SEMICONDUCTOR MEMORY

The semiconductor is the most prevalent computer memory medium in use. **Semiconductor memory** is composed of thousands of micro-scopic transistors manufactured in groups or arrays on a small chip of silicon. A transistor is a solid state device that can either amplify signals or behave much like a switch, remaining in an on or off posi-tion. Figure 5-6 illustrates an enlarged view of a section of metal oxide semiconductor (MOS) memory.

There are several types of semiconductor memory systems, among them metal oxide semiconductor (MOS) transistors and bipo-lar transistors. These systems use the two-state characteristic of tran-sistors as a switching device to store data in binary form. Each cell or transistor is either not charged (the digit 0) or charged (the digit 1). Data are written into the devices in the form of electrical pulses that

One megabyte of storage capacity would occupy the same space as

Figure 5-5   Reduction in Size of
Computer Memory.

1990

Die

1980

Orange

1975

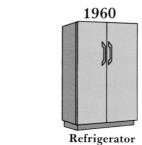

Basketball

1970

Microwave oven

1960

Refrigerator

1950

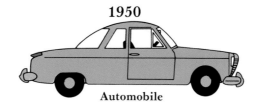

Automobile

Figure 5-6 Metal Oxide Semiconductor (MOS) Memory. MOS memory relies on the two-state switching characteristics of transistors. Arrays of transistors manufactured on a silicon chip, shown here much enlarged, are mounted on a printed circuit board.

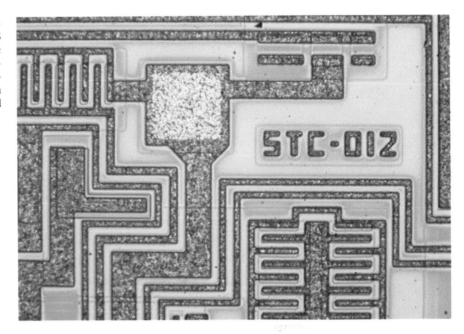

place them in either the 0 or 1 state. They remain in that state until they are changed by another pulse. Data are read out by sensing the electrical characteristic or the state of each semiconductor in the array. Reading data out does not destroy the data in memory.

Semiconductor memory is fast and reliable. Because it uses integrated circuits, it is very compact, so thousands of bytes of data can be stored on a single chip.

The major limitation of semiconductor memory is that it is **volatile** (also called **dynamic**), that is, its contents are erased when it is disconnected from its electrical power source for even a short time, because the storage depends upon the presence of a charge. Therefore, standby electrical power, or an uninterruptible power system, must be provided at all times in order to avoid loss of data.

BUBBLE MEMORY

One of the newest memory systems is **bubble memory**, also called **magnetic bubble storage**. This system uses a solid state material that provides a surface on which magnetic areas store or represent data.

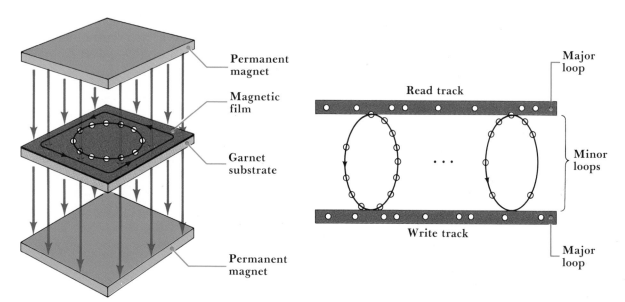

Figure 5-7 Bubble Memory. A memory chip is a magnetic device consisting of layers of material. Two coils of wire wound around the garnet produce a rotating magnetic field that causes the bubbles to circulate in loops. Data are placed in storage as bubble sites in the minor loop are transferred to the major loop, run past a write station, and then returned to the minor loop. Data are retrieved as bubbles are transferred to the major loop that carries them past the read track.

Several sheets of material are overlayed so that, by controlling a current flow to each, it is possible to generate a magnetic "bubble" which can be moved about. The presence of a bubble represents a 1 and its absence a 0 (Figure 5-7). Up to 4 million bits of data can be stored on a chip 1 centimeter square.

The advantage of bubble memory is that it provides a low cost medium capable of storing large amounts of data in a small area. Bubble memory is nonvolatile; its contents remain intact, even after power is removed.

Bubble memory has both primary and secondary storage applications. Further research promises reductions in cost which will make such systems competitive with semiconductor memory. Researchers have attempted to increase the volume of data stored in memory, yet reduce its physical size, and cost.

JOSEPHSON JUNCTION SYSTEM

One memory system under development, the **Josephson junction** system, uses a type of solid state switch to represent 0s and 1s. To work properly, these switches must be kept at temperatures near absolute zero (about $-459°F.$) This requires a liquid helium cooling system. The system holds promise for a compact and high-speed memory and may well become the preferred system of the future.

FERRITE CORE MEMORY

An early form of computer memory was the **ferrite core**. Because of its high cost of manufacture and physical size, it has been largely replaced by semiconductor systems. However, since it is still found in some computers, its operation should be understood.

Ferrite core memory is composed of thousands of cores, strung on wires to form a plane. The cores are tiny, doughnut-shaped objects pressed from iron ferrite. Each core may be magnetized in either a clockwise or counterclockwise direction. Cores magnetized in the clockwise direction represent the 0 state; cores magnetized in the counterclockwise direction, the 1 state. Once charged, the cores hold their direction of magnetism, or flux, until new data are read in.

MEMORY ADDRESSES

STORAGE LOCATIONS

The primary memory areas of the CPU are divided into small units, or storage modules, composed of groups of storage locations, each of which has its own address (Figure 5-8). Usually, the first position or location in storage is assigned the address 0, the next 1, the next 2, and so on.

The number of bytes in a storage location varies from one computer to another. All the bytes stored in one location are treated as a unit and form a **computer word**. In some machines each word has its own address. These machines are **word addressable**. In other machines the address of a word is the location of either the first or last byte of the word. Such machines are **byte addressable**.

A computer is built to store fixed-length computer words,

Figure 5-8 Memory Addresses. Each primary memory location in the CPU is assigned its own address, or identifying number, which remains the same regardless of the storage location's contents.

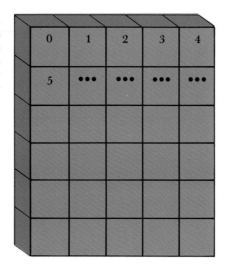

variable-length computer words, or both. **Fixed-length computer words** all have the same number of bytes. In other words, each location holds the same number of bytes. **Variable-length computer words** vary in the number of bytes they contain, that is, different locations in a computer may store a different number of bytes (Figure 5-9).

We address storage modules in a way similar to the way we address apartment buildings. One street address refers to the whole building and all the apartments in it. The number of rooms in an apartment may differ. In a fixed-length building each apartment would have the same number of rooms. In a variable-length building apartments would have different numbers of rooms.

A clear distinction exists between the data stored in a given location and the address itself. Let us return to the apartment building analogy. An apartment has an address and an occupant. They are not the same thing. The address refers to the location and does not change, but the occupant may change from time to time.

In the same way a computer address refers to the location itself and not to data stored in that location (Figure 5-10). The data it holds will change, but the address will not. Each storage location is, in effect, a reusable container. Different data may be read in and out of one location several times during the run of a program. To call

Fixed–length Word

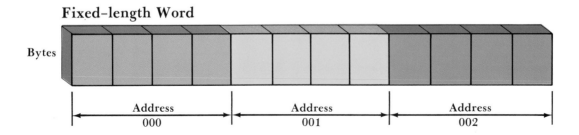

Bytes

Address
000

Address
001

Address
002

Variable–length Word

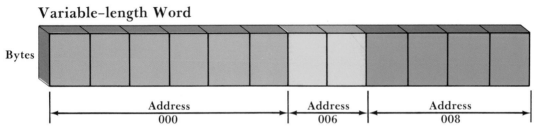

Bytes

Address
000

Address
006

Address
008

Figure 5-9 Word Length. Computers may be designed for either fixed word-length or variable word-length storage or both. This affects the number of bits that can be stored in a given location.

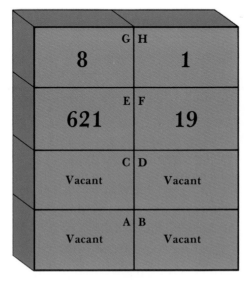

Figure 5-10 Data in Memory Addresses. Memory addresses refer to specific locations, not to the data stored. Here the addresses are the capital letters and the numbers are the data. When new data are stored in an address location, data previously stored there are erased and replaced. For example, the item of data number 8 in location G might be replaced by any other number or the location might be left empty.

data from storage, the programmer need not know the actual data, but only the address at which they are stored. The circuitry will locate the desired item by its location number and relay it for processing.

USE OF ADDRESSES IN PROGRAMS

The ability to locate data by their addresses is one of the most important characteristics of the CPU. The programmer can instruct the computer to perform a series of operations on the contents of an address. In this way operations can be repeated many times during a job, each time on a new piece of data read into a particular storage location. The programmer merely instructs the computer to store the data in the proper location.

For example, suppose a program directs the computer to read two numbers into addresses 001 and 002. The numbers are to be added, and the answer is to be sent to address 003 and then printed out on the line printer. Then the computer is to return to the beginning of the program and repeat the cycle on two more numbers.

In executing the program the CPU will read the two numbers, say 10 and 15, into storage addresses 001 and 002 (Figure 5-11). Next it will call them out and transmit them to the arithmetic unit for processing. Here they will be added and the result transmitted to address 003. Following instructions, the computer will then print out the contents of address 003 on the line printer. The number 25 will be printed out. Then the CPU will begin the next cycle. It will bring in two new numbers, say 50 and 25, write them into addresses 001 and 002, add them and send the result (75) to address 003, and print it out. The cycle will be repeated until all numbers have been added.

ARITHMETIC AND LOGIC UNIT

The **arithmetic and logic unit (ALU)** of the central processing unit performs the arithmetic and logic functions of the system. The ALU is equipped with a series of registers and gates that perform logical comparisons and mathematical operations in binary arithmetic.

First data is read into memory, and ADD performed

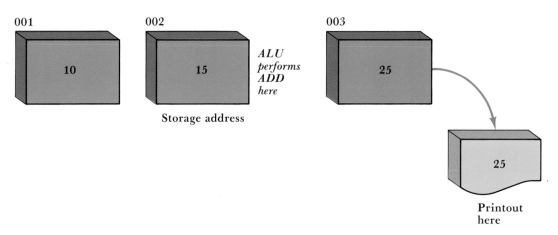

Then new data is written over old data, and ADD performed

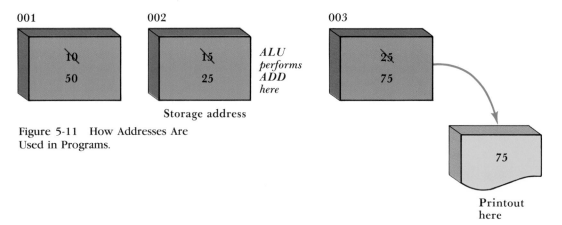

Figure 5-11   How Addresses Are
Used in Programs.

REGISTERS

The CPU contains a group of storage areas called **registers**. These
are similar in concept to semiconductor memory, but hold only a few
bytes of data or a limited number of words. Registers are electrical
circuits made up of transistors or integrated circuits. As we have
seen, transistors are either on or off in either a conducting or a nonconducting state. A conducting transistor represents the value 1

stored in that position; a nonconducting transistor the value 0.

Registers serve different purposes. Some are used by the control function of the CPU, some by the arithmetic and logic unit, and others serve as temporary storage places. Data can be read out and written into registers in billionths of a second. The system of registers is an indispensable part of the CPU.

Registers give the CPU its ability to process data. The electrical changes that take place in the register transistors give the computer the ability to count, store data, compare electrical pulses, and perform mathematics. There are several kinds of registers in computers.

GENERAL-PURPOSE REGISTER   As the name indicates, a general-purpose register can be used for many functions. For example, it may act as a counter or an accumulator and hold addresses or data for processing. In most systems general-purpose registers are available to the programmer.

INSTRUCTION REGISTER   One instruction at a time is pulled from primary storage by the CPU and placed in registers for execution. The instruction register holds the part of an instruction that indicates what process is to be performed. An instruction may direct the computer to add numbers, move data from point to point, print out numbers, and so forth.

ADDRESS REGISTER   The address register holds the part of an instruction that indicates where the data to be used are stored.

STORAGE REGISTER   A storage register acts as a temporary holding area for data awaiting processing. Actual processing does not take place in a storage register. It is more like a waiting room where data needed for the next step in an operation are kept ready. While part of the CPU is operating on one piece of data, another part can retrieve the next piece from memory and have it ready in an accessible storage register.

ACCUMULATOR REGISTER   The accumulator register holds results of calculations. It holds binary bits of data, such as numbers, sums, quotients, and products. Each time a new value is added to a running

THE SUPERCHIP

Quietly, often in secrecy, scientists at dozens of laboratories in Europe, Japan and the United States are racing toward yet another revolution in the speed, size and reliability of computers.

They are on the verge of shrinking the present generation of room-sized supercomputers down to the size of a baseball through a new technology that will allow the complex circuitry of hundreds of silicon chips to be etched onto a single, thin wafer.

While many of today's chips carry thousands of transistors, a single wafer could hold millions.

In addition to enormous advances in computer speed and reliability, the result will be a dramatic decrease in cost, according to scientists in the field. . . .

It is believed that the wafer and its supporting hardware will enable the creation of computers hundreds of times faster and more powerful than anything now in existence. Small desk-top computers based on a wafer will easily outperform large "main frames" that now occupy whole rooms.

The stakes in the race are high: Today, for example, no computer is powerful enough to simulate the airflow around an entire aircraft, and the first country to build a machine to do so "will undoubtedly produce superior planes," according to the National Science Foundation.

So too, the Government wants more powerful computers in order to excel at forecasting weather, building weapons, breaking codes and developing new sources of energy.

The push to master the wafer is occurring at universities, Federal laboratories, fledgling companies and virtually all the major semiconductor manufacturers, although the work is often closely guarded. Gordon E. Moore, chairman of the Intel Corporation, has reportedly warned his employees, "I don't want anyone from Intel saying anything to anyone about wafer-scale integration."

The allure of wafer-scale integration is that it removes, in one fell swoop, a host of problems usually associated with the production of silicon chips and their assembly into computers.

For years, the manufacture of silicon chips has started with plain old sand, which is heated and formed into thin silicon wafers a few inches in diameter. In a complex series of steps, using light, chemicals and special masks not unlike tiny photographic negatives, the surface of these wafers is etched with "chip" patterns, typically about 200 of them. These tiny chips are then tested, broken apart from the wafer, encased in carriers, hooked into printed circuit boards and wired into the complex assemblages known as computers.

"You chop the wafer apart and then the first thing you do is put it back together," noted Dr. Robert R. Johnson, president of Mosaic Systems Inc., a company in Troy, Mich., that is developing the wafer-scale technology. "It's sort of nutty, but that's how the industry grew up."

In a large computer, the big draw-back is that all these separate chips slow things down tremendously. It takes time for electrical signals to travel back and forth along the miles of wires that connect all the chips.

A single large wafer can eliminate this time lag, and several other problems as well, such as the huge expense of housing separate chips in a large computer cabinet and wiring them together, often by hand.

What has now changed is the emergence of such new technologies as ultra-precise lasers that insure eventual success, according to experts in the field. "The key is really the whole emerging field of micro engineering," said Dr. Richard M. Osgood, director of the micro-electronics laboratory at Columbia University.

Approaches to creating a monster wafer range from the ambitious to the conservative. At Mosaic, scientists are using a hybrid approach—taking individual, already tested standard memory and logic chips and assembling them on special wafers that can be programmed to make the myriad connections. . . .

The ultimate wafer—and the most powerful of all—will have its entire surface covered with working circuits. That means every circuit will have to be tested, and faulty ones corrected, before the whole wafer is ready to go to work. . . .

---

total, for example, it is added to the accumulator register, updating the total. When the calculations have been completed, the results in the accumulator register can be written into storage or another register for further processing.

GATES

The mechanics of addition, subtraction, and logical decisions are performed by a group of specialized circuits within the ALU. These circuits use **gates**. Gates are semiconductors wired in special arrangements that open different pathways, depending on the pulses they receive.

Many kinds of gates wired in different arrangements and combinations are used in a CPU. Gates are designed to add and subtract binary numbers, compare values to determine whether a value is equal to or greater than another, and so forth. Gates are the heart of the computer's mathematical and logical ability. Some common CPU gates are the AND gate, OR gate, and NOR gate.

The use of gates can be illustrated with a brief description of a circuit used to perform addition (Figure 5-12). This is a special semiconductor circuit with two input wires, one output wire, and one

Figure 5-12 Addition Gate. The addition gate diagrammed here is able to add binary numbers following the rules of binary addition.

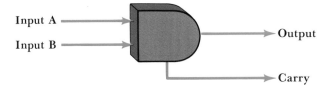

Input A   Output

Input B   Carry

Truth Table			
Input A	Input B	Output	Carry
0	0	0	0
0	1	1	0
1	0	1	0
1	1	0	1

carry wire. The circuit behaves according to the rules of binary addition. To understand this example, you may wish to look at Appendix B in which binary addition is explained in more detail. If a pulse is sent to either input A or input B, the carry line remains at 0 and the output wire conducts a signal. (This corresponds to $1 + 0 = 1$ or $0 + 1 = 1$ in binary addition.) If signals are sent to both input A and input B, the carry line conducts a signal and the output line is 0. (This corresponds to $1 + 1 = 10$ in binary addition.) Figure 5-12 has a truth table illustrating the conditions possible with this circuit.

To perform a mathematical operation, the numbers to be processed are called out from storage and fed into registers. Electrical pathways are then set up that feed the pulses representing these numbers to the proper gates. The output from the gates passes through other circuits and into accumulator registers. From there, the pulses may be sent back to storage, be used for other processing, or be sent to an output device.

Logic decisions are made in gates similar to the arithmetic gates. Logic gates test the voltage from one value against another. They can indicate whether a given value is equal to, greater than, or less than the other value. This result is then used by the CPU to branch control to one of several paths specified in a program.

Figure 5-13   Cycle Clock. A cycle clock is an electronic circuit that emits millions of timed pulses per second.

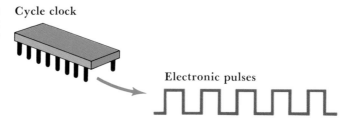

CONTROL UNIT

The last major element of the central processing unit is the control unit. It includes a cycle clock, counters, decoders, and other components necessary to control the overall operation of the CPU. The control unit schedules and directs the movement of data within the CPU between primary memory and the ALU and between registers and gates in the ALU. It also governs the instruction and execution cycles described later in this chapter.

CYCLE CLOCK

A major component of the CPU is the **cycle clock**, which sends out pulses at a rate of many millions of cycles per second (Figure 5-13). These electrical pulses are sent to parts of the CPU to control its operations and timing. The pulse causes electronic circuits to open or close. Completed circuits create new paths for the pulse to follow and, in turn, these open other paths. All operations of the CPU are actually only a matter of different paths that the circuitry opens. Each change in the electrical condition within the CPU is in time with and in response to the pulses from this clock. Each step the computer takes to solve a problem is governed by this internal clock.

COUNTERS

CPUs contain circuitry called **counters**, which have only one function: to count and remember the number of pulses sent to them. They are groups of transistors and other components arranged in a **flip-flop circuit** (Figure 5-14). Flip-flop circuits increase the count by one each time they receive an electrical pulse.

Figure 5-14   Flip-Flop Counter.

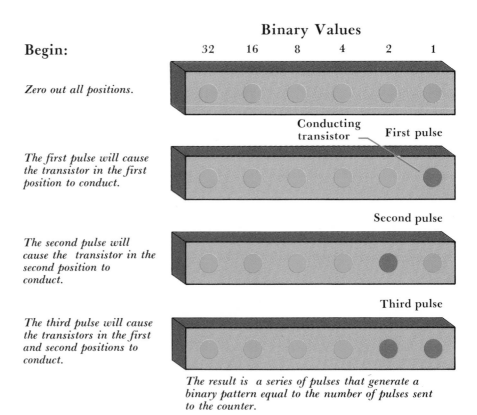

Binary Values

| 32 | 16 | 8 | 4 | 2 | 1 |

Begin:

Zero out all positions.

Conducting transistor — First pulse

The first pulse will cause the transistor in the first position to conduct.

Second pulse

The second pulse will cause the transistor in the second position to conduct.

Third pulse

The third pulse will cause the transistors in the first and second positions to conduct.

The result is a series of pulses that generate a binary pattern equal to the number of pulses sent to the counter.

A transistor in a flip-flop circuit reverses its electrical state when a pulse is received. If it is already conducting and is fed another pulse, it passes the current on to the next transistor and changes to a nonconducting state.

At the beginning of the counting cycle, all transistors are set to zero and are nonconducting. The first pulse turns on the first transistor (creating a binary 01). The second pulse causes it to flip-flop, turn on the next transistor, and turn off (creating a binary 10). The next pulse turns on the first transistor again (creating binary 11), and so on. Counters can work in a positive or negative direction, that is, they can either add to or subtract from the number in the counter.

Counters are controlled by the CPU and serve specific functions during the processing of a job. For example, counters keep track of the number of times a given series of steps is carried out. If the computer is to repeat a cycle, say 100 times, the counter will add 1 each time a cycle is completed. When the counter reaches 100, the computer goes on to the next instruction. Or if a number is to be multiplied by itself (raised to a power), for example, increased from 10 to 10^6, a counter will add 1 each time the number is multiplied, until the limit 6 has been reached.

Counters also keep track of instructions. Instructions are assigned consecutive storage spaces in primary storage. The **instruction counter** is indexed to the address of the first instruction. This counter increases each time the CPU processes an instruction, indicating the address of the next instruction to be processed.

DECODERS

A **decoder** is an electronic device in the CPU that sets up an electrical pathway in response to a specific instruction. **Operation decoders** convert an instruction into the electrical paths or circuits that will perform the proper operation. Suppose that the computer is directed to perform addition and that in the computer language being used the word ADD is the code for addition. In binary language ADD might be expressed as 0101 1010. This collection of binary bits is sent to a decoder. The decoder senses the bit pattern and prepares the circuit to perform addition. It will allocate storage registers to hold the numbers to be added and the sum.

Command decoders prepare the proper pathways for program instructions that have been input to the computer. Other decoders convert expressions from a code to a more easily understood form. For example, decoders convert groups of binary numbers to their decimal equivalents.

HOW COMPUTERS PROCESS INSTRUCTIONS

How are all three functions of the CPU integrated to actually execute a program? In the rest of this chapter you will read about program

Start Program

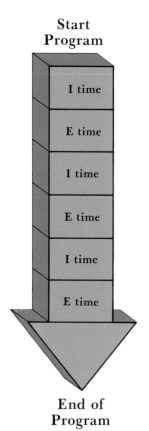

End of Program

Figure 5-15 Machine Cycles. The computer always begins with an I cycle (instruction time) and continues to alternate between I time and E (execution) time until the end of the program is reached.

execution and how the registers, gates, and other circuitry work as an organized whole.

PROGRAMMING INSTRUCTIONS

A program containing the set of instructions a computer is to follow is entered into the computer's primary memory. Each instruction, whether to add, subtract, move data, or compare, is stored in sequential locations. Programming instructions have several parts. In some languages, such as assembler, the first part of the instruction, called an **operation code (op code)** directs the machine to carry out a specific action, such as add or compare data. The second part of the instruction, the **operand**, describes the location where data will be found and where the results will be sent.

High-level languages, such as BASIC, COBOL, or Pascal, use different forms. Their instructions are more like common English or mathematical notations. The computer converts these instructions into machine-readable operations together with descriptions of where data will be found and where they must be sent after processing.

MACHINE CYCLES

The procedure for executing programming instructions involves two cycles that are synchronized by pulses from the cycle clock. These cycles are the **instruction (I) cycle**, which sets up circuitry to perform a required operation, and the **execution (E) cycle**, during which the operation is actually carried out (Figure 5-15).

Computers alternate between the I and the E cycles millions of times per second, in time with the pulses from the cycle clock. The first cycle is always the instruction cycle, and it is always followed by the execution cycle. The time spent on the instruction cycle is called **I time**; that spent on the execution cycle is called **E time**.

During the instruction cycle the computer locates the instruction in storage and places it in a storage register. The operation code is sent to the instruction register and the operand to the address register. The operation decoder converts the op code into the specific circuitry necessary to perform the job. During I time the address counter increments, informing the computer of the location of the next instruction.

The function of the execution cycle is to manipulate the data as specified in the op code of the instruction. The data specified by the operand is pulled from storage and sent to the proper devices by the circuitry initiated by the op code. During the execution cycle the computer may move data electronically from primary storage to register and vice versa. It adds numbers, moves data, subtracts values, and so forth. The results of these or other operations are placed in appropriate registers or storage.

After execution is completed, the cycles are repeated for the next instruction. This process continues until the last instruction in the program has been executed.

PROGRAM ILLUSTRATION

Suppose a series of 30 instructions are held in primary memory in locations 000 to 029, as shown in Figure 5-16. They are part of a program that has been entered into the computer. When the operator directs the machine to execute the program the following steps will be performed.

1. The computer sets the instruction counter to 000. The instruction counter is now pointing at the first instruction (READ).
2. The CPU calls up the contents of storage register 000 and performs the READ function. The call up is done in two phases. During I time the instruction is set up and decoded; during E time it is actually carried out.
3. The instruction counter is incremented to 001.
4. The computer pulls the ADD instruction from location 001 and performs the necessary addition. This, too, is done in two phases, first I time, then E time.
5. The computer continues to retrieve instructions, decode them, execute them, and increment the program counter until each instruction in memory has been executed.
6. When the computer executes the instruction stored in location 029, execution terminates.
7. The result is output on a line printer or CRT.

Figure 5-16 How the Computer Processes a Program. In this example, 30 instructions, 000 through 029, are held in memory. The computer will execute each instruction in sequence. After all instructions have been executed, the computer will stop.

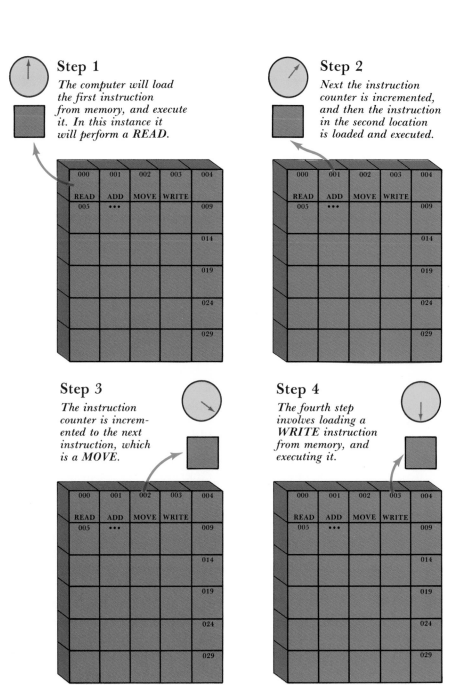

Step 1

The computer will load the first instruction from memory, and execute it. In this instance it will perform a READ.

Step 2

Next the instruction counter is incremented, and then the instruction in the second location is loaded and executed.

Step 3

The instruction counter is incremented to the next instruction, which is a MOVE.

Step 4

The fourth step involves loading a WRITE instruction from memory, and executing it.

In this chapter we looked at the central processing unit and its functions. While the CPU's functions can be easily understood, they are performed by complicated electronic circuitry. The CPU does its job quietly, tirelessly, and virtually without moving parts. It is a modern electronic marvel, challenged only by the human brain.

SUMMARY AND KEY TERMS

- The heart of the computer system is the **central processing unit (CPU)**. The CPU contains the control unit, primary memory, and logic unit.

- **Primary memory**, or **main storage**, holds source programs, data files, and frequently used programs. Memory capacity is rated in **kilobytes (KB)** or **megabytes (MB)**.

- Computers equipped with **virtual storage** use direct access secondary storage devices in addition to primary memory to expand their memory capacity.

- In **random access memory (RAM)** data can be written in, read out, and changed. In **read only memory (ROM)** data can be read out as often as desired, but new data cannot be written in its place.

- **Programmable read only memory (PROM)** is a form of memory chip that the user can change by removing it from the CPU and reprogramming it. The data cannot be changed while they are in the computer.

- Data are erased from the **erasable programmable read only memory (EPROM)** using ultraviolet light, and then new information is written in.

- **Semiconductor memory** is composed of thousands of microscopic transistors manufactured on a single chip of silicon.

- In **bubble memory** systems, a solid state material provides a surface on which magnetic areas store or represent data.

- The **Josephson junction** system uses solid state switches that function at absolute zero.

- One of the earliest forms of computer primary memory was **ferrite core**. It has been largely replaced by semiconductor systems.

• The computer's primary memory is organized into **computer words**. Machines may be either **word** or **byte addressable**, and words may be either **fixed** or **variable** in length.

• The **arithmetic and logic unit (ALU)** performs its functions using a series of registers and gates.

• A **register** is a semiconductor device that can hold a limited number of words for processing. Modern computers are equipped with **general-purpose, instruction, address, storage**, and **accumulator registers**.

• Mathematics and logical decisions are performed in circuits using **gates** which are semiconductors wired in arrangements to perform various tasks.

• The **control unit** contains a **cycle clock** that emits pulses to control the operation and timing of the computer. It also contains **counters**, which keep track of operations and perform binary counting tasks, and **decoders**, electronic devices that set up electrical pathways to carry out specific instructions.

• Computers execute a program by alternately moving through an **instruction (I) cycle** and an **execution (E) cycle** until the end of the program is reached.

EXERCISES

1. What functions does primary memory perform?

2. What are the advantages of virtual storage systems?

3. How do RAM and ROM memory systems differ?

4. What are the differences between semiconductor memory and bubble memory?

5. Draw a storage system capable of holding 20 bytes of data. Label storage positions and assign addresses.

6. What are the differences between fixed-length and variable-length word memory?

7. Briefly define the functions of the following: address register, instruction register, storage register, accumulator register.

8. In what ways does register storage differ from primary memory?

9. What are gates and what is their function?

10. What is the function of the cycle clock?

11. How is counting performed in the CPU?

12. Arrange a group of dominos or other objects into a flip-flop counter. Increase this counter by manipulating the dominos.

13. What are the differences between the instruction and execution cycles?

6

Learning Objectives

After studying this chapter, you should be able to
1. List the advantages and limitations of secondary storage
2. Contrast sequential and random access
3. List the factors that affect access time
4. Describe the major forms of secondary storage
5. Explain how data are written on and read from magnetic tape
6. Describe different disk storage systems in use

Chapter Outline

Advantages and Limitations of Secondary Storage
Access Time
Access Methods
  Sequential Access
  Direct Access
  Indexed File Access
Data Transmission Codes
  American Standard Code for Information
    Interchange (ASCII)
  Extended Binary Coded Decimal Interchange
    Code (EBCDIC)
  Parity Check
Magnetic Tape Storage
  Tape Reels
  Recording Data
  File Organization
  File Identification
  Processing Tape Files
  Magnetic Tape Cassette
Magnetic Disk Storage
  Rigid Disks
  Recording and Accessing Data
  Processing Disk Files
  Winchester Disks
  Flexible (Floppy) Disks
Mass Storage
  Cellular Mass Storage
  Magnetic Bubble Storage
  Laser Beam Storage
Comparison of Storage Media

Secondary Storage Systems

Did you ever stop to think how much paperwork is generated when you do something as commonplace as opening a new checking account? A single business transaction may generate dozens of documents. Each document may contain many pieces of data and information which must be treated as a unit. Large business enterprises must store millions of records generated by marketing, personnel, inventory, production, distribution, and financial operations.

In the previous chapter we discussed the computer's primary memory capability, located within the CPU. Primary memory is easily accessible storage from which data can be retrieved quickly, but its capacity is limited. **Secondary storage** systems give the computer greatly expanded memory capability. Figure 6-1 illustrates a computer system with several different forms of secondary storage media. Information flows back and forth between the CPU and the secondary storage devices. Without such systems, computers would have to rely totally upon their primary memory to store information.

The capacity to store large amounts of data in a small amount of space has greatly increased over the past several decades. A measure of storage capacity is **recording density**, or the number of bits per square inch. Three decades ago it required a magnetic surface about the size of a double bed to store a million bytes of data. Today the same amount of information can be stored on a magnetic surface the size of a postage stamp. It is estimated that by the year 2000 the same amount of data will fit on a surface the size of a grain of salt. This represents roughly a 3000-fold increase in storage density (Figure 6-2).

In this chapter we will look at secondary storage and see how magnetic disk, tape, and other storage media are used to supplement the computer's primary memory.

Figure 6-1 Secondary Storage Media. Modern computers use a variety of secondary storage devices to provide fast access, large capacity, and low cost data retrieval.

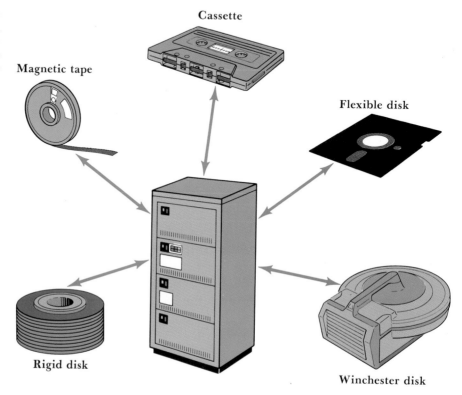

Cassette

Magnetic tape

Flexible disk

Rigid disk

Winchester disk

ADVANTAGES AND LIMITATIONS OF SECONDARY STORAGE

Secondary storage is an efficient, compact means of storing millions of characters ready for retrieval or further processing. It is substantially less expensive to store a million bytes of data in secondary storage, such as in a magnetic disk, than it is to put the same data in primary memory semiconductors.

Secondary storage is much like a giant electronic scratchpad available to the computer. Data can be written into secondary memory at the rate of millions of characters per second and later read out or erased. Since it relies upon expendable or reusable media, such as tape and disk, the capacity is virtually unlimited.

Secondary storage devices simplify moving and storing data. Thin plastic disks or reels of tape can be sent through the mails or conveniently stored in file cabinets. Information is easily exchanged

Figure 6-2 Recording Density. Recording density is measured by the number of bits that can be stored on a square inch of a magnetic surface, such as a disk or tape. The graph anticipates technological advances and projects densities that will soon be available to users.

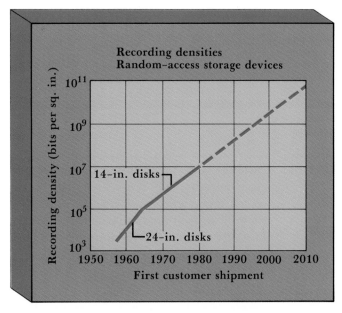

with other data centers or computers by exchanging reels of tape, cassettes, or disk packs. Backup files can be generated and stored in a safe place. Duplicate files may be distributed to many computer users simultaneously. Disks and tape may be sent where they are needed instead of bulky physical records, documents, or files such as checks, tax reports, and other items on paper.

One limitation of secondary storage is that its retrieval time is slower than that of primary memory. It takes more time for a computer to retrieve data from a rotating disk or reel of tape than from a directly accessible semiconductor memory. Another limitation is that some secondary storage devices require delicate and precisely positioned moving parts. Also, fingerprints, dust particles, or even the presence of magnetic fields can destroy valuable data (Figure 6-3).

ACCESS TIME

The time required to locate and retrieve a given piece of data from storage is known as the **access time**. To illustrate, estimate how long

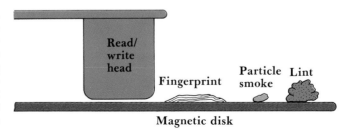

Figure 6-3 Contamination on a Recording Surface. It is obvious how lint or dirt particles, finger-prints, moisture, or any other substance can cause errors in reading or writing data. Although the illustration is not drawn to scale, it makes clear the fact that a smoke particle, which might measure 250 millionths of an inch in diameter, would seriously disturb the space between the head and the magnetic surface.

it would take you to find a particular piece of information in your class notes. If your notes are with you in class and they consist of only a few pages, it will take less time than if they are at home and they fill several notebooks. Access time is a function of (1) the location of the data, (2) the amount of data to be searched, and (3) the speed of the hardware.

Primary memory is already within the CPU. Being limited in capacity it usually contains fewer data than all the secondary memory in a system. Primary memory is usually solid state electronic, while secondary storage is electromechanical in nature, usually involving slower moving parts. These factors combine to make primary memory faster than secondary storage.

Access times differ among secondary storage devices according to the medium and retrieval mechanism used.

A piece of data located at the end of a reel of tape, for example, will take longer to locate than a piece at the beginning of the tape. The greater the volume of data to be searched, the longer the time necessary to retrieve the data. If the memory system requires positioning a magnetic head over a disk or track, if time elapses while the disk rotates until the information moves under the head to be read, or if a tape must be repositioned, then access will be slowed down.

ACCESS METHODS

Several different methods are used to access information from secondary storage. These include sequential access devices, direct access storage devices, and indexed file systems.

SEQUENTIAL ACCESS

Devices that locate a given piece of data in a file by searching the storage medium in sequence from beginning to end are called **sequential access devices**. Magnetic tape is a commonly used form of sequential access storage. Data are stored on magnetic tape in the order in which they were recorded. They need not be in any logical order. To find a piece of data, the computer rewinds the reel of tape to the beginning and checks each item on the tape until it finds the specified data.

DIRECT ACCESS

Direct access storage devices (DASD) can retrieve data directly from storage without searching in sequence. The storage medium is divided into storage locations, and each location is given an address. Each piece of data is assigned to one of these addresses as it is written into storage. Given the address, the computer can locate a specific piece of data without searching through every item in the file. It can go directly to the item.

Data stored on direct access devices can, of course, be accessed sequentially as well. Magnetic disk systems are common direct access devices. Understandably, direct access devices are faster than sequential access systems.

INDEXED FILE ACCESS

Indexed file access is a cross between sequential and direct access. In this method all records in the file are stored sequentially. Each record has a primary and a secondary key. The **primary key**, which may be a social security number, part number, or other identification, serves as a file or record locator number. Within a given block of sequenced data, specific records may be stored at random. An index at the beginning of each block is used to locate the random records. To access a record, the computer searches sequentially for the primary key or record locator number. It then looks up a **secondary key** in the index which tells it specifically where the out-of-sequence record can be found. This arrangement allows both sequential and direct access of the same file.

Mrs. Robner says she loved her murdered husband, but you know she is lying. The proof is in the love note you just intercepted. Ask her about the man who wrote it, and she says she never heard of him. Confront her with his letter, and she changes her tune: "You have certainly stooped to a new low, Inspector, opening other people's mail!" Then she spills her story.

Not all mysteries these days appear in paperbacks or movies. The tale above scrolled up the screen of a personal computer. The story, titled *Deadline*, is part of the latest craze in home computing: programmed fiction. Machines that were used mainly for blasting aliens and calculating monthly budgets are now also churning through adventure tales and murder-mystery plots. "It's like reading a novel, only you are the protagonist," says Science-Fiction Writer Linda Bushyager. While arcade-style games like Pac Man are losing popularity, these complex programs are winning more and more fans.

In *Deadline*, one of ten computer "novels" produced by Infocom, a Cambridge, Mass.-based software publishing house, the player is given a casebook of evidence, a floppy disc containing the plot, and twelve hours to unravel the mystery. If the murderer is not found in the allotted time, a character named Chief Inspector Klutz takes the player off the case. The program shuts down automatically and must be replayed from the beginning.

As *Deadline* opens, a wealthy businessman has been found dead in the library of his mansion from a mysterious drug overdose. The player, who takes the role of inspector, has been called in to investigate. He types commands into the computer, and the machine responds with descriptions of people and places and snatches of dialogue that develop the story. Suspects duck in and out of rooms; clues appear and disappear; characters lie low or kill again, depending on the player's actions. The story can unfold in literally thousands of ways. A typical investigation, including starts and restarts, can run 40 hours or longer. "It takes me three to six months to get completely through one," says Craig Pearce, 31, a building manager from Berwyn, Ill. "It's unbelievable how you can get hooked on these things."

The concept of interactive fiction is not totally new. The hit of the Czechoslovak pavilion at Expo 67 in Montreal was an experimental movie that let the audience vote on the course of the action. But it took the computer, with its awesome power to store and sort text, to turn the concept into a popular art form.

DATA TRANSMISSION CODES

Several codes have been developed to encode data on magnetic tape, magnetic disk, or paper tape. These codes can represent up to 256 different characters in any given byte.

In the early years of telegraph transmission, paper tape was

Figure 6-4 Lost Bits (No Check Present). This five-bit code has no provision for detecting lost bits. The loss of a bit means a character would not be transmitted accurately.

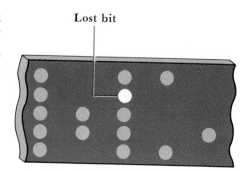

Lost bit

used to transmit data. The code combination was punched in the tape with no provision for accuracy checks (Figure 6-4). This early code system contained only five **tracks** or **intelligence channels**. Each bit in a coded character is stored in one of the five tracks running the length of the tape. Adjacent bits (five, in this case) make up a character such as a letter or number. Modern coding systems use seven or eight such intelligence channels and also have an additional track used for error checking procedures.

There are two main codes used to transmit data between the CPU and input and output devices and to store data on secondary storage devices.

AMERICAN STANDARD CODE FOR INFORMATION INTERCHANGE (ASCII)
The term **ASCII** (pronounced ask-key) stands for **American Standard Code for Information Interchange**. This code, shown in Figure 6-5 as it looks punched on paper tape, consists of seven intelligence channels and an eighth channel for checking accuracy. The channels are numbered 1 through 8. Because it uses 7 channels for intelligence, it can represent 128 characters. This is possible because 7 bits can be rearranged in 128 different ways. ASCII is widely used for transmitting data to computers and for transmitting data between remote terminals and CPUs.

EXTENDED BINARY CODED DECIMAL INTERCHANGE CODE (EBCDIC)
The **EBCDIC** code (pronounced ebb-see-dick) is an extension of the ASCII code. It has nine tracks, eight for intelligence and one for

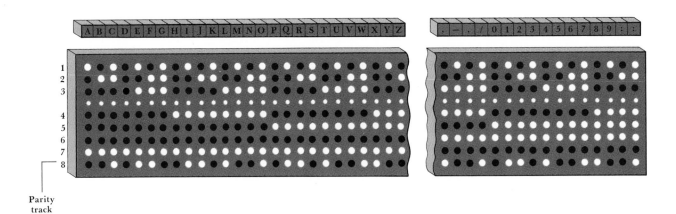

Figure 6-5 American Standard Code for Information Interchange (ASCII). In this example even parity is shown. Notice that an even number of bits is always punched out or recorded for each byte.

checking (Figure 6-6). It is capable of representing 256 characters. (The 8 bits can be arranged in 256 permutations.) EBCDIC allows both upper- and lower-case characters, many special symbols, and control characters to be transmitted.

PARITY CHECK

Early data transmission codes had a serious problem in that a bit could be lost or gained in transmission because of an electrical or mechanical failure. If the loss went undetected, the character received on the other end of the line was incorrect.

To prevent this from happening, a **parity check system** was developed. Each character is represented by a byte consisting of a combination of **intelligence bits** (seven bits in ASCII and eight bits in EBCDIC) and an additional bit called a **check** or **parity bit**.

Even parity codes place a check bit with each byte that contains an uneven number of 1 bits. (Remember that a bit is either 1 or 0.) Because the check bit is transmitted only with characters composed of an uneven number of 1 bits, all characters transmitted will have an even number of 1 bits (Figure 6-7a). The check bit is transmitted to and from the computer along with the character code. If a bit is lost (or added) in transmission, the system will detect its loss. An uneven number of 1 bits received in a code string composed of even bits will signal an error.

Odd parity codes add a check bit to code combinations that

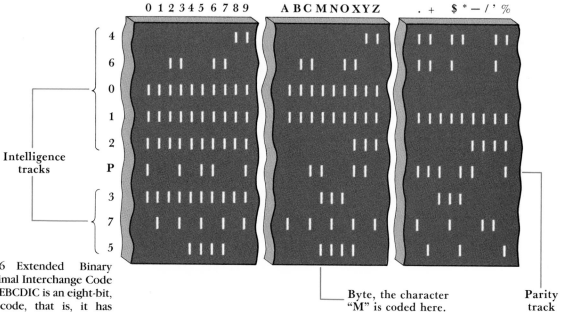

0 1 2 3 4 5 6 7 8 9   A B C M N O X Y Z   . + $ * − / ' %

Intelligence tracks

4
6
0
1
2
P
3
7
5

Figure 6-6 Extended Binary Coded Decimal Interchange Code (EBCDIC). EBCDIC is an eight-bit, nine-track code, that is, it has eight intelligence tracks or channels and one parity track. There are 256 possible permutations available, representing up to 256 different characters.

Byte, the character "M" is coded here.

Parity track

have an even number of 1 bits (Figure 6-7b). Thus, all characters transmitted have an odd number of bits. Odd and even parity are similar in nature. They are both designed to signal an error in the event that data are lost or added.

Longitudinal parity is used to check accuracy when recording and transmitting on magnetic tape. All characters in a track are tallied along the length of the tape. At the end of each track a check bit is added to maintain even or odd parity (Figure 6-8). Longitudinal parity can be used in addition to the parity system used to check each byte. The system is sometimes called a **horizontal redundancy check**.

MAGNETIC TAPE STORAGE

Magnetic tape is a sequential access storage medium. One or more tape units may be connected to the CPU to give the computer access to data stored on more than one reel of magnetic tape at a time.

Figure 6-7   Parity Bits. The figure on the left shows the letter A in an even-parity system. Because it consists of an even number of 1-bits, no check bit is necessary. The figure on the right shows the same character in an odd-parity system. In this case the two 1-bits require a check bit to make the total an odd number.

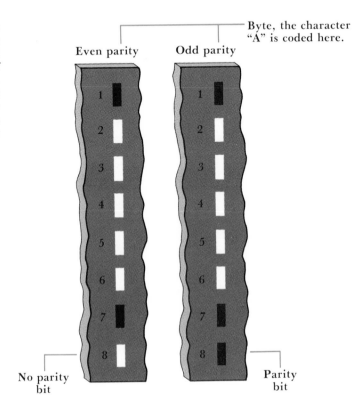

Figure 6-8 Tape with Parity Checks. A horizontal redundancy check involves a longitudinal check at the end of the length of tape and a vertical check for each byte.

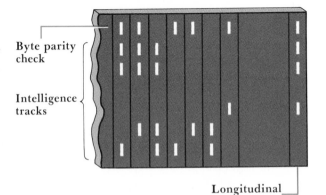

Figure 6-9 Magnetic Tape. A thin ribbon of plastic or Mylar is coated with a ferromagnetic material so that data can be recorded on the surface of the tape.

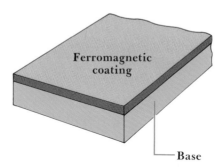

Figure 6-10 Reel with File Protection Ring. The presence of the ring means that data can be written onto the tape. Its absence means that no new data can be recorded and so precludes accidental erasure.

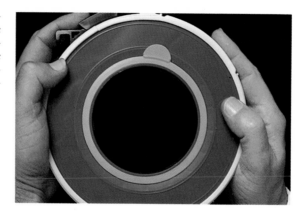

TAPE REELS

Magnetic tape is ½-inch-wide plastic ribbon that has been coated with a thin layer of ferromagnetic material and wound on reels (Figure 6-9). The two most common reel sizes are 10½ inches in diameter, holding 2,400 feet of tape, and 8½ inches, holding 1,200 feet.

Each reel of magnetic tape contains two indicator marks, the **load-point mark** and the **end-of-reel mark**, which note the beginning and end of usable recording tape on the reel. The indicators are small pieces of reflective foil bonded to the edge of the tape so that they can be sensed by photocells in the drive mechanism.

The tape reel is equipped with a special plastic ring, called the **file protection ring** (Figure 6-10). When the ring is in place on the hub of the reel, new data can be recorded or old data erased from the tape. When the ring is removed, no new data can be recorded

Figure 6-11 Recording on Magnetic Tape. Data are written as magnetic areas along the length of the tape.

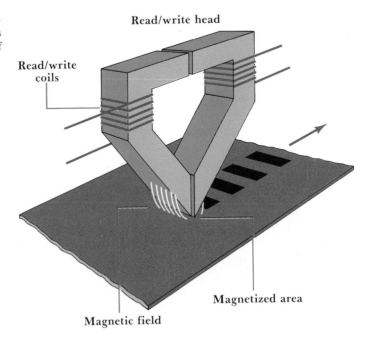

over the existing bits of information. The removal of this ring serves as a protection against accidental destruction of important data, because it requires a deliberate act by the computer operator to replace the ring. In other words, "No ring, no write."

RECORDING DATA

Data are recorded by magnetizing areas of the coating as the tape passes under a write head. The head converts electronic pulses (representing alphabetic and numeric characters) into magnetized areas on the moving tape. Data are read from the tape by a reverse procedure. The read head senses the magnetized areas on the tape, induces a current in a pickup coil, and converts the magnetic fields to electronic pulses. These pulses, representing coded data, are sent to the CPU for processing. The same head may be used for both writing and reading and is often referred to as a **read/write head** (Figure 6-11).

Figure 6-12 Interrecord Gap (IRG). The tape drive stops at the end of each record. An IRG is placed between records to allow the drive to come up to speed before reading or writing the next piece of data.

Inter-Record Gap (IRG)

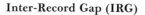

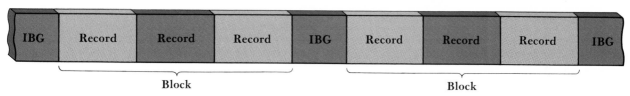

Figure 6-13 Blocking Records. To save the space taken up by interrecord gaps, records may be run together to form a block.. The blocks are separated by an interblock gap (IBG).

FILE ORGANIZATION

A tape **record** is a group of bytes relating to a single transaction. Tape records can be either fixed or variable in length. A record can be only one byte or as many as several thousand. Each record on the tape is separated by a 0.6-inch-wide space, called the **interrecord gap (IRG)**, shown in Figure 6-12. When a computer reads a file, the tape drive comes to a stop after each record, starts again, moves to the next record, stops again, and so on. Approximately 0.6 inches of tape will be reeled during the time required for the drive to go from a stopped position to the proper speed for reading or writing.

Interrecord gaps occupy space on the tape that cannot be used for data storage. One method of avoiding this loss is to combine several records into a **block** without IRGs, as shown in Figure 6-13. Blocks are separated by an **interblock gap (IBG)**. Records within the block are separated by a **group mark** inserted during recording.

FILE IDENTIFICATION

A reel of tape may contain all or part of the records for one or more files. Because of this, in any file maintenance procedure care must be taken to see that the correct files are being processed. For example, updating the wrong inventory file or posting charges to the wrong list of customers would cause serious problems. A file identification system is especially important in secondary storage systems, where

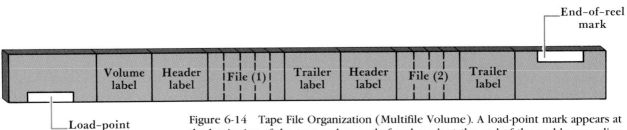

Figure 6-14 Tape File Organization (Multifile Volume). A load-point mark appears at the beginning of the tape and an end-of-reel mark at the end of the usable recording area. Computer-readable internal labels identify the data on the tape.

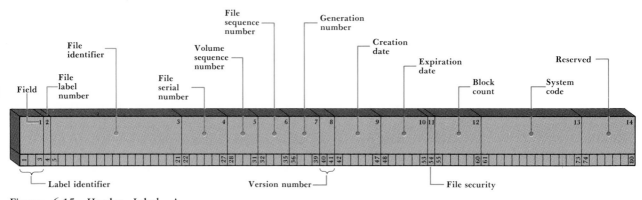

Figure 6-15 Header Label. A header label appears before each file and gives a variety of information relative to that file.

data are stored in a magnetic code that a human operator cannot read to verify identification.

Labeling techniques have been developed to identify files accurately and prevent errors. The labels are similar to a book's table of contents. They contain information on the contents and location of the files stored on a reel of tape or a disk.

In order to assure that the correct reel of tape is loaded for processing, a system of external and internal labels is used. The **external label** is written in a form readable by the human operator. It is applied to the outside of the reel. **Internal labels** are magnetized bits of information recorded on the tape. They contain identifying information that is readable by the computer (Figure 6-14).

Each reel of tape has three types of internal label. It has a **volume label** just after the load-point mark to indicate the number of that reel. Before each file on the reel is a **header** or **file label** that identifies the file and gives information such as the file name and the date after which it can be erased (Figure 6-15). The **trailer label** ap-

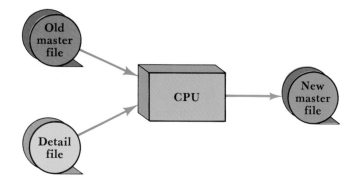

Figure 6-16 Magnetic Tape Storage Drive. Some computers are equipped with several tape drives in order to process a master file and many detail files.

Master record

Account No.	Account Name	Address	Balance

Detail record

Account No.	Account Name	Transaction Code	Amount

Figure 6-17   Tape File Processing. The information from the old master file and detail file are merged in the CPU and a new master file is generated. The next time file processing takes place, the new master file becomes the old master file.

pears at the end of each file and gives the same information as the header label, along with a count of the blocks of records that are in the file. This is used during processing to assure that all records are processed.

PROCESSING TAPE FILES

Magnetic tape can be used for both input and output during processing and to generate backup files. Often **detail files**, recorded on magnetic tape or punched cards, will be merged with a **master file** recorded on magnetic tape, and a new, updated master file will be output on another magnetic tape. A tape drive is required for each tape file involved (Figure 6-16).

Figure 6-17 illustrates the updating of a master file for department store charge accounts, where both the master and detail files are on magnetic tape. The input master file contains the master records, each of which includes an account number, name, address, and a balance amount. The account numbers are in sequential order. The input detail file contains records of transactions that have occurred during the month. Each record shows the account number and name, the kind of transaction, and the amount. Some accounts may have more than one transaction to be posted; others may have none. The records in the detail file are also in sequential order by account number (having been previously sorted and merged in another operation), with records for the same account grouped together.

The program will merge the two input files and produce a new master file. Documents such as reports or statements could also be produced at this time. Because tape is a sequential access medium, each record must be read in turn before the next one in line can be read.

The computer first reads a record from the old master file and one from the detail file into primary memory and checks to see if the account numbers match. If they do, the transaction is posted. The next detail record is read and the account numbers checked. After all transactions for that account have been posted, the new updated master record is written onto the output tape file. If the account numbers do not match, it is assumed that no transactions have occurred within the month and the old master record is copied onto the new master file. In either case the next master record is read in and the process continues until all records have been posted and written.

MAGNETIC TAPE CASSETTE

Another form of magnetic tape storage is a system that uses common Phillips-type cassettes (Figure 6-18). Data are stored in a plastic cassette similar to those used for sound recording tape. The cassette contains a reel of ⅛-inch-wide tape (3.785 millimeters), capable of storing several hundred thousand bytes of data.

Cassette tape storage is convenient and inexpensive. Cassettes can be mailed and easily filed. They can be erased and reused. Some microcomputer systems rely entirely on this secondary storage system. An ordinary, inexpensive cassette player can be used to record

Figure 6-18 Phillips-Type Cassette. This type of cassette is similar to those used on domestic tape recorders. It is compact and helps protect the tape from dust, humidity, temperature changes, or other factors that might cause reading or writing errors.

Figure 6-19 Rigid Disk Storage System. Rigid disk storage is a common means of storing files on large computer systems.

and play back digital tapes. This type of system makes secondary storage available for under $100, with cassettes costing only a dollar or two.

Accidental erasure of the cassette can be prevented with a system similar to the file protection ring. When a small plastic tab is broken off from the cassette, no new data can be recorded over the existing contents. Once the tab is removed, data can be read out repeatedly.

MAGNETIC DISK STORAGE

A variety of disk storage systems are used for secondary storage. These include rigid (Figure 6-19), Winchester, and flexible (floppy) disks.

RIGID DISKS

The **rigid magnetic disk** is a round metal plate with a thin coating of ferromagnetic material. Each disk is approximately 14 inches in diameter and has from 200 to 500 concentric **tracks** on each surface.

Figure 6-20 Disk Pack. The disk pack contains several rigid disks mounted on a common core. Information is written on both sides of the disk. Data are recorded on concentric tracks. The vertical alignment formed by tracks in the same position on all disks is called a cylinder.

Data are recorded one byte at a time along each track. Depending on the system used, from 3,625 to 7,294 bytes of data can be recorded on each track. Each track holds the same amount of data. Rigid disks are sometimes known as hard disks, particularly on microcomputer systems.

A **disk pack** is a collection of two or more disks (usually six) mounted on a common shaft. The vertical alignment formed by tracks in the same position on all disks in the pack is called a **cylinder** (Figure 6-20). A **disk drive** rotates the pack at 2,400 revolutions per minute. Each disk pack weighs about 10 pounds and can be removed from the drive mechanism and stored in a filing cabinet. Disk packs can store up to 571 million bytes of data, depending on the particular system. The data-transfer rate from the disk to the CPU ranges from 156,000 bytes per second to almost 2 million bytes per second.

RECORDING AND ACCESSING DATA

Data are recorded on both the top and bottom surfaces of each disk, except for the top and bottom surfaces of the pack. A disk pack with 6 disks has 10 recording surfaces.

A group of read/write heads attached to either movable or fixed arms record and read data on the disk pack (Figure 6-21). In the **movable head** system the arms move back and forth across the surfaces of the disks. Two read/write heads attached to one arm service the bottom of one disk and the top of another.

In the **fixed head** system a single read/write head is positioned over each track. Data are recorded or read as the track rotates beneath the stationary head. Average access time in this arrangement is 5 milliseconds. Although the movable head system is more economical to manufacture than the fixed head, its access time which is 30 milliseconds, is slower.

Disk storage is a direct access medium. To locate a given piece of data, the arms advance across the disks to the appropriate track. A read head senses the magnetized areas on the revolving disk and converts them into electronic pulses. Average access time to locate a given record ranges from 30 to 60 milliseconds, depending upon the equipment.

Figure 6-21   Disk Access Mechanism. Information is read from or written on the disk by read/write heads positioned near the surface of the disk. Multiple access arms move together in and out of the disk pack. The program supplies the record's disk address including the cylinder number, surface number, and record number. Multiple heads reduce seek time, or time required to position a head over the proper track.

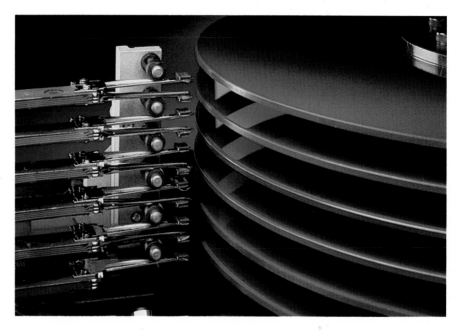

PROCESSING DISK FILES

Records stored on a disk can be either fixed or variable in length. They are usually separated by gaps. Storage locations on a disk pack are identified by the disk surface number, the track number, and the address of the location on the track.

Records in a disk file can be processed sequentially, directly (randomly), or by the indexed file method, depending upon the needs of the user. If the records are to be processed sequentially, they must be sorted numerically or alphabetically. To save space on the disk and processing time, these records may be blocked, that is, entered with no gaps between records. If files are to be processed randomly, an addressing system must be used to give the location of the required data, and additional space must be provided between records. In the indexed file method, records may be stored sequentially by their primary key and randomly within any given block based upon a secondary key.

Figure 6-22 illustrates a file updating procedure where the master file and the detail or transaction file are both stored on disks.

Figure 6-22 Disk File Processing. File processing on disks is different than tape. The old master file is updated, creating a new master file.

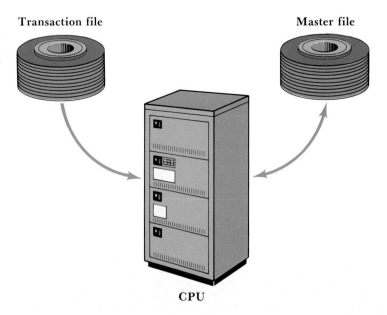

Transaction file

Master file

CPU

The computer processes each item in sequence from the transaction file. Because the master file is stored on a random access medium, the computer can go directly to the master record with the same account number. It can copy the data into primary memory, post or update the data, and write out a new master record over the old. Gaps are provided in recording the master file to allow for the addition of information. The direct access disk method is considerably faster than the sequential method of processing tape files.

WINCHESTER DISKS

Winchester technology is a system in which data are recorded on a permanently mounted revolving disk (Figure 6-23). The 14-, 8-, or 5¼-inch-diameter metal disk is sealed in a tamper-proof and contamination-free metal or plastic case. The Winchester is named after the Winchester 30-30 rifle, because the earliest model, developed by IBM Corporation, stored 30 megabytes in each of two drives.

Data are recorded on a revolving disk in much the same way as on the rigid disk. The system can be made to store 100 megabytes or more per drive. The disks may have up to 300 tracks. High re-

Figure 6-23 Winchester Technology. The Winchester disk provides mass storage capability for many small computer systems. The disk, vertical shaft, access mechanism, and read/write heads are enclosed in the sealed cartridge. The heads ride a fraction of an inch above the disks, in effect floating on a cushion of air created by the rotation of the disks.

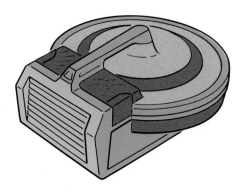

Figure 6-24   Floppy Disk. Floppy disks come in various sizes. Those shown here are 5¼″ wide and are mounted in protective plastic envelopes.

cording densities are possible because the distance between the recording head and the disk can be reduced to less than a thousandth of an inch. Dust or dirt that would normally collect between the disk and the recording head is eliminated by the protective case.

The high cost of Winchester drives as compared with flexible disks and their bulk make them unsuitable for convenient shipment through the mails. For this reason they are used mostly to maintain extensive backup files.

FLEXIBLE (FLOPPY) DISKS

The **floppy disk**, sometimes called a **diskette**, is a thin, flexible plastic disk, 8 or 5¼-inches in diameter with a coating of ferromagnetic ma-

Figure 6-25 Flexible (Floppy) Disk Drive. Floppy disks are inserted into the drive which rotates the disk at about 300 revolutions per minute.

terial (Figure 6-24). It is housed in a square plastic envelope with an aperture that allows a read/write head to access the disk with the envelope in place. Concentric tracks on each side of a 5¼-inch floppy disk can store approximately 1.6 megabytes of data.

Floppy disks are similar to phonograph records. They can be removed from the disk drive, filed, mailed, or otherwise easily handled. Their low cost makes them competitive with other storage media.

The floppy disk drive shown in Figure 6-25 has provisions for mounting the floppy disk, which is always kept in its envelope. The drive rotates the disk under a read/write head. Typically, data can be transferred at the rate of 500,000 bytes per second. The average access time is approximately 6 milliseconds. Floppy disk drives are smaller and more economical to manufacture than rigid disk or Winchester systems.

To record data, the disk, still in its envelope, is inserted in a drive. The disk rotates within the envelope at several hundred revolutions per minute, and data are recorded by a read/write head through the aperture in the envelope.

Records and files are organized and processed in the same way as with rigid disk systems.

DISKETTES MAKE A FASHION STATEMENT

Source: Ira Mayer, *New York Post,* July 19, 1984, p. 56.

Designer diskettes in decorator colors?

It sounds silly at first, but for PC users with different clients or several distinct applications, colored diskettes can help you spot what you are looking for quickly.

Sentinel Technologies has diskettes in 10 colors, while Allenbach Industries' Kaleidiskettes come in four. If you have more than, say, 15 diskettes, you might want to explore this simple, lo-tech, time-saving device.

With color diskettes, you can color-code all your word processing, spreadsheet and database files–or match colors to particular customers (green for those you envy, red for those you . . . ?)

MASS STORAGE

Many computer systems must store hundreds of millions of records, each containing thousands of bytes of data. Examples are extensive social security, driver registration, and income tax files. Thousands of flexible disks would be needed to store that amount of information. Therefore, **mass storage** systems have been developed specifically for storing extensive files, where instantaneous access is not critical.

Figure 6-26   IBM 3850 Mass Storage System. Data are recorded on tape mounted in cartridges. The cartridges are housed in a honeycomb storage facility. When the data are needed, the cartridge is withdrawn from its cell, positioned under a read/write head, and its contents read or changed. When processing is completed, the cartridge is returned to its cell.

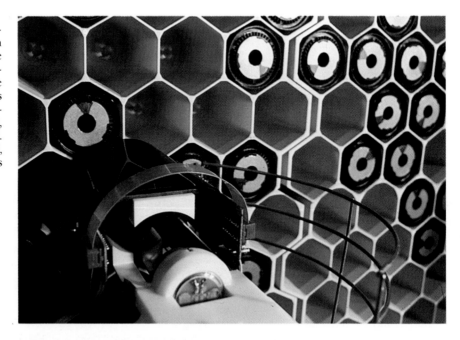

CELLULAR MASS STORAGE

The IBM 3850 is a mass storage device based on **cellular** (or honeycomb) **storage** (Figure 6-26). Data are stored in specially designed cartridges that are housed in cells in a honeycomb. Strips of magnetic tape are mounted on a length of flexible plastic which is placed in the cartridge. The cellular drive positions itself in front of a cell, withdraws a cartridge, and positions it under a read/write head. These systems can store 50 megabytes of data per cell. Average access time is about 10 seconds. Its large capacity and slow access time make this system suited for large files where pieces of data are not accessed frequently.

MAGNETIC BUBBLE STORAGE

Other mass storage systems use the **magnetic bubble** principle discussed under primary memory, although the physical devices are different. The medium used is a garnet substrate coated with a thin magnetic film. In magnetic bubble storage the presence or absence of a bubble-shaped magnetic domain represents either a 1 or a 0. The bubbles or data are read from the substrate using specially constructed magnetic pickup coils. One system, called "plug-A-bubble," developed by Intel Corporation, uses cassettes that hold over 130,000 bytes of data. This is comparable to a floppy disk and provides non-volatile mass storage.

LASER BEAM STORAGE

Laser beams are used to record and read data encoded on a revolving plastic or metal disk. The system is similar to the video disks used to record television and motion picture features (Figure 6-27). Information is written onto the disk by a process that uses a laser beam to melt holes in a tellurium surface (Figure 6-28) or by a system that heats up the surface of the disk, causing gas bubbles to deform the surface layer. The information is read from the disk by scanning the changed reflectivity of the surface in the presence of a reflected laser beam.

Since laser systems rely upon optics, they are not prone to erasure from magnetic fields as are magnetic disks or tapes. Laser disk storage has the advantages of random access, permanence, low cost, and great storage capacity, with up to 4 billion bytes of data stored on a single 12-inch disk.

COMPARISON OF STORAGE MEDIA

An organization that has millions of records to be filed needs a large secondary storage system. In choosing storage media the user must consider whether files are in sequential or random order, cost of hardware, data access speeds, and primary storage capabilities. Most computer installations use a combination of media to provide high-peed access for certain files and high-capacity storage for others. Table 6-1 compares average access time, capacity, and access method of various secondary storage devices.

A reel of magnetic tape, which weighs about 4 pounds, will hold an amount of data equivalent to what could be stored on 200,000 punched cards. A reel of magnetic tape about 2,400 feet long costs less than $20. The punched cards needed to store the same amount of data would cost approximately $250. There is far

Figure 6-27 Laser Beam Storage. The erasable optical memory disk system employs (a) a single-layer recording medium on a plastic substrate and (b) two laser beams, one to record and play and the other to erase.

Magnified view of optical disk

Record/playback and erase mechanism

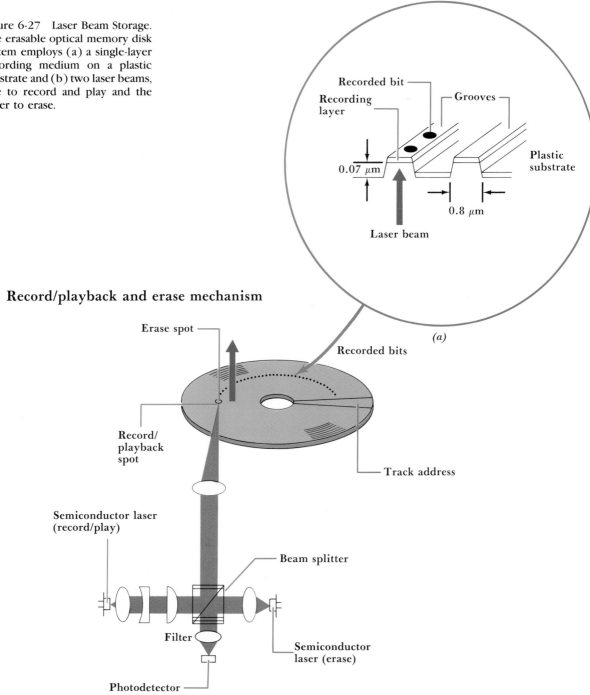

 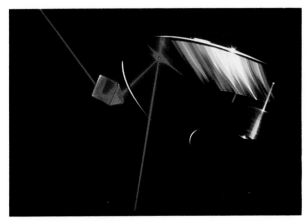

Figure 6-28 Laser Beam Disk. (*Left*) A laser beam melts holes in the disk surface. Information is read by detecting the changed reflectivity of the surface of the disk. (*Right*) A disk such as this can store as much data as 25 tape reels.

TABLE 6-1 Comparison of Secondary Storage Devices

MEDIA	AVERAGE ACCESS TIME	CAPACITY	METHOD
Magnetic tape	5 seconds	40 megabytes	Sequential
Rigid disk			
Fixed head	5 milliseconds	11.2 megabytes	Random
Moveable head	30 milliseconds	571 megabytes	Random
Flexible disk	6 milliseconds	1.6 megabytes	Random
Winchester disk	60 milliseconds	100 megabytes	Random
Cellular mass storage	10 seconds	472 megabytes	Random

less chance of a record being lost or damaged on tape than on punched cards. Magnetic tape can be erased and reused.

Magnetic tape is, however, subject to damage, is limited to sequential access method, and it has a much slower access time than a magnetic disk. Magnetic disks can be accessed sequentially or directly, are less apt to be damaged, and have a fast access time.

Both magnetic tape and rigid disks are being replaced by floppy disks for certain purposes. Floppy disks are inexpensive, costing only a couple of dollars each. They are lightweight and can be sent through the mail easily. They are suitable where a relatively small amount of data must be stored or transmitted.

Winchester disk storage, while bulkier than flexible disks, is less prone to equipment failures and provides high-density storage at relatively low cost. Cellular storage, bubble memory, and laser beam technologies have proven to be effective methods of mass storage, but equipment costs have not yet dropped low enough for wide use of these systems.

A little over 500 years ago Gutenberg printed his first Bible. His masterpiece weighed over 20 pounds. Today the entire contents of the Bible could be stored on a floppy disk weighing only a few ounces with plenty of room to spare.

SUMMARY AND KEY TERMS

• The computer's **secondary storage** system is designed to supplement primary memory capacity using magnetic disk, magnetic tape, or other media.

• **Access time** is a function of the location of the data, the amount of data to be searched, and the speed of the hardware.

• In **sequential access** a file is searched record by record.

• In **direct** or **random access** data are retrieved directly from storage without searching in sequence by using location addresses.

• The **indexed file access** method uses a **primary key** to locate sequentially stored data and a **secondary key** to give direct access to randomly filed data.

• The **American Standard Code for Information Interchange (ASCII)** consists of seven **intelligence channels** and a **check bit** or **parity channel.** The **Extended Binary Coded Decimal Interchange Code (EBCDIC)** system uses eight intelligence and one check channel.

• **Even parity**, **odd parity**, **longitudinal parity**, or **horizontal redundancy** are methods to determine whether information has been accurately recorded along the length of a tape.

• A magnetic tape reel may contain up to 2,400 feet of tape. The tape on each reel has a **load point mark** and an **end-of-reel mark.** A **file protection ring** prevents accidental erasure of data.

• Records are grouped together, or **blocked**, to save space on tape. Records are separated by an **interrecord gap (IRG)** and blocks by an **interblock gap (IBG)**. Reels of magnetic tape include **volume**, **header**, and **trailer labels**.

• **Cassette tape storage** uses ⅛-inch-wide tape stored in a plastic case.

• Data are stored on **magnetic disks** in concentric **tracks**. A **disk pack** is a collection of two or more disks mounted on a common shaft. Data are organized in **cylinders** on disk packs.

• The **Winchester technology** uses a permanently mounted revolving disk protected by a sealed case.

• The **floppy disk** system uses a thin, flexible disk housed in a plastic envelope.

• In **cellular mass storage** specially designed **cartridges** are housed in honeycomb storage compartments. Other mass storage systems are **magnetic bubble memory** and **laser beam storage**.

EXERCISES

1. Define primary and secondary storage.

2. Give three uses for secondary storage.

3. Explain storage capacity and why it is important in secondary storage systems.

4. Define average access time. What factors affect it?

5. Ask a friend to look up five words in the dictionary at random. Using a stop watch, record the minimum and maximum access times. Calculate the average.

6. What are the advantages of direct access storage and sequential access storage?

7. What is the purpose of labeling files?

8. What features do magnetic disk, magnetic tape, and Winchester storage devices have in common?

9. What kinds and types of secondary storage are available on the system in use at your data center?

10. Select one storage device used in your data center. Determine how it is used, what its average access time is, and how it is called in and out by the programmer.

7

Learning Objectives

After studying this chapter, you should be able to
1. Contrast soft and hard copy output
2. Contrast serial and parallel printing
3. List the principal hard copy output devices in use
4. List the major forms of computer output microforms (COM)
5. List the principal soft copy output devices in use
6. Describe audio response unit output

Chapter Outline

Hard Copy Devices
   Character Output Sequence
   Impact Printers
   Thermal Printers
   Ink Jet Printers
   Laser Printers
   Photographic Printers
   Computer Output Microform (COM)
   Punched Output
   Plotter Output
Soft Copy Devices
   Video Display Terminals (VDT)
   Liquid Crystal Display (LCD)
   Audio Response Units

Data Output

When you go to the supermarket, you can't pay for your purchases with a strip of magnetic tape that contains a record of how much money you have in your checking account. You must give the clerk something, in this case a check, that is in a physical form suitable for use in the ordinary business world. Data output by the computer is of little value unless it is in a form comprehensible and usable by people. In this chapter we look at the variety of media produced by the computer as output. This includes the display of characters or graphics on a screen, printed reports and graphics, and sounds or spoken words.

All data output devices perform the same basic function: they convert the electrical pulses processed by the CPU into a usable form. Early computers used a modified electric typewriter as their sole form of output. These devices could output a couple of lines a minute. Modern printing devices can output over 20,000 lines a minute. In addition, modern computers can convert pulses into spoken words and into characters and moving objects displayed on a screen.

Figure 7-1 shows the major categories of computer output media, including both hard and soft copy machines—printers, punches, plotters, CRTs, and many others. **Hard copy** output devices generate a permanent physical copy or printout of the data that may be read by humans and may be filed, duplicated, mailed, or otherwise processed manually. Examples include punched cards, printed reports, and forms. **Soft copy** output devices provide a temporary display of the data, such as spoken words or an image on a CRT.

Generally, hard copy output devices operate more slowly than soft copy devices. Because they require paper and other supplies, they are more expensive to run. Soft copy devices can display large volumes of data quickly and at a low cost, but because soft copy is not permanent, its usefulness for certain applications is limited. Computer systems often include a combination of hard and soft copy output devices that can be switched in and out as the work in process requires.

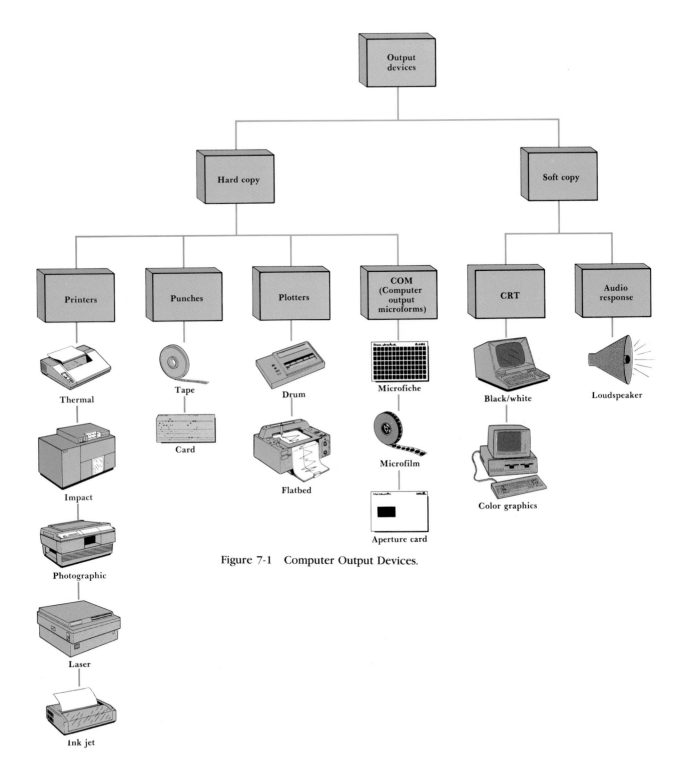

Figure 7-1 Computer Output Devices.

CROSSWORD PUZZLE ON HARDWARE

ACROSS

1. Delays
5. Debby Boone's dad
8. Shove
12. Above
16. Talk with each other
17. On _____ with (equal to)
19. Draft status
20. Italian money
21. A systematic sequence of operations performed upon data
24. Big smile
25. A body-builder might take this
26. Fat sometimes fed to birds
27. Small, pointed beard
29. A VDT looks like a TV _____
30. White lies
31. Statute
32. Employ
33. Random access memory (abbrev.)
36. Church councils
38. Eye layer
40. Tall spring flower, often purple
42. Ice cream _____
43. Rear
44. Slender
47. Magnetic ink character recognition (abbrev.)
48. Batter's feat
49. A group of adjacent bits that form a character
50. Social class in India
51. Enthuses
53. Run away
54. A person who sulks
55. Boxing victory: abbr.
57. Frost a cake
58. Reagan, to friends
59. _____ puddle
60. Ending for twos or fours
61. Fill a suitcase again
63. Coolidge or Moreno
64. ". . . bombs bursting ___ _____ gave proof . . ."
66. Eagle's nest
67. Pizza _____
68. Tender loving care (abbr.)
69. Direct access storage device (abbr.)
72. Trudge slowly
73. Fish propellers
74. Former ruler of Iran
75. Grew older
76. Giving up to
78. Black eye
80. Lamb's mom
81. Make a knot
83. Horse's snack
84. Ventilates
85. Hoover or Grand Coulee
87. Beginnings
89. Competent
90. Finger pointer
94. Space agency initials
95. What CRT means
98. "Country" Slaughter
99. Another word for margarine
100. Mix
101. Cupid
102. Dry; parched
103. Fortune teller
104. To _____ records to a file
105. Dispatched

DOWN

1. Liquid crystal displays: abbr.
2. At the drop of __ _____
3. An electronic circuit that performs a math or logical operation
4. They come out on Oscar night
5. System for detecting the loss or gain of a bit during transmission
6. Like two peas in __ _____
7. Tic- _____ -toe
8. Sits to have a picture taken
9. _____ record
10. Member of congress: abbr.
11. Tired and worn
12. Gymnast Korbut
13. Computer memory expanded beyond primary memory capacity
14. New York State indians
15. Raja's mate
18. Dwell
22. Edgar Allen's kin
23. Undersea ships, for short
28. Possess
30. A set of characters molded on a printing element
31. Single
33. Edge
34. Aristotle Onassis's nickname
35. The central processing unit manufactured on a small silicon chip
37. Din
38. Give credit to
39. Jacob's brother
41. Mrs., in Madrid
43. Laughing _____ (zoo animal)
45. Short newspaper account
46. Nothing more than
49. Soaks up ink
50. Musical ending
52. _____ president
53. French _____ (potatoes)
54. Another term for this is unit record
55. Ensnare
56. On an even _____
59. No. Italian city
62. Assistant
63. File protection _____
65. Actress Lupino
67. Half-quart
68. "What Is _____ Thing Called Love?"
70. Hem or baste
71. White House monogram, 1953-61
73. Complete failures
74. Tears to bits
77. _____ matrix
78. Grain storehouse
79. Risque; off-color
81. Tints
82. Senseless
84. Hate
86. Trumpet mufflers
88. Relax, as a grip
89. To __ _____ (right on target)
90. Lacking water to grow crops
91. Positive
92. Black, to poets
93. Take a breather
96. Pub beverage
97. Estimated time of arrival (abbrev.)

The solution for this puzzle immediately precedes the index.

Figure 7-2 Serial and Parallel Output.

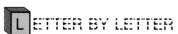

In parallel printing, the entire line is struck at one time. This generates a high volume of output.

LETTER BY LETTER

In serial printing, one letter is struck at a time. This results in a low output speed.

HARD COPY DEVICES

Many devices produce hard copy output from the computer. Printers, punches, plotters, and computer output microforms (COM) produce data in the form of typewritten characters, punched holes, photographic images, and graphs.

CHARACTER OUTPUT SEQUENCE

There are many techniques for creating output in the form of character images. Characters are output in two modes: serial and parallel (Figure 7-2). In **serial output** characters are struck one at a time. For example, a line of 100 characters would be printed character by character, usually from left to right. The ordinary typewriter follows this principle. Generally, the serial mode is not used for high-volume computer output. Because it is economical from a machine design standpoint, it is often used for low-cost or low-volume output systems.

In **parallel output** all characters on a line are struck at the same instant. The type wheel printer uses this principle. To produce a line 100 characters wide, the output device turns 100 type wheels across the page so that the desired character is in position to be printed. At a signal 100 hammers strike the page at the same instant. Naturally, parallel printing is much faster than serial printing.

IMPACT PRINTERS

The **impact printer** uses the **type bar** principle similar to a typewriter. Type hammers form the images by striking a ribbon which

Figure 7-3 Type Element. The set of characters that constitutes a type font is molded on a "golfball" element that is inserted in a typewriter terminal. To change fonts the operator removes the typeball and replaces it with a different one.

Figure 7-4   Daisy Wheel. Each wheel contains a different type font and is easily snapped into or out of place in the teleprinter terminal.

imprints on a sheet of paper. In this system each hammer has a character in relief. Because type bar output is slow, it is not suitable for high-volume computer output.

Another impact device used to print characters is a **type element** or **type ball** (Figure 7-3). A set of numbers and characters (called a **font**) is molded on each type element. To print a character, the element is indexed to the proper position, that is, moved to bring the proper character into position, and struck against the ribbon onto the page. Type element output is used on some console typewriters and small computers. Type element printers can produce up to 30 characters per second—too slow for high-volume computer output. The advantage of the type element is that type sizes and styles can be easily changed simply by changing elements.

Several kinds of printers use a similar principle. The **daisy wheel** consists of a set of spokes arranged in a flat, circular pattern around a central core, similar to the arrangement of the petals of a daisy (Figure 7-4). Each spoke contains a different character. The wheel rotates to bring the desired spoke into position to be struck by a hammer so that the character is imprinted on the page. Daisy wheel printers produce high-quality images at speeds up to 50 characters per second. Because of their low cost and the high quality of the images they produce, these printers are used on many word processing systems.

A slightly different design that works on the same principle is the **thimble** printer. The thimble is constructed of molded plastic curved spokes, each with a different character on it. As the thimble rotates, a hammer strikes an individual spoke against a sheet of

Figure 7-5   Thimble. The thimble works on the same principle as the type element and daisy wheel. Characters and line spacing are easily varied and the type font is easily changed.

Figure 7-6 Dot Matrix Image. Images are formed from a rectangular matrix of dots. The number of wires in the matrix, for example, 5 x 7 or 7 x 9, determines the density or quality of the characters. Some impact printers of this type can print 560 lines per minute.

paper (Figure 7-5). Thimble printers are also used in word processing machines because of the high quality image they produce and their economical design.

Printed characters can also be generated with a **dot matrix** (Figure 7-6). A group of wires or rods is arranged in a 1 × 7, 5 × 7, or other matrix pattern. Each rod prints a dot when struck. Characters are formed by patterns of dots. To print the digit 4, for example, the rods that form the image of the number are struck from behind and forced against the paper. A ribbon inserted between the rods and the page provides the ink. Keypunch machines and some computer printers use this principle. Dot matrix printers are less expensive than other impact machines because they do not require carefully machined type fonts (Figure 7-7).

The **type wheel** printer is yet another method of generating characters (Figure 7-8). Each type wheel contains a full font of characters. To print a character, the wheel is rotated until the appropriate character is in position. An image is made by striking the page from behind with a hammer or moving the type wheel forward against the page. Some systems are set up for parallel printing, with one type wheel in each print position. Others output serially, using one wheel that travels across the page. Type wheel printers are faster than type element or type bar machines. They can print 200 to 300

 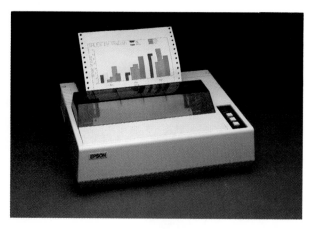

Figure 7-7 Dot Matrix Printer. Dot matrix printers can generate multicolor output ranging from letters and numbers to drawings and illustrations.

Figure 7-8 Type Wheel. Still another type of impact printer uses one or more type wheels. The font of characters is cast around the wheel's perimeter.

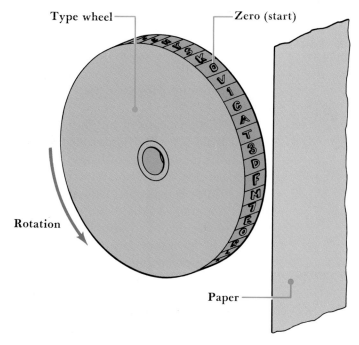

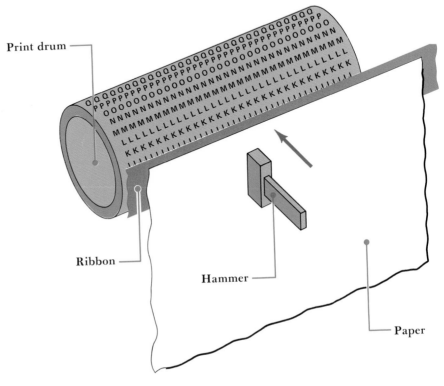

Figure 7-9 Drum Printer. Embossed characters extend the length of the drum with a complete character set in a band for each print position. Drum printers are reliable because they have few moving parts, they range in size from 120 to 144 positions per line, and some can print up to 2,000 lines per minute.

lines per minute. However, they are still too slow for high-speed data output.

A faster means of output is the **drum printer** (Figure 7-9). The drum is a metal cylinder around which characters are cast. It contains as many bands of letters around its perimeter as there are print positions. Each band contains all the characters in the font. The drum printer is equipped with a ribbon transport mechanism and an impact hammer. As the drum rotates, the hammer moves down the length of the drum, striking the appropriate letters to form the line of printed characters. Drum printers are faster than type wheel printers. However, the type faces cannot be changed easily because the drum is permanently mounted in the machine.

High-speed output is possible with a **chain printer** (Figure 7-10). Type slugs are mounted on a moving train, or type chain. Gears move each slug into printing position. A ribbon is placed be-

Figure 7-10   Chain Printer Mechanism. A series of hammers strikes the character slugs as the train moves. The more copies of the set of characters on the train, the faster the printing. Individual characters or the entire train can be changed to print with a particular character set.

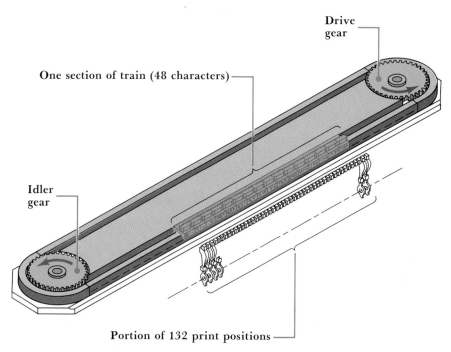

Drive gear

One section of train (48 characters)

Idler gear

Portion of 132 print positions

Complete train composed of 5 sections
(80 type slugs with 3 characters per slug)

tween the page and the train. To print a character, a hammer behind the paper forces the sheet up against the moving type chain. When the sheet is brought into contact with the moving train, a letter image is transferred to the paper. Chain printers can produce up to 2,200 lines per minute. One or more full fonts of characters are available on each train.

A similar printer uses the type band. The **band printer** replaces the rotating chain with a steel belt or band. The band rotates and is struck by hammers. Bands are easily changed, thus providing different type faces.

THERMAL PRINTERS
The **thermal printer** produces characters by using heat and heat-sensitive paper. Character forms are generated by heating selected

Figure 7-11 Ink Jet Printer. Charged ink droplets leave the nozzle, pass between charge and deflection plates, and strike the sheet forming a dot-matrix image. Type fonts are changed electronically, and output in several colors is possible. High quality print is achieved with extremely high matrix density.

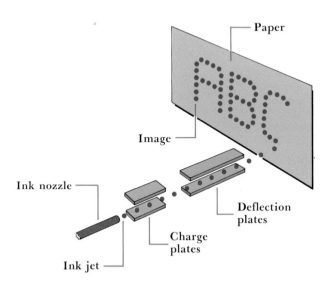

rods in a matrix with an electronic heating element. When the ends of the selected rods touch the heat-sensitive paper, the image is generated. While paper is more expensive for this printer, the printer is very quiet, making it suitable for use where noise is undesirable.

INK JET PRINTERS

Ink jet printers are becoming widely used because they can output black and white or color images quickly and inexpensively. Many different types of ink jet printers are manufactured. These can output lines of text through to full color graphic images, including drawings, figures, and illustrations. The simplest ink jet printer, sometimes known as a drop-on-demand device, contains a print head that has a group of ink jets formed into a matrix. A piezoelectric crystal is used to energize the system. When the crystal receives a pulse, it vibrates, causing a small droplet of ink to leave the jet squirting onto the page. The letter is formed by a combination of ink jets simultaneously squirting the pattern of the letter onto the page. Different colors of ink may be used, and in combination they can create a variety of additional colors. The ink sets quickly upon touching the page.

More sophisticated ink jet printers form the image from a continuous stream of ink droplets sprayed across a page (Figure 7-11).

Figure 7-12 Laser Printer. Laser printers can print thousands of lines per minute. The high quality of the print results from a resolution of over 25,000 dots per square inch.

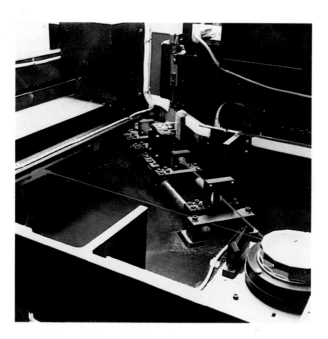

The ink droplets, which have been charged, move between another set of plates which deflect the stream as it moves across the page. These devices are capable of forming images on many different materials, such as paper, plastic, and fabric. Up to 200 characters per second are produced from a stream of more than 100,000 droplets per second.

LASER PRINTERS

One of the fastest printers is the **laser printer** (Figure 7-12). These machines can produce up to 20,000 lines per minute. They are capable of outputting lines of text as well as drawings and figures. These devices operate on a principle similar to a Xerox copying machine. A laser beam sweeps back and forth across the length of a drum. The beam is switched on and off as it sweeps across the drum. The drum, which has been electrostatically charged, responds to the moving light beam, causing areas of the drum to lose their charge. The drum then rotates past a brush, which transfers a toner to selected areas of the drum. Much like an ordinary office copier, the toner, now forming an image, is transferred to a sheet of plain paper. Finally, the paper passes under fuser rollers which permanently set the image.

These printers can combine computer output with a predesigned form and produce both enlarged and reduced images. Working with collating, punching, and binding machines, laser printers can turn computer-generated information into finished booklets or manuals.

PHOTOGRAPHIC PRINTERS

Photographic techniques are also used to create output images, **Photographic printers** produce high-quality text composition on photographic film or paper. A focused beam of light is projected through a rotating disk that contains a full font of characters. The image of the character is projected onto photographic film or paper. The print or negative is then developed and fixed, similar to ordinary photographs. Type styles can be changed easily and images can be created in different type sizes and line widths. This form of output prints high quality, letter perfect characters, and is often used in book and magazine production.

COMPUTER OUTPUT MICROFORM (COM)

Computer Output Microform (COM) units transfer output data from the computer to microform media. A magnifying viewer is used to display the images. Common microforms are microfilm, microfiche, and aperture cards. **Microfilm** is a strip of film containing extremely small photographic images (Figure 7-13). **Microfiche** is a single piece of film, 4×6 inches, holding hundreds of images. The **aperture card** is a standard 80-column punched card upon which a microfilm image is mounted in a window cut into the card.

COM has several advantages over paper output. It requires substantially less storage space, it is easy to mail, and data can be retrieved easily.

COM output machines print upwards of 14,000 lines of data per minute. A 1-inch stack of microfiche records may contain the

Figure 7-13 Computer Output Microfilm (COM). A microfilm recorder can transfer information from the CPU directly onto microfilm, reducing the amount of space necessary to store data, or it can read information stored on tape and transfer it to film. Most recorders project the information on a CRT and then a high-speed camera films the image.

same amount of data as 25,000 pages of computer printout. COM costs approximately one-tenth as much as line printer output and is generated approximately ten times as fast. However, COM requires microform readers in order for people to be able to read the small images. The microfilming process also calls for film processing equipment and supplies.

PUNCHED OUTPUT

Some machines produce output in the form of holes punched into paper tape or cards. A principal advantage of punched output is that it is machine readable; the output can be read back into the computer via its input system.

PLOTTER OUTPUT

Plotters convert data sent from the CPU into graphic shapes, such as lines, curves, drawings, charts, and diagrams (Figure 7-14). The plotter is equipped with a movable pen and carriage mechanism and a chart paper holder. The carriage, holding one or more pens, moves across the page. In a **drum plotter** the paper is mounted on a drum that rotates to move the paper at the same time the carriage is mov-

LASER PRINTERS FOR COMPUTERS MAY DOMINATE INDUSTRY

Someday, in the automated offices of tomorrow, video screens may take the place of ink and paper. Today, however, office automation is producing more paper, not less. The printers that help computers create much of this paper have become a $2.4 billion industry, and printer sales should more than double before the decade ends.

But the nature of printers is changing. During the next several years, printers that write with heat, beams of light, or jets of ink are expected to supplant those that work like typewriters. "The change will be almost complete by the end of the decade," says Roger Kiel, a Xerox Corp. vice president.

At present, almost all printers use what is called impact technology. In some machines, a hammer strikes a piece of metal or plastic type, pressing it against a ribbon and transferring its image to paper. Other impact machines replace the type with a matrix of needles. By hitting the needles in the appropriate patterns, hammers print arrays of dots that look like letters or numbers.

Impact printers are simple. Some sell for as little as a few hundred dollars. But they are slow and noisy. Non-impact printers, all those that don't rely on hammering, are fast and quiet but, until recently, much more expensive.

Consider the most well-developed of the non-impact technologies, laser printing. Laser printers work like copying machines. In a copier, light reflecting from an original document creates a pattern of electrical charges on a rotating drum. The drum turns through a tray of black powder. The powder adheres to the charged pattern, and is transferred to paper, creating a copy. A copier is transformed into a printer by replacing the light-reflecting mechanism with a laser beam that, under the control of a computer, can write directly on the rotating drum. . . .

Laser printers may be vital to the success of some new computers, such as Apple Computer Inc.'s Macintosh. At a time when most personal-computer-makers are pursuing the business customer by offering echoes of International Business Machines Corp.'s products, Apple is trying to sell Macintosh as an IBM alternative. Apple concedes that IBM has won the contest for personal-computer sales to large corporations but believes that Macintosh can become the standard machine for an even more substantial market—the millions of people in small businesses and professional offices who haven't yet bought a computer. However, although most early reviews have been favorable, the Macintosh system has some shortcomings for business users.

The most important may be the system's present inability to produce letters that look as if they had been written on an electric typewriter. The edges of letters or numbers that contain curves or diagonal lines are jagged because the printer sold with Macintosh (the only printer with which the computer operates now) prints letters as patterns of dots and can't space the dots closely enough to form the smooth edges that most business-quality machines produce. . . .

"Unless you are a graphic-arts professional, it's difficult to tell the difference between the output of this printer and pages that have been typeset," says Hideo Yamamoto, director of Canon's laser-beam printing division. There is a catch, however: the laser printer may cost almost twice as much as the Macintosh itself.

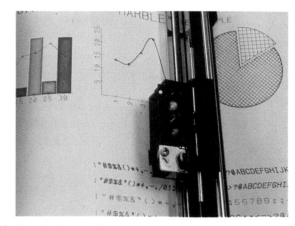

Figure 7-14   Plotter With Sample Output. Many forms of output can be produced by a plotter—maps, engineering drawings, architectural layouts as well as charts and graphs. Shaded drawings and 4-, 6-, or 8-color output can be produced. Some devices print electrostatically instead of with pens.

ing. In a **flatbed plotter** the paper is held in a stationary position and only the carriage moves.

Digital information received from the CPU causes the drum to rotate or the pen to move. These movements create a line representing the output data. Precise charts, lines, and drawings can be prepared because the CPU provides exact horizontal (x) and vertical (y) coordinates to direct the position of the pen.

Drum printers can produce plotter charts of just about any length. Flatbed plotters are limited to the size of sheet that can be conveniently positioned under the carriage mechanism.

The plotter is used to plot many different kinds of business and scientific data, such as stock market curves, utility price curves, and analog wave forms, and to construct figures, symbols, pie charts, and bar graphs.

SOFT COPY DEVICES

Figure 7-15   Video display terminal (VDT). VDT output is inexpensive since paper, ribbons, and other supplies are not required.

Figure 7-16   Light Pen Display Console. When the light pen is pointed at a lighted area on the CRT, the computer is able to determine which part of the display the pen is pointing to and thus change the data on the screen.

Soft copy devices provide output in the form of visual images or audible signals.

VIDEO DISPLAY TERMINALS (VDT)

The **cathode ray tube (CRT)** is frequently used to output soft copy. The process is similar to the process of forming images on an ordinary television screen. An electron beam is scanned back and forth across the face of a phosphor-coated tube at high speeds. The beam is modulated (turned on and off) as it swings back and forth. When the beam is on, it activates the phosphor coating on the inside of the tube, causing it to glow. The glowing spots on the tube create patterns visible from the front of the tube. Letters, numbers, tables, curves, lines, and other figures can be generated in this manner.

The **video display terminal (VDT)** shown in Figure 7-15 resembles an ordinary television set with an attached keyboard. It converts electronic pulses into visual images and displays them on a cathode ray tube. Such devices may display several thousand characters on the screen at one time and can load a screen with characters in a fraction of a second. They are virtually silent. Formatted images, blank forms, and operator cues can be displayed. Video display terminals are widely used where formatted data or an inquiry and response are to be displayed.

The **light pen display console** is another form of video display terminal. A unique feature called a light pen is used to change or replace data displayed on the screen. When touched to the screen, a light beam from the pen modifies the data as desired (Figure 7-16). Data remain on display until replaced by new output from the CPU or until the unit is turned off. No hard copy is generated.

Instead of the light pen, some video display terminals are equipped with paddles or joysticks. These devices position a pointer on the screen. They can also be used to detect operator responses. Many popular video games use joysticks or paddles along with the CRT.

COLOR GRAPHICS TERMINALS   The **color graphics terminal** has a screen capable of displaying a variety of lines, shapes, curves, and

2.2.10, DNA Double Helix

Figure 7-17   Color Graphics Output. These examples of color graphics output show many different applications.

printed letters in full color. Some microcomputers use ordinary color television sets to display color graphic data. These terminals allow drawings, illustrations, graphs, charts, and moving images to be created from data input by the user and displayed on the screen as output (Figure 7-17). On some units the images appear to be three-dimensional. Images can be rotated as they are displayed on the screen. The user interacts with and directs the terminal from a console keyboard. Associated software routines allow the user to edit output from the keyboard by inserting, deleting, adjusting, and changing the color of displayed elements.

Color images can be displayed in two different modes: the ras-

Figure 7-18   Color Graphics Imaging. On the left, the image is formed by a vector display. The electron beam is steered continuously to form a visual image. On the right, the image is formed by raster display. The electron beam traces out a regular raster pattern of horizontal scanning lines.

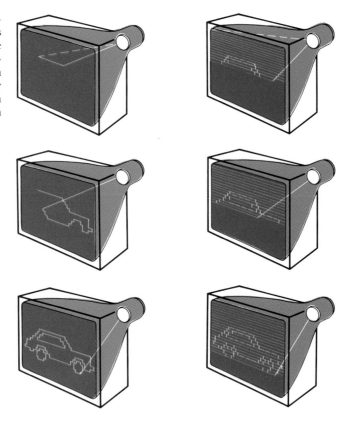

ter pattern and the vector display (Figure 7-18). The **raster pattern** is the method used to create images on an ordinary television set. As an electron beam swings back and forth across the face of the screen, light and dark spots are created by variations in the beam's intensity. Each spot or dot that makes up an image is called a picture element or **pixel**. In **vector display** a continuous electron beam is directed in straight lines over the face of the screen. This lays down a pattern of lines or shapes, creating the image.

The advantage of the raster pattern is its ability to generate high-resolution color graphics. The more pixels making up the final image, the greater its detail or resolution. (Figure 7-19). The principle is the same in reproducing photographs in print media in either color or black and white. If you look at a photograph in this book

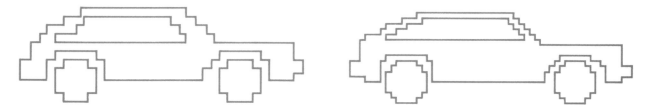

Figure 7-19 Image Resolution. The greater the number of pixels, the greater the resolution. A less jagged effect is obtained as more bits of information are used to generate a figure.

under a magnifying glass, you will see that it is made up of many small dots. Each dot, corresponding to a pixel, blends with the others to create a final image. Compare this photograph to a photograph in a newspaper and you will see how the number of dots per square inch affects the quality of the image.

LIQUID CRYSTAL DISPLAY (LCD)

Liquid crystal display (LCD) uses a liquid suspended in an electrical field. A voltage applied across the liquid causes a change in its optical characteristics. By applying a voltage selectively, an image, in the form of characters, can be made to appear. You are familiar with a liquid crystal display if you own a pocket calculator or digital watch. LCDs are inexpensive and rugged compared to CRTs and other forms of output, but they lack the brightness and intensity of a CRT.

AUDIO RESPONSE UNITS

The **audio response unit**, sometimes referred to as an audio synthesizer, converts data output by the CPU into an audible signal. It can output data as spoken language, musical tones, or other audio signals. The device synthesizes the human voice or the sound of a musical instrument using an oscillator and data stored in the computer's memory system.

Audio response units are particularly useful in conjunction with a Touchtone telephone. A caller can dial a computer from a Touchtone telephone and key an inquiry into the system. The computer will respond to the inquiry and then synthesize a verbal reply that is sent back over the telephone line.

You have probably already been exposed to an audio response

SPEECH SYNTHESIZERS BRING SIMPLE MACHINES TO LIFE

Source: Ira Rifkin, *Daily News of Los Angeles*, October 13, 1984.

"Your weight is 150. You have gained 5 pounds. Have a nice day."

As if gaining the weight is not enough, there is now a bathroom scale on the market that lets you know how much additional ground has been lost in the continuing battle of the bulge.

Have a nice day indeed! It takes nerve to wish you a nice day after ruining it for you. And this from a machine!

"We're not insulting anyone," said Kenneth Burnett, president of Technasonic Electronics Inc., the Chicago-area firm that markets Weight Talker, the scale that has the capability to utter the above mentioned phrase. "People wouldn't stand for that."

The Weight Talker . . . is a recent addition to the list of consumer products that are outfitted with speech synthesizing microchips. The technology, first applied to consumer products a decade ago, has popped up in everything from cars to clocks, video games to security systems.

"Applications for the (speech) synthesizer are limited only by the imagination," a press release from Mitsubishi, a producer of speech synthesizer microchips, proclaimed not long ago.

Vending machines, toys, automobiles, cameras, automated banking machines and high-end appliances, which is what the industry euphemistically calls its more expensive products, will soon be replete with speech synthesizers, according to Mitsubishi executives.

Although most speech synthesizers available so far are limited to just about 15 seconds of electronic-sounding speech taken from a vocabulary of a few dozen words, Whirlpool Corp. has developed prototype washers and dryers that both talk and respond to voice commands.

Consumer resistance could, however, put the brakes on the expanded use of speech synthesizers. A lot of people apparently do not like machines talking to them.

"The biggest stumbling block is consumer acceptance," Don R. Vander Molen, a senior researcher at Whirlpool, said recently. "People are self-conscious talking to a dryer, and we really aren't convinced they want to listen to one either."

Some higher-priced Nissan car models come equipped with speech synthesizers that alert drivers to doors left ajar, lights and emergency brakes left on, keys left in ignitions and dwindling fuel supplies. But George Yasso, a salesman at Miller Imports in Van Nuys, said customers are often relieved when told the speech systems can be shut off.

Even Azmat Malik, product marketing manager for Mitsubishi's component marketing branch, expressed doubts about speech synthesizers. . . .

"I bought a camera that tells you if film speed or exposure is wrong. I returned it. I couldn't stand the idea of this machine telling me what to do," he added. . . .

One possible application is a typewriter that writes in response to dictation,

Malik said, although problems remain with getting the microchips to understand the difference between homonyms like their and there and to decipher words spoken by someone with a heavy accent or nasal congestion.

Kurt Bartsch, director of product planning for Nissan Motors in the U.S., said the automobile manufacturer is experimenting with voice responsive systems that open and close windows and adjust car radios upon voice command. The technology already is available to consumers in Japan, where Nissan first introduced speech synthesizer systems five years ago.

unit without being aware of it. In most major cities the telephone company uses audio response units to handle telephone number changes. When you dial a number that has been disconnected or changed to a new number, it is processed by a computer and an audio response unit. The computer looks up the old number, locates the new number in memory, and then synthesizes a response. What you hear over the telephone is a sentence composed by a computer.

SUMMARY AND KEY TERMS

- The function of data output devices is to convert electronic pulses processed by the CPU into a usable form. **Hard copy** output devices generate permanent physical copies, while **soft copy** devices produce only a temporary display.
- Characters may be output in **serial** fashion, with one letter struck at a time, or in **parallel** fashion, with all characters in the line struck at the same instant.
- Types of printers include **impact printers**, **thermal printers**, **ink jet printers**, **photographic printers**, and **laser printers**.
- Common types of impact printers are **type bar**, **type element**, **daisy wheel**, **thimble**, **dot matrix**, **type wheel**, **type drum**, **chain**, and **band**.
- **Computer output microforms (COM)** include **microfilm**, **microfiche**, and **aperture cards**.
- Other output devices are **paper tape** and **card punches** and **plotters**.
- **Video display terminals (VDTs)** use an electron beam to scan a phosphor-coated tube to display characters. The **light pen display**

console is a form of VDT in which the display can be modified by a light beam from the pen.

• In **color graphics terminal** output images are formed from a series of dots called **pixels**.

• In **liquid crystal display (LCD)** characters are formed by a liquid suspended in an electrical field.

• **Audio response units** convert data from pulses to audio signals such as musical tones or human language.

EXERCISES

1. What are the advantages of hard copy output?

2. How does serial printing differ from parallel printing?

3. Compare the advantages and disadvantages of type bar, type wheel, and type element printers.

4. Describe the principle used in laser printers.

5. What are the advantages of computer output microforms?

6. What are plotters and what kinds of information do they display?

7. What are the advantages of soft copy output?

8. List three applications for which video display terminals are suited. List three applications for which they are not suited.

9. How does the audio response unit respond to queries from a user?

10. Visit a data center and determine what kinds and types of output devices are on the system.

Part 3   Microcomputer Systems

8

Learning Objectives

After studying this chapter, you should be able to
1. Define key terms related to microcomputer systems
2. Summarize the reasons for the increasing use of microcomputer systems
3. Describe several microcomputer hardware systems
4. Describe several business applications for microcomputers
5. Discuss the goods and services offered by computer stores
6. Discuss how to shop for a home computer system

Chapter Outline

The Advent of Microelectronics
Types of Small Systems
    Microprocessor
    Microcomputer
    Minicomputer
Limitations of Small Systems
Microcomputer Hardware
    Popular Models on the Market
    CPU Chips
    Expanded Systems
Personal and Business Applications
    Home Use
    Business Use
Computer Stores
How to Shop for a Home Computer System

Microcomputer Hardware and Applications

In a short time the microcomputer has evolved from an exotic machine used by a handful of engineers and hobbyists to a basic tool of business and industry. Microcomputers have found their way into offices, schools, homes, and game rooms. Because so many microcomputers are now in use, an enormous number of applications programs are being written for them. This, in turn, means still more use of these small systems.

Few people predicted the monumental growth of and interest in microcomputers that began just a few years ago. The first microcomputers were sold to engineers or, because of their low cost and entertainment value, to hobbyists. These small computers had instant appeal and spawned a whole new industry. Companies such as Tandy Corporation (Radio Shack), Apple Computers, Commodore Business Machines (PET), and later IBM Corporation, entered the microcomputer marketplace.

In 1981 there were 344,000 personal computers shipped for business applications. By 1987 it is expected that this figure will reach 5,245,000 machines. Home computer applications have enjoyed an even more spectacular increase in sales and shipments. In 1981 only 143,000 computers were shipped for home applications, and the figure will exceed 10,000,000 by 1987. Both scientific and education applications of personal computers are expected to enjoy similar increases. Figure 8-1 shows the increased number of machines in use for these four important categories.

This chapter will cover microelectronics and microcomputer hardware. It will describe typical applications of these systems and give you some advice on how to shop for a personal computer. The next chapter will go into microcomputer software and programs.

THE ADVENT OF MICROELECTRONICS

The low cost and great capacity of microcomputers are made possible by the modern technology of **microelectronics**. Microelec-

	1981	1982	1983	1984	1985	1986	1987
U.S.							
Business	344,000	926,000	1,850,000	2,775,000	3,524,000	4,335,000	5,245,000
Home	143,000	1,977,000	3,544,000	5,670,000	7,258,000	8,710,000	10,016,000
Scientific	37,000	80,000	122,000	153,000	183,000	214,000	248,000
Education	87,000	147,000	190,000	220,000	249,000	276,000	304,000
TOTAL U.S.	611,000	3,130,000	5,706,000	8,818,000	11,214,000	13,535,000	15,813,000

Figure 8-1 Microcomputer Usage (in units shipped) (*Source:* International Data Corporation.)

tronics is the science of designing and constructing subminiature electronic components using integrated circuits and solid state technology. Before the development of microelectronics most electronic circuits were hand assembled; individual components were connected by wires soldered point to point by hand. The circuits were bulky, expensive, and unreliable.

During the 1960s efforts were made to find ways to package electronic components that were more reliable and cheaper to manufacture. At first, individual electrical components such as transistors were manually soldered on printed circuit boards. Later, new technology made the **integrated circuit (IC)** possible. The integrated circuit is a complex collection of hundreds of transistors, diodes, and other electrical components and their connections manufactured on a small chip of silicon.

Further research led to the development of the **large scale integrated circuit (LSI)**. An LSI circuit is a microelectronic circuit containing thousands of electronic components that form a complete functioning device (Figure 8-2). An entire computer can be manufactured on a microelectronic chip no larger than a 25 cent piece. When wired to input/output devices, microelectronic computers can perform all the tasks previously done by machines occupying hundreds of square feet of space.

Figure 8-2 Large Scale Integrated Circuit (LSI). On an LSI thousands of electronic components are manufactured on a single chip to form a complete functioning device.

The importance of microelectronic technology lies in its high reliability, small size, low power consumption, and economy of manufacture. Microelectronic circuits are extremely reliable partly because their manufacture does not depend on hand assembly. A circuit is laid out as a piece of artwork measuring at least 3 × 4 feet. The artwork is reproduced in greatly reduced size in a form that resembles a photographic negative. The design is repeated many times on a piece of film called a photomask. The mask is used in manufacturing hundreds of microcircuits on a small wafer a couple of inches in diameter. The individual circuits, or chips as they are called, are cut apart and mounted on small plastic carriers with electrical contacts.

Electronic devices, such as computers, communications equipment, and message switching equipment, are mass produced using automated manufacturing and testing techniques. Devices that once cost tens of thousands of dollars are now produced on a small microelectronic chip for only a couple of dollars. This reduction in cost by several orders of magnitude has stimulated the sale of computer and electronic equipment.

TYPES OF SMALL SYSTEMS

Although there are no industry standards to define specific characteristics of types of small systems, certain general distinctions can be made. The prefixes *micro* and *mini* emphasize their small physical size. However, their small size does not imply that their speed or processing capability is necessarily limited. We described classes of computer systems in Chapter 3. Let's review some of their characteristics here.

MICROPROCESSOR

A **microprocessor** is an entire central processing unit (CPU) manufactured on a single silicon chip (Figure 8-3). This microscopic piece of circuitry is about the size of a dime and costs between $5 and $60. Microprocessors are combined with other components, such as memory chips, to form the devices that make up complete computer systems.

Figure 8-3 Microprocessor Chip. This example of very large scale circuit integration (VLSI) contains an entire microprocessor on a single chip.

The low cost of the microprocessor makes it particularly suited for integration of computer systems into machines and other products. In such cases, the computer is built directly into another piece of equipment and sold as an integral part of that equipment.

For example, microprocessors installed in an automobile dashboard can provide information about elapsed time, miles traveled, es-

Figure 8-4 Microcomputer with Dual Floppy Disk Storage. This unit includes a CRT, dual floppy disk drives, a CPU with primary memory, and a keyboard in one unit.

timated time of arrival, fuel level, and the status of the car's electrical and power systems. More and more frequently, microprocessors are being integrated into business machines, word processing systems, children's toys, and electrical appliances.

MICROCOMPUTER

A CPU alone is not a computer, but rather a part of a system. The term **microcomputer** refers to a CPU (the microprocessor) and at least one input/output device. The microprocessor is coupled to memory and input/output circuits that are manufactured on one or more chips. A microcomputer system is capable of input, processing, output, and primary storage. A complete small system, such as that illustrated in Figure 8-4, may cost between $600 and $2,000, but it may be capable of performing the same tasks as much larger and more expensive systems.

Two other machines are closely related to microcomputers. A programmable calculator is a computing device with limited input, output, and processing capabilities. Because it can store programs, it is usually considered a simple version of a computer. It is most fre-

Figure 8-5 Hand-Held Calculator. This device possesses input and output capability and is the product of modern microelectronic technology.

quently used in mathematical applications. A hand-held calculator is a solid state computing device that performs the functions of input, output, and processing and possesses a limited amount of storage (Figure 8-5). Only those calculators that can follow a set of instructions and are self-directing may be classified as computers.

MINICOMPUTER

It is difficult to distinguish a minicomputer from a microcomputer because many minicomputer systems have microprocessor CPUs. In practice, the term **minicomputer** refers to a desktop digital computing device with a microprocessor as its central processing unit, at least one input/output device, a minimum primary storage capacity of 32KB to over 128KB, and provision for connection to a variety of peripheral devices for secondary storage and additional processing capabilities (Figure 8-6). Minicomputers may cost less than $5,000 to over $20,000 fully equipped. They operate on the same principles as do larger systems.

Figure 8-6 Minicomputer System. Linking five work stations to a single processor takes full advantage of the processor's ability to handle a high volume of data at high speeds.

LIMITATIONS OF SMALL SYSTEMS

The reductions in size and cost provided by small systems are obvious advantages to small business and personal users. However, the virtues of the smaller system may be somewhat offset by their limitations. In general, the smaller the system, the more limited its capabilities. Some limitations of a typical low-priced system are:

1. Limited input/output capacity. These systems may have only one or two input/output devices. This limits the amount of information which can flow in and out of the system.

2. Limited storage capacity. Many important programs require more memory than is available and cannot be run on small systems.

3. Limited program language capability. Internal design may limit the number or type of languages that can be used to program the equipment.

4. Incompatibility with large computer mainframe peripherals. The inability to interface with other computers limits a machine's utility.

5. Lack of industry standards and the great diversity of machines, creating system incompatibilities. This limits the ability to transfer programs from one machine to another.

Many of these limitations can be and are overcome by expanded and more elaborate microcomputer systems. As competition in the marketplace continues, there will be a shakeout of manufacturers. This should result in fewer manufacturers who will provide higher quality machines with greater capacity and more compatibility with other machines. The evolution of automobile design illustrates this point. Early automobiles used many nonstandard parts and components. Each automobile used unique tires, hoses, and belts. This made maintenance difficult and therefore limited the vehicle's utility. Today, a degree of industry standardization has reduced the problem to some extent. Parts dealers can stock fan belts, lamps, hoses, and other items that can be used on many different kinds and types of automobiles.

MICROCOMPUTER HARDWARE

POPULAR MODELS ON THE MARKET

Over 150 companies manufacture microcomputers. These companies range from small firms that assemble standard components to large computer mainframe companies such as IBM Corporation. The leading desktop computer manufacturers in terms of worldwide shipments in dollars are IBM, Apple Computers, Commodore Business Machines, Hewlett-Packard, and Tandy Corp. which have 28, 14, 8, 6, and 6 percent of the market respectively (Figure 8-7). This figure shows both world wide shipments in dollars as well as the number of units sold. AT&T is one of the newest entries into the microcomputer field. The major small business computer manufacturers are IBM, Wang, and Digital Equipment Corporation. Digital Equipment, Data General, and IBM lead the field in sales of minicomputers.

There are dozens of microcomputers on the market. Listed below are a few of the most popular.

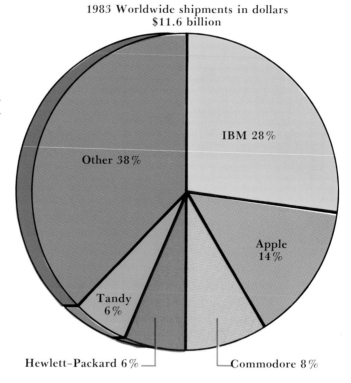

1983 Worldwide shipments in dollars
$11.6 billion

Figure 8-7 Computer Manufacturers Market Share (*Source:* International Data Corporation.)

IBM 28%

Other 38%

Apple 14%

Tandy 6%

Hewlett–Packard 6%

Commodore 8%

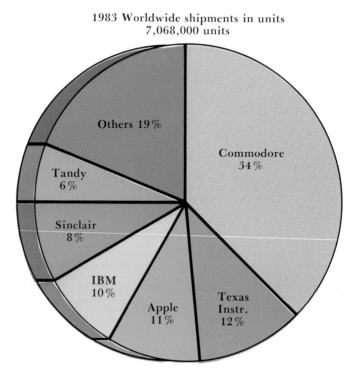

1983 Worldwide shipments in units
7,068,000 units

Others 19%

Commodore 34%

Tandy 6%

Sinclair 8%

IBM 10%

Apple 11%

Texas Instr. 12%

Figure 8-8 DEC Rainbow 100. This system includes a keyboard, CPU, monitor, and mass storage capability.

Figure 8-9 Commodore Computer, Model 64. This system includes a printer, disk drive, monitor, and communications modem.

DIGITAL EQUIPMENT CORPORATION (DEC)   The Rainbow 100 is manufactured by Digital Equipment Corporation, a computer firm that has sold minicomputers for many years. The Rainbow 100 is equipped with a dual drive that handles two 5¼-inch floppy disks, each able to store 400KB of data (Figure 8-8). At the buyer's option the system may be equipped with a 5 MB Winchester disk and a color monitor. The computer's CPU is equipped with a minimum of 64KB of random access memory.

COMMODORE   Commodore Business Machines' initial entry in the microcomputer market was a desktop computer called the PET. Their best seller is the VIC 20, which sells for under $200. Other Commodore systems, such as the Commodore 64, sell for less than $300, and can be coupled to an ordinary telephone line to interface with other computers (Figure 8-9).

COMPAQ   The Compaq Plus, which was introduced in 1982, is an example of a popular transportable microcomputer. It is equipped with a rigid disk drive and weighs approximately 26 pounds. The system

WOULD COMPUTER STANDARDIZATION HELP OR HURT U.S. FIRMS?

Source: Thomas B. Rosenstiel, *Los Angeles Times*, June 21, 1983.

A recent decision by several Japanese computer companies to build a "standard" home computer focuses attention on two of the murkiest questions in the computer industry:

Will home computers ever be standardized enough that programs will run on virtually any machine, and if standardization does come, how will it affect consumers?

Computer makers and analysts say standards will lead to more competition and lower prices. But they also say standards could hurt American manufacturers and benefit the Japanese.

It is also unclear whether such standards will inhibit or enhance the creativity now so lauded in the computer field.

In any case, while *de facto* temporary standards may come and go, changing the computer market for a time, it will likely be years before any firm standards emerge. . . .

The Japanese, who make little software of their own, believe that a standard system is needed to persuade American software makers to design for them. But for now at least, the plan apparently is aimed at launching a market for home computers in Japan, not for penetrating the competitive U.S. market.

Most American home-computer companies, on the other hand, make operating systems that run only their machines, so each brand of computer generally runs only software made specially for it. . . .

All this diversity is confusing, but is it all bad? For consumers, most analysts said, the answer is yes.

"Standards mean the consumer can go to the store and buy a cassette and not worry about whether its for Atari, or Coleco, or Tandy machines," said Pamela Edstrom, a spokeswoman for Belevue, Wash.-based Microsoft Corp., the company that makes MS DOS and has proposed a system for the Japanese home computer.

Standards also tend to bring down prices, said Chris Kirby, a securities analyst for Sanford C. Bernstein & Co., a New York investment firm. A standardized industry is easier for consumers to understand, so standards broaden the marketplace. When that happens, more companies enter the field, which brings more competition and lower prices.

Retailers also will benefit from standards, analysts said, because they won't have to stock 10 versions of the same program. . . .

But many in the industry agree that standardization will not come to the U.S. market until consumers demand it, probably by overwhelmingly supporting one format over any other. To some extent that has happened already with the success of MS DOS for the more expensive personal computer. Yet even that *de facto* standard may be short-lived.

Technology is changing so quickly that within another five years the MS DOS system probably will be superseded by some new technology, said Michele Preston, a securities analyst with New York-based L.F. Rothschild.

"This industry is so young and so vast and changing so quickly, it would be foolish to make a prediction about what will become the standard," said Stan DeVaughn, a spokesman for Apple Computer. "It's going to take time, and its probably going to take some technological breakthrough we don't know about yet."

Figure 8-10 Compaq Computer. The Compaq is a self-contained unit designed to be easily carried about.

can run either MS-DOS or the CP/M operating system and can be programmed in BASIC to run a variety of programs with personal applications. The machine sells for less than $2,500, and its utility is greatly expanded because it is easily carried about (Figure 8-10).

TANDY   Tandy Corporation's first machine, the TRS-80 Model I was introduced in 1978 and sold through Tandy's Radio Shack stores. The popularity of Model I led the company to develop Models II and III. Today the Model 4 sells for less than $2,000, can be programmed in BASIC, and can be connected to a variety of peripheral devices (Figure 8-11). Other computers in Tandy's line include the

Figure 8-11 Radio Shack TRS Model 4P. Tandy Corporation was one of the earliest entries into the microcomputer field. Systems such as this may cost under $2000.

Model 100, a hand-held, completely portable computer that operates on batteries.

APPLE   Apple Computers entered the market offering a desktop computer priced under $1,400, with color capability. The machine's success led to the introduction of the Apple II, Apple III, and Apple IIc. The IIc personal computer weighs less than 8 pounds and costs under $1,300 (Figure 8-12). The system comes with 128KB of primary memory and a built-in 5¼-inch diskette drive.

Another popular Apple machine is the Macintosh. The Macintosh is equipped with a 9-inch CRT display, 128KB of primary memory, and a 3½-inch built-in disk drive. It is a computer that uses a **mouse** as an input device (Figure 8-13). The mouse is used to position a pointer on a list of icons (Figure 8-14). The computer in turn executes the function pictured in the icon.

IBM   One of the later companies to enter the home computer market was IBM Corporation with its Personal Computer (PC). The basic IBM PC costs under $4,000 (Figure 8-15). The IBM PC has a 16-bit microprocessor and its basic 64KB primary memory can be expanded to 640KB. The system can be equipped with either one or two floppy disk drives, in addition to a mass storage rigid disk. A

Figure 8-12 Apple IIc. This system, a portable version of the popular Apple II, weighs less than eight pounds, and is priced under $1300.

Figure 8-13 Apple Macintosh. Hardware capable of producing high-resolution graphics, an extensive software package, and easy manipulation using a mouse allow inexperienced users to produce complex graphic displays.

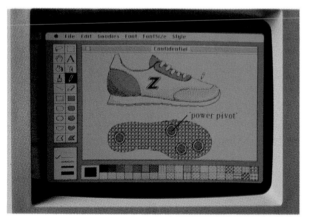

Figure 8-14 Display Screen with Icons. The list of icons (symbols) representing various functions is displayed down the left side of the screen. The user points to the appropriate icon, which in turn causes the computer to execute the function pictured.

Figure 8-15 IBM Personal Computer. This system, which features dual floppy drives, is one of the most popular of the IBM series of microcomputers, with particular appeal to business establishments.

large variety of software is available for this system, which greatly expands its utility. IBM markets several different varieties of its personal computer with different memory, keyboard, and disk storage facilities.

OTHER MANUFACTURERS   A number of other firms enjoy a share of the market. Sharp, Sony, Fujitsu, Hewlett-Packard, and NEC have introduced small desktop microcomputers. Microcomputers are also sold by North Star, Cromemco, and others. The common characteristics of all these machines are their low price, small size, and adaptability to small business and home use.

CPU CHIPS

Most microcomputer manufacturers assemble their systems from common components and subassemblies. The most important component of the microcomputer is the CPU chip. These chips give the microcomputer its unique characteristics.

CPU chips are manufactured by a number of integrated circuit manufacturers. Several competing microcomputers may use the same brand of chip. Entire computer systems are built from chips such as the Z80 made by Zilog, Inc., the M68000 made by Motorola, and the TI9900 made by Texas Instruments. Other CPU chip manufacturers are Digital Equipment Corporation and National Semiconductor. The Z80 is one of the most popular CPU chips. It appears in the TRS-80 and NEC microcomputer systems.

The advantage of a common CPU chip is that programs written for one microcomputer can be run with little or no change on any other brand or model that is equipped with the same processor chip. This gives many microcomputers common characteristics and the ability to use similar programs and software.

CPU chips are sometimes categorized by the number of bits of information they can process simultaneously. The Zilog Z80 is called an 8-bit chip because it can manipulate 8 bits of data at one time. About 39 percent of personal desktop computers are equipped with the Z80 8-bit processor. More powerful chips can manipulate 16 or 32 bits of information simultaneously. The Motorola M68000, Intel 8086, and Zilog Z8001 are in this class.

EXPANDED SYSTEMS

The smallest microcomputer system consists of only a central processing unit, one input, and one output device. A keyboard for input may be attached to the CPU, which is housed beneath a CRT for output. A slightly larger system equipped with one secondary storage device, such as a cassette recorder or floppy disk drive, is still limited in capacity. However, the low cost of such minimal systems—between $500 and $3000—makes them suitable for many homes and small businesses.

In general, the capabilities of a small system increase in proportion to the number of **peripheral devices** available. Figure 8-16 diagrams an expanded microcomputer system with disk drives, tape storage devices, cathode ray tube terminals, line printers, and so on. Expanded systems such as these have many business applications. In fact, such computers are often referred to as small business computers rather than as personal computers.

A complete line of low-cost, light-weight, portable peripheral devices has been developed for use with microcomputer systems. Figure 8-17 gives an idea of the reduced size of a line printer designed for use with microcomputer equipment. In addition to line printers, peripheral devices for small computers include flexible and rigid disk storage devices, card readers, CRTs, paper tape readers, optical scanners, and audio output devices.

PERSONAL AND BUSINESS APPLICATIONS

Throughout the text we have mentioned many commercial microcomputer applications. We will now list a few typical microcomputer applications in the home and small business.

HOME USE

GAMES AND RECREATION   The microcomputer is often used as a toy or recreational device. There are programs that simulate standard games such as backgammon, blackjack, chess, bridge, and checkers. Many new games, capitalizing on the computer's graphic and mathematical capabilities, have been created (Figure 8-18).

PERSONAL INFORMATION FILES AND PROCESSING   The computer can store a variety of personal information that can be maintained elec-

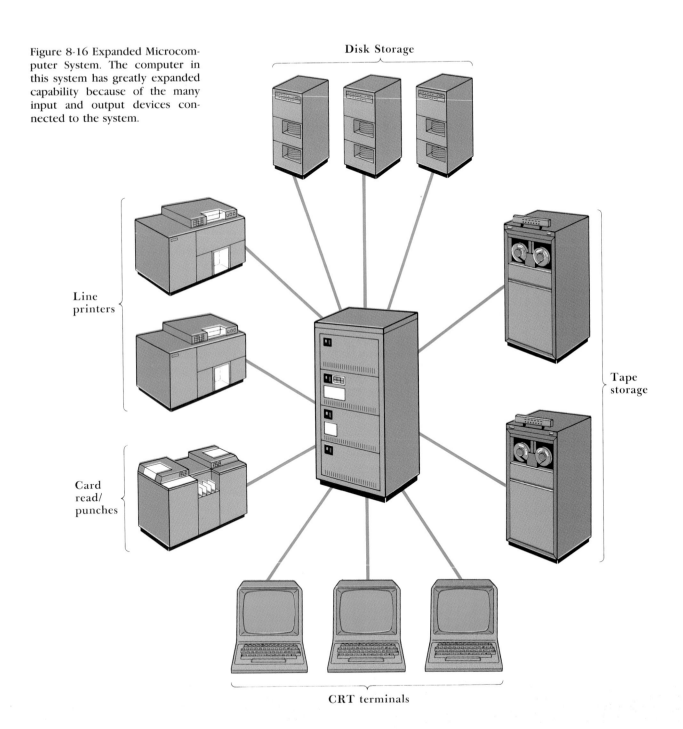

Figure 8-16 Expanded Microcomputer System. The computer in this system has greatly expanded capability because of the many input and output devices connected to the system.

Disk Storage

Line printers

Card read/ punches

Tape storage

CRT terminals

Figure 8-17 Line Printers for Microcomputer. Many models of small line printers are available for use with microcomputers. They vary in speed, print-out size, and letter quality.

Figure 8-18 Microcomputers in Recreational Games. Many new games are possible because of the graphic and visual capabilities of the microcomputer. Games are the first hands-on contact with computers for many people.

tronically. For instance, it can maintain up-to-date lists of names, addresses, and telephone numbers, investment portfolios, lists of personal possessions, and so on (Figure 8-19). Systems such as these require one or more floppy disk drives to store the large volumes of information involved.

Because of the computer's excellent ability to manipulate numbers, it has become widely used for personal accounting. The computer can balance the checkbook and keep track of the family budget. It can prepare basic tax records, print out reminders of bills to be paid, and categorize information for income tax purposes.

LEARNING AND SELF-IMPROVEMENT   The microcomputer has many learning applications. It has superb capabilities for drill practice in mathematics, foreign languages, spelling, and history. It gives instant feedback on accuracy, provides encouragement, evaluates progress, suggests alternate plans of study—and has eternal patience.

COMPUTER ART   One of the most exciting applications of the computer for personal use is in the area of graphic design. The small

Figure 8-19 Family Business Usage. The computer can maintain extensive files of information and is useful in small, family-run businesses.

computer can be coupled to a color television set to output a variety of brilliant, moving color images (Figure 8-20). These patterns can be rotated, shifted, or moved about on the screen. Color graphics can be used to test color harmony, to generate artistic designs for interior decorating or print design, or to provide an outlet for creative expression.

WORD PROCESSING   Microcomputers have become popular in the home to handle a variety of word processing tasks. Home computers equipped with printers act as a replacement for ordinary typewriters. With them the user can manipulate words and phrases in composing letters, reports, or other writing. The machine can then produce pages of accurately typed and properly arranged material. Computers are now widely used by students in preparation of homework, reports, and other class assignments.

Figure 8-20 Computer Art. Many creative and interesting visual and artistic designs can be created using computer color graphics.

CONTROL OF APPLIANCES   Microcomputers can be adapted for a variety of control applications around the home. They have been wired to domestic lighting systems, air conditioning and heating equipment,

Figure 8-21 Computer Accounting and Record Keeping. Accounting is a major task for small computers in many business establishments.

and security and burglar alarm devices. The computer can monitor for fire and break-ins and actuate a telephone dialer to call the police or fire department.

BUSINESS USE
The list below contains a few of the many ways microcomputers are being used by business.

ACCOUNTING   Perhaps the most common application of the computer in small business is for accounting and record keeping (Figure 8-21). Microcomputers are used to maintain the general ledger and to process accounts receivable and payable files. They keep track of inventory and fixed assets. They print out payroll and tax records and perform cash and credit control.

MANUFACTURING AND PROCESS CONTROL   Microcomputers have found their way into manufacturing plants and machine shops (Figure 8-22). They schedule work in process, monitor inventory

Figure 8-22 Microcomputers in Manufacturing. Microcomputers are often found near assembly lines to help monitor inventory and keep track of parts and production schedules.

quantities, and keep track of orders. They aid in assembling, testing, shipping, and designing goods. Microcomputers prepare schedules showing how equipment, personnel, or supplies are to be used for a given operation. They also maintain records so that the business proprietor can analyze unit cost, cost by department, or by the entire shop.

Process control applications include managing laboratory processes that require monitoring or recording of output (Figure 8-23) and managing continuous or batch processes that are part of the manufacture of plastic, chemicals, glass, and textiles.

INFORMATION NETWORKS   Microcomputers provide small business users with access to large information networks (Figure 8-24). Firms such as Dow Jones or CompuServe maintain enormous data banks of useful information that can be accessed through microcomputers. For example, a small investor may use the Dow Jones information network to obtain historical data on stocks or bonds and to compute trends, highs and lows, or other useful data. The services are priced to the user on a minute or hourly basis.

Figure 8-23 The Microcomputer in the Laboratory. The microcomputer is found in many scientific, medical, and industrial laboratories to monitor and control processes.

COMPUTER STORES

During the last few years hundreds of computer retail shops have opened across the country. These stores specialize in small computers for home or office use. Some major features of these computer stores are:

1. System selection assistance. Many retailers will help prospective buyers define their needs, demonstrate hardware and software, and assist in system selection (Figure 8-25).
2. Programming classes. Some computer stores offer classes in programming, hardware, and operation of systems.
3. Books and periodicals. Computer stores sell a variety of textbooks, instruction manuals, and magazines to help users get the most out of their equipment.
4. Software. Most computer stores carry a variety of software and programs. These may be available on floppy disks or cassette tape or as program listings.
5. Paper and supplies. Many computer stores sell ribbons, paper,

Figure 8-24 Information Networks. The microcomputer often serves as a principal means of accessing large central computers. This local computer is equipped with local storage and can access the master data base that serves the host computer.

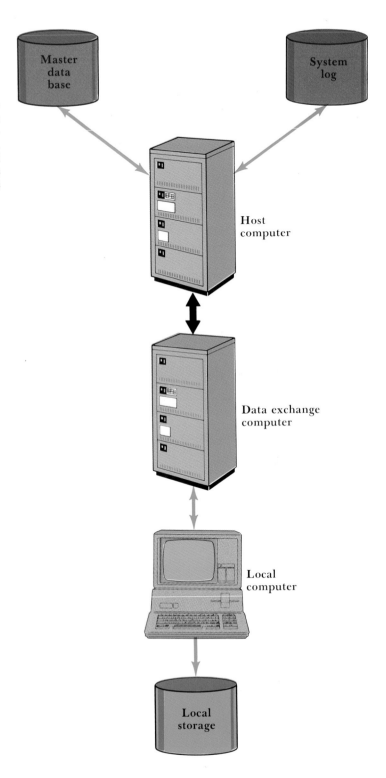

Figure 8-25 Retail Computer Store. Many retail computer outlets display goods and assist customers in defining their needs and purchasing new equipment.

punch tape, floppy disks, and other supplies. They can sometimes order expansion boards, additional memory, or special plugs and connectors for customers.

HOW TO SHOP FOR A HOME COMPUTER SYSTEM

Many students, homemakers, hobbyists, and small business proprietors are buying microcomputer systems. There are hundreds of sizes and types of microcomputers on the market. Each has special characteristics. Some have black and white displays, others have color graphics, and still others provide voice synthesized output. Some can be coupled with a modem to telephone lines.

The search for a home computer should be approached systematically. Begin by analyzing your needs, your budget, and available software. Ask yourself what business, personal, or recreational tasks you know you want your computer to do now, and try to anticipate what other services might be useful to you. Sometimes buyers find unexpected uses that they did not think of when they bought their

FAMILY COMPUTER: THE BYTE THAT FAILED

Source: Art Buchwald, The Los Angeles Times Syndicate, July 14, 1983. Reprinted with permission of the author.

The home computer business is in a lot of trouble. It would be nice to blame the Japanese for it all, but they never really got into the action.

One of the reasons the business got into difficulty is the female gender problem. Women still don't appreciate the value of a home computer and what it can do to make their lives easier.

When I set up my brand-new computer one night, my wife asked why I bought it.

"This is going to change our lives. We can do our taxes on it."

"H & R Block did them already."

"Well, we can do them next year," I said. "We also can compute our household expenses on this machine. Give me all our bills and I'll start programming them."

"You have to be kidding. It will take me three months to find all our bills. Would you take my word for it that we spent $10,000 more than you made in 1982?"

"All right, I'll put that into the computer."

"What does the computer say about that?"

"It says we spent $10,000 more than I made. Why don't I try balancing your checkbook? Give me all your stubs."

"What for?"

"The bank's computer could have made a mistake and we can take our computer printout to the president and show it to him."

She came back and threw her check stubs on my desk, and stomped out of my study.

Three hours later she came back. "How are you doing?"

"I'm up to Lord & Taylor's stub for March. So far everything checks out. Maybe I'll make up your calendar for the week. What have you got on for the next few days?"

"I have a hairdresser's appointment on Thursday."

'Good, now I'll just feed that information into the computer, and then when you want to know what you've got on for Thursday, you just put this floppy disc into this slot, put your finger on CODE, then hit this button, and you'll know you have a hairdresser's appointment on Thursday."

"I already know it."

"OK, forget the calendar. Let's take an inventory of everything we have in the house."

"At 11 o'clock at night?"

"Why not? Once we record it on a disc, and we have a fire, we'll know what was lost."

"Suppose the computer gets burned up in the fire?"

"We won't keep the disc in the house. We'll put it in my office, and a printout in the bank's safety deposit box."

"What else can your computer do?"

"I can key into a bulletin board and talk to anyone in the United States who has a compatible communications terminal."

"You can do that by phone. You still haven't told me why you bought this computer."

"If you must know, I bought it for the children. Kids have to grow up these days with computer knowledge."

"Our children are all grown up and they don't live here anymore."

"You never know when they'll come back home."

The home computer is still in my study, but I don't seem to use it as much as I thought I would. I made a friend in Minneapolis with it one night, but just when we were getting to know each other, his wife made him come to bed.

machines. A woman who buys a computer so her family can play games may find that the machine soon becomes indispensable in her small home business. A man who purchases a microcomputer to keep track of bills and do accounting tasks may discover that its word processing capability is even more useful to him than the accounting applications.

Cost is a major consideration. If your budget is limited, you might consider a machine equipped with basic components that can be added to later. You can build up your system if you acquire standard pieces of equipment that can be easily interfaced to other systems. Some manufacturers reduce prices by selling machines with only a minimum amount of manuals and instructions. It is true that the expense and effort of preparing adequate user manuals and documentation increases the price of a system. However, the higher initial cost may mean that you will have fewer problems in using the system.

Visit several computer stores to discuss available hardware and software. Compare systems, looking at price, capability, flexibility, and expandability. When the choice has been narrowed down in terms of hardware, run several test programs to evaluate speed and capacity.

The following questions focus on the major factors you should consider when choosing a personal computer system.

1. Cost. What is a system's basic cost? What additional charges are involved in expanding the input/output and storage systems?

2. Software. What languages, games, operating systems, and other software are available for the system? Software is an important consideration, since not all software works on every machine.

3. Expandability. Can the system be expanded easily? Is the computer upwardly compatible with other models? Upward compatability means that a user can trade in a machine for a larger or faster model without reprogramming or installing new communications equipment.

4. Storage capacity. How much and what type of primary memory is available on the system? Can floppy disks and other secondary storage devices be added easily?

5. Documentation. Is a set of manuals, diagrams, and instructions available for the machine? Are the user guides and language and reference manuals clear and easy to understand?

6. Service and maintenance. Are maintenance and repair facilities conveniently available? What warranty and service provisions come with the computer?

7. User groups. Are there user groups in your vicinity so that you can share information and software with others who have the same make of computer? Do these user groups publish a newsletter or have meetings?

8. Networking. Does the computer come with adequate hardware and software so it can function in an information network? Can it be connected through telephone lines? Are the proper programs available to allow access to remote data banks?

Some of these questions are easily answered. Others may require more research. The size and type of computer ultimately selected should meet your needs. Too much capacity raises the cost unnecessarily, but inadequate equipment may not serve its intended purpose. Finally, the field of home computers is undergoing great and constant change. You will need up-to-date information to make your best judgment.

SUMMARY AND KEY TERMS

• The low cost and high capacity of microcomputers is possible because of **microelectronics**. Microelectronics involves the design and construction of subminiature electronic components using **integrated circuits** and **solid state electronics**.

• A **microprocessor** is an entire central processing unit manufactured on a single silicon chip. A **microcomputer** includes a CPU and at least one input/output device. A **minicomputer** is usually defined as a desktop or rack-mounted device that has a CPU, at least one I/O device, a minimum primary storage of 32K, and various peripheral devices for secondary storage and processing.

• Some major companies that manufacture and sell microcomputers are IBM, Tandy Corporation, Apple, Commodore Business Machines, and Digital Equipment Corporation.

• The major manufacturers of CPU chips include Zilog, Motorola, Texas Instruments, Digital Equipment Corporation, and National Semiconductor. The Z80 (Zilog), M68000 (Motorola) and TI9900 (Texas Instrument) are popular CPU chips. Chips are classified by the number of bits of information they can process simultaneously as **8-bit, 16-bit**, or **32-bit** chips.

• A minimal microcomputer system may contain only a keyboard, central processing unit, and cathode ray tube for ouput. Expanded systems include disk drives, tape storage, line printers, color graphic displays, optical scanners, audio output, or other **peripheral devices**.

• Personal computer applications include recreation, personal information files and processing, self-teaching, computer art, word processing, and control of appliances.

• Common business applications include accounting, manufacturing and process control, and information networks.

• Among the services offered by computer stores are system selection assistance, classes, and the sale of books and periodicals, software, and paper and other supplies.

• Major factors to be considered in selecting a computer system include cost, available software, expandability, storage capacity, documentation, service and maintenance provisions, existence of user groups, and networking capacity.

EXERCISES

1. Define the terms minicomputer and microcomputer.

2. Contrast the capability of the microcomputer with hand-held calculators.

3. Describe how microprocessors are integrated into finished goods.

4. Diagram an expanded microcomputer system.

5. List some common microcomputer peripheral devices.

6. Give several examples of personal applications for small computers.

7. Describe some applications of color graphics.

8. Give several examples of business applications for microcomputers.

9. What are some of the services offered by computer stores?

10. Describe how to buy a home computer system.

9

Learning Objectives

After studying this chapter, you should be able to
1. Contrast applications and system software
2. Contrast batch, multiuser, and real time operating systems
3. List the major functions of operating systems
4. Describe the function of word processing software
5. Describe the function of data base management system software
6. Describe the function of communications software

Chapter Outline

Applications and System Software
Operating Systems
   Function of Operating Systems
   Resident Storage Devices
   Structure of Operating Systems
Types of System Programs
   Control Programs
   Service Programs
Types of Operating Systems
   Batch Operating Systems
   Multiuser Operating Systems
   Real Time Operating Systems
Applications Software
   Spread Sheet Programs
   Word Processing Programs
   Data Base Management System (DBMS) Programs
   Graphics Programs
   Communications Programs
   Combination Packages

Microcomputer Software

S oftware includes the programs; codes, sets of instructions, languages, and commands that enable a computer to perform its functions. As computers evolved, it soon became apparent that software was as important as hardware in getting the best out of the systems. Microcomputers originally used software adapted from minicomputers or larger systems, but as the market for microcomputers expanded, programs, operating systems, and other software were developed specifically for these smaller machines.

Because of the large number of microcomputers now in use, thousands of programs have been and are being written. Many small software houses are currently in the business of developing and selling applications programs and software specifically aimed at microcomputers. In addition, users exchange programs and information through microcomputer user groups.

This chapter focuses on applications and system software. It explores operating systems, spread sheet analysis packages, word processing, data base management systems (DBMS), graphics, and communications software. A later chapter describes BASIC and other languages used on microcomputers as well as larger systems.

APPLICATIONS AND SYSTEM SOFTWARE

All computer programs can be divided into two major categories: applications software and system software (Figure 9-1). **Applications programs** are designed to solve end user problems. They are either written by computer manufacturers or software companies for a general purpose or written by users to solve a specific, or local, problem. Examples of applications programs include programs to prepare payrolls, perform accounting or financial functions, compute business ratios or profits, manage personnel files, or keep track of inventory. Businesses buy computers so that they can run an applications program to solve a problem, perform a task, or carry out a function that might otherwise be performed by a human operator.

Applications programs are often sold as packages. These in-

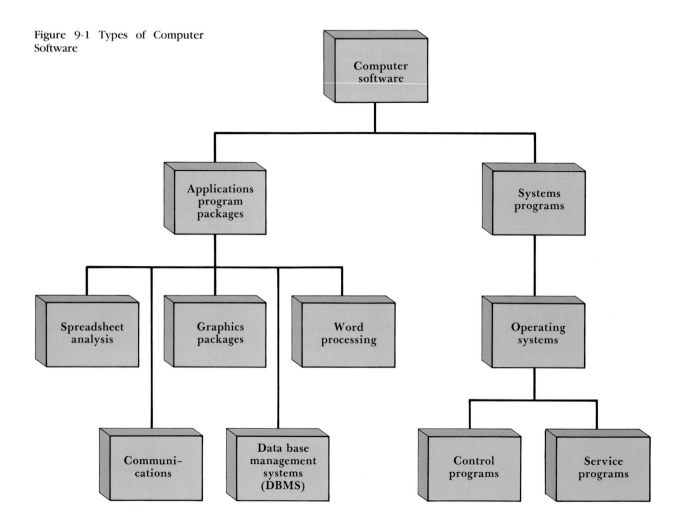

Figure 9-1 Types of Computer Software

clude (1) already tested and debugged instructions entered on a disk and ready for use in the computer and (2) program **documentation**, that is, flowcharts, sample input data, output specifications, program listings, and other written material that describes and explains the program. Some of the most popular applications packages are graphics, word processing, communications, data base management systems (DBMS), and spread sheet analysis.

A second category of software, called **system software**, is an essential part of computer operations. System programs do not solve end user problems. Instead, they manage the resources of the computer, automate its operations, and facilitate programming, testing, and debugging. Most applications programs run under the control or direction of a system program.

System software is generally provided by the computer manufacturer or a firm specializing in system programs, rather than written by the user. The writing of system software requires a great deal of technical knowledge of specific hardware details. These specialized programs may take thousands of hours to write and cost hundreds of thousands of dollars to develop.

Once finished, a piece of system software may be used by many computer owners. It enables them to run applications programs which in turn solve local problems.

OPERATING SYSTEMS

The most complex and extensive pieces of system software on many microcomputers are **operating systems (OS)**. In this chapter we discuss operating systems as they relate to microcomputers. The reader should understand, however, that operating systems are not limited to microcomputers. In fact, they were originally written for large mainframe machines. The study of the microcomputer gives us a good opportunity to learn about how operating systems work. Many of the principles discussed in this chapter are applicable to mainframes as well as to microcomputers.

In some respects the operating system performs functions that are transparent to the user. It is something like the services performed by the public utility that provides electricity to your home or office. One need not understand the inner workings of the power generation plant to use the electric power that is provided. Operating systems differ and are often tailored to include features unique to a particular computer system. There are many programs that do not require the user to understand the computer's operating system or employ any system commands. Thus the reader may wish to skip the following discussion on operating systems, or rely upon the specific documentation provided by the computer manufacturer. One does need, however, to understand specific operating system commands to use a computer for many applications.

SIZING UP THE SOFTWARE AVALANCHE

Source: Gene McMahon, *New York Post*, March 5, 1984.

Software has become the dominant factor in the business-PC marketplace. . . .

The purchaser of any microcomputer is faced with an avalanche of software to choose from. The hardware manufacturers know it and are soliciting software developers to help make their machines competitive. . . .

To understand how the right software contributes to the ultimate success and usefulness of a PC, let us examine how the software and the hardware fit together.

Software is anything that is not exclusively hardware. If you think I'm hedging my bets you're right! With so much software being burned into the ROM (read only memory) of virtually all microcomputers, the line which separates hardware and software tends to get fuzzy.

To get a clearer picture of what software is and what it does for the computer, let us step back in time and place to a chance meeting in 1945, at the Aberdeen, Md., railroad station between John von Neumann, a famous mathematician who was working on the design of nuclear weapons, and Herman Goldstine, a member of the team that was building ENIAC, the world's first digital electronic computer.

As they waited for the train both men were discussing the problems of their respective jobs. Von Neumann was bogged down with the delays caused by routine checking and rechecking of mathematical calculations. Goldstine told him of the lightning speed they hoped to achieve with ENIAC.

From that moment, von Neumann took an interest in the ENIAC project. In 1946 he became a special consultant to the team.

In theory ENIAC was programmable—capable of switching from one task to another. In practice this switching of programs was difficult and time consuming.

Von Neumann developed a solution to this problem. He set down the precepts of the "stored program"—keeping the instructions to ENIAC inside the computer along with the data. Thus, ENIAC could use its great speed to change programs itself and, more important, programs could call other programs and pass information among themselves. Software was born.

The stored-program concept is the heart and soul of today's digital computers—from mighty mainframe to mini micro.

What hath von Neumann wrought? When a computer chip designer such as Intel designs a chip, they build into the computer a set of instructions in "machine language"—a series of binary digits. When a microcomputer manufacturer uses this chip to build a new machine, the unit uses these instructions as the basic raw materials from which the whole house of software will be built.

But programming in machine language is arduous and error-prone. So, the first program to be built is an assembler, a program which will translate symbolic assembly-language statements into machine language instructions. . . .

To allow the computer to run a large selection of available software, the manufacturer will contract software firms, such as Microsoft (developers of PC-DOS and MS-DOS), to build a special version of the operating system and high-level languages such as BASIC or COBOL.

However, the manufacturer must now build an application software base, because, at this point there is nothing in the new machine's bag of tricks that is of much interest to the bulk of micro purchasers.

Micro buyers usually want to use the desktop computer as tools for their careers. They don't want to become programmers. They would be overjoyed if the micro was as easy to use as a telephone. . . .

Thus, today's hardware manufacturers are constantly trying to convince the software developers to create versions of their software that work for their machines. For the public, this means an outpouring of software.

FUNCTION OF OPERATING SYSTEMS

An operating system is a complex group of programs and routines that resides all or in part in the computer's memory. It controls the computer's overall functioning, manages its resources, monitors its status, handles interruptions, schedules its work in an efficient manner, and enables it to communicate with input/output devices. The operating system switches in and out peripheral devices, calls programs from storage, and links parts of programs together into larger programs. System software includes language translators, programs that sort and merge files, and programs that assist in program developing and debugging, to name just a few.

Operating systems, sometimes called **monitors** or **supervisor programs**, are provided by most manufacturers. Such software was not available on early computers. To appreciate its role, one need only look at how early machines were operated before its development. In the absence of an operating system, a user had to read a set of handwritten instructions from the programmer for each job, load in the appropriate language translator, and then load the job and the data set. The operator then had to stand by and keep a close eye on the machine while it ran the program. If the program contained an error and stopped executing part way through, or if a printer ran out of paper, or an input device jammed, the operator had to diagnose the cause of the failure and decide what to do. He or she had to log all jobs in and out so that accounting records could be kept on usage and had to schedule jobs according to priority. It became impossible for operators, even with help, to keep up with the hundreds of programs to be run through a computer in one day. It was obvious that the weak link in the chain was the human operator.

Computer engineers designed a master control program to replace these functions of the human operator. Operating systems have proven so successful that almost all modern computers have them. Some of the tasks they perform are:

Schedule input and output operations

Schedule jobs according to priority

Communicate with the human operator

Handle interruptions

Log jobs in and out

Monitor system status

Control system access and data security functions

Combine phases of a job into a complete run

Facilitate debugging and locating of errors

Handle multiprogramming so that several programs may be run concurrently

Coordinate multiprocessing, the activities of two or more computers

Load compilers or language translators

Maintain the computer system's library of programs

Facilitate generation of new systems

RESIDENT STORAGE DEVICES

A nucleus of operating system instructions is always stored in primary memory (Figure 9-2). However, the bulk of the instructions may occupy several hundred thousand bytes and so is too big to be kept in primary memory. It is therefore necessary to rely upon secondary storage, such as disk or tape, to hold the main part of the operating system. The nucleus in primary memory can call special routines in from secondary storage as needed. This means that the operating system can perform many complicated tasks without tying up primary memory with infrequently used instructions.

Operating systems are classified according to the nature of the

Figure 9-2 Resident Storage Device. The nucleus of the operating system resides in primary memory, while the balance is kept on a secondary storage device.

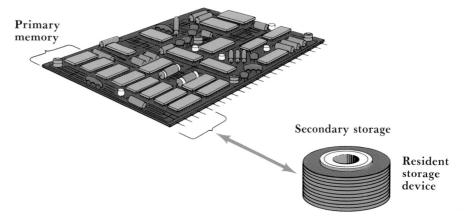

Primary memory

Secondary storage

Resident storage device

storage devices that hold the operating system. A **disk operating system (DOS)** stores the bulk of its commands on a magnetic disk. A **tape operating system (TOS)** stores the main part of the program on tape. When a microcomputer system is equipped with several floppy disk drives, one drive is usually reserved to hold the operating system disk.

STRUCTURE OF OPERATING SYSTEMS

At the center of the operating system is the **kernel** (Figure 9-3). The kernel contains the basic core of the operating system. All or part of the kernel resides in the CPU at all times and calls other routines in and out. These other routines are located in the **shell** surrounding the kernel. Programs in the shell are either **control programs** or **service programs**. They include compilers, interpreters, assemblers, editors, and program debuggers. **I/O driver routines** that program specific input/output devices are also located in the shell.

Surrounding both the kernel and the shell are the security and file protection programs. They prevent unauthorized users from accessing the shell or kernel programs. Data base management systems (DBMS), word processing, communications, graphics, and spread sheet analysis programs may be available at this level. These are described in more detail at the end of this chapter. These programs can

Figure 9-3 Operating System Structure. The kernel contains the nucleus of the operating system's instructions. It is surrounded by a shell of control and service programs that in turn is surrounded by an outer shell of user programs.

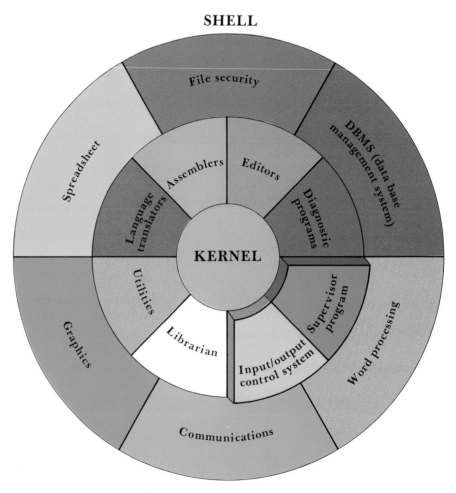

SHELL

be accessed by users directly without the need to learn a programming language.

TYPES OF SYSTEM PROGRAMS

CONTROL PROGRAMS

Control programs manage overall operations, schedule work, communicate with the operator, log jobs, and monitor system status. These tasks are done using the following modules.

SUPERVISOR PROGRAM   The **supervisor program** controls the overall scheduling of the computer's operations. It pulls required routines from the resident storage device (disk, tape, etc.) and loads them into primary memory. It also conveys messages to the computer operator, indicating error conditions, I/O devices that need attention, and so on. The programs are located in the shell.

Interruptions caused by errors or input/output problems are processed in an orderly way to reduce time loss. If an error is detected, the computer prints out a message and goes on to the next job without delay.

The supervisor program keeps a list of jobs run and clocks them in and out. It records and prints out the elapsed compilation and execution time.

INPUT/OUTPUT CONTROL SYSTEM (IOCS)   Careful and efficient scheduling and operation of input/output devices such as card readers, line printers, card punches, and tape units are essential, if the computer is to run at maximum processing speed and without interruption. In most computers the **input/output control system (IOCS)** performs these functions rapidly.

The IOCS continually monitors the I/O devices. If the line printer is out of paper, for example, the IOCS sends a message to the operator. If a device is not functioning or not available, it substitutes another device that is available so that processing will not be interrupted.

The IOCS prepares input and output devices for use. For example, it checks identification labels and indexes reels of tape to the required point. It opens the circuitry that permits data to flow between the I/O devices and the computer. It checks parity of data being transmitted in and out of the computer.

SERVICE PROGRAMS

Service programs are subprograms that perform frequently used routines and functions for the programmer. They save much programming time and effort by making a great variety of procedures available. The specific program needed is called out by the operating system as directed by the job control instructions.

The computer's ability to store and call out these service programs gives it much of its power and capability. Some common service programs are as follows.

LIBRARIAN PROGRAM The **librarian program** maintains the system library. It allocates a storage area in the computer system for any program or part of a program that a programmer wishes to save and keeps track of where that program has been stored for future use. A system library is usually kept on disk or tape.

The **system library** contains programs from many sources. Some are frequently accessed programs or modules cataloged by users; others are cataloged by the manufacturer. These programs have wide applications in the routine processing performed by many users.

UTILITY PROGRAM Much of data processing involves preparing and maintaining files that must be merged, updated, or sorted. Programs stored in the operating system that perform these common tasks are called **utility programs**. They are called out by job management commands. Sort and merge programs are usually general in nature and serve multiple functions. Other utility programs perform such tasks as transferring data from disk to disk or from tape to disk and reformatting data.

LANGUAGE TRANSLATOR Computers are able to execute instructions only if they are coded in machine language. Since most people write programs in a high-level language such as BASIC or COBOL a **language translator** is necessary (Figure 9-4). A translator converts statements into instructions the computer can execute. A **compiler** is a translator that converts an entire program into machine instructions before the computer begins executing, while an **interpreter** translates instructions into machine language line by line as the computer executes the program. In addition, an operating system may include an **assembly program** or **assembler** to convert programs written in assembler language into machine instructions.

Each translator can convert only one programming language into a form the machine understands, so a separate translator is needed for each language. Some operating systems include only one

Figure 9-4 Language Translator. The language translator converts high-level instructions into machine-executable language.

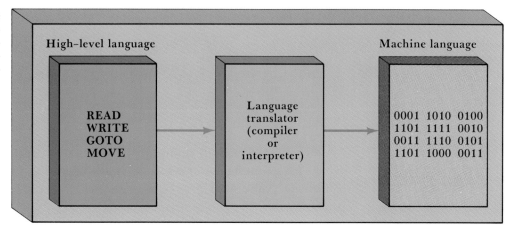

High-level language

READ
WRITE
GOTO
MOVE

Language translator (compiler or interpreter)

Machine language

0001 1010 0100
1101 1111 0010
0011 1110 0101
1101 1000 0011

or two language translators, such as BASIC or Pascal, while others are equipped with dozens of translators.

DIAGNOSTIC PROGRAMS   A **diagnostic program**, or debugger, facilitates locating errors or bugs in a program.

Some diagnostic programs check primary memory by writing information into memory, reading it out, and comparing it for accuracy. Others echo back characters from a keyboard or display them on a screen to verify that input/output devices are functioning properly.

TYPES OF OPERATING SYSTEMS

Many different types of operating systems have been developed for microcomputers. UNIX was developed by the Bell Telephone labs and has become widely available on 16-bit computers, such as Digital Equipment Corporation's PDP-11 family. One of the most common operating systems for the 8-bit microcomputers is the Control Program for Microcomputers (CP/M), developed by Digital Research Corporation. CP/M-86 is another important operating system developed by Digital Research. Microsoft Corporation's MS-DOS is widely used

Figure 9-5 Batch Operating System. In a batch system, jobs are processed in sequence without regard to priority.

JOB QUEUE

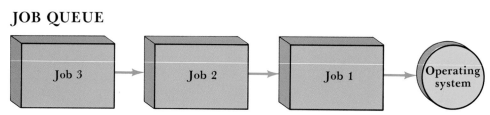

on the IBM Personal Computer and other 16- and 32-bit systems.

Operating systems can be characterized as being batch, multi-user, or real time.

BATCH OPERATING SYSTEMS

As the name indicates, **batch operating systems** are designed to control batch processing. They accept and process jobs in sequence, without regard to priority (Figure 9-5). While they can process several jobs concurrently, they do not allow computer terminals to share the computer's resources at the same time.

Batch operating systems are directed by control statements submitted at the beginning of each job in the form of one or more punched cards or program instructions. The statements give the computer the necessary instructions regarding data sets, output devices, and so on.

Batch operating systems are often found on small computers for which only a few input devices are used and no time sharing is involved. Examples of batch processing are the preparation of payrolls and student grade reports.

MULTIUSER OPERATING SYSTEMS

Multiuser operating systems are designed to run several programs at one time. The process is called **multiprogramming**. The operating system partitions its memory and shares it among several jobs (Figure 9-6). Once jobs are assigned priority, the computer allocates memory and I/O devices accordingly. Jobs are broken down into tasks and segments of the program are written into memory. By sharing memory and I/O devices, the computer can run several applications programs concurrently.

Figure 9-6 Multiprogramming. A multiuser operating system breaks memory into sections, divides jobs into tasks, and allocates I/O devices among jobs, so that several programs can be run at once.

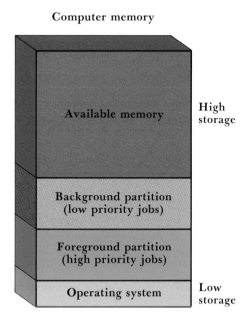

Computer memory

Available memory — High storage

Background partition (low priority jobs)

Foreground partition (high priority jobs)

Operating system — Low storage

REAL TIME OPERATING SYSTEMS

The **real time operating system (RTOS)** is designed to respond to requests from many users as they occur and usually to execute several batch or interactive programs concurrently from online devices. For example, a real time operating system is required when remote terminals are connected online to the computer. The system must be able to respond promptly to the requests of each terminal user.

This type of system processes jobs in a hierarchical order rather than in sequence, that is, jobs with higher priorities are executed before jobs with lower priorities. An RTOS is capable of beginning execution on one job, suspending operations on that job to execute a job with a higher priority, then resuming execution of the suspended job where it left off (Figure 9-7). An RTOS can also schedule jobs at a preset time. For example, it can schedule the preparation of an inventory report at the end of each working day.

Some operating systems are designed to handle batch and real time tasks at the same time. The computer can process a stream of batch programs fed into a local card reader or terminal and at the same time respond to real time terminals, such as a remote automatic teller machine (ATM).

Figure 9-7 Real Time Operating System. This type of operating system supports remote terminals and processes jobs according to priority. The system's ability to satisfy multiuser requirements depends on the speed at which the system components operate, both hardware and software.

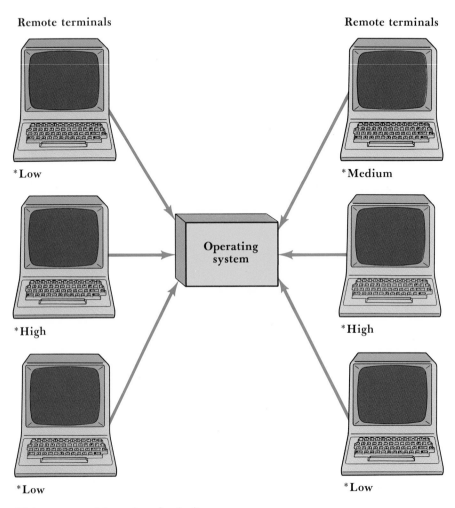

Remote terminals

*Low

*High

*Low

Remote terminals

*Medium

*High

*Low

Operating system

*Jobs processed in order of priority

APPLICATIONS SOFTWARE

A great deal of time and money has gone into developing applications software packages for microcomputers. The applications packages described below usually contain one or more floppy disks and an instruction manual. This software runs under the control of an operating system such as CP/M or MS-DOS. The programs can pro-

Figure 9-8 Spread Sheet Display. Spread sheets are electronic ledger sheets. Data are manipulated and updated from the keyboard.

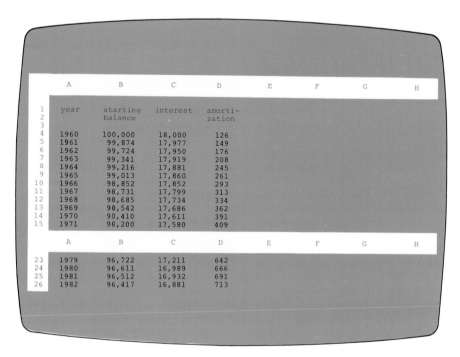

	A	B	C	D	E	F	G	H
1	year	starting	interest	amorti-				
2		balance		zation				
3								
4	1960	100,000	18,000	126				
5	1961	99,874	17,977	149				
6	1962	99,724	17,950	176				
7	1963	99,341	17,919	208				
8	1964	99,216	17,881	245				
9	1965	99,013	17,860	261				
10	1966	98,852	17,852	293				
11	1967	98,731	17,799	313				
12	1968	98,685	17,734	334				
13	1969	98,542	17,686	362				
14	1970	98,410	17,611	391				
15	1971	98,200	17,580	409				

	A	B	C	D	E	F	G	H
23	1979	96,722	17,211	642				
24	1980	96,611	16,989	666				
25	1981	96,512	16,932	691				
26	1982	96,417	16,881	713				

duce color graphic images, print out reports, letters, and memos, make economic projections, and perform many other tasks. Let's review some of the most widely used applications packages.

SPREAD SHEET PROGRAMS

Spread sheet packages are computer software specially designed to display information graphically and allow files and data to be manipulated easily. Spread sheet packages are essentially electronic versions of a pencil, paper, and calculator.

A spread sheet is an electronic ledger sheet on which data are entered (Figure 9-8). The information can be changed, revised, or updated by keyboarding in new data.

Spread sheet packages allow the user to scan any section on the electronic page quickly and conveniently. The page can be **scrolled** up or down, the display area can be positioned horizontally or vertically, or on some packages the screen can be split. With the

Figure 9-9 Spread Sheet Grid. Information on a spread sheet is arranged in rows and columns. Intersecting points make up a cell which in turn holds data.

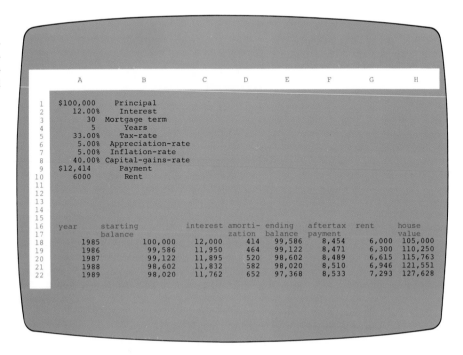

	A	B	C	D	E	F	G	H
1	$100,000	Principal						
2	12.00%	Interest						
3	30	Mortgage term						
4	5	Years						
5	33.00%	Tax-rate						
6	5.00%	Appreciation-rate						
7	5.00%	Inflation-rate						
8	40.00%	Capital-gains-rate						
9	$12,414	Payment						
10	6000	Rent						
11								
12								
13								
14								
15								
16	year	starting	interest	amorti-	ending	aftertax	rent	house
17		balance		zation	balance	payment		value
18	1985	100,000	12,000	414	99,586	8,454	6,000	105,000
19	1986	99,586	11,950	464	99,122	8,471	6,300	110,250
20	1987	99,122	11,895	520	98,602	8,489	6,615	115,763
21	1988	98,602	11,832	582	98,020	8,510	6,946	121,551
22	1989	98,020	11,762	652	97,368	8,533	7,293	127,628

split screen, up to four separate sections can be displayed simultaneously.

The information displayed on the page is arranged in rows and columns (Figure 9-9). A **row** is a horizontal division on the worksheet, usually identified by a number. A **column** is a vertical division on the worksheet, usually identified by a letter. The rows and columns together make up a **matrix**. The entire matrix is called a **grid sheet** or simply a **grid**. Each intersecting point or coordinate is called a **cell** or **entry position**. A cell can contain data in any position on the grid. The actual information located in a cell is called an **entry**. A **cursor**, or flashing pointer, can be moved about to identify a particular entry position that the user wishes to change or modify.

The **window** is the area displayed on the screen. Figure 9-10 illustrates a split screen display using six sections. Several different types of displays are shown. The user can change the contents of the screen.

Perhaps the most important feature of spread sheet packages is the computer's ability to remember calculations and formulas. A

Figure 9-10 Split Screen Display. Split screens display several different types of information at one time.

change in one cell will automatically cause the computer to search its memory and revise all related information. Spread sheet packages also allow users to replicate formulas easily. Once a formula has been entered in one position, it can be picked up and moved to another or duplicated in several places.

Sometimes information stored in a given cell must be protected from change. Provision is made in the software for **cell protection**. This allows information to be locked in so that it cannot be changed.

Spread sheet software is marketed by Hewlett-Packard, VisiCorp, Microsoft, Context, Lotus, and other companies. Some popular spread sheet packages are VisiCalc, SuperCalc, and Multiplan. These easy-to-use packages allow business and personal computer users to manipulate complex data bases and to prepare reports with visual or tabular material quickly and easily. Spread sheet packages are especially useful in preparing business forecasts, budgets, and projections.

WORD PROCESSING PROGRAMS
Word processing software allows the user to manipulate words rather than just numbers. This software is sometimes referred to as a

Figure 9-11 Marked-Up Draft of Stored Text. Changes marked by hand on a checking copy of a preliminary draft can be quickly and easily made on a word processor, resulting in a final, error-free document without extensive retyping.

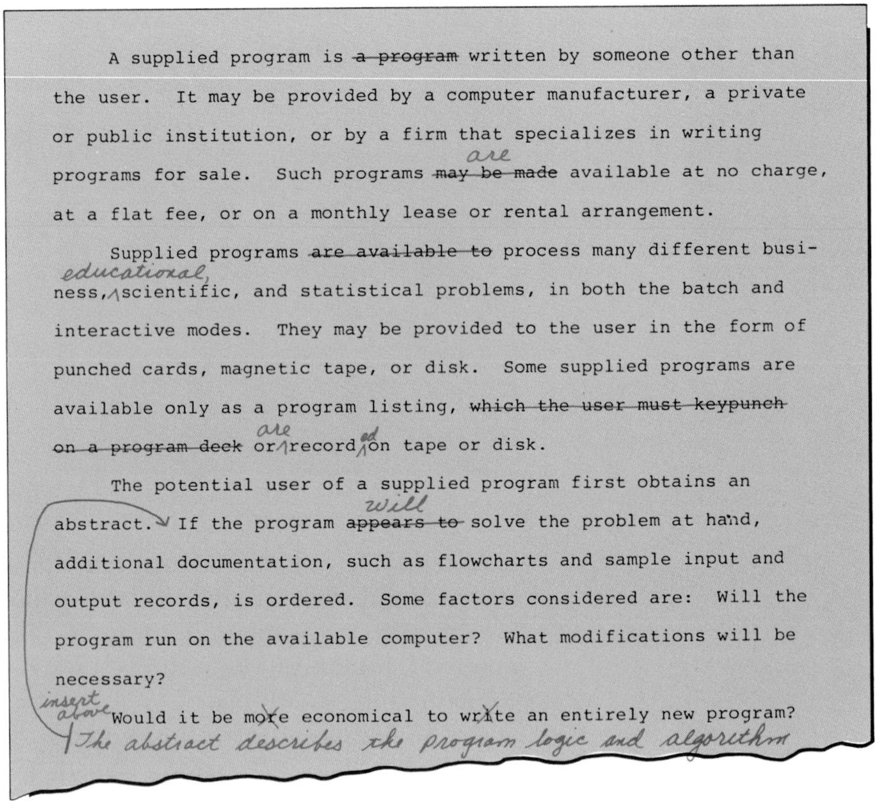

```
A supplied program is a program written by someone other than

the user.  It may be provided by a computer manufacturer, a private

or public institution, or by a firm that specializes in writing
                                                        are
programs for sale.  Such programs may be made available at no charge,

at a flat fee, or on a monthly lease or rental arrangement.

     Supplied programs are available to process many different busi-
        educational,
ness, scientific, and statistical problems, in both the batch and

interactive modes.  They may be provided to the user in the form of

punched cards, magnetic tape, or disk.  Some supplied programs are

available only as a program listing, which the user must keypunch
                      are             ed
on a program deck or record on tape or disk.

     The potential user of a supplied program first obtains an
                              will
abstract.  If the program appears to solve the problem at hand,

additional documentation, such as flowcharts and sample input and

output records, is ordered.  Some factors considered are:  Will the

program run on the available computer?  What modifications will be

necessary?
insert
  above  Would it be more economical to write an entirely new program?
         The abstract describes the program logic and algorithm
```

text editor. It can be purchased and loaded into a computer. The program enables the user to prepare reports, bulletins, letters, or other written documents easily. Word processors are particularly valuable when extensive editing or revisions are needed.

Some word processing programs make document preparation easier by checking spelling against a dictionary stored in the machine. Others maintain address files and prepare labels or shipping tags. Still other programs are designed for text editing. Text editors eliminate most or all of the retyping usually needed in revising.

Some examples of word processing software on the market are WordStar, SpellGuard, VisiWord Plus, EasyWriter, Mail Merge, and DataStar.

Data to be processed by the text editor are typed in without

Figure 9-12 Final Draft Printed Out. This final draft includes all of the changes and revisions that were marked on the checking copy.

A supplied program is written by someone other than the user. It may be provided by a computer manufacturer, a private or public institution, or by a firm that specializes in writing programs for sale. Such programs are available at no charge, at a flat fee, or on a monthly lease or rental arrangement.

Supplied programs process many different business, educational, scientific, and statistical problems, in both the batch and interactive modes. They may be provided to the user in the form of punched cards, magnetic tape, or disk. Some supplied programs are available only as a program listing, or are recorded on tape or disk.

The potential user of a supplied program first obtains an abstract. The abstract describes the program logic and algorithm. If the program will solve the problem at hand, additional documentation, such as flowcharts and sample input and output records, is ordered. Some factors considered are: Will the program run on the available computer? What modifications will be necessary?

regard to line width or spacing. Errors are corrected by backspacing and retyping. The text as typed and corrected is stored in the computer's memory. After all the text is entered, a draft may either be displayed on a screen or printed out. At this stage words, phrases, or sentences can be replaced, rearranged, or deleted by the operator. The computer inserts the revisions into the stored text. At the press of a key the machine prints out an updated draft. The operator can tell the computer to print out drafts with different formats, line width, or page depth. Text editor programs can automatically center lines, provide page numbers, or insert heads or footnotes.

After text editing is completed and the format decided upon, the operator instructs the computer to print out a finished draft. This version contains headings, page numbers, and so forth, is evenly spaced, and neatly typed. Figure 9-11 shows a piece of copy that has been keyboarded, stored in memory, printed out, and then marked with corrections to be made in the final draft. Figure 9-12 shows the reformatted printout as it appears with all changes and alterations made.

Figure 9-13 Graphics Output. Graphic software extends the range and forms in which information can be displayed. Using simple commands the user with little or no artistic ability can easily create charts or graphs of presentation quality.

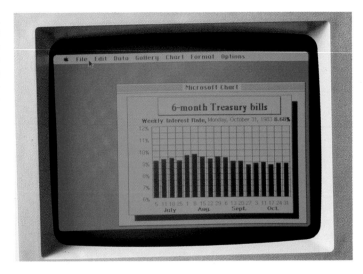

DATA BASE MANAGEMENT SYSTEM (DBMS) PROGRAMS

A large portion of the work performed on microcomputers involves the updating, querying, or retrieval of information from a data base. You will recall that a data base is an organization's total collection of records, files, and libraries of useful information. Special programs, called **data base management systems (DBMS)**, facilitate the processing and manipulation of a data base. (These programs are discussed more fully in Chapter 11.) Among the more popular microcomputer data base management packages are dBase II, DataFax, and VisiFile.

A data base management system manages large files and permits users to locate records, search for data, and display information quickly and easily. An electronic DBMS replaces filing card systems or other manual methods and allows thousands of records to be searched in a second or two.

GRAPHICS PROGRAMS

Graphics software is designed to prepare various types of graphic display such as bar charts, graphs, line charts, scattergrams, pie charts, and plots (Figure 9-13). Some popular graphics packages are Graphwriter, VisiTrend/Plot, and SuperChartman II.

Figure 9-14 Computer Graphics Design. Three-dimensional objects can be displayed, rotated, and viewed from different perspectives using computer graphic output.

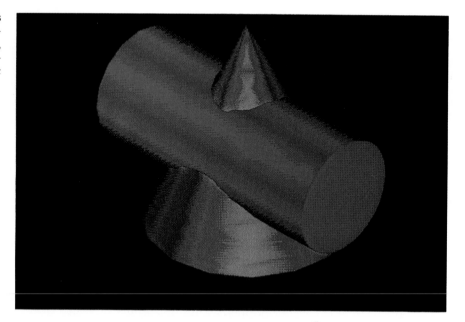

Graphics software allows the user to generate charts and graphs in eight or more different colors (Figure 9-14). The charts may also include elements of different textures, as well as labels and headings. Some packages prepare three-dimensional displays. The quality of the display depends upon the capability of the specific output unit used as well as on the program. Once the display has been generated, it can be edited. Finished art can be displayed in different sizes, widths, or colors.

Graphics packages, together with spread sheet software and word processing software, makes it possible for the microcomputer user to create a wide variety of pictures, text, and tables quickly and easily.

COMMUNICATIONS PROGRAMS

Today many microcomputers are connected to other computers located hundreds or even thousands of miles away. They are linked by telephone lines, satellite relay stations, or microwave circuits. More

Figure 9-15 Integrated Software. A single software package such as Lotus 1-2-3 integrates spread sheet, graphics, and data base management capabilities. For example, data entered in spread sheet form may be used to create charts and graphs.

than elaborate hardware is needed to allow communication between two machines; the appropriate software is also necessary. (We will talk about data communications in more detail in Chapter 10.) Some popular communications software packages for microcomputers are Mail-Com, Smarterm, and SNA Protocol.

Communications software allows computers to originate transmissions and answer messages. It establishes the switching routine needed to establish contact between distant computers and assures that data will be sent in the proper format and at the proper speed.

It detects transmission speeds and codes and routes information to appropriate hardware. This is usually done through a **front end communications computer** and **front end software**. Communications software also checks for errors in transmission and handles interruptions or transmission priorities.

Communications software is essential if the computer is operated as part of a network. The computer manages the flow of data throughout the network, balances system loads, and performs file security and access protection.

COMBINATION PACKAGES

Some software publishers are integrating several of these programs into a single package. Lotus Development Corporation's Lotus 1-2-3 (Figure 9-15), Lotus's Symphony, and Context Management System's

The MBA are integrated software. These pieces of software generate spread sheets with from two to four windows and allow the user to edit material while it is on the screen. They include data base management functions. They prepare bar, line, pie, and other graphs. They have text editing capability.

Integrated packages perform more functions than any one individual software package, but as yet none provides the full range of capabilities provided by separate, individual pieces of software.

In a sense a microcomputer is like a stereo system. The more records and tapes you own, the greater enjoyment and use you will get from your system. Microcomputers equipped with word processing, graphics, communications, and data base management system software serve a broad range of uses and make the computer a more valuable tool.

SUMMARY AND KEY TERMS

- **Applications programs** are written to solve a specific user problem. They are written by the user or sold as packages containing a disk and **documentation**. **System programs** manage the resources of the computer, automate its operations, and facilitate programming, testing, and debugging.

- Among the tasks handled by operating systems are scheduling I/O operations, communicating with operators, handling interruptions, logging jobs, monitoring status, combining phases, handling multiprogramming, loading compilers and interpreters, maintaining the program library, and coordinating the activities of two or more computers.

- The **nucleus** of the operating system is stored in primary memory and the balance on the **resident storage device**.

- Operating systems include two types of programs. **Control programs** manage the operation of the system, and **service programs** perform frequently used routines.

- A **language translator** converts program statements into commands the computer can execute. A **compiler** converts an entire program into machine instructions before the computer begins executing, while an **interpreter** translates each line of code as it is executed. An **assembler** converts assembly language into machine language.

• **Diagnostic programs** facilitate locating errors in a program.

• **CP/M** is a common 8-bit microcomputer **operating system, CP/M-86, UNIX,** and **MS-DOS** are 16- and 32-bit computer operating systems.

• The three common types of operating systems are **batch, multiuser,** and **real time**.

• **Spread sheet packages** enter information for manipulation and display on an electronic ledger sheet.

• **Word processing packages** are used to write, revise, and arrange textual matter such as correspondence and reports.

• **Data base management system (DBMS) software** is used to manage large files of records and data.

• **Graphics packages** are used to prepare bar charts, graphs, line charts, pie charts, and other visual displays.

• **Communications software** handles communication between computers, detects transmission errors, and routes signals through a network.

EXERCISES

1. Define operating system.

2. Summarize the functions of an operating system.

3. Compare the major types of operating systems.

4. How do control programs and service programs differ?

5. What are the functions of service programs? How do they save time and programming effort?

6. What language translators are available on the microcomputer available to you?

7. What service and utility programs are available on your system?

8. Describe the function of spread sheet software.

9. Describe the function of word processing software.

10. Describe the function of communications software.

Part 4   Communications and Information Systems

10

Learning Objectives

After studying this chapter, you should be able to
1. Explain what the three telecommunications domains are
2. Define key terms related to networks and data communications
3. Summarize the history of data communications
4. List the advantages and limitations of data communications
5. Contrast types of data transmission circuits
6. Describe local area networks (LANs)

Chapter Outline

What is Telecommunications?
Evolution of Telecommunications
Distributed Data Processing
   Advantages and Limitations
Data Communications Applications
   Electronic Banking
   Information Retrieval Systems
   Electronic Word Processing
   Electronic Mail
   Electronic Shopping
   Teleconferences
   Monitoring and Metering
Data Transmission Principles
   Data Transmission Circuits
   Channels
   Communications Media
   Transmission Modes
   Couplers
Types of Data Communications
   Multiprocessing
   Remote Job Entry
   Data Inquiry
Networks
   Network Architecture
   Factors in Network Design
Examples of Teleprocessing Networks
   Local Area Networks
   Common Carriers

Networks and
Data Communications

W hen Alexander Graham Bell cried out over a twisted cable to his associate in the next room, "Watson, come here! I want you!" he almost certainly did not foresee that his invention would one day be part of a worldwide communications system. He could not have imagined today's communications network that links hundreds of millions of telephones, business and home computers, and television sets.

In this chapter we will look at the field of telecommunications. We will see how satellites, microwave electronics, fiberoptics, and telephone networks are being integrated into a vast system that moves data and information, human voices, and television pictures.

Telecommunications is the process of moving data, audio information (sound), and video information (pictures) over long distances by means of transmission lines such as telephone cables, microwave channels, and fiberoptic circuits.

Telecommunications has three major domains (Figure 10-1). One domain is audio transmission, that is, the transmission of sounds, including the human voice, by telephone through long distance lines, local circuits, or private board exchanges (PBX). A second domain is video transmission, or the moving of pictures, using airwaves or cable access television (CATV). The third domain is **data communications**, or the transmission of information in digital form, through a network of computers, terminals, and transmission lines.

The first efforts at telecommunications involved transmitting sound; then video and data transmission came on the scene. Today, the three domains are merging into a single technology, with pictures, voice, and data transmitted interchangeably.

Business data processing is primarily concerned with data communications. Data communications systems process data remotely and may involve computers, terminals, transmission lines,

Figure 10-1 Domains of Telecommunications. Voice, data, and video comprise the three major types of information handled by telecommunications systems.

Voice

Data

Telecommunications network

Video

telephone or telegraph lines, or microwave circuits to transmit digital information. Data communications is sometimes known as **teleprocessing**.

An integral part of the data communications system is the **communications link**, the physical means of connecting elements of the system in order to transmit and receive information. The communications link consists of the hardware and circuitry that integrates one or more computers and one or more terminals and permits the flow of data between them.

EVOLUTION OF TELECOMMUNICATIONS

Before the age of modern data communications, how was information moved from one place to another? It was usually physically carried; papers, cards, record books, or tapes were moved from point to point to be processed. The invention of the telegraph and the telephone made the movement of data easier. Information could be converted into electronic signals and sent over wires. During the past hundred years, homes and offices across the United States and throughout the world have become linked through the development of a vast network of telephone lines.

Data communications took a step forward after World War II with the military's development of Semi-Automatic Ground Environment (SAGE) in which telephone lines and later radio circuits were used to send information from remote terminals to a computer. This availability of real time data processing increased the military's ability to make rapid, accurate air defense judgments.

Seeing the success of military data communications, business firms began to use data communications as a tool for solving business data processing problems. One early system was Semi-Automatic Business Research Environment (SABRE), which processed airline reservations. A listing of available seats was stored in a central computer. Terminals were placed in airline ticket offices. Ticket agents could query the system to learn the number of unsold seats on any given flight. This reliable and highly successful method of handling seat reservations pointed the way toward other data communications applications.

During the 1960s the Advanced Research Projects Agency of the U.S. Department of Defense established the **ARPA network**. This network tied together the computers of several dozen university and research institutions in the United States and Europe. UCLA, Stanford, MIT, and other schools were able to transmit data through the ARPA network.

At the same time a video network began to emerge. **Cable ac-**

Figure 10-2 Point-of-Sale Terminal. Point-of sale terminals collect data at a remote point, and transmit them to other locations where they are processed.

cess television (CATV) became a major force in bringing television to millions of homes throughout the country. These television cables originally served areas that could not be reached by ordinary television signals. Soon cable networks expanded to other areas. They continue to grow and now offer such diverse services as electronic newspapers, teletext, home security monitoring, and shop-at-home ordering.

During the 1970s several government and private communication satellites were put into orbit, allowing radio, television, voice, and data to be transmitted around the world. Such firms as Satellite Business Systems, RCA, Southern Pacific Communications, and AT&T now offer services via satellite.

Today, data communications is invaluable to businesses with big inventories or a large flow of data from remote points and makes possible new processes such as electronic metering, monitoring, and mail. Much of the recent growth in data communications has been in point-of-sale (POS) terminals (Figure 10-2). These terminals are connected to a central computer via a communications link. As we have seen, POS terminals are already widely used in retail establishments. Their applications will continue to increase as more retail establishments install them.

In the 1980s hundreds of thousands of microcomputers were installed in homes, schools, and offices across the country. At first they were confined to local processing, but then users began requesting access to large data banks such as those offered by Dow Jones, CompuServe, and others. Access to these data banks became available through ordinary telephone lines.

The next step in the evolution of telecommunications seems to be the integration of video, voice, and data transmission. It is likely that the computer, telephone, and cable television will eventually be merged into a single system, tying together almost every home and office in this country as well as many nations around the world.

DISTRIBUTED DATA PROCESSING

The availability of the low-cost microcomputer changed the direction of data processing markedly. The installation of low-cost computers in businesses across the country reduced the need for large central computer installations. Businesses moved toward a new concept called **distributed data processing (DDP)**. In distributed data processing, large central computers are replaced by a network of small, stand-alone processors (Figures 10-3 and 10-4). The smaller computers can communicate with each other through data communications circuits.

ADVANTAGES AND LIMITATIONS

Networks of computers that distribute data processing resources over a large geographic area have both advantages and limitations.

Data communications makes real time processing applications available to almost any business. It does away with the need for physically carrying records or data to a computer center. Many users can share the same system or the same data base, thereby reducing costs. Since several CPUs can be integrated into one system, each user has

Figure 10-3 Centralized Data Processing. In a centralized system, information from many branch terminals is sent to a single central computer for processing.

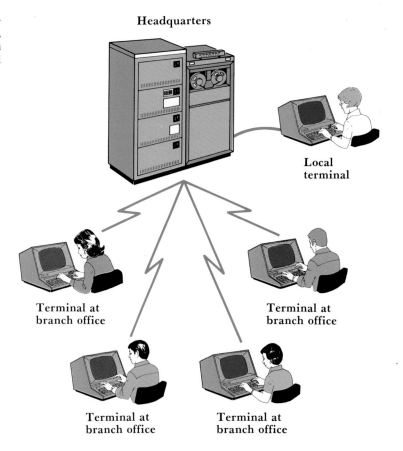

Headquarters

Local terminal

Terminal at branch office

Terminal at branch office

Terminal at branch office

Terminal at branch office

access to greater available resources. System loading can be controlled and balanced to get the most out of all computers in the network.

Distributed data processing systems cost less to operate than central systems. There is no need to install large computers with extensive secondary storage systems. There is less likelihood of a total network breakdown or failure, since processing is spread among many small computers. Response time is reduced, with users accessing local information rather than large central computers located some distance away.

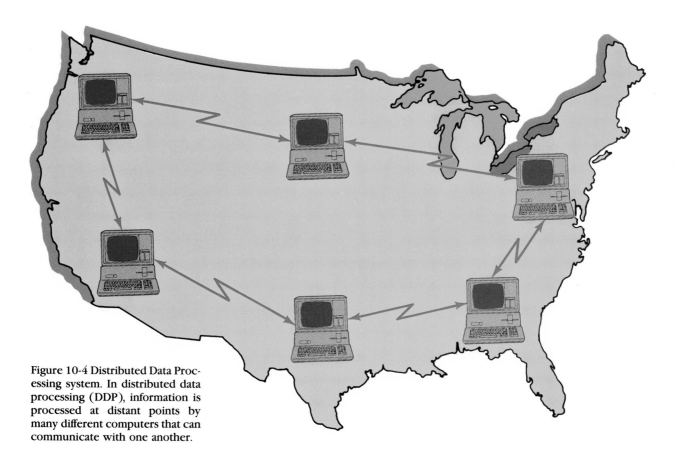

Figure 10-4 Distributed Data Processing system. In distributed data processing (DDP), information is processed at distant points by many different computers that can communicate with one another.

But distributed systems are not without their problems. Although there is less likelihood of a total system failure, the use of many communication links increases the chances of subsystem failures. Telephone lines, microwave links, and relay satellites do break down.

When data are stored and processed at many points, it is more difficult to maintain security and protect the integrity of the system. Measures must be taken to keep unauthorized users from querying the system or accessing files.

Cost accounting procedures must be designed to handle and control usage on the system. Data processing costs can rise substantially if not controlled, because of the many users who have access to the system.

DATA COMMUNICATIONS APPLICATIONS

Before discussing how data are transmitted through a network, let us look at some of the more common applications for which data communications is used. Data communications is a vital and rapidly changing technology and new applications are being discovered almost daily. Here are some major applications of data communications systems.

ELECTRONIC BANKING

The entire banking industry has benefitted from data communications. **Electronic funds transfer (EFT)** systems are becoming widely used, with funds, debits and credits, and charges and payments electronically routed between banks and their customers. EFT is fast. It eliminates delays associated with sending hard copy documents. It can handle the large volume of transactions generated by the banking industry. Data communications adds flexibility to banking. Using home terminals, customers will soon be able to transfer funds, pay bills, or ask about the status of their accounts. **Automated teller machines (ATM)**, using communications links, are being installed in shopping centers and storefronts, allowing individuals to make deposits or withdrawals from their accounts 24 hours a day.

INFORMATION RETRIEVAL SYSTEMS

Data communications networks make large data bases of information available to users all over the country. Stock market information, news wire service reports, or comprehensive banks of statistical data can be accessed from remote terminals. For example, Susan Smith can use her microcomputer and telephone to access the Dow Jones data base for information she needs on the history and earnings of a given stock in order to make an informed purchasing decision.

ELECTRONIC WORD PROCESSING

Electronic word processing has come into its own as a result of modern data communications. Business people can write letters, memos, and reports through remote processing. Using terminals located in homes, offices, or automobiles, they can send messages to word processing centers that result in the generation of finished letters or reports. For example, a sales representative can compose a letter on a remote terminal connected to a data communications network. A supervisor can access the draft, make changes, and then electronically forward it to a division manager for checking. After other interested people have reviewed and revised the letter, a finished hard copy, incorporating all the changes and revisions, can be printed out.

ELECTRONIC MAIL

By the use of data communications, letters are sent electronically rather than through the mails. The sender sits at an electronic terminal and keyboards the date, time, and person to whom a message is directed and the message itself. The system automatically routes the message to the recipient. At the receiving end a hard copy may be printed out or a signal may flash indicating that a message is waiting for the recipient.

Electronic mail can be sent simultaneously to many people. Data can be received at one point, revised or updated, and sent on to other points. Electronic mail eliminates time delays and other problems associated with physically delivered mail.

ELECTRONIC SHOPPING

Computer terminals located in homes or offices can be tied to closed circuit cable systems through which customers can see and order goods. Shopping from home is being test marketed now. Such a system would be of great use for shut-ins and invalids.

TELECONFERENCES

A **teleconferencing network** using hard copy printers, video terminals, or picture phones allows participants at different locations to have access to the same information, to make individual contributions to the meeting, and to interact. Such conferences are easier to arrange and much less expensive than flying individuals around the country.

Teleconferencing may take several forms. In a voice-only conference, information is exchanged through a conference telephone call. In a data communications conference, participants interact through a network of terminals. Video techniques may involve the transmission of still pictures or graphics to each member of the conference or full motion video. In the most elaborate system all the participants are linked together through real time circuits enabling the exchange of voices, illustrations, full-motion pictures, and data.

MONITORING AND METERING
Many homes, businesses, and factories are equipped with digital communications monitoring equipment that reports fire, break-ins, flood, or other emergency conditions to a central agency or police department. Other equipment measures use of utilities. Consumption of gas, water, or electricity is metered and reported to a central billing computer through closed circuit cable.

DATA TRANSMISSION PRINCIPLES

In a data communications system data are transmitted between terminals and computers or between several computers over telephone or telegraph lines or through fiberoptic, microwave or radio wave circuits. The transmission mode selected for a teleprocessing system depends upon what the user needs.

DATA TRANSMISSION CIRCUITS
Communication lines or circuits for teleprocessing systems are categorized according to the direction of data flow and volume of transmission.

DIRECTION OF DATA FLOW Circuits can be categorized according to the direction in which data can flow through them. Three types of circuits are in common use. They are (1) simplex circuits, (2) half-duplex circuits, and (3) full-duplex circuits.

In the **simplex circuit**, data can flow in only one direction. A

COURTING BY COMPUTER

Source: Los Angeles Times, February 4, 1983.

"Before I met Chris, I was fonder of Sinbad (a 500-pound gorilla) than most people I knew," said Zebra 3, the code name for Pam Jensen, a shy primate keeper at Chicago's Lincoln Park Zoo. Chrisdos (Chris Dunn), was a computer technician in New York. They courted via a linkup that connects computer terminal users the way CB radio links truck drivers. Dunn could type a message at his terminal and all who were connected to the CB simulator program would receive the message on their screens, signing them with the "handle" of their choice. "With CB (the program) you can reveal whatever you want about yourself, no voice problems," said Dunn, 26. "I could give as much of myself as I wanted, or nothing. Every woman is a 10, every man is a 10," said Jensen, 30. Dunn later moved to Chicago and now is helping out around the zoo. April 23—a year after they first met—is the tentative wedding date. They aren't planning a family just yet. "I'm very interested in my career," Zebra 3 said, and they still have their computers. "Instead of children," she said, "I'll settle for a couple of primates."

Simplex

One way only

Half duplex

Send or receive alternately

Full duplex

Send and receive simultaneously

line either receives or transmits data; it cannot do both. The simplex circuit is therefore a limited means of data transmission. A terminal coupled to a simplex circuit that only transmits data is called a **send-only terminal**. A terminal coupled to a simplex circuit that only receives data is called a **receive-only terminal**.

A **half-duplex** circuit can receive and transmit data, but can do only one thing at a time. The half-duplex line can be shifted from one direction of data flow to the other, but its utility is still limited. If a terminal is transmitting data over a half-duplex circuit, the computer cannot interrupt the input flow to send back an important message. It must wait until the terminal shifts the circuit to the receive mode before delivering the information.

A **full-duplex circuit** is obviously the most efficient, because it allows a concurrent two-way transmission of data. Suppose an operator is entering data through a terminal to the computer and is unaware that the system's storage capacity has reached its limit. With a full-duplex circuit, the computer can signal the terminal to stop inputting data before the system becomes overloaded.

VOLUME OF DATA TRANSMITTED   Communication lines are also classified by the volume of data they can transmit. Volume is, of course, the number of characters transmitted, so it can be measured by the speed of transmission, or the number of characters transmitted per second. The grade of a line refers to its capacity for volume; the higher the volume, the higher the grade of the line.

The standard measure of line capacity or data transmission speed is **bits per second (bps)**. (The term *baud* is sometimes inaccurately applied here. Baud refers to a measure in the teletypewriter industry.) The higher the bps, the more data the line can move per given interval of time.

Three grades of lines used for data transmission are
(1) narrow-band line, (2) voice-grade line, and (3) wide-band line.

Narrow-band lines have a maximum transmission speed of about 300 bps. These lines are not widely used. They are, however, more economical to lease than other grades.

Voice-grade, or **voice-band**, **lines** can transmit more than 300 bps. They are called voice grade because they are commonly used for ordinary telephone conversations.

Wide-band lines are capable of transmitting data at 18,000 bps or higher. Of the three grades of lines, wide-band lines have the greatest capacity for moving data and are the most expensive to lease.

Thus, we see that the most versatile and expensive circuit would be a full-duplex, wide-band line. A simplex, narrow-band line would be less expensive, but more limited in capacity.

CHANNELS

Channels are the paths between terminals and computers or between computers. A computer that services 10 terminals concurrently would require 10 channels. (Figure 10-5). In theory each channel would require a separate line, a considerable expense in setting up the system. Further complicating the problem are the differing speeds at which data are transmitted. It is inefficient and expensive to connect several slow-speed terminals to a distant computer on one line. They would not use the full capacity of the line or the computer. Obviously, methods must be found to allow many channels on one line and to accommodate differing circuit speeds. Two devices that help solve these problems are data concentrators and multiplexers.

Figure 10-5 Channels. In this system, ten individual channels or paths are provided so that the computer can serve the ten remote terminals.

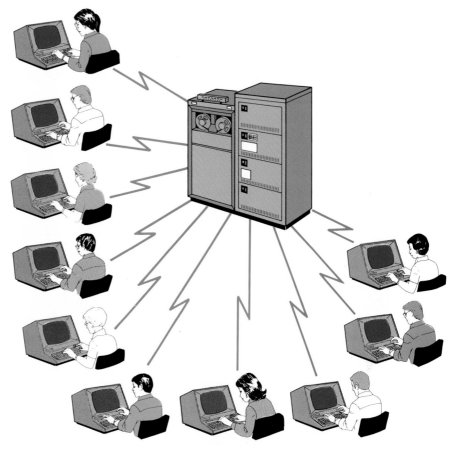

Ten channels

CONCENTRATORS   A device that makes it efficient for a slow-speed terminal to operate on a high-volume transmission line is a **data concentrator**. A data concentrator stores characters and then transmits them all at once over a line in a high-speed burst. High-volume transmission lines cost more money to operate and lease than lower bps lines. It is therefore most economical to send the maximum amount of information possible over the line to take advantage of the line's capacity.

Data concentrators increase transmission efficiency through

Figure 10-6 Data Concentrator Transmission. A data concentrator receives electronic pulses representing characters from several devices and stores them in a buffer located within the concentrator. At timed intervals the data concentrator emits a pulse train that contains blocks of information from each of the devices connected to the concentrator.

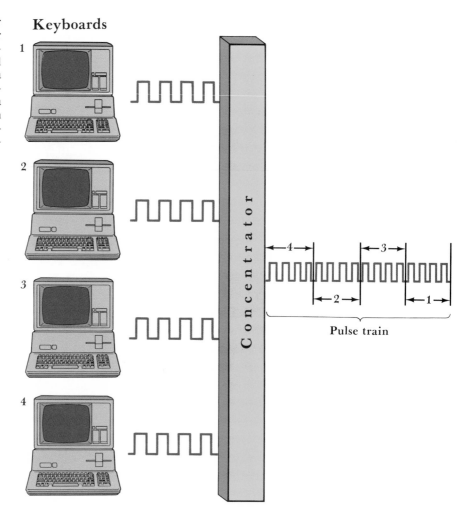

Keyboards

buffering. Built-in buffering circuits store up characters from a slow-speed device. When sufficient data are accumulated, they are sent over the line at once. Suppose four operators working at ordinary typing speed feed data to a computer over one channel (Figure 10-6). Each of the four keyboards is connected to one concentrator. The concentrator stores up the characters in a buffer and then transmits them in a burst. This makes the best use of the facilities.

Figure 10-7 Multiplexers. In this system, a multiplexer is connected to each end of a transmission line. The multiplexer at the terminal end of the line interleaves pulses from the terminals and sends them over the line. At the other end of the line the pulses are separated by another multiplexer and processed by the computer.

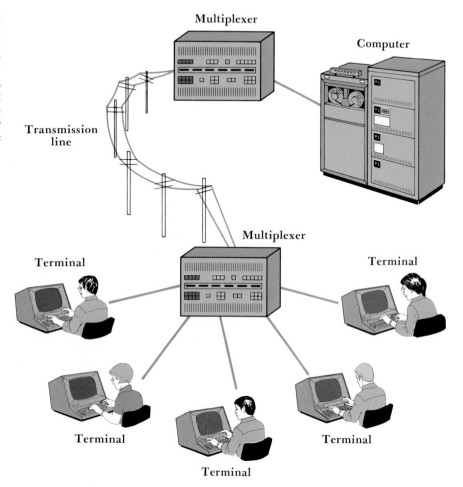

MULTIPLEXERS   Another means of sending data from several sources over one line is a **multiplexer**. A multiplexer interleaves data from several devices and sends them over a single transmission line. Figure 10-7 illustrates a system with a multiplexer at each end of a transmission line. The multiplexer on one end sets up channels over which to transmit the data coming in from the terminals. The multiplexer at the other end of the line separates the data and sends them to the computer. This arrangement provides a low-cost means of coupling

Figure 10-8 Multiplexer Transmission. The multiplexer interleaves data from the four terminals and sends the signals in sequence over the line.

Keyboards

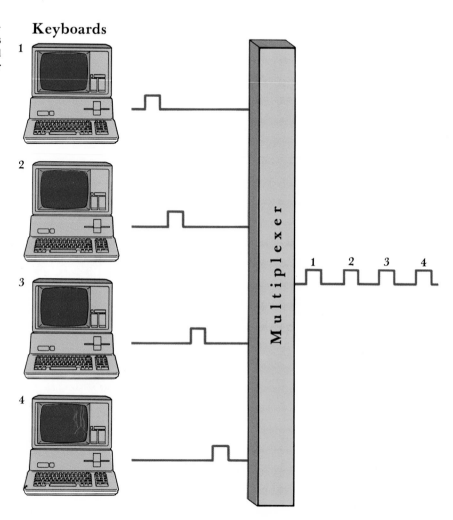

dozens of online terminals to a computer using only a single transmission line.

Figure 10-8 shows how four keyboard-speed devices are tied to a single transmission line using a multiplexer. As each key is struck, an appropriate pulse is sent to the multiplexer. The multiplexer sends the pulses in sequence over the line. Thus, by rotating time slots all four keyboards can transmit data over one line concurrently.

Multiplexers differ from concentrators in their principle of operation. Concentrators save up characters in a buffer and then transmit them in a burst. Multiplexers interleave data, sending one character or more from each device in rotation. In either case, these devices establish multiple channels on a single line. This enables many slow-speed devices to transmit data concurrently over a single circuit. It also greatly reduces line charges, since many devices can share the same line at no extra cost.

COMMUNICATIONS MEDIA

The following list summarizes the major media used to transmit data.

1. The most common medium for transmitting data is the ordinary **telephone line**, or **twisted pair**, as it is sometimes called. Lines are already in place in most businesses. There are wired networks of telephone lines in most countries. However, all instruments must be physically wired to the system.

2. There are networks of privately owned wires linking point to point. **Private wire systems** are expensive, since they are not shared by other users as is a telephone line.

3. A network of **coaxial cables** may be used instead of conventional twisted pair wiring. Data may be transmitted at low frequency and voltage (base band) or at high-speed radio frequencies (broad band). Coaxial cable systems may not be compatible with conventional circuits.

4. Fiberoptics are cables made of bundles of glass or plastic fibers that are able to transmit light along their entire length (Figure 10-9). Each filament, or strand, of glass in the cable carries an individual data or voice transmission in the form of light (as a series of flashes). There are no interference problems, particularly from radio waves, and access is easily protected.

5. Radio circuits (AM and FM) are a major means of transmitting information. Possible problems include broadcast interference, sun spot interference, and security.

6. A system of orbiting **satellites** allows information to be relayed between points on the globe. Satellite transmission is subject to interfer-

Figure 10-9 Fiberoptic Cable. A fiberoptic cable consists of many strands or filaments, each of which can carry a separate signal. Information is sent through the filaments as light waves, not electrical pulses.

Figure 10-10 Communications Satellite. A satellite in orbit around the earth relays information to distant points. Satellites in place today allow a high volume of data to be transmitted internationally.

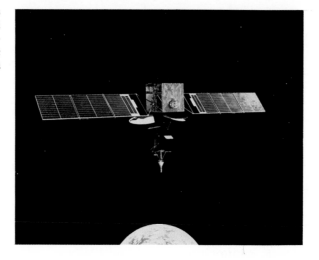

ence from sun spots and has security problems (Figure 10-10).

7. Data may be transmitted over a **laser beam**, a specially focused, coherent beam of light (Figure 10-11). Wires or cables are not required. However, such transmissions are limited to line of sight.

Figure 10-11 Laser Transmission. Digital or voice information can be transmitted over a laser. Information is encoded by modulating or changing the intensity of the beam.

TRANSMISSION MODES

Once a communication channel has been established, data can be transmitted in two modes. The **asynchronous** mode is the transmission of data character by character without any reference to a clock. Generally, a **start bit** precedes the transmission of the character and it is followed by a **stop bit**. Such systems require relatively inexpensive hardware, but they are limited in speed.

The **synchronous** mode is the transmission of information in a format that is synchronized to a clock at both the transmitting and receiving ends. Stop and start pulses are not used. Instead, the circuit transmitter and receiver are synchronized and operate in phase. Synchronous transmission equipment is more expensive than asynchronous, but it can transmit a higher volume of data per second.

COUPLERS

A **coupler** is a device to connect a terminal or a computer to a transmission line. It is also called a **modem** (MOdulator-DEModulator) or **interface facility** (Figure 10-12). Couplers may be either hard wired

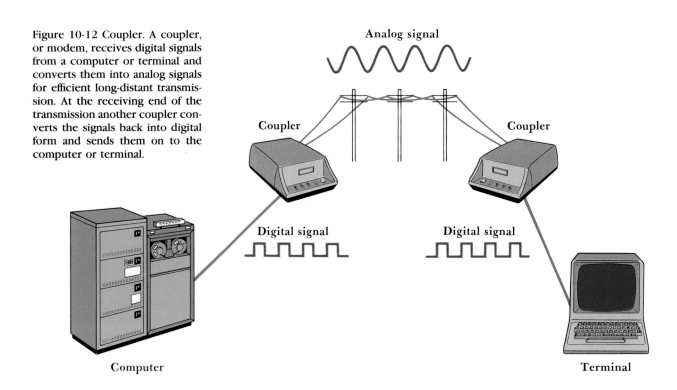

Figure 10-12 Coupler. A coupler, or modem, receives digital signals from a computer or terminal and converts them into analog signals for efficient long-distant transmission. At the receiving end of the transmission another coupler converts the signals back into digital form and sends them on to the computer or terminal.

or acoustic. A **hard-wired coupler** is permanently connected to the telephone line and the data transmission device. It forms a direct physical and electronic path between the elements on the circuit. Couplers at the computer end of a system are usually hard wired.

Acoustic couplers are not permanently connected to the computer, the terminal, or the telephone line. This independence allows a terminal to be connected to any telephone line in the field. Acoustic couplers convert signals from the terminal into an audible tone for transmission over ordinary telephone lines (Figure 10-13).

TYPES OF DATA COMMUNICATIONS

MULTIPROCESSING

One of the most important advantages of data communications is the ability of the computer to do **multiprocessing**. In a multiprocessing

Figure 10-13 Acoustic Coupler. This terminal is connected to the telephone line through an ordinary telephone handset. The coupler converts signals into audible tones for transmission, and no direct connection to the telephone wire is required.

system two or more CPUs are tied together. With appropriate software and transmission circuits, CPUs can share the processing, thereby balancing the load. Storage, CPU, and communications equipment can be shared by all computers on the system. Complex networks involving many central processors have greatly expanded capability.

REMOTE JOB ENTRY

Data communications brings the power of the computer to users in remote locations. Through **remote job entry (RJE)** terminal users can process data in much the same way as if a large computer were available on the site. Data in the remote job entry system are input to a computer and output from it through an elaborate terminal system consisting of many input/output devices. With remote job entry users thousands of miles away from a computer can maintain large files, prepare monthly billing, or compute a payroll, just as if they were at the CPU site.

DATA INQUIRY

Some data communications systems designed to output data are called **inquiry systems** (Figure 10-14). Remote users can request the computer to output information from a file accessible to the CPU.

Figure 10-14 Data Inquiry System. Each display terminal is able to access the central computer and make inquiries. Each can receive output from the CPU, but cannot input data. Any changes in the files are made from an input device located near the main computer.

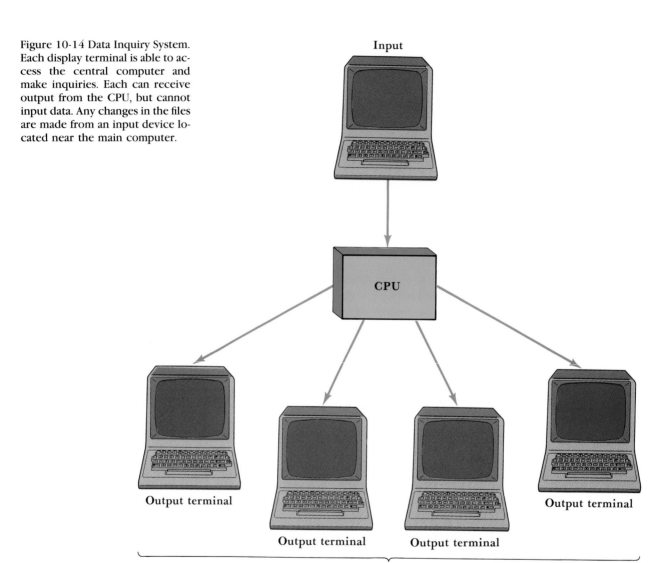

Input

CPU

Output terminal

Output terminal

Output terminal

Output terminal

Video display terminals

Data inquiry systems generally do not allow users to update, add data, or otherwise change a file. File maintenance and data input are done at the site of the CPU.

Examples of data inquiry systems include stock market quotation and inventory inquiry systems. In these systems the user asks the computer about the status of a given file. Files can be queried either through a telephone inquiry with an audio response or a keyboard inquiry with a video display output.

In telephone inquiry with audio response the user calls the system and inputs a key number, such as a part or item number. The computer then accesses the master file and locates the requested record. It assembles a verbal message, which is fed back over the telephone line to the terminal. The user receives a spoken reply to the query over the telephone.

In keyboard inquiry with video display the user keyboards in the descriptive data and the computer processes the request. The results of the processing are sent back to the terminal and displayed on a video screen.

NETWORKS

A **telecommunications network** is an arrangement of communications facilities that links together users who may communicate voice, digital, or video information. A telecommunications network may be limited to a few users at nearby points, or it may extend to thousands of users in local clusters or scattered around the globe.

A telecommunications network may be specialized, allowing the transmission of only one type of information—video, voice, or digital. Some CATV networks transmit both video and digital information. Systems that combine both voice and digital are more efficient and flexible. For example, some systems enable a telephone and data terminal to be serviced by a single existing telephone line.

In a data communications network users access the system through terminals or **work stations**. These are entry points to the system, referred to as **ports**. A group of local ports may be clustered about a point known as a **node**. Nodes are connected together through long-distance facilities called **long-haul circuits** (Figure 10-15). The switching, monitoring, and control of the network is done through a system of data communications computers.

NETWORK ARCHITECTURE

The structure, design, and layout of the network and transmission facilities are called the **system architecture**, or its **topology**. The ar-

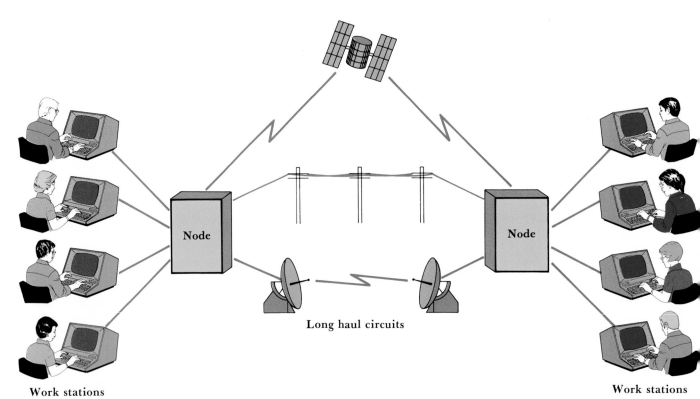

Figure 10-15 Long Haul Circuits. Satellite relay, microwave, or ordinary telephone circuits may be used to connect two nodes on a system. Some systems use a combination of transmission facilities to connect distant points.

chitecture of systems takes many forms, depending upon the needs of the system users (Figure 10-16). There are five major topologies in use.

1. In the **tree** or **hierarchal** configuration all terminals are tied to, and communications are routed through, a central host computer. The host computer monitors and controls the movement of data throughout the network. It performs major data processing functions and serves as a backup computer. The terminals do not communicate with each other directly. The design resembles a tree with branches.
2. In the **star** design all computers are tied to a central computer, but the major processing is done by the satellite processors rather than

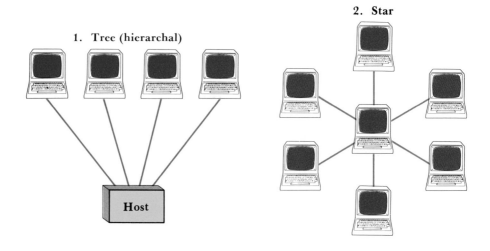

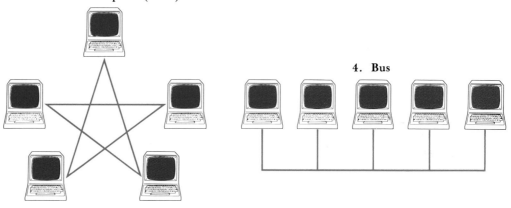

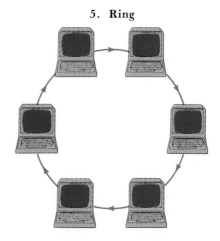

Figure 10-16 Topologies. The topology of a communication system is its design or layout. Five common layouts are the tree, star, point-to-point, bus, and ring.

the host. All computers, including the central one, are on equal level with all others on the system.

3. In a **point-to-point** design all computers are tied to each other in a mesh of point-to-point wiring with no central computer.

4. In the **bus** configuration all computers are tied together in a single line with no host computer. Each has access to the data on the bus.

5. In the **ring** design computers are integrated into an active loop. Information is transmitted from station to station through a series of repeaters. There is a continuous flow of data around the ring.

FACTORS IN NETWORK DESIGN

When laying out a data communications network, system designers must consider many factors. For example, should all switching be controlled by a single host computer? Which computer should do the switching? How will loads and delays be handled? How should system interruptions be dealt with? What functions should be delegated to each work station? Which computers should serve as backup? How can backup facilities be provided and still keep equipment duplication and transmission line costs to a minimum? What security provisions should be provided to control unauthorized system access? What method should be used to control or limit users?

EXAMPLES OF TELEPROCESSING NETWORKS

Networks are evolving in two directions as new data communications technology and equipment emerge. There are networks of local users, within a few miles of each other, who share common data base and communication facilities (Figure 10-17). These are called **local area networks (LANs).** There are also complex, large national and international networks that incorporate extensive data bases and are maintained by companies that offer long-range communications circuits.

LOCAL AREA NETWORKS

A **local area network (LAN)** is a communications system that enables users in a geographically limited area to share computer resources

Figure 10-17 Teleprocessing Network. Each local area may contain dozens of devices connected into a local area network (LAN). These local systems in turn may be tied together into a larger network through satellite, microwave relay, or telephone line communications circuits.

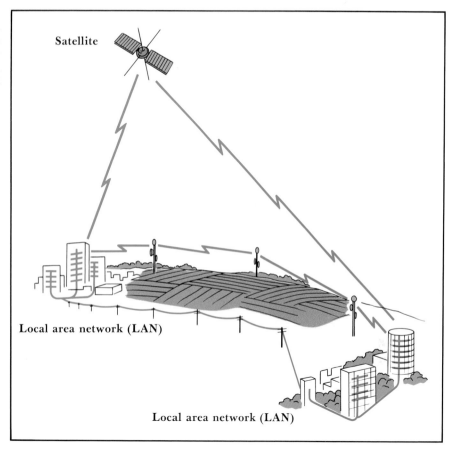

Satellite

Local area network (LAN)

Local area network (LAN)

and communications equipment (Figure 10-18). LANs are usually limited to 5 miles or less in range and rely upon coaxial cables. Users are added to or dropped from a system by connecting to or disconnecting from the coaxial cable. LANs are usually limited to users in one company or perhaps in a government agency or university.

One of the most successful LAN systems is called **Ethernet**. It was developed by Xerox Corporation, in conjunction with Digital Equipment Corporation and Intel Incorporated. Ethernet is a standardized package of hardware, communications lines, and system software. Ethernet users are tied together through a single coaxial cable. A user can query other users on the network, move data from one point to another, or direct information to be printed out on printers

Figure 10-18 Local Area Network (LAN). In this typical situation three buildings are operated by one company. Microcomputers in the three building are integrated into a network by coaxial cable connections. A computer in any of the buildings can communicate with any other computer in the three buildings, allowing them to share or exchange information.

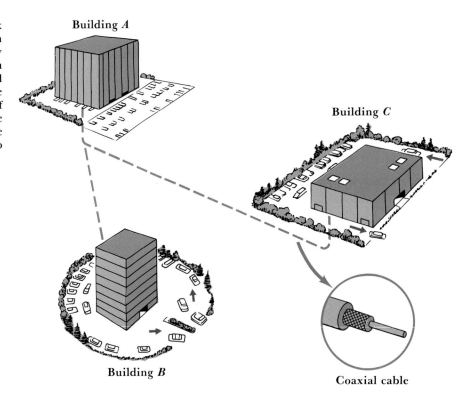

Building *A*

Building *C*

Building *B*

Coaxial cable

throughout the system. Services on the system include EtherLink Exchange, EtherShare, EtherPrint, and EtherMail.

LANs can be interfaced with other LANs through long-haul transmission circuits (Figure 10-19). A user in one LAN who wants to communicate with a work station in another LAN gains access through a port which in turn selects the appropriate long-haul network. This may be a telephone, microwave, or satellite link. Information can be routed between work stations in different LANs as though they were in the same local network.

COMMON CARRIERS

Many firms have entered the long-haul communications field. Organizations that offer transmission facilities to the public and are controlled by state or federal regulations are called **common carriers**.

NETWORK LINKS FOR COMPUTERS

Most major computer manufacturers deny they are in the computer business any more. Instead, they profess to be leaders in the "systems business," selling "system solutions" that insure customers will not be left with a bunch of disparate components, unable to communicate with one another.

Despite the reassuring words, however, the most promising systems for tying the hottest-selling desktop and personal computers into truly efficient "networks" are still on the electronic drawing board. "It's one thing to provide people with the wires, the connectors and the jacks," said Dixon Doll, president of the DMW Group, a telecommunications consulting firm in Ann Arbor, Mich. "People are just beginning to realize that these systems require a much higher level of coordination."

Communications in the office was rarely a problem when companies relied almost exclusively on some large mainframe computer, buried in the basement. Workers needing the computer worked at terminals—machines with no computational power of their own—and shared the power of the central system. But only a limited number of terminals can be hooked up to a central processor, and when demand is at a peak, the response time of the main computer can slow tremendously.

Microcomputers, however, can fend for themselves. They are more flexible, less expensive, and because they usually serve only one user they are quick. But manufacturers have realized that they must be able to share information without resorting to a central computer to act as "traffic cop."

Thus the rise of "local area networks" that link desktop computers with nearby printers and other equipment. The first in the race was Xerox, which in 1980 agreed on standards for its Ethernet system with the Digital Equipment Corporation and the Intel Corporation. It licensed more than 100 other manufacturers to make Ethernet-compatible equipment.

While specific characteristics of those systems vary, they operate on the same principle: The computers are linked by a central "pipeline," and each can shoot a message—in a "packet" that is best envisioned as a tennis ball—to any other computer in the network. If one tennis ball collides with another, they both retreat to their point of origin, to be shot out again at a random time.

Xerox says more than 5,000 Ethernet systems have already been installed. "It was a good idea, but it has its limitations," said Douglas Wilson, the manager of system operations for Project Athena, a Massachusetts Institute of Technology project that is attempting to link several types of local area networks.

Common carriers provide communications, message switching, and access to extensive data bases and program libraries to their customers. The major companies are international in operation, using microwave, satellite, and surface communications facilities.

Figure 10-19 Interfaced LANS. Several LANs at distant points can be tied together through long-haul communications circuits. A computer in one LAN can access data in a distant LAN through entry points into the long-haul network.

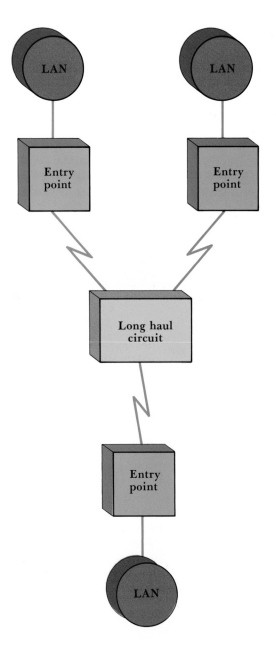

CompuServe Incorporated is a leader in the development of an international network for remote computing and data base access. CompuServe customers may access their network through a local telephone call from more than 200 international locations. A wide variety of programs and data is available to users. For example, there are programs dealing with money market and bond portfolio management, analysis for mining engineers and geologists, and statistical techniques for biomedical researchers.

Control Data Corporation offers Cybernet service. Cybernet is an international communications network, tying together dozens of large computers in major cities in this country and abroad. Cybernet's extensive communications network includes wide-band and satellite transmission facilities. It offers communications, remote computing, and data base access services.

Other entrants into the common carrier arena include Hughes Communications, Southern Pacific Communications, Xerox, MCI, and Western Union. They provide various combinations of local dial-up, long-haul, or other network capabilities. As more businesses expand into international markets, there will be a greater reliance upon common carriers such as these.

Data communications is one of the most dynamic areas of computers and data processing discussed so far. The breakup of AT&T into smaller competing companies and the entry of many new common carriers into the marketplace means new jobs and changing technology. Students who understand data communications and its impact have an advantage in the labor market of the future.

SUMMARY AND KEY TERMS

- **Telecommunications** is the science of moving information by means of transmission lines, telephone cables, microwave channels, or fiberoptic circuits. The three major domains are **audio** or **voice** transmission, **video** transmission, and **data communications** or **digital** transmission.

- Data communications is also known as **teleprocessing**.

- A **communications link** is the physical means by which elements of the system are connected and by which information is transmitted or received.

- Telecommunications was first used by the military and then adopted by airline, hotel, and other reservation systems. The **point-**

of-sale terminal is an example of a teleprocessing application.

• **Distributed data processing (DDP) systems** involve a network of small, stand-alone processors and data communications circuits that allow many users to share the same resources. Such systems are limited by communications costs and potential failure of communications links.

• Modern data communications applications include electronic banking, information retrieval systems, electronic word processing, electronic mail, electronic shopping, teleconferences, monitoring, and metering.

• Three types of transmission circuits in common use are **simplex**, **half-duplex**, and **full-duplex**.

• The standard measure of data transmission speed is **bits per second (bps)**. Three common grades of lines are **narrow band**, **voice grade**, and **wide band**.

• A **channel** is a path between a terminal and a computer or between several computers. **Data concentrators** use **buffering** circuits to get maximum use of high-volume lines with slow-speed terminals. **Multiplexers** allow data from several sources to be sent over one line.

• Major communications media include telephone lines, private wire circuits, coaxial cables, fiberoptics, radio circuits, satellites, and laser transmission systems.

• **Couplers** connect terminals or computers to transmission lines. These devices, also known as **modems**, and interface facilities, may be either hard wired or acoustic.

• A **network** is an arrangement of facilities linked by communications lines. They include **work stations**, **ports**, and **nodes** tied together through **long-haul lines**.

• Common network **topologies** are the tree, star, point-to-point, bus, and ring.

• **Local area networks (LANs)** use coaxial cables to link computers in a geographically limited area. National and international communications networks can be accessed by many users all over the country and abroad.

EXERCISES

1. Define the term telecommunications.

2. Summarize the major advantages and limitations of teleprocessing.

3. List some major data communications applications.

4. Explain how teleprocessing differs from conventional or local processing.

5. How does data communications differ from telecommunications?

6. List the three kinds of transmission circuits used in teleprocessing and explain how they differ.

7. How do narrow-band, voice-grade, and wide-band lines differ?

8. What are the advantages of an acoustic coupler? Suggest several applications for portable terminals with acoustic couplers.

9. List some common communications media.

10. Visit a stockbroker's office, business firm, or small engineering company that uses data communications. Determine what online equipment is involved and how it is used, how the system is used by the company, and the advantages of the system.

11

Learning Objectives

After studying this chapter, you should be able to
1. Summarize the evolution of information systems
2. Define key terms in file terminology
3. List the major advantages of data base management systems.
4. Contrast four common data base schemas.
5. Describe the function of data dictionaries.
6. Describe how commercial data base services operate.

Chapter Outline

Data Base
Management Systems (DBMS)

For information to be useful to businesses in problem solving and decision making, complete and accurate data must be available at the right time and place. They must also be processed at a reasonable cost.

A **data base** is the total collection of information accumulated by an organization and structured in a systematic way to eliminate duplication and to facilitate use by several users for several applications. A **data base management system (DBMS)** is the most efficient way to process the data base. It includes the software, hardware, and structures necessary to maintain and manipulate files of information so they can be accessed by one or more users.

In this chapter we shall look at the procedures and techniques for collecting, storing, and reporting data in a systematic way. We will study data base principles and software and commercial data base vendors.

EVOLUTION OF INFORMATION SYSTEMS

One logical way to organize data is simply to put them in a file. A file, in general terms, is a collection of related information. For example, you may maintain a file on the courses you take at school. This file might include grade cards, schedules, and other records related to your school work.

For years businesses have maintained files that are organized to serve the needs of particular departments. For example, an accounting department keeps accounts receivable and accounts payable files; a personnel department, employee roster and hourly wage files; and a production department, finished goods in inventory and raw materials in inventory files. Information can be retrieved from these files and from the files of other departments by physically checking the records.

The technique of looking up information in a file, making use of it (reading or changing it), and returning it to the file is called **file processing** (Figure 11-1). When the computer came

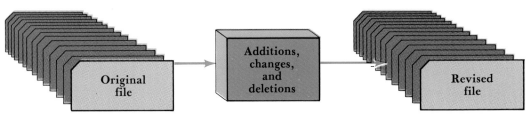

Figure 11-1 File Processing. File processing consists of searching for information, using it, and returning it to storage. The user may make additions, changes, or deletions in the original file to generate a revised file.

on the scene, it was logical to use it to process data in ways that had already proved reliable. In effect, the computer was used like a giant electronic filing cabinet. However, the computer added a new element of speed and convenience to processing. Electronics replaced the physical files and physical checking. A user could rapidly search a file, update its contents, and print out records electronically. The needs of organizations with large volumes of data led to the development of **data base processing**.

The early data base management systems were designed to serve a single user (Figure 11-2). Later systems allowed a group of users to share a common data base (Figure 11-3). They could revise, update, or query information in the common data base. Soon organizations began installing data bases that could be shared by dozens of users with different types of terminals and varied applications.

As data communications technology improved, business organizations turned to **distributed data base processing** in which a common data base is geographically distributed throughout the system and users share data through a data communications network (Figure 11-4).

At first businesses built data base management systems for their own use. However, it soon became clear that the vast collections of data built up by some companies, for example, Dow Jones, Reader's Digest, and the New York Times, could be extremely useful for many other firms and individuals, and so two types of DBMS began to develop. A **proprietary DBMS** is maintained exclusively for the inhouse users of one company (Figure 11-5). Proprietary DBMS are generally not accessed by or available to outsiders. A **commercial data base**, on the other hand, offers access to its resources through communications networks. Such data bases are operated by vendors such as CompuServe, Mead Corporation, and Control Data. Anyone who wishes to access these data bases may do so, paying usage

Figure 11-2 Single User Data Base. In this configuration, only one user has access to the data base.

Figure 11-3 Shared Data Base. In this arrangement, many users share a common data base.

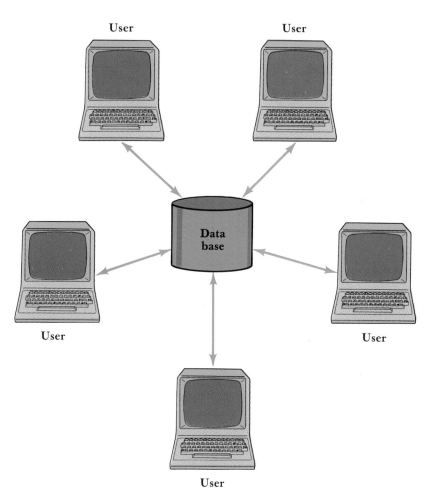

charges. Today, many companies use commercial data bases as well as maintain their own proprietary systems.

Low-cost microcomputers and DBMS programs have brought information systems within reach of home and small business users. Now anyone with a microcomputer, a coupler, and a telephone line can access a commercial data base.

MANAGEMENT INFORMATION SYSTEMS (MIS)

A **management information system (MIS)** is a form of data base management system. It is designed to provide information to man-

Figure 11-4 Distributed Data Base. In this configuration, the data base is distributed geographically at many sites and can be accessed by many users.

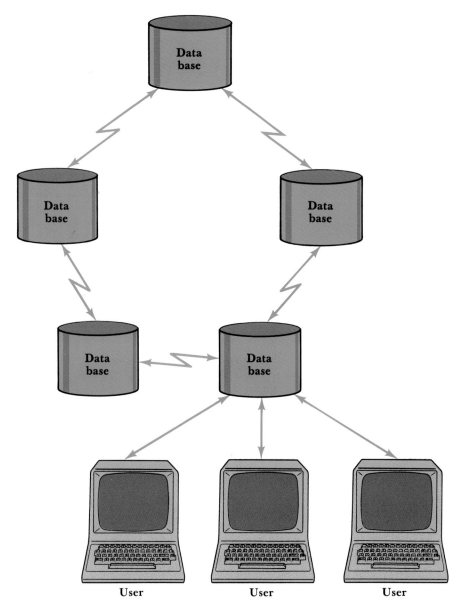

agement for the effective control and decision making necessary to operate an organization. Management information systems are an

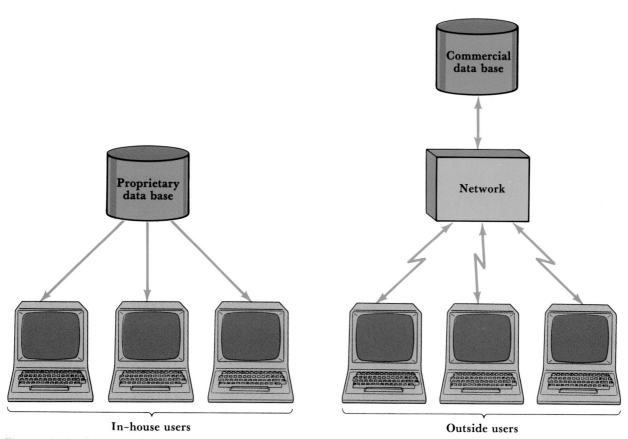

In-house users

Outside users

Figure 11-5 Commercial Data Base Users. Proprietary data bases contain information relevant to an organization's activities solely for the use of the organization's members. Commercial data bases are vast files of information for sale. The data are made available to outside users through communications networks for a fee.

outgrowth of file processing systems. They generate reports, printouts, and documents that help managers at all levels in an organization make better decisions. Virtually any kind of information can be managed by an MIS, ranging from engineering, manufacturing or raw material costs, to labor, promotion, advertising, or transportation data. For example, reports can be generated for such matters as cash flow, trends in accounts payable and receivable, earning ratios, and turnover ratios.

The MIS can give management data concerning distribution functions. These reports can provide information on finished goods in stock or in transit, goods in production, or backlogged orders. It can prepare shipping schedules, routing data, and shipping cost tables. This type of information decreases late deliveries, misrouted goods, and over- or underproduction of goods.

Investment planning and management of capital assets can be included in a management information system. For example, managers can receive reports on capital outlays, returns on investment, cost centers, depreciation schedules, and equipment maintenance and installation costs. This facilitates planning the acquisition of new capital goods or the sale of outdated or unproductive equipment.

DECISION SUPPORT SYSTEMS (DSS)

As computers became more prevalent in business offices, it was inevitable that people who are not computer oriented would turn to them for their decision-making tasks. Some of these managers preferred to work in an unstructured decision-making environment, one that did more than merely rely on historical reports or data generated by computers. They needed systems that emphasized long-range goals and future orientation.

This need led to the development of **decision support systems (DSS),** an outgrowth of file processing and management information systems. Decision support systems are a form of data base management that emphasizes decision making. They are generally implemented using color graphics terminals that access a data base in real time and display information for the manager. Instead of simply generating printed reports for decision makers, DSS allow the manager to query the system, structure relationships, and then display the results. It is not necessary to learn formal programming rules or complicated system details.

A feature of decision support systems is their ability to deal in relationships. Organizations are represented as mathematical models that can be manipulated, tested, and experimented with. In implementing a DSS, pertinent data are gathered in a data base and the relationships of business variables are defined. Reports can be generated that aid in decision making, and relationships can be altered and new information displayed instantaneously. With a DSS, the manager does not rely on just printed reports, but instead, on a real time assessment of a model that shows future trends and graphically displays key data.

The following contrasts the different emphasis between the MIS and DSS:

MIS	DSS
Relatively structured procedures	Unstructured procedures
Emphasizes reports, printouts	Emphasizes decision making
Focuses on collection of data	Future oriented
Historical reporting	Real time reporting
Bound by system constraints	User friendly, visual display

FILES AND FILE PROCESSING

TERMINOLOGY

You may recall from an earlier discussion that the smallest unit of data is a **bit**, and that bits go together to make up a character or **byte**. A **field** is a group of related bytes, such as the name of a customer or a part number. Fields are combined to form a **record**. A record may be a punched card or an area on tape or disk that stores a group of related fields. For example, a student record may contain a name field, identification number field, and class enrollment field.

A **file** is a collection of two or more records in the same category (Figure 11-6). A file in business may contain personnel lists, accounts payable lists, parts lists, inventory, and so forth. Related files make up a **library** (Figure 11-7). An organization may maintain a library in several different cities, with each place containing files pertinent to that location. All the libraries in an organization are referred to collectively as its **data base**. The data base is the total collection of all information related to an organization. It may be located at one or more sites.

To help you remember the relationship of these terms, think of them as a hierarchy as shown on the next page. The smallest piece of information is a bit, while the most global and encompassing structure is the data base.

DATA BASE

↑

LIBRARY

↑

FILES

↑

RECORDS

↑

FIELDS

↑

BYTES

↑

BITS

Figure 11-6 File. A file is a collection of related records and may be composed of information stored on punched cards, magnetic tape, or magnetic disk.

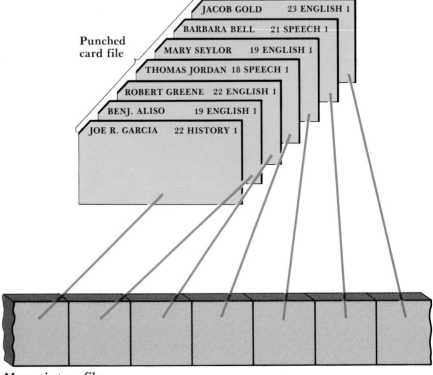

Punched card file

JACOB GOLD   23 ENGLISH 1
BARBARA BELL   21 SPEECH 1
MARY SEYLOR   19 ENGLISH 1
THOMAS JORDAN 18 SPEECH 1
ROBERT GREENE   22 ENGLISH 1
BENJ. ALISO   19 ENGLISH 1
JOE R. GARCIA   22 HISTORY 1

Magnetic tape file

Figure 11-7 Libraries. A library is a collection of related files. A data base is a collction of an organization's libraries.

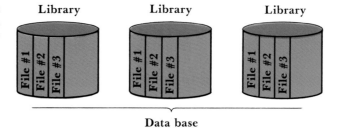

FILE-BASED PROCESSING LIMITATIONS

There are several problems associated with an information system based on files, even if they are maintained by computers, as compared to one that is structured around the entire data base. If different parts of an organization each maintain their own files, there is likely to be a lot of duplication. There is also likely to be little standardization of the format or content of information stored in files. These inconsistencies lead to errors and inaccurate output.

Many file-based systems are program dependent. That is, the files are structured in such a way that they can be used only by a given computer program. Some systems are hardware dependent, that is, they can be accessed only by a specific piece of hardware, such as a selected terminal or disk drive.

If files are maintained in many different departments, security and file protection are difficult to maintain.

ADVANTAGES OF DATA BASE MANAGEMENT SYSTEMS

Data base management systems are program and hardware independent. The information in the files is organized in a way that allows for generalized access. This means sets of data can be reached via programs written in many different computer languages. The same data base can also be accessed through a simple language, similar to spoken English, in which no program need be written. Finally, file updating and maintenance is simplified since data are routinely collected, managed, updated, or purged.

Organizations that use data base management systems have experienced many benefits. Cost saving is a major benefit of DBMS. It is more economical to maintain a large data base where there is little or no redundancy of records or duplication of equipment. Access is available to many, but the integrity of confidential data can still be preserved through a security system. Collections of information can be expanded, be kept up-to-date in a logical and systematic way, and be routinely eliminated according to the needs of the organization.

DBMS do have limitations associated with personnel and equipment. DBMS installations require a high level of data processing sophistication in the personnel who manage them. Some firms find it necessary to employ special DBMS administrators and programmers to oversee and control the growth of their data base, although some companies manage to reduce the personnel demands by buying ready-made DBMS software. There are operating costs associated with maintaining large files. Another limitation is that distributed DBMS are subject to problems of network and communication failures.

STRUCTURE OF DATA BASES

Let us now take a look at how data bases are set up and the various types of files and means of accessing them.

One of the first tasks of an administrator assigned to establish and maintain a data base is to structure the data base system. Part of this task involves setting standards so that data will be collected, stored, and maintained in a consistent and logical manner. This in turn involves the development of a plan or schema. The data base administrator must then coordinate data collection efforts and see that use of the system is monitored and controlled.

For example, suppose an organization decides to set up an inventory file of goods purchased from various suppliers. Item names may be spelled differently by different vendors. Some suppliers might use metrics, while others use U.S. standard sizes and weights. The same color may be called by different names by various suppliers. It is the administrator's responsibility to establish uniform nomenclature for each item and to describe a common weight and measuring system. In the absence of standardization, errors in handling data, duplications, and shortages could occur.

SCHEMAS

A **schema** is the logical structure, plan, or method by which data are organized in a system. Schemas include a model of the basic data elements or attributes. The **data model** defines all data elements. It spells out precisely what information is contained in a field, how many characters it will hold, and whether alphabetic or numeric information will be entered. The data plan assigns standard numbers or identifiers used to reference individual pieces of data.

A major factor in planning the data model is what it is going to be used for. Data models begin with an assessment of the needs of the organization and its users. Some schemas are structured for only local processing, that is, only local users are allowed access to the data within the structures. Other schemas provide for a distributed data base in which data are maintained at many different locations. Still others involve both local and remote users within one company. In such a schema the data base manager must decide what information can be accessed locally and what information can be accessed by all users. A schema could make available to all users on the system, regardless of location, names and addresses of all employees. These would be defined as **global data elements**. Information about employees' salaries could be restricted to local access from selected terminals. These would be defined as **restricted local data elements**.

The design of data base structures is a complex task. There are many different approaches to organizing data in files so that information can be accessed from the data base quickly and easily. Large files containing thousands of records cannot be easily sequenced. Imagine if a file with 10,000 names in alphabetical order had to be completely redone every time a name was added or deleted! In order to get around this, a plan or schema is set up that allows records in a file to be located when they are not numerically or alphabetically in order. Provision must also be made to add, modify, and delete records from a file.

Let us look at four common data base schemas.

LIST STRUCTURE

One frequently used schema is the **list structure**. The list structure enables out-of-sequence records to be treated as though they were in sequential order. Records can be added or deleted at any point without file reorganization. This is done by a system of numeric **pointers** that direct the computer to the next record, even though it is not in sequence. All records in the file must, however, be stored in serial

Figure 11-8 List Structure. In this list structure, pointers direct the computer to the next record to be located, even though it may not be in sequence.

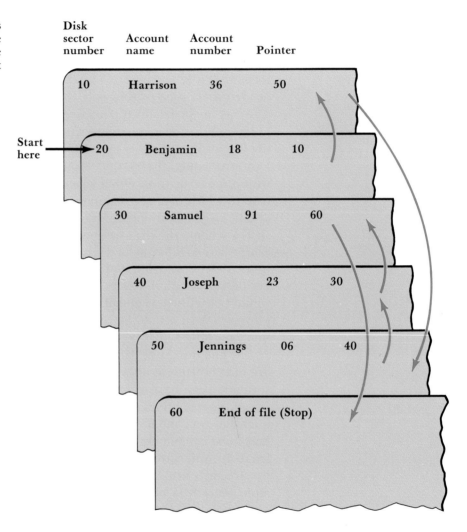

Disk sector number	Account name	Account number	Pointer
10	Harrison	36	50
20 (Start here)	Benjamin	18	10
30	Samuel	91	60
40	Joseph	23	30
50	Jennings	06	40
60	End of file (Stop)		

form on a direct access disk so they can be located at random.

Suppose a programmer wishes to print out alphabetically a group of names stored in a list structure file, such as shown in Figure 11-8. For various reasons the records are not in alphabetical order. Each record is stored on a different area of the disk and includes the account name and number and, most important, a pointer or **linkage address**. This address is automatically assigned by the system. To begin, the computer goes to the entry point in the file, in this instance disk sector 20, and prints out the first alphabetical name, Benjamin. Then it follows the pointer to the next alphabetical record in the file. In this instance it is physically the first record on the disk, but logically the second. After printing out the name Harrison, the computer moves to the name Jennings, then to Joseph, and then Samuel. At Samuel's record, the pointer finally directs the computer to the end of file record, where it stops.

This basic arrangement allows the computer to hop and skip through an unsequenced file using the pointer to produce a neatly alphabetized list.

TREE OR HIERARCHAL STRUCTURE

The **tree** or **hierarchal structure** contains a group of master records, sometimes known as **parents** or **owners**, and a group of subordinate records, sometimes known as **children**. Each subordinate record has only one owner or master record. There are times when it is necessary to locate information on several different physical records that are related to one logical entity. Each master record may therefore have to direct the computer to a number of subordinate records to obtain all the needed information.

The computer always accesses the master record first and then goes to one or more subordinates to obtain the necessary data. Figure 11-9 illustrates this concept. Suppose a programmer wishes to obtain data on a specific automobile, engine, and water pump. This information related to one logical entity is actually stored on one master and two subordinate records. Using a hierarchal data base, the computer first seeks the master record "automobile." It then branches to the subcategory "engine" and finally moves down the hierarchy to the detail record "water pump." Thus, all related information is brought together, even though stored on different physical records.

NETWORK STRUCTURE

The **network structure** provides still another mechanism by which records in a data base can be accessed. The network file is composed of

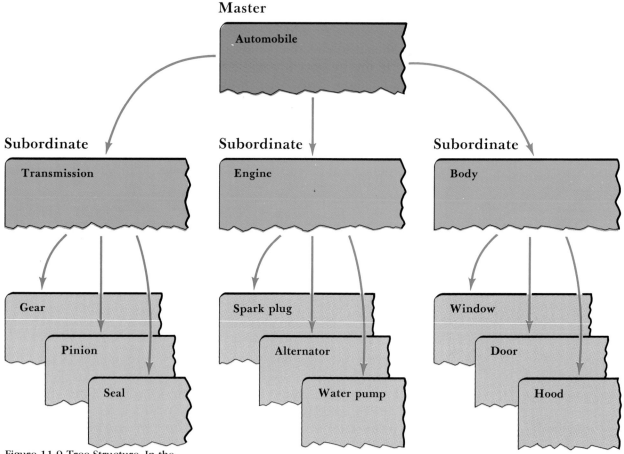

Figure 11-9 Tree Structure. In the tree structure, each subordinate record has only one owner or master record. Each master record may direct the computer to several subordinate records to obtain information.

both master and subordinate records. A master record may have several subordinate records, and a subordinate record may be linked to more than one master record. Thus the network differs from the tree, in which all subordinates are linked to only one master record.

Figure 11-10 is a simplified illustration of computing order charges using a network structure. Two master records direct the computer to seek information from five subordinate records. Some charges are common to both retail and wholesale orders, while others are related to one or the other. If a retail order is being processed, sales tax and retail commission are obtained from two detail records

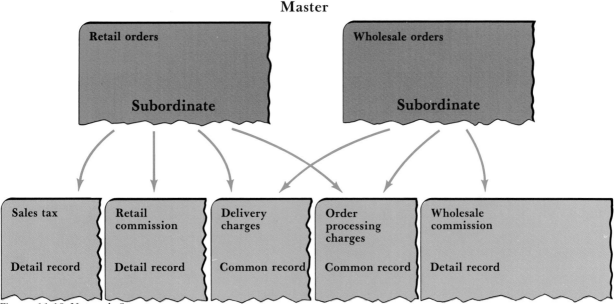

Master

Retail orders

Subordinate

Wholesale orders

Subordinate

Sales tax	Retail commission	Delivery charges	Order processing charges	Wholesale commission
Detail record	Detail record	Common record	Common record	Detail record

Figure 11-10 Network Structure. In the network structure, a subordinate record may be linked to more than one master record, and each master record may be linked to several subordinate records.

and delivery and order processing charges from two common records. If a wholesale order is being processed, wholesale commission is pulled from one detail record and delivery and order processing charges from the two common records. The network structure enables records to be linked to one or more master records without the one-to-one constraint of the tree structure.

RELATIONAL STRUCTURE

The **relational structure** is the most flexible data base schema. The elements to be searched need not be defined before the data base is constructed. Pointers are not used. Instead, the schema uses a group of tables to show relationships. Once the table or file is constructed, any relationships can be searched out.

Figure 11-11 shows four files. The first file lists accounts by type of store. It relates customers and the type of store they operate. A second table lists customers and type of goods they purchase. The third table relates customers and the monthly volume of goods they

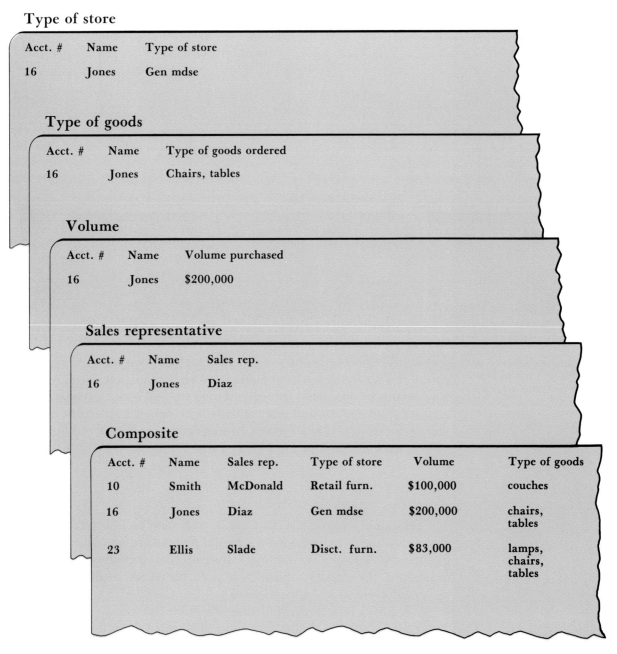

Figure 11-11 Relational Structure. The relational schema is flexible, since pointers are not used. Instead, tables show relationships.

purchase. The fourth keys the customer to the sales representative. There are so many types of relationships between customers and aspects of their business that it would be impractical to keep all the information in one file. By using the relational schema, the user can locate all customers who buy a given type of goods or all those who purchase a given volume of goods. It is easy to isolate customers by type of store, salesperson, territory, or any other attributes stored in the data base. Thus, it would be possible to locate the customer who buys only a certain quantity of a specific item from a particular salesperson in a given area. The computer branches from the customer file to the type of goods file to other files to obtain the necessary information.

DATA BASE SOFTWARE

DATA DICTIONARIES

In ordinary languages a dictionary is a reference book containing words arranged alphabetically, giving information about their form, function, meaning, and syntax. In a data base management system a **data dictionary** is a comprehensive list or collection of information, usually arranged alphabetically, giving the form, function, meaning, and syntax of data. Data dictionaries describe standard field sizes, coding schemas, and the kind and type of data to be managed by the system.

Data dictionaries are a prerequisite to setting up a functioning system. They establish consistency and eliminate repetitions and omissions. They may also contain a security function, that is, they may define which files or fields may be accessed by specific users and which may be changed or modified. Once the data base dictionary has been prepared, the DBMS administrator can set about the task of actually setting up the files, entering data, and implementing the system.

The value of a data dictionary is illustrated by the following example. Suppose two managers in the same company, located in different cities, wish to establish address files on their local accounts. According to company policy they must refer to the data dictionary before establishing new files. The files must conform to specified field width, number of characters, format, and so forth. Later the managers decide to merge the two files, giving both a broader data base. Had they not consulted the dictionary, the managers might not be able to merge their files because the formats or field widths might be inconsistent.

DATA BASE CAPABILITIES

The simplest data base management systems support only one user who can access the data base only through a procedural language such as COBOL or BASIC. The more sophisticated DBMS may support hundreds of users in a distributed system with a variety of means of accessing the data base. Figure 11-12 diagrams some DBMS software.

The following programs or capabilities may be written into data base management systems.

1. Single user capability. The most elementary data base management systems support one user. The software allows one terminal to access, change, or modify the information in the data base. Software such as this is available for small microcomputer systems.

2. Multiuser capability. Multiuser software gives many terminals concurrent access to a single data base. Users may be restricted to only querying the data base or may be permitted to update or change information, depending upon the needs of the users.

3. Distributed data base capability. Using special software, users are able to access, query, or modify data bases distributed over a wide geographic area. The software must allow concurrent use of the data base. It must also provide for system recovery in the event of transmission failure.

4. Procedural language access. A DBMS may provide access to information only through a high level procedural language. This means the user must write a program in COBOL, FORTRAN, or BASIC, for example. The user must be trained in the use of a high-level language in order to access data.

5. Query language access. A query language allows an untrained user to access information in the data base. A program does not need to be written. Instead, an easy-to-learn, English-like query language is

Figure 11
is made,
play a su
down the

Figure 11-12 Data Base Management System Software. The core of the data base includes a data dictionary and pieces of software that specify type of access, such as single user, multiuser, or distributed data base capability. The software also sets the means of access, that is, the query is protected by a peripheral piece of security software that screens and limits users.

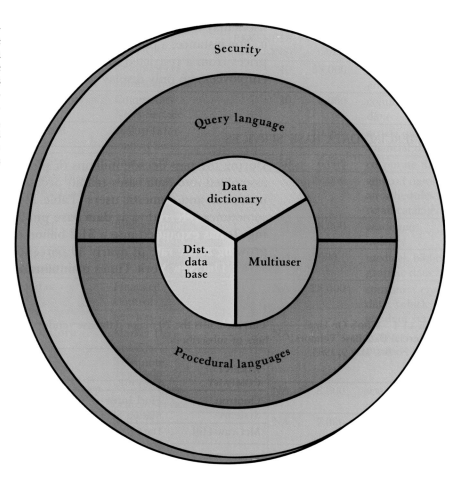

used. Other software may enable unsophisticated users to prepare reports or print out data by entering only a few simple commands from the keyboard.

6. Relational data base management. One of the most flexible means of accessing data bases is through relational files. Relational files allow users to structure different data paths without the necessity of restructuring the files. Special software is necessary to process relational files in place of ordinary list files using pointers.

7. Security facilities. Security programs allow only selected users to access the data base. Some files, records, or fields are restricted to selected users by means of passwords or user numbers. Only qualified

Figure 1
cial Data
mercial
through
phone lii
compani
the FCC
tions ser
dition tc
lies, su
compani
ized co
private-l
data trai

DIALING A DATA BASE

Source: Forbes, May 9, 1983, p. 204.

Using an on-line database is a relatively simple procedure—if you know exactly what you want and where to find it. Looking up AT&T's five-year sales and earnings history, for example, takes only minutes. The information is on several services, including Lockheed's Dialog, Mead Data Central and The Source. Here's how we got it from Dow Jones:

1. We connect our computer terminal to a telephone and make a local call to a packet switching network, in this case Telenet.

2. Telenet answers and asks what equipment we are using, to provide a clearer signal. We punch in the code "A8," signifying Digital Equipment Corp.'s Decwriter III, a so-called dumb terminal.

3. On flashes the symbol "@," Telenet's way of telling us to name a database vendor. We answer with the "address" for the Dow Jones News/Retrieval service in Princeton, N.J.

4. Telenet tells us we are connected with Dow Jones.

5. We are now communicating with an IBM mainframe computer at Dow Jones that asks which of the company's several services we want. We answer: "DJNS," the product that carries corporate financial data.

6. DJ asks for our paid-subscriber password. Since this also tells the computer whom to bill, the word is blanked out by the computer.

7. DJ's copyright notice appears, and the vendor asks what database we would like to access. We enter "DSCLO," for a specific bank of computers containing SEC reports compiled by Disclosure Inc.

8. After logging on with Disclosure, DJ asks what company we are interested in. "T," we reply, using stock symbol code, and DJ affirms that we want AT&T. DJ's computer is now ready to "read" the proper section of its database disks. (Like a researcher referring to an index, the computer need not search the entire file.)

9. DJ now asks what part of the file we are interested in. It offers 15 choices. We request number six.

10. Instantly the computer reads that section of the database and prints out the information.

11. We disconnect from the database, vendor, Telenet and local phone lines.

Doing all this took two minutes on-line, probably the minimum time for any database request. Our bill came to roughly $8.55. About $4.20 goes to Dow Jones for computer time. Another $4 goes to Disclosure Inc. for the information. Telenet gets 25 cents, and 10 cents goes to New York Telephone for the local call.

The entire contents of Grolier's *Academic American Encyclopedia* have been entered into a computer data base. This electronic encyclopedia consists of 21 volumes, 28,000 articles, and approximately 9

Figure 11-12 Data Base Management System Software. The core of the data base includes a data dictionary and pieces of software that specify type of access, such as single user, multiuser, or distributed data base capability. The software also sets the means of access, that is, the query is protected by a peripheral piece of security software that screens and limits users.

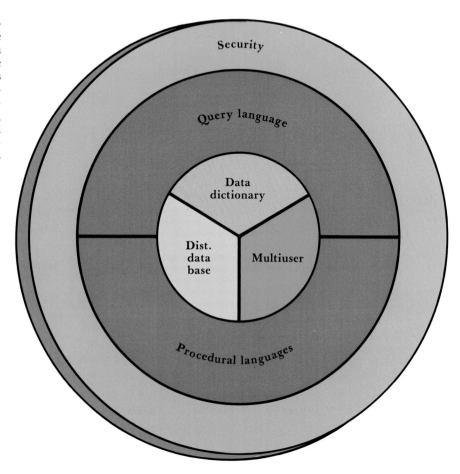

used. Other software may enable unsophisticated users to prepare reports or print out data by entering only a few simple commands from the keyboard.

6. Relational data base management. One of the most flexible means of accessing data bases is through relational files. Relational files allow users to structure different data paths without the necessity of restructuring the files. Special software is necessary to process relational files in place of ordinary list files using pointers.

7. Security facilities. Security programs allow only selected users to access the data base. Some files, records, or fields are restricted to selected users by means of passwords or user numbers. Only qualified users may change the contents of the data base, while all may access it. For instance, a department supervisor may be permitted to change prices from a restricted terminal, using a special password, while line employees can only display prices in the data base.

COMMERCIAL DATA BASE SERVICES

During the past decade millions of pieces of information have been assembled into data bases readily accessible to business, industrial, educational, and domestic users (Table 11-1). This new industry is sometimes referred to as **data base publishing** or **electronic publishing**. It has expanded into a $1.2 billion a year industry which is growing at the rate of nearly 30 percent per year.

The New York Times maintains a data base of over 2 million

TABLE 11-1   Who's On-Line: Commercial Data-Base Vendors (*Source: Forbes*, May 9, 1983, p. 200.)

This table lists the 20 major database vendors, their services, revenues, and numbers of subscribers.

PARENT COMPANY	SERVICE	EST 1982 REVENUES (MILLIONS)	SUB-SCRIBERS 1/1/83	PRINCIPAL INFOR-MATION
Quotron Systems	Fincl Information Svcs	$120	50,000	corporate data
McGraw-Hill	Data Resources	100	3,000	business, economic data
Dun & Bradstreet	DunSprint	75	6,000	corporate credit reports
Reuters	Monitor	65	13,000	general news, commodity data
Mead Corp	LEXIS/NEXIS	62	4,000	legal citations, articles, general news
Dow Jones	Dow Jones News/ Retrieval	50	60,000	general news, corp data
Planning Research	Multiple Listing Service	40	9,000	real estate listings
OCLC, Inc	OCLC	40	5,000	bibliographic data

TABLE 11-1 *Continued*

PARENT COMPANY	SERVICE	EST 1982 REVENUES (MILLIONS)	SUB-SCRIBERS 1/1/83	PRINCIPAL INFOR-MATION
H&R Block	CompuServe Information/Service	40	38,000	general news encyclopedia
Knight-Rider	Commodity News Service	30	8,000	commodity data
Lockheed	Dialog Information Svcs	30	19,000	article index, financial data
I P Sharp	Sharp APL	20	6,000	corporate data
Reader's Digest/ Control Data	The Source	7	27,000	general news, air schedules, retail catalogs
Thyssen	Bibliographic Retrieval Svcs	7	8,000	academic indexes
Natl Library of Medicine	Medlars	4	3,000	medical, biblio-graphic data
Equifax	Financial Control Services	NA	28,000	consumer credit data, vehicle accident reports
Allied Corp	Market Decision Sys 7; Telequote, Teletrade	NA	25,000	stock prices
Burroughs Corp	Sys Dev Corp Search Service	NA	8,000	scientific, technical data
General Electric	Mark III	NA	7,000	financial, sci-entific data
British Telecomm	Prestel World Service	NA	25,000	general news

abstracts of newspaper articles. Dow Jones has a subscriber base of over 60,000 customers, the largest in the industry, who rely upon its general news and corporate data. The Dow Jones corporate profiles include income and balance sheet statements for major industrial companies and extensive reports on their financial operations, officers, directors, and ownership of subsidiaries. LEXIS, offered by Mead Corp., and a competing data base offered by West Publishing Company contain citations on thousands of Supreme Court and appellate decisions. CompuServe Information Service, owned by H & R Block Company, has 38,000 subscribers. Lockheed's Dialogue, Read-

Figure 11-13 Accessing Commercial Data Bases. Access to commercial data bases is gained through common carrier telephone lines. Common carriers are companies that are authorized by the FCC to provide communications services to the public. In addition to the authorized monopolies, such as the telephone companies, there are now specialized common carriers that offer private-line services for voice and data transmission.

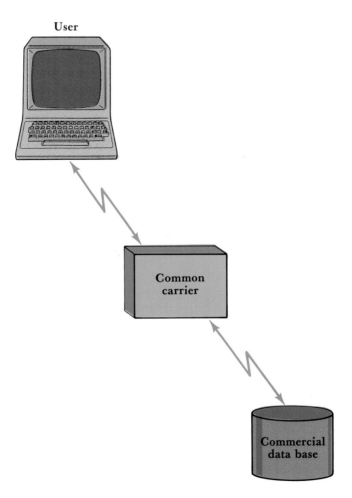

er's Digest's The Source, and Equifax's Financial Control Services collectively contain files ranging from general news and air line schedules to credit reports, medical bibliographies, and stock prices.

ACCESS TO COMMERCIAL DATA BASES

To access a commercial data base, a user must go through a common carrier such as AT&T, GTE, or MCI (Figure 11-13). GTE, for example, offers its Telenet service to users. Telenet is a common carrier that enables users to access the network from hundreds of cities across the country or from over forty foreign countries. Telenet can

Figure 11-14 Menu. After a choice is made, the computer may display a submenu to help narrow down the selection.

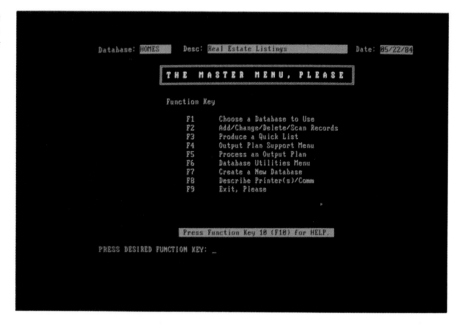

be accessed via terminals having many different speeds, formats, or data codes. Tymshare, Inc., offers its Tymnet service. These firms provide access to commercial data bases, and some even operate data bases of their own.

The cost to the user depends on the communications network's access charge and a data base usage fee based on how long a terminal is connected to the network, the amount of central computer time taken, or the amount of data accessed.

Once the user is connected to the data base, a list of options is presented. This list is called a **menu** (Figure 11-14). The user selects an option from the menu. The computer may then display **submenus**, narrowing down the selection. Through a system of menus and submenus, a user with no programming skills can easily access complex data bases.

COMMERCIAL DATA BASE EXAMPLES

We'll conclude with a description of how two different kinds of data bases are used. The discussion should help you grasp the depth and scope of data base applications.

DIALING A DATA BASE

Source: Forbes, May 9, 1983, p. 204.

Using an on-line database is a relatively simple procedure—if you know exactly what you want and where to find it. Looking up AT&T's five-year sales and earnings history, for example, takes only minutes. The information is on several services, including Lockheed's Dialog, Mead Data Central and The Source. Here's how we got it from Dow Jones:

1. We connect our computer terminal to a telephone and make a local call to a packet switching network, in this case Telenet.

2. Telenet answers and asks what equipment we are using, to provide a clearer signal. We punch in the code "A8," signifying Digital Equipment Corp.'s Decwriter III, a so-called dumb terminal.

3. On flashes the symbol "@," Telenet's way of telling us to name a database vendor. We answer with the "address" for the Dow Jones News/Retrieval service in Princeton, N.J.

4. Telenet tells us we are connected with Dow Jones.

5. We are now communicating with an IBM mainframe computer at Dow Jones that asks which of the company's several services we want. We answer: "DJNS," the product that carries corporate financial data.

6. DJ asks for our paid-subscriber password. Since this also tells the computer whom to bill, the word is blanked out by the computer.

7. DJ's copyright notice appears, and the vendor asks what database we would like to access. We enter "DSCLO," for a specific bank of computers containing SEC reports compiled by Disclosure Inc.

8. After logging on with Disclosure, DJ asks what company we are interested in. "T," we reply, using stock symbol code, and DJ affirms that we want AT&T. DJ's computer is now ready to "read" the proper section of its database disks. (Like a researcher referring to an index, the computer need not search the entire file.)

9. DJ now asks what part of the file we are interested in. It offers 15 choices. We request number six.

10. Instantly the computer reads that section of the database and prints out the information.

11. We disconnect from the database, vendor, Telenet and local phone lines.

Doing all this took two minutes on-line, probably the minimum time for any database request. Our bill came to roughly $8.55. About $4.20 goes to Dow Jones for computer time. Another $4 goes to Disclosure Inc. for the information. Telenet gets 25 cents, and 10 cents goes to New York Telephone for the local call.

The entire contents of Grolier's *Academic American Encyclopedia* have been entered into a computer data base. This electronic encyclopedia consists of 21 volumes, 28,000 articles, and approximately 9

```
 1  TELENET
    212 117N

 2  TERMINAL = AS

 3  OC 609 42

 4  609 42 CONNECTED

 5  WHAT SERVICE PLEASE ????
    DJMS
 6  ENTER PASSWORD
    XXXXXXXXXXXXXX
          DOW JONES NEWS/RETRIEVAL
             COPYRIGHT (C) 1983
          DOW JONES & COMPANY, INC.
             ALL RIGHTS RESERVED.

    ENTER QUERY
       //DSCLO
    DISCLOSURE II
    COPYRIGHT (C) 1983
    DISCLOSURE INC.

 8  TO CONTINUE, ENTER COMPANY STOCK SYMBOL AND PRESS RETURN
          T
    COMPANY NAME:   AMERICAN TELEPHONE & TELEGRAPH CO.

 9  ENTER        FOR
       1          CORPORATE PROFILE
       2          BALANCE SHEETS FOR 2 YEARS
       3          INCOME STATEMENTS FOR 3 YEARS
       4          QTRLY INC STATEMENTS (CUR FY)
       5          LINE OF BUSINESS DATA
       6          5-YR SUMMARY DATA (REVS, INCOME, EPS)
       7          FULL FINANCIAL DATA (2 THRU 6)
       8          OFFICERS AND DIRECTORS
       9          OWNERSHIP AND SUBSIDIARIES
      10          OTHER CORPORATE EVENTS
      11          MANAGEMENT DISCUSSION
      12          CORPORATE RECORDS (1 THRU 10)
      13          FULL CORPORATE RECORD (1 THRU 11)
      14          2-YR LIST OF REPORTS ON FILE WITH THE SEC
      99          HOW TO ORDER FULL TEXT OF SEC REPORTS

          6
10                     FIVE YEAR SUMMARY
                          SALES          NET INCOME    EPS
        1981   59,229,000,000   6,888,000,000   8.55
        1980   51,755,000,000   6,058,000,000   8.17
        1979   46,183,000,000   5,655,000,000   8.01
        1978   41,744,000,000   5,262,000,000   7.73
        1977   37,003,000,000   4,466,000,000   6.84
          DISC
11  LOG ON:   10 13 LOG OFF:   10 15 EASTERN TIME MARCH 17, 1983
    609 42 DISCONNECTED
```

DAY'S PRICE & CHANGE	NAME & CITY OF BANK	DIVI DEND	% YIELD	P-E RATIO	SALES
14 1/4 + 1/4	Affiliated Bankshs; Boulder	1.00	7.02	4.6	1900
3 1/8 − 1/8	Alaska Bancp; Anchorage	0.00	0.00	52.1	3400
22 7/8 + 1/4	Allied Bancshares Inc; Houston	0.92	4.02	7.6	39000
13 ...	Amer Bancorp Inc; Reading	1.00	7.69	5.1	700
29 1/2 + 1/4	AmeriTrust Corp; Cleveland	2.72	9.22	4.7	3600
15 3/4 + 1/4	American Fletcher Corp; Indianapolis	1.32	8.38	4.7	2700
18 1/4 − 1/4	American Secur Corp; Washington	1.30	7.12	5.0	1700
24 1/2 + 1/4	Ancorp Bankshares Inc; Chattanooga	1.32	5.39	11.8	2000
12 ...	Arizona Bk; Phoenix	0.80	6.67	5.3	7400
25 ...	Atlantic Bancorporation; Jacksonville	1.16	4.64	3.5	2200
39 1/2 + 1/4	Banc One Corp; Columbus	1.80	4.56	8.7	12000
12 1/4 + 1/4	BancOhio Corp; Columbus	1.00	8.16	3.6	10400
12 3/4 ...	BancOklahoma Corp; Tulsa	0.70	5.49	3.8	3700
16 1/2 + 1/4	Bancal Tri St Corp; San Francisco	1.20	7.27	7.0	4700

Figure 11-15 Bank Stock Prices. A listing of bank stock prices, updated daily, is an example of the type of statistical information available from commercial data base sources. The user pays a fee for access to the data.

million words. Customers gain access through computers connected to the data base by coaxial cable or telephone wires. The fee for the service is under $1 per minute, with a monthly access charge. Several hundred schools and libraries are among the thousands of subscribers to the service.

The computer allows different levels of coverage to be presented. A rather simple and untechnical discussion of various topics is available for the elementary school student. A more advanced user can direct the computer to print out or display a more complex discussion.

American Banker News Service's Innerline is a data base of information for bankers and financial institutions. When a banker or investor wishes to use Innerline, he or she first accesses a menu. The computer displays the options, including the day's banking news, morning market comments, bank stock prices, and even legislation pending before Congress or lawsuits before the courts. The user selects one of the options and receives a display. Figure 11-15 illustrates a display of bank stock prices, and Figure 11-16 is an example of current opinion and analysis available on the system. Innerline charges users by the minute to access the system and has a small additional report charge. This service allows bankers and financial man-

DEREGULATION COMMITTEE DISCRIMINATES AGAINST SMALL BANKS

By JACK W. WHITTLE
Chairman
Whittle, Raddon, Motley & Hanks
Chicago

Throughout history, whenever a ground swell of demand has arisen for a particular service or product, someone, somewhere, somehow has devised a solution that meets the demand.

During the last four years, the ground swell in the financial services industry has, of course, been the need for an instrument that couples a high rate of return with liquidity. Most financial institutions -- but not all of them -- are prohibited by regulation from fulfilling this current need.

Because there is a nonregulated segment of the financial industry, the lucky institutions in this group are free to design, plan, scheme, and connive with the goal of delivering products which closely meet the public's needs.

ENTER MORE, SELECTION #, INDEX, OR DONE--

Don't get me wrong. The banking industry does have a product-development team. Unfortunately for us, however, these people are highly trained in legalese and the skills of negotiation.

Figure 11-16 Current Opinion and Analysis. Not only statistical information, but also opinions and analyses on a variety of subjects are available to help decision makers.

agers to make important decisions based upon current information readily available through the Innerline data base.

SUMMARY AND KEY TERMS

• A **data base** is a collection of common records structured in a systematic way to serve one or more users. **File processing** involves updating records and returning them to the file. In **data base processing** records are searched electronically and updated by computer.

• In a **distributed data base** arrangement many users share information dispersed geographically throughout the system.

• A **library** is a collection of files. A **file** is made up of **records**. A record is composed of **fields** which are made up of **bytes**.

• A data base is constructed from a collection of libraries.

• The advantages of **data base management systems (DBMS)** are cost savings, elimination of duplication, and access by many users to information that can be controlled and secured.

• A **schema** is a logical plan or structure around which data are organized. It includes a **data model** that defines all **data elements**. Data base structures in use include the **list**, **tree**, **network**, and **relational** structures. These structures use **pointers**, **linkage addresses**, or other means of locating records.

• A **data dictionary** is a comprehensive list of information describing the field size, coding schema, and other details related to files and records.

• Data base software includes programs for **single user**, **multiuser**, and **distributed data base** capabilities. Some provide for access by high-level languages, such as COBOL or FORTRAN, while others use an English-like **query language**.

• Commercial data bases are available via electronic publishing systems. They first display to the user **menus** and **submenus** that describe various services or areas of data from which the user chooses.

EXERCISES

1. Define the term data base.
2. Contrast file-based processing with data base processing.
3. List the major terms used in describing files.
4. Define the term file.
5. List the advantages of data base management systems.
6. Define the term schema.
7. How are pointers used in the list structure?
8. Describe the information contained in a data dictionary.
9. What is the purpose of a query language?
10. Who may access commercial data bases?
11. How are commercial data bases accessed?

12

Learning Objectives

After studying this chapter, you should be able to
1. List the steps in preparing a computer program
2. Summarize the objectives of problem analysis
3. Describe the purpose and function of decision tables
4. Describe the function of pseudocoding and program coding
5. Describe the function of program documentation
6. List several kinds of errors that occur in preparing programs

Chapter Outline

Stored Program
Problem Analysis
   Define the Problem
   Describe Variables in Quantitative Terms
   Reduce Operations to Specific Steps
   Establish Relationships
Algorithm, Flowcharting, and Pseudocoding
Coding
   Coding Forms
Keyboarding
Running and Debugging
   Compilation and Initial Run
   Types of Bugs
   Debugging Procedures
Documentation

Program Planning
and Development

People and computers differ in the way they go about solving a problem. Generally, people try to solve problems in an "all-at-once" fashion. They don't spell out all the procedures before actually beginning to execute them, and they usually carry out the first steps before structuring the last. Their plan for solving a problem becomes intermixed with and responsive to the results. This feedback-response activity allows humans to solve problems creatively.

The resources of the computer can be used for problem solving only after the method for solving the problem has been reduced to a series of individual steps and instructions stated in a language the computer understands. The computer must be told where to find the required information, what calculations to perform, and what form the answer should be given in. It cannot change its approach or evaluate its progress.

In this chapter we will look at the basic steps in preparing a computer program designed to solve a given problem.

STORED PROGRAM

Before preparing a program, a computer programmer studies a problem or procedure and sets up a plan of action. The programmer decides what steps the machine must take to reach the results and specifies the forms of input and output. Then this plan of action is converted into a set of instructions, coded in a programming language, that are input to the computer. The set of instructions is called a **stored program**, a **source program**, a **problem program**, or simply a **program**.

The computer has a degree of self-direction in that it can follow the instructions of the stored program without further human intervention or direction. But it can *only* follow the steps in the program. At the present time the computer cannot examine its own output, decide if something is wrong, or change the procedure it is following if something is wrong.

This limitation has advantages and disadvantages. If the pro-

Figure 12-1 Symbolic Names. A symbolic name is a name that stands for a quantity. In a program, the programmer can refer to the symbolic name rather than the address where the quantity is stored.

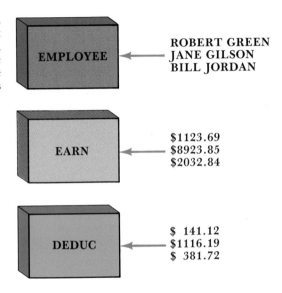

grammer has made an error in procedural logic, the output may be incorrect, sometimes without the programmer realizing it. On the other hand, once a program is known to be logically sound and accurate, the procedural steps and level of accuracy will not vary from one run of the program to another.

The stored program has another major advantage. A program can be written and tested before the data to be processed are available. The programmer assigns **symbolic names** to the quantities manipulated in the program (Figure 12-1). For example, instructions could tell the computer, first, that the values keyboarded from a terminal, referred to as EARN, are the amounts an employee has earned and, second, that the employee's deductions, called DEDUC, can be found on a magnetic disk storage device. The computer can then be instructed to subtract the value at location DEDUC from the value at location EARN and print out the contents of location PAY on the check form in the line printer. This use of symbolic names gives the computer a great deal of power and flexibility.

Figure 12-2 lists the steps involved in writing a computer program. Generally, the evolution from problem to program includes:

1. Problem analysis
2. Algorithm, flowcharting, and pseudocoding

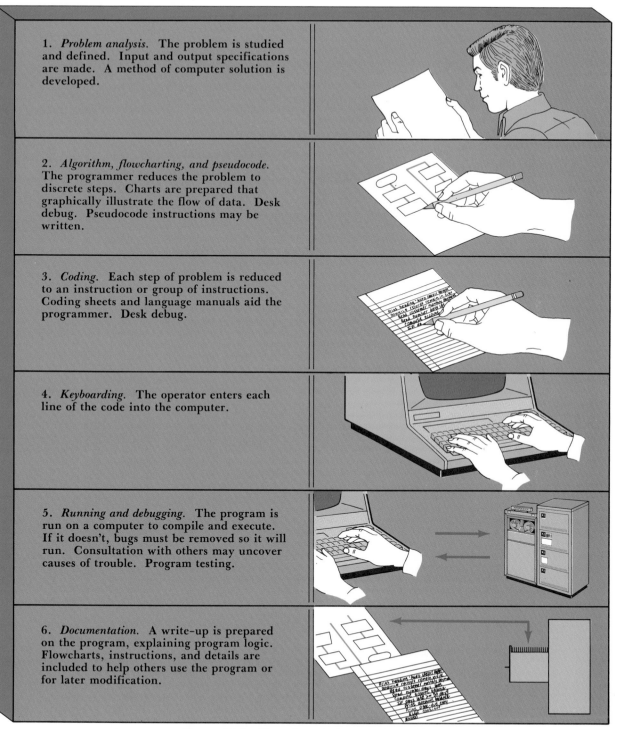

1. *Problem analysis.* The problem is studied and defined. Input and output specifications are made. A method of computer solution is developed.

2. *Algorithm, flowcharting, and pseudocode.* The programmer reduces the problem to discrete steps. Charts are prepared that graphically illustrate the flow of data. Desk debug. Pseudocode instructions may be written.

3. *Coding.* Each step of problem is reduced to an instruction or group of instructions. Coding sheets and language manuals aid the programmer. Desk debug.

4. *Keyboarding.* The operator enters each line of the code into the computer.

5. *Running and debugging.* The program is run on a computer to compile and execute. If it doesn't, bugs must be removed so it will run. Consultation with others may uncover causes of trouble. Program testing.

6. *Documentation.* A write-up is prepared on the program, explaining program logic. Flowcharts, instructions, and details are included to help others use the program or for later modification.

Figure   12-2   Major Steps in Program Preparation.

Figure 12-3 Problem Analysis. Problem analysis involves definition of the desired output, analysis of available information, and assessment of the best way to manipulate the available information to achieve the desired output.

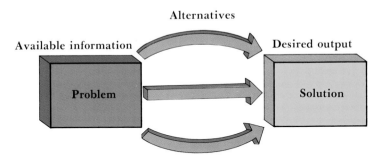

3. Coding
4. Keyboarding
5. Running and debugging
6. Documentation

These steps may vary from one computer installation to another or with the needs of different firms. Some installations allow the program to be entered on a terminal while others still require keypunching. Some organizations require extensive documentation; others may not. In all cases all steps must be considered.

PROBLEM ANALYSIS

The problem to be solved by the computer must first be analyzed carefully and defined in terms of desired results. The programmer must determine what data are needed, what form they are to be in, what information is to be output, and how the data are to be manipulated to produce this output (Figure 12-3).

Problem analysis begins with considering whether it makes sense to use the computer at all. Cost, error, and time factors must be weighed. It does not always pay to use the computer, especially if the problem is a simple one that will not be repeated. If computer solution seems economically practical, then the programmer proceeds.

The programmer generally follows a series of steps: Define the problem, describe variables in quantitative terms, reduce operations to specific steps, and establish relationships (Figure 12-4).

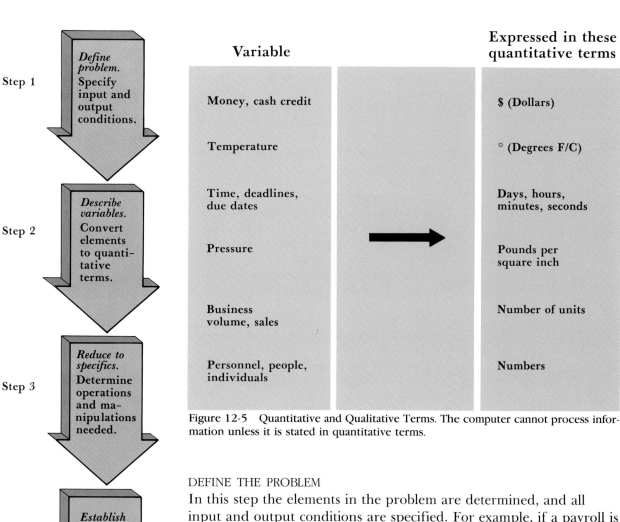

	Variable		Expressed in these quantitative terms
Step 1	**Define problem.** Specify input and output conditions.	Money, cash credit	$ (Dollars)
		Temperature	° (Degrees F/C)
Step 2	**Describe variables.** Convert elements to quantitative terms.	Time, deadlines, due dates	Days, hours, minutes, seconds
		Pressure	Pounds per square inch
Step 3	**Reduce to specifics.** Determine operations and manipulations needed.	Business volume, sales	Number of units
		Personnel, people, individuals	Numbers
Step 4	**Establish relationships.** Select actions to be taken.		

Figure 12-5 Quantitative and Qualitative Terms. The computer cannot process information unless it is stated in quantitative terms.

Figure 12-4 Steps in Problem Analysis.

DEFINE THE PROBLEM

In this step the elements in the problem are determined, and all input and output conditions are specified. For example, if a payroll is being computed, one decision that must be made is what specific items are to be deducted from the employee's paycheck, such as contributions to retirement fund, state or federal taxes, credit union, and so forth.

DESCRIBE VARIABLES IN QUANTITATIVE TERMS

Next, the programmer converts all elements to be processed into quantitative terms (Figure 12-5). An element stated in **qualitative**

PIONEERING PEOPLE: GRACE MURRAY HOPPER

Source: Reprinted with permission of *DATAMATION*® magazine, © Copyright by Technical Publishing Company, a Dun & Bradstreet Company, 1982—all rights reserved.

Call her Captain Hopper. Call her, as she has called herself, slightly ancient. Call her the discoverer of the first computer bug (a real moth). Call her one of the pioneers. Call her anything you want, but take a minute to remember that if you're using a computer in business, she's made your job immeasurably easier. Capt. Grace Murray Hopper is the progenitor of COBOL.

"Nobody believed it could be done," she remembers of her first efforts to get backing for a business compiler that would be largely system independent. "It was all so obvious. Why start from scratch with every single program you write? Develop one that would do a lot of the basic work over and over again for you."

And that's how COBOL got started.

Grace Hopper got started in 1906. She's hoping to be around to celebrate New Year's Eve on Dec. 31, 1999. "I have two reasons," she says. "The first is that the party will be one to end all New Year's Eve parties. The second is that I'll want to point back to the early days of the computer and say to all the doubters. "See, we told you the computer could do that."

Grace Hopper is a grand old gal, a Navy career officer as tough as any captain ever was. The military runs in her blood: her antecedents include a minuteman and a Civil War captain and admiral. Getting from binacles to binaries is her own doing.

Hopper has been in the computer business since 1943, when the Navy sent her to Harvard to work with the Mark I. In 1946, she joined the Harvard faculty and worked on the Navy's Mark II and Mark III. It was the Mark II that bears the distinction of containing the first computer bug. It was the summer of 1945, as Captain Hopper tells it, and the Mark II was still under construction. Something was inexplicably wrong with the monster machine. A little poking around inside the hulk's innards revealed a moth, which had somehow gotten stuck in the circuitry.

In 1949, Hopper went with the Eckert-Mauchly Computer Corp., which was building UNIVAC I. She stayed there through its merger into Remington and then into Sperry. She didn't retire from the company until December 1971. "I seem to do an awful lot of retiring," she says today, "but I don't think I will ever be able to really retire."

Hopper has published more than 50 papers, stood watch on the first (and many subsequent) meetings of Codasyl, and served on the ANSI X3.4 committee. The list goes on.

Some of what she's seen keeps Hopper hopping, and it sometimes makes her hopping mad. "It's costing this country $450 million a year because we're not using a standard high-level computer language," she has complained. At another time, she told the industry she has tried to lead through stormy seas, "I'm going to shoot somebody for opposing change because 'we've always done it the old way' someday. In the computer industry, with changes coming as fast as they do—and they're coming all the time—you just can't afford to have people saying that."

But most of the time, Capt. Grace Murray Hopper isn't really mad at all. She just likes to make people think. Her famous counterclockwise clock—it runs backwards—symbolizes her attitude. When people first see it, they're confused. After a moment, they realize it does indeed tell the time, just in a different way. Its message, and Hopper's, is that there is more than one way to solve a problem.

terms, is described by qualities or characteristics. An element stated in **quantitative terms** is described by numbers and is rather precise. For example, qualitative terms such as "poor credit," "Christmas bonus," "good employee," and "best accounts" must be stated in terms of measurable quantities, such as "delinquent more than 45 days," "$50," "absent less than five times," and "purchases over $10,000." The expected outcomes are expressed in terms of these quantitative variables.

REDUCE OPERATIONS TO SPECIFIC STEPS
In this phase the programmer determines how the data are to be manipulated to produce the desired output. These operations are expressed as specific, discrete steps, such as read, write, add, compare, move. At the same time the programmer determines the order in which the steps are to be taken. For example, in preparing a payroll, the number of hours worked by each employee, pay rate, and number of exemptions must be input before income tax calculations can be made.

ESTABLISH RELATIONSHIPS
In this phase relationships are established among all the elements. The programmer determines what action the computer is to take if certain conditions exist. For example, when customers make payments or add purchases to their accounts, the program must go to the appropriate routine to record the transactions as either debits or credits.

DECISION TABLES   There are several ways that programmers establish relationships. Some use decision tables. The student may wish to skip or only lightly review the discussion on decision tables, if the instructor does not emphasize this method of delineating relationships. (The discussion is included for those who wish to become familiar with decision tables.)

If there are many possible alternatives and relationships in a problem, the programmer may organize them by setting up a decision table. A **decision table** is a tabular representation of the alternatives and branches in a program (Figure 12-6). It displays in a table format all possible conditions and the actions to be taken in each case. The programmer refers to the decision table when writing instructions in programming language to be assured that all possible conditions and actions are accounted for.

Decision tables for computer programs are based on the IF-THEN relationship. For example, IF a customer orders more than 1,000 units of an item, THEN a "restock inventory" message must be sent to the stockroom. IF an employee works more than 40 hours, THEN overtime must be added to the paycheck. Each entry is translated into coded instructions in the program.

A decision table is divided into four parts (Figure 12-6a). The **condition stub** (upper left) lists all possible conditions that may be encountered. Possible conditions are stated quantitatively. Symbols such as = (the same as), < (less than), > (more than), and <= (less than or the same as) are used to express relationships. The **condition entry** portion (upper right) shows the various combinations of conditions that may be present. Condition entries are usually Y (yes) to indicate that the condition exists or is true or N (no) to indicate the negative condition. These Ys and Ns are arrived at by analyzing the various conditions that must be dealt with. Obviously, the more complex the problem, the greater the number of variables to be considered.

The **action stub** (lower left) lists all possible actions to be carried out in the program. The **action entry** portion (lower right) indicates the actions to be taken for a given set of conditions. Action entries are usually Xs.

Each vertical column (containing Ys, Ns, and Xs) is called a **rule** or alternative. Each rule represents a given set of conditions (IF) and the actions that must be taken for that set (THEN). It is the programmer, or other person familiar with the problem to be solved,

Figure 12-6 (a) Parts of a Decision Table. (b) Decision Table for Holiday Bonus Program. Rule 1 reads: If an employee has a low absence rate, a high volume of production, and a low rejection rate, then he or she will receive a $200 bonus check, a certificate for a $30 turkey, and a holiday greeting letter. On the other hand, rule 2 reads: If an employee has a low absence rate, a high volume of productivity, but a high rejection rate, he or she will receive only a $100 bonus and a holiday greeting letter.

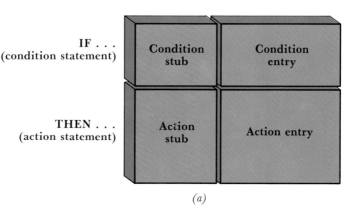

IF . . .
(condition statement)

THEN . . .
(action statement)

(a)

	Rule 1	Rule 2	Rule 3	Rule 4	Rule 5	Rule 6	Rule 7	Rule 8
IF . . .								
Low absence rate	Y	Y	Y	Y	N	N	N	N
High volume of production	Y	Y	N	N	Y	Y	N	N
Low rejection rate	Y	N	Y	N	Y	N	Y	N
THEN . . .								
$200 bonus check	X							
$100 bonus check		X	X		X			
Certificate for $30 turkey	X			X		X	X	
Greeting letter	X	X	X	X		X	X	
Notice to improve				X	X	X	X	
Notice of termination								X

(b)

Figure 12-7 Algorithms. An algorithm is a series of finite steps that will solve a problem. Problem: It is 10 a.m. and you decide to enjoy an afternoon at the beach. How do you get there? There are several possible algorithms that will solve the problem, each involving a series of actions and a series of prerequisites, such as availability of a car, money for carfare, or time required for the trip. Each series can be planned, step by step, and the most practical or desirable can be chosen.

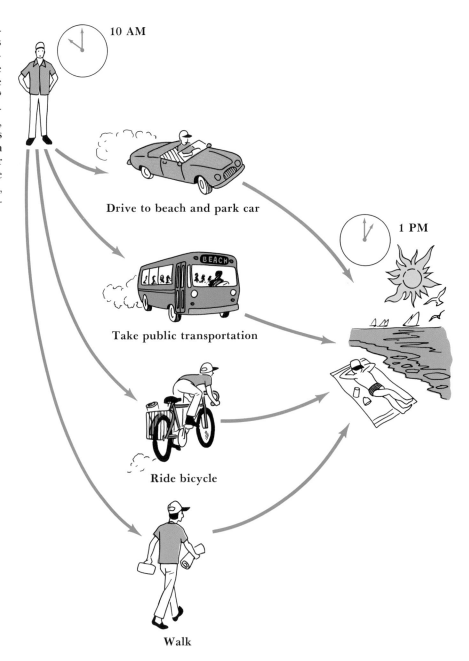

10 AM

Drive to beach and park car

1 PM

Take public transportation

Ride bicycle

Walk

that sets out the number of rules and distributes the Ys and Ns according to the needs of the organization. To use a decision table, the programmer locates the rule for a given set of conditions and programs the computer to carry out the action entries indicated by that rule.

Figure 12-6b is a decision table for a program to prepare a holiday bonus mailing to employees. Bonus checks, holiday greetings, certificates for turkeys, and letters from management or the personnel department are to be mailed to each employee, depending on certain conditions. These conditions are employee absenteeism, level of production, and rejection rate.

ALGORITHM, FLOWCHARTING, AND PSEUDOCODING

After all elements and relationships in the problem have been analyzed and defined in quantitative terms, they must be expressed as steps that the computer can perform. This sequence of steps, a strategy for solving the problem, is called an **algorithm**. The programmer usually designs several alternative algorithms and selects the one most suited to the particular problem and system (Figure 12-7).

One way the programmer illustrates the sequence of steps in an algorithm is with a **flowchart**, a graphic representation of the sequence of operations a computer is to perform (Figure 12-8). Flowcharting allows the programmer to detect errors in an algorithm (desk debug) and facilitates coding, which is the next step to be performed. (Problem solving logic and flowcharting techniques are discussed in more detail in the next chapter.)

Many programmers prefer to write instructions in pseudocode before actually writing the code. **Pseudocode** is a version of the instructions describing each step the computer must follow. It is written in an abbreviated form of spoken language and lies somewhere between commands written in ordinary English and those in a computer language. Pseudocode helps the programmer work out programming details and logic without the constraints and rigor of a formal language (Figure 12-9).

Figure 12-8 Program Flowchart. A program flowchart illustrates each step in the algoritm showing what is to be done in sequence.

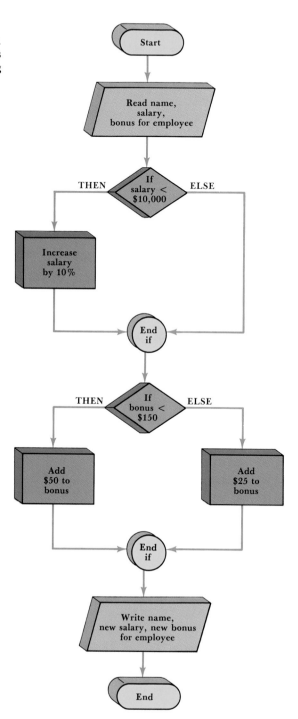

Figure 12-9 Pseudocode. Pseudo-code instructions are similar to ordinary English. They are useful in the preliminary stages while a programmer is planning a program. In the final version, the programmer must translate the pseudocode into a specific formal computer language.

```
Print heading "AGED CREDIT REPORT"
DOWHILE records remain in file
    Read customer's monthly payment
    Read number days late
    Compute account balance
    IF days late >= 30 days
        Print account balance
        Print past-due entry
    ELSE continue
ENDDO
```

CODING

After a solution has been designed, it must be converted into a set of instructions understandable to the computer. **Coding** is the process of converting the steps in the algorithm to a set of commands written in a programming language.

We cannot simply give a computer an instruction like "Please figure out wages paid and cash received from last month's books. Add them together and give them to the controller." In the future computers may be able to accept instructions given in casual English, but at present programming instructions must follow a precise format. The instructions must direct the computer through each step in the algorithm and define each calculation in detail. They must give

```
10 REM GRADE AVERAGING PROGRAM
20 DIM N$(10)
30 PRINT "PLEASE ENTER 3 SCORES FOR EACH NAME"
40 LET C=0
50 FOR I=1 TO 10
60 LET T=0
70 READ N$
80 PRINT
90 PRINT N$
100 INPUT S1,S2,S3
110 LET T=S1+S2+S3
120 LET C=C+T
130 IF T>170 THEN 160
140 PRINT "TOTAL SCORE IS: ";T
150 GOTO 170
160 PRINT "*** TOTAL SCORE IS: ";T;" ***"
170 NEXT I
180 PRINT
190 PRINT
200 PRINT "THE AVERAGE TOTAL SCORE IS: ";C/10
210 DATA "N. BARTON","P. DENNIS","V. DIAZ","L. GREEN","K. LIU"
220 DATA "J. MCCADE","S. SILVA","R. SMITH","A. THOMAS","T. WHITE"
230 END
```

Figure 12-10 BASIC Listing. Actual programming commands must be written in a specific style and must conform to the rules of spelling, structure, and punctuation for a specific language, in this instance BASIC.

the computer such information as the size and type of numbers to be read in and out, their location on the records, and the exact form and layout of the output.

The programmer writes the commands in COBOL, BASIC, or any other programming language. The instructions must conform precisely to the rules of spelling, structure, syntax, and punctuation for a particular language. (You probably remember from your English course that syntax refers to the rules for sentence structure and grammar.) Figure 12-10 is an example of a program coded in BASIC.

CODING FORMS

Programming statements are sometimes coded on a standard printed form ruled off in columns and rows. Each coding form is designed to conform to the conventions of a specific programming language. Each column on the form corresponds to one character; each row corresponds to an individual instruction. Figure 12-11 shows several forms now in use. All the forms serve the same function: they provide uniform pages on which to write computer instructions. These instructions are essentially a preliminary draft of what will eventually be keyboarded into the computer.

Coding forms are usually used with languages that have fixed formats such as COBOL, in which certain information must appear in specific columns. Forms can be particularly helpful when the input media are punched cards. They are not generally used with free-form languages such as BASIC.

KEYBOARDING

In **keyboarding** the coded instructions in the program are converted to a code readable by the computer. Keyboarding is done either online or offline, depending on the type of language used and the design of the system (Figure 12-12). For example, a program written in COBOL is usually best handled offline due to its length.

In **online processing** programs are input directly to the computer for immediate processing. As each instruction is keyboarded on a terminal, it is relayed directly to the computer. In some systems the computer will immediately indicate if an error is present in the instruction and wait for the programmer to make corrections. After all instruction lines have been entered, they are listed on the terminal and checked for accuracy by the operator. Additions or changes are made at this time, using various editing techniques.

In **offline processing** the instructions are prepared for later entry and processing by the computer. This method is sometimes called **batch programming**. Instructions are keypunched into punched cards or keyed onto magnetic tape or disk. Each line in the program is converted into one punched card or is recorded on tape or disk. Or there may be direct input via a computer terminal into a file stored in primary memory, which is manipulated or edited and then run later.

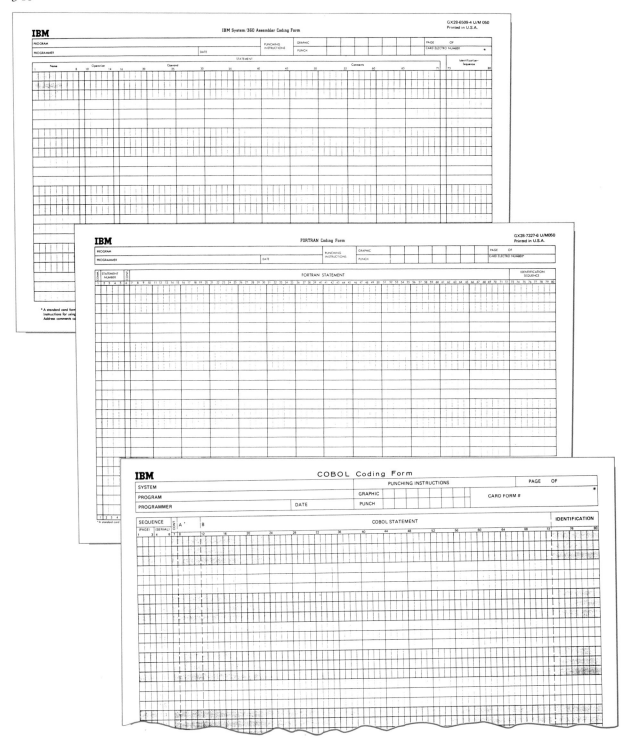

Figure 12-11 Coding Forms. Coding forms are needed when programming in a language that requires certain commands or items of data to appear in specific columns. They may be helpful in other languages without such requirements to aid in producing neat, readable programs.

Figure 12-12   Online and Offline Processing. In online processing (*above*), key strokes are transmitted directly to the computer and the program is entered line by line. In offline processing, instructions are stored on magnetic tape or disk and entered into the computer in a batch.

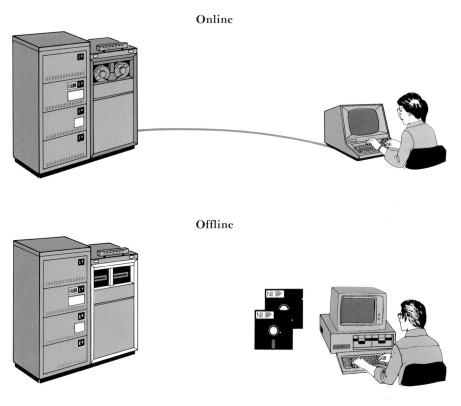

Online

Offline

RUNNING AND DEBUGGING

After the instructions in a program have been converted into machine-readable form and input to the computer, the execution of the program is tested.

COMPILATION AND INITIAL RUN

Instructions must be translated into machine language before they can be executed. The translation is done either by a compiler or an interpreter program (Figure 12-13).

A **compiler** is a special program for each programming language that is loaded into the computer when that language is used. It translates each line of code into machine instructions that the com-

Figure 12-13 Compilers and Interpreters. A program in a high-level language such as BASIC can be compiled or interpreted. If it is compiled, the list of program statements is known as source code. The compiler translates source code into a block of machine executable code known as object code. The computer then uses only the object code when the program is executed. When a program is interpreted, the list of program statements is entered one line at a time, and the interpreter translates lines into machine executable code as it executes the program.

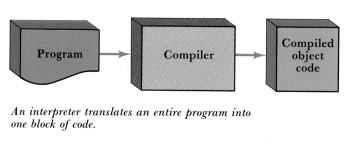

An interpreter translates an entire program into one block of code.

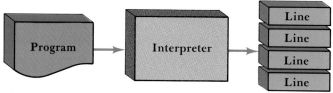

An interpreter translates and executes an entire program into object code one line at a time.

puter can carry out. An entire block of translated code is called an **object program**. It is executed in a block after the compilation is complete. During compilation the computer checks each instruction to see that it follows the rules of the computer language and uses the proper punctuation, spelling, and syntax. Only correctly written instructions are compiled.

An **interpreter** program performs a similar task, but translates and executes programs line by line rather than by generating an object program. As with the compiler, the computer must be equipped with the appropriate interpreter in order to execute programs written in a given language. An interpreter, like a compiler, checks the accuracy of spelling and syntax and executes only statements conforming to the rules of the language.

When a computer discovers errors in a program, it communicates this information to the operator by printing out or displaying a **diagnostic message**. These messages usually appear on a CRT, line printer, or other output device along with a listing of the program instructions.

With an interpreter, the diagnostic messages are listed on the output device, either as each line is entered or at the end of the listing. One disadvantage of using a compiler is that errors and incorrect statements are not detected until the entire program has been

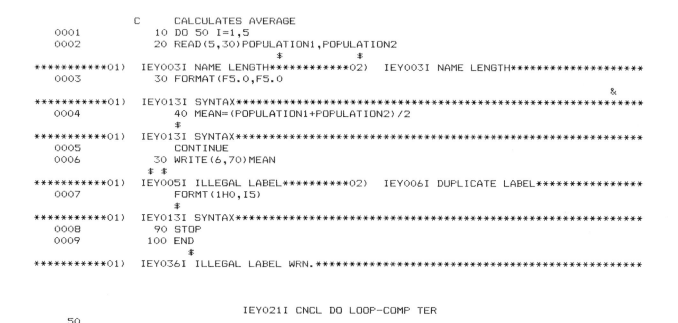

```
                  C      CALCULATES AVERAGE
     0001              10 DO 50 I=1,5
     0002              20 READ(5,30)POPULATION1,POPULATION2
                               $             $
***********01)   IEYOO3I NAME LENGTH************02)   IEYOO3I NAME LENGTH*****************
     0003              30 FORMAT(F5.0,F5.0
                                                                              &
***********01)   IEYO13I SYNTAX********************************************************
     0004              40 MEAN=(POPULATION1+POPULATION2)/2
                               $
***********01)   IEYO13I SYNTAX********************************************************
     0005                 CONTINUE
     0006              30 WRITE(6,70)MEAN
                       $ $
***********01)   IEYOO5I ILLEGAL LABEL**********02)   IEYOO6I DUPLICATE LABEL***************
     0007                 FORMT(1HO,I5)
                               $
***********01)   IEYO13I SYNTAX********************************************************
     0008              90 STOP
     0009             100 END
                               $
***********01)   IEYO36I ILLEGAL LABEL WRN.*********************************************


                        IEYO21I CNCL DO LOOP-COMP TER
     50


                        IEYO22I          UNDEFINED LABEL
     50                  70                        100
```

Figure 12-14 Diagnostic Messages. This figure shows how the computer prints out diagnostic messages. Each message has a reference number and descriptive term. Dollar signs points to places where the compiler has detected errors.

keyboarded and submitted to the computer for running.

Figure 12-14 contains some typical error messages. The errors were noted by the computer as the program was entered. As each instruction was read, the computer checked to see that it conformed to the language rules. Those that did not conform were flagged.

An error-free compiled program will have no diagnostic messages to print out. Once instructions have been corrected, translated, and stored, the program can be executed.

Most source programs manipulate a collection of data. For example, a program that prepares a company's payroll operates on the file of employees' payroll records. This file is the **data set**. When running the job, the data set is entered in the computer after the source program has been compiled. The combination of a source program and one or more data sets is called a **job** in a batch processing system.

Once compiled, a source program can be run on many consec-

Figure 12-15   Program Bugs.

Correct	Incorrect
PRINT	**PRNT**
PRINT	**OUTPUT**
READ A,B	**READ, AB**

Errors occur when the computer receives erroneous data, misspelled words, or instructions containing errors in punctuation or syntax.

utive data sets. This is an important advantage of the computer. Once written, the program can be saved and used as many times as required. For each run the program is copied into the computer, followed by a data set.

TYPES OF BUGS

If, as often happens, the initial run of a program is unsuccessful, that is, it does not compile or execute as planned, it is said to **blow up**, **crash**, or **bomb** or simply that it doesn't run. Few programs with more than a dozen instructions compile and execute the first time through. The fault lies not with the computer, but with bugs in the program. **Bugs** are logical or clerical errors that prevent the computer from properly compiling or interpreting the program. The programmer must change the program to correct errors in logic and coding in a process called **debugging**.

There are many types of programming bugs (Figure 12-15). If errors are present, the program will not run, or it may run but give inaccurate results. Some of the most troublesome errors are generated by programs that compile or translate properly, but give incorrect results.

Compilation errors are discovered by the compiler or interpreter and include spelling errors, syntax errors, improperly sequenced statements, improperly labeled statements, conflict in variable names, illegal names or statements, invalid statements, and missing punctuation.

Some **logical errors** are discovered by the computer during the execution of the program. Among them are numbers too large

Figure 12-16   Logical Errors.

Correct	Incorrect
READ A	READ A
READ B	ADD A TO B GIVING C
ADD A TO B GIVING C	READ B
PRINT C	PRINT C

or

PRINT C
ADD A TO B GIVING C
READ A
READ B

or

READ A
READ D
ADD A TO B GIVING C
PRINT C

> *Logical errors occur when the computer is directed to carry out an illogical task such as adding two numbers together when they have not been entered properly into the machine.*

for a storage area, incorrectly placed input statements, and miskeyed characters in the data set (Figure 12-16). Other logical errors must be detected by the programmer.

DEBUGGING PROCEDURES

Debugging requires patience and insight. It can be the most frustrating part of programming. One small clerical or logical error can mean many hours at the computer running the program, checking the results, keyboarding changes, and rerunning the program until the error is found.

A programmer looks for and corrects errors in keyboarding, coding, syntax, and so on. If all these errors are corrected and the job still does not run, the programmer considers logical errors. For example, a program may direct the computer to read in two numbers, sum them, and display the answer. But wrong instructions may

FORTY DAYS AND FORTY NIGHTS

When Michael Wise sits down at a keyboard, he never knows when he will get up. The plump, bearded computer programmer often works twelve, 24, even 36 hours without a break, filling a green screen at the San Rafael, Calif., offices of Broderbund Software with words and numbers that only he and his computer completely understand. Since December, Wise has written 40,000 lines of instructions for a video game he calls Captain Goodnight, after the old *Captain Midnight* radio series. By the time the program is ready for release this summer, it will have grown to 50,000 lines and swallowed up some 900 hours of programming time, or nearly 40 days and 40 nights.

The lines of code Wise types into his Apple IIe may look like a meaningless string of letters and numbers, but they are the crucial link between computers and the people who use them. At the heart of every machine are thousands of on-off switches. Wise's 64K Apple has 524,288. Software tells the switches when to turn on and off, and those switches control the machine.

Wise's first task in writing his program was to create the objects displayed on the screen. These are actually just patterns of colored dots, with each dot controlled by an individual on-off switch. Wise sketched the images on an electronic drawing tablet that translated his lines into patterns of ones and zeros, where one represents a dot of color and zero a blank space. The image of Captain Goodnight's airplane is stored in the computer as a list of 798 zeros and ones that look like this: 11111100 0000000110000000 . . .

After the objects were drawn, Wise began creating a series of small, self contained miniprograms called subroutines. One subroutine, for example, moves the captain's jet. Another controls the enemy planes. A third fires a missile. In all, the finished program will have 400 different subroutines. Wise writes it one subroutine at a time, making sure that each new one works before continuing. A typical section of coding reads:

```
EMIS-HIT?   LDA JETY
            SBC EMISY
            CMP #10
            BGE EMISEXIT
PLAYR-HIT?  LDA #01
            STA JETCOND
```

Those commands tell the computer to determine the jet's altitude (JETY) and subtract the altitude of the enemy missile (EMISY). If the result is ten or more, the two objects have missed each other. If it is less than ten, the program puts a one in a special switch called JETCOND that sends the jet into a flaming crash.

As the pieces of the program fall together, their interrelationship becomes maddeningly complex. Even one letter misplaced in 10,000 lines of code is enough to throw the whole program out of kilter. At one stage in the game's development, the computer had the captain walking in mid-air because one subroutine was inadvertently modifying another subroutine's instructions. "I almost went blind trying to find that bug," Wise recalls.

Wise has been dabbling in software since the age of 14, when he learned FORTRAN on an IBM at Stewart Junior High School in Tacoma, Wash. He dissected nearly every radio and television set in the house and then skipped college to take a series of odd jobs on the periphery of the computer world. He repaired video arcade games. Xerox machines and personal computers, and at one time ran the ComputerLand store in Renton, Wash. In 1979, convinced that there were fortunes to be made, he bought an Apple II Plus and began churning out video games, working as a building manager by day and programming at night.

Wise still does his best work at night. Every evening after dinner he picks up where he left off at work. "My wife is a computer widow," he confesses. During the past month, he has been working until dawn with increasing regularity. "When I'm done, we're taking a vacation," says the 29-year-old programmer. "I'm almost getting too old for this."

actually direct it to read in two numbers, print out the sum, and then add the two numbers together. A repeated sequence of actions may begin the cycle at the wrong statement, or an error in logic may cause the computer to skip an important step.

A programmer tries to find and eliminate such bugs by carefully checking the listing of the set of computer instructions and by reexamining the program logic. The programmer traces a piece of test data through the program manually, checking the results of the computer run at each step. The program may be modified to have the computer print out the intermediate results after performing each operation.

When all errors are corrected and the job executes properly, it is considered a running program ready for documenting.

DOCUMENTATION

Completing documentation is the last step in implementing a program. Final documentation consists of explanatory material—flowcharts, instructions to the computer operator, sample test data, and other information relating to the details of a program—filed as a permanent record.

Documentation explains the program algorithm. It is a record of logic, details, and input and output specifications—all easily forgotten items. Programmers find documentation of older programs useful when writing new programs. Well-documented programs are a source of notes, routines, algorithms, and other pertinent information. Documentation is essential if programs are to be modified later. It is much easier to retrace logic and follow through calculations with the help of documentation. Also, there is less chance of creating a logical error if the logic is clearly outlined on paper.

It is good practice to prepare documentation as each programming step takes place. This avoids the need to retrace steps after a program is running so as to get the documentation in order.

There are no standard rules about what must be placed in a documentation file, although many companies have strict documentation policies. The file should be complete enough to allow the programmer to make changes and modifications in the program easily. Here are some typical items that are often placed in the file.

1. **Abstract.** A one- or two-paragraph summary of the purpose of a program and its major features and options, the abstract may include an overall view of the algorithm and general procedures followed. The sample abstract in Figure 12-17 includes sufficient information to explain the basic program without unnecessary detail.

2. **Descriptive narrative.** The narrative defines the problem and explains the algorithm, methodology, and logic followed in the program. All mathematical calculations and formulas are shown. Any options are listed, such as whether a short or long report will be generated or whether decimal numbers will be rounded off, with an explanation of how they are called out or used.

3. **Graphic narrative.** Graphic and visual devices, such as program flowcharts, system flowcharts, and block diagrams, illustrate a program and its relationship to the system. (These are explained in detail in the next chapter.)

4. **Program listing.** An accurate program listing serves as the master record against which copies and revisions of the program are checked.

5. **Description of input and output records.** The file should contain a complete set of specimen input and output records. Any alphabetic

Figure 12-17 Abstract. A program abstract provides a brief description of an available program. More information can be obtained by reviewing the program's documentation file.

```
Program Name:   Medical Record Screening Program
                _____

Program Author:  Susan Tyler
                _____

Inquiries Handled By:    Susan Tyler, Med. Rec. Div.,
                _____
  Eastern Hospital, X 233
_____


DESCRIPTION:

     This program performs a data screening and
sort routine on medical records.  The program
screens data for selected characteristics.
Common data input to the program include
patient's name, medical record number,
descriptive physical information, number of
days lost, type of injury, and class of
coverage.

     Program outputs a group of reports
categorized by type of injury, number of
days lost, and occupational class.  A summary
report is also prepared, giving descriptive
data on the selected population, by age,
height, weight, and other parameters.


SOFTWARE SYSTEM:

     This program operates under a disk
operating system, with interactive terminal
support.


MINIMUM HARDWARE CONFIGURATION:

     CPU with 128K of memory, including 2
disk drives, line printer, and CRT.


LANGUAGE:   BASIC
```

or numeric codes used to group data should be described and explained. If several data records, such as master and detail records, are used, they should all be shown and described in detail.

Specifications for output records should be shown and described. Sometimes a preprinted form, such as a printer spacing chart, is used for this purpose. The fields for each piece of data on the records should be indicated. If output is to be printed, a sample should be included, along with a note about the size of the form and type of paper on which it is to be printed.

6. Test data. Test data sets are valuable testing and debugging aids. They should include data that forces the computer to execute all branches and possibilities in the program. Carefully checked printouts should be included as known standards for checking future runs.

In this chapter we have surveyed the major steps in developing a program. In the next chapter you will learn more about one especially important aspect of program planning and development—flowcharting.

SUMMARY AND KEY TERMS

• A computer **programmer** studies a problem and lays out a sequence of steps leading to its solution.

• In **problem analysis** the problem is defined in terms of end results, variables are reduced to quantitative terms, manipulations are reduced to specific steps, and relationships between conditions and actions are established.

• **Decision tables** list all possible conditions and define what actions are to be taken in each case.

• An **algorithm** is the sequence of steps or strategy to solve a problem. The logic in a program may be illustrated in a **flowchart**, which is a graphic device using standard symbols.

• **Pseudocode** is a set of English-like instructions used as a step preliminary to actually writing the code.

• **Coding** is the process of converting steps in an algorithm into a set of instructions in a programming language.

• In **keyboarding** the instructions in the program are converted into machine-readable form. Keyboarding may be done online or offline.

• A **compiler** translates a program into an entire block of machine instructions, while an **interpreter** translates a program line by line into executable instructions.

• When an error is encountered in a program, the computer prints out **diagnostic messages**. **Compilation** and **logical errors** sometimes occur. A job containing errors, or **bugs**, is said to **blow up**, crash, or bomb, or not run. **Debugging** is removing errors in spelling, syntax, and logic.

• **Documentation** is descriptive material on a program. A documentation file may include an **abstract**, **descriptive narrative**, **graphic narrative**, **description of input and output records**, **program listing**, **test data**, and other information related to the program.

EXERCISES

1. List and describe the six major steps in implementing a computer program.

2. Define coding. What is its purpose and how is it done?

3. List three instructions that are too general to be coded. List three commands that are specific enough to be coded.

4. Select a simple business problem, such as calculating interest or figuring a bank balance. Break the problem down into a series of discrete steps.

5. Obtain several coding forms for different languages. How do they differ?

6. What is the purpose of running and debugging a program?

7. List three types of compilation errors.

8. How do compilation errors differ from logical errors?

9. What are diagnostic messages? How are they indicated by various computers?

10. How do programmers debug a program?

11. What is the function of documentation?

12. List some items normally found in a documentation file.

13

Learning Objectives

After studying this chapter, you should be able to
1. List the major kinds of flowcharts
2. Contrast the functions of system and program flowcharts
3. List and draw the major flowchart symbols in use
4. Describe some common structured programming algorithms
5. Draw simple program flowcharts
6. Use flowcharts in program planning

Chapter Outline

Function of Design Diagrams
Types and Functions
   System Flowchart
   Program Flowchart
   Block Diagram
   Detail Diagram
   Structured Design
Standard Flowchart Symbols
Algorithms
Structured Programming
   Sequence Structure
   Selection Structure
   Loop (Iteration) Structure
Some Design and Logic Examples

Program Design
and Logic

Once a problem has been defined and reduced to quantitative terms, the initial steps of program planning are completed. The programmer must then work out the logic and design and algorithm to solve the problem. One of the most efficient ways to do this is to start by preparing a program flowchart or design diagram. A flowchart is a graphic representation of the program logic and an essential part of the planning process.

This chapter explains the standard technique for preparing the most common design diagram, the flowchart, and the universal symbols used in drawing it. The chapter also illustrates fundamental logic that may be adapted to a variety of programs.

FUNCTION OF DESIGN DIAGRAMS

Flowcharts or other diagrams of the program design are always prepared *before* a program is coded, not after. A flowchart is like a road map. Most people who drive across the country use a road map to find the correct route. Getting a map after the trip is over wouldn't help them find their way. The road map guides the driver, helps avoid wrong turns, and saves time by eliminating trial and error. In much the same way, professional programmers make flowcharts to help them work out correct program logic and plan the most efficient way to solve a problem.

A flowchart is a diagram, prepared by the programmer, of the sequence of steps involved in solving a problem. It can provide either an overview or a detailed picture of the program. It is like a blueprint, showing the general plan and essential details of the proposed structure.

A flowchart diagrams the strategy and thread of logic followed in a program. It allows the programmer to compare different approaches and alternatives on paper, and it often reveals interrelationships that would otherwise not be immediately apparent. Figure 13-1 is a flowchart of a washing machine's cycles showing the sequence and relationship of steps the machine follows in performing its task. A series of data processing steps may be diagrammed in a similar way.

Figure 13-1   A Sample Flowchart: Washing Machine Cycles. This chart shows both the sequence of events and relationships of cycles as a washing machine performs its functions.

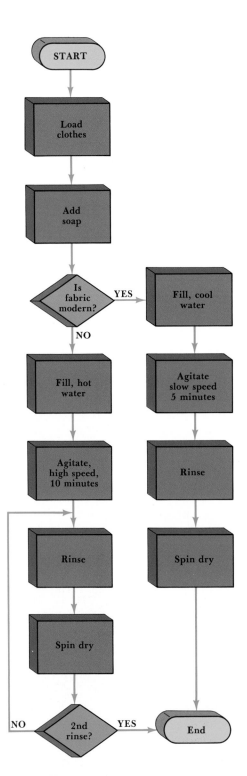

The flowchart is an essential tool for the programmer. By forcing him or her to lay out the logic in clear terms and to state essential details, it helps the programmer to avoid fuzzy thinking and accidentally omitting steps. The flowchart is also a tool to help the programmer, the program user, the systems analyst, and the computer operator communicate with one another.

TYPES AND FUNCTIONS

Flowcharts are divided into two basic types: the system flowchart and the program flowchart. Either of these may be drawn in the form of a block diagram or a detail diagram, discussed later.

SYSTEM FLOWCHART

The **system flowchart** presents an overview of all aspects of a data processing system. It covers human activities and documents as well as computer operation. It shows the data flow between various departments and work stations. It describes data inputs, the stages through which they will be processed, and their outputs.

Figure 13-2 shows the channels of data flow and processing in a merchandising system. It includes activities such as generation of source documents, order entry, and computerized sorting and processing. Some of the steps are performed by a human operator.

PROGRAM FLOWCHART

A **program flowchart** is used to prepare a computer program. It shows the sequence of steps the computer will follow in executing a program. Figure 13-3 is a flowchart for a program that calculates a salary and prints out a paycheck and voucher.

A program flowchart differs from a system flowchart in that it shows input and output operations and the computational steps performed by the computer only. The system flowchart includes steps that may be performed by people, such as answering a telephone or physically checking an item in inventory. Both system and program flowcharts can be further categorized as block diagrams, or detail flowcharts.

Figure 13-2 Program Flowchart. This flowchart shows the major steps followed in calculating a salary and printing out a paycheck and voucher.

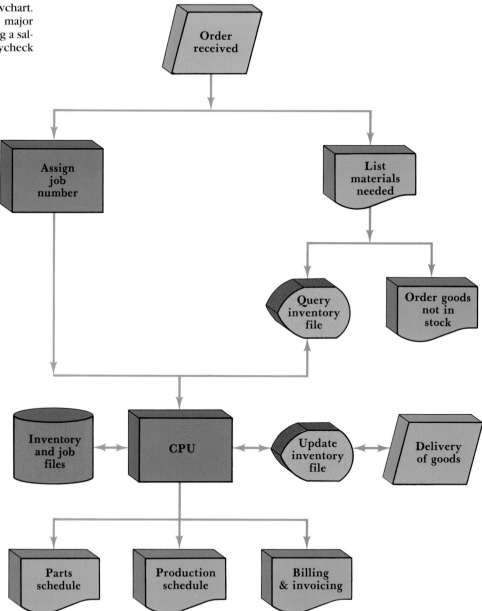

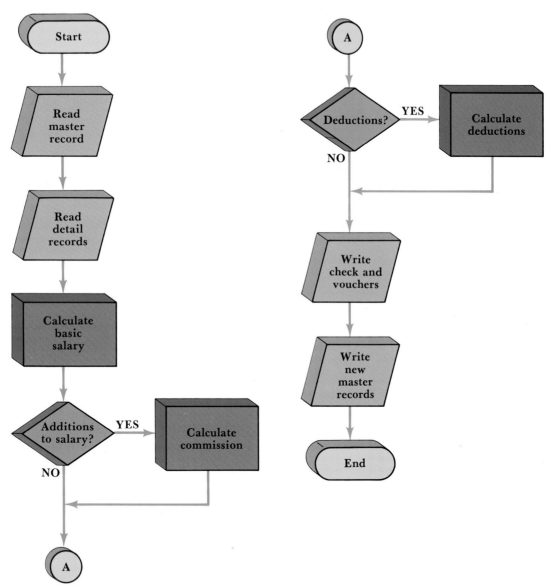

Figure 13-3 Block Diagram Flow-chart. This type of flowchart, also called a macroflowchart, shows only the major steps or blocks in a process. It provides an overview that may be supported by other more detailed charts.

BLOCK DIAGRAM

A **block diagram**, sometimes called a **macroflowchart**, shows only the gross phases of the solution; it does not include details. Each block in the flowchart represents a major step in the process. It provides the programmer with a broad picture of the strategy and flow of data in a particular program. In a system flowchart it shows the major activities or operations to be carried out at each work station. In a program flowchart it summarizes operations. For example, the program flowchart in Figure 13-3 shows "Calculate basic salary" in one block. This one operation may involve dozens of steps that will be diagrammed in a separate detail program flowchart.

More refined and detailed flowcharts are prepared from the block diagram for use in writing a program or laying out a business system.

DETAIL DIAGRAM

A **detail diagram**, sometimes called a **microflowchart**, outlines each step, calculation, test, and comparison involved in solving a problem. It provides a microscopic view of each element in the system.

The detail program flowchart expands the elements in the block diagram into programmable steps and is used as a guide for writing the program. Such a flowchart helps the programmer be sure that all steps are included, that branches refer to the correct points in the program, and so on. In Figure 13-4 the programmer has drawn in each decision point, branch, and calculation.

STRUCTURED DESIGN

Good programming practice suggests that programs be **structured**, or **modular**, that is, that each major step in the program be developed as an independent **module** and represented as a separate block on a flowchart. (Each of these blocks can be expanded into as many programming steps as needed.) In programming terms this means avoiding the use of GOTO statements. GOTO statements tend to make programs confusing and the logic hard to follow.

Each module is concerned only with its own task. It does not communicate with any other module. These modules are sometimes called **subroutines**. A control program ties all the individual modules

Figure 13-4 Detail Program Flow-chart. A detail diagram, or micro-flowchart, may contain dozens of precise steps showing each calculation and decision in the program.

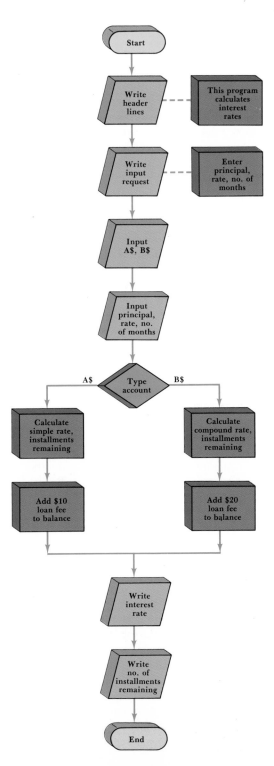

WILL DESIGNERS GOTO STRUCTURED PROGRAMMING?

Source: Electronic Design, July 19, 1980, p. 72.

In recent years, every promoter of a new language has emphasized that the newcomer offers structured programming and top-down (or, sometimes, bottom-up) design and will stamp out the evils of "spaghetti code" once and for all. Lost in the clamor is the distinction between languages and programming techniques.

While some languages (like Pascal) do encourage certain techniques (like structured programming), bad code can be written in any language, with or without GOTO statements. On the other hand, structured programs can be written even in assembly.

What are these modern programming techniques? *Top-down design* is nothing more than good software engineering: An overall task is broken down first into its major, and then into its lesser components.

Often, top-down design is combined with *structured programming*. Its zigzag arrangement of statements indicates program layers—for instance, nesting levels. "Bills of materials" have used the concept of indentation for decades to show which parts form which subassembly. Indentations can be used in any language that permits free-form coding. Like GOTO statements, indentation can be overdone, turning programs into messy eyesores, and defeating its very purpose—improving readability.

The proponents of *bottom-up design* also have a valid case. A purist top-down truck designer might find—too late—that there's no space left for the engine. Bottom-up design starts with the building blocks of a software system, which are often tied into specific hardware features like interrupts or dedicated processors.

The favorite buzzword for the bottom-up school is *modular programming*, but there's little agreement on such basics as optimum module size. A bottom-up modular program often consists of a large number of functions and subroutines, tied together by a skeleton main program. But such a program, consisting of nothing but procedure and subroutine calls, can become meaningless—and inefficient to boot.

What does all this mean to program selection? In *applications programs*, the concept of reusable modules is largely academic. If any modules can be lifted from previous programs, that's a nice bonus—but in the diversified environment in which most design engineers work, it happens rarely. So a language supporting the top-down, structured approach is usually best.

For *operating systems*, however, module commonality is much more feasible and will continue to gain importance as systems get more complex. Multi-tasking, parallel processing and the intricacies of realtime operation in general all make the argument for "building block" operating systems even more persuasive. Here, bottom-up design has many advantages.

Does that mean structured programming is useless for systems programmers? Not at all, but he will use it in the sense of tactics rather than strategy. For software systems, modular design is emerging as the strategy of the future, because its potential benefits are immense. So, in picking a systems language, ask not whether it suppresses GOTO statements, but whether it supports modularity.

MAIN MODULE

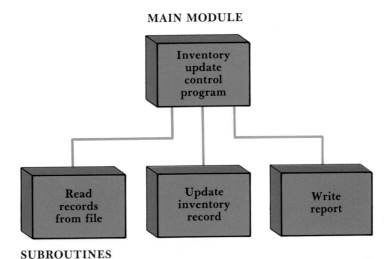

SUBROUTINES

Figure 13-5   Structured or Modular Diagram. The main module calls in subroutines in sequence. First a record will be read, then it will be updated, and finally a report will be prepared.

or subroutines together, calls each one in as needed, and controls the transfer of data between it and the individual modules.

This concept of individualized modules adds flexibility and portability to programs. The individual modules can be called from other programs by the control modules to perform their tasks on other files and in other programs.

The structure chart shown in Figure 13-5, consists of a main module and three subroutines, and shows the relationship of the modules in the program. This particular program updates an inventory control file. The **main module**, or **core** of the program, calls in each subroutine in sequence. The first subroutine reads records from a file, the second updates an inventory record, and the last writes out a report. Since each subroutine is a module independent of the others, it can be called back in by the main module as frequently as needed. In such a structured approach, entry and exit to subroutines are always through the main module.

The subroutines may themselves call in other subroutines. In all instances entries and exits to the sublevel routines are made systematically through the next higher level module. This arrangement leads to a more standardized and logical approach to programming.

Figure 13-6 Flowcharting Template. This template conforms to the ANSI X3.5 standard. Each symbol represents a specific task. There are symbols to represent manual operations as well as computer tasks.

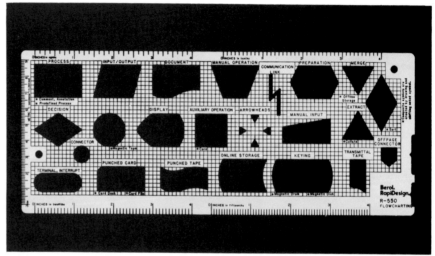

STANDARD FLOWCHART SYMBOLS

Each operation the computer performs is indicated by a different shape, called a **flowchart symbol**. Both the symbol and the words written within it explain what activity is being performed. About two dozen standard symbols cover the most common flowcharting situations (Figure 13-6). These symbols have been adopted by the American National Standards Institute (ANSI).

A flowchart may be drawn informally in longhand, lettered in pen or pencil, or typed on a sheet of paper. It can be drawn either horizontally or vertically and may take from one to several dozen pages. Most programmers prepare working flowcharts with a **template** (a pattern for the outline of the symbols), pencil, and scratch paper. Permanent flowcharts are usually drawn in ink, although a computer can be used to print them. Straight lines, called **flow lines**, connect the symbols on a flowchart. Arrows along the flow lines show the direction of program flow, which should be from top to bottom and left to right. A brief description of the step is written within the symbol.

Figure 13-7 shows a few symbols and how they are used. The most common symbols are shown on the next pages.

1. Terminal. The terminal symbol is an oval; the words START, STOP, HALT, or EXIT are usually written in it. START in the first

Figure 13-7 Symbols in Use. This figure illustrates how symbols are used. Descriptive information is written within the box to explain what operation is being performed in the step.

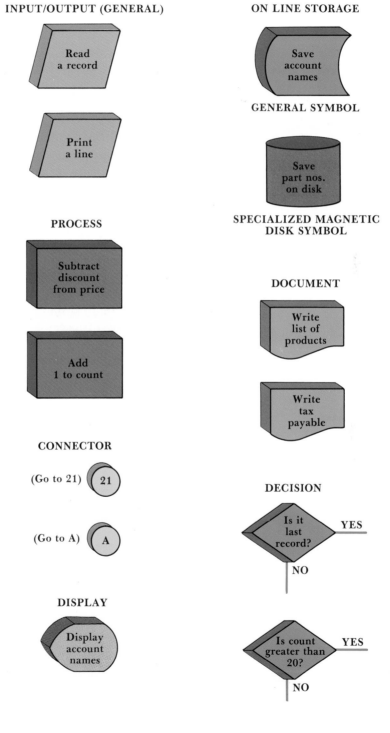

INPUT/OUTPUT (GENERAL)

Read a record

Print a line

PROCESS

Subtract discount from price

Add 1 to count

CONNECTOR

(Go to 21)   21

(Go to A)   A

DISPLAY

Display account names

ON LINE STORAGE

Save account names

GENERAL SYMBOL

Save part nos. on disk

SPECIALIZED MAGNETIC DISK SYMBOL

DOCUMENT

Write list of products

Write tax payable

DECISION

Is it last record?   YES

NO

Is count greater than 20?   YES

NO

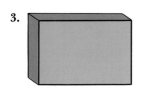

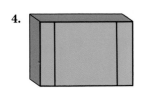

2.

3.

4.

5.

6.

7.

8.

symbol on a flowchart marks the beginning of the program sequence. STOP or EXIT in the last symbol of the flowchart marks the end of the logic train. The oval also appears at points where branches terminate or where the program is to stop due to an error condition.

2. Input/output (general). A parallelogram indicates the input or output of data during a program. It is a general form, used for all input/output media, such as punched cards, line printers, or CRTs. A few words in the symbol describe the input or output action and the data involved.

3. Process. The process symbol, a rectangle, indicates an operation to be performed by the CPU. It may be a mathematical operation such as add, subtract, compute, or find the square root. The specific action is written in.

4. Predefined process. The predefined process symbol is a rectangle with a second vertical line drawn at each side. It indicates that an entire module or predefined process is to be executed elsewhere. Once these steps have been executed, control always branches back to the predefined process box in the main flowchart. This symbol is particularly helpful in preparing structured flowcharts.

5. Connector. The connector symbol, a small circle, ties parts of a flowchart together. It allows the programmer to draw portions of a chart elsewhere on the page or on a separate page. Keys such as GOTO 19 or GOTO READ RECORD help the reader follow the continuity of the program. The connector symbol is handy when charts have many branches or run onto many pages.

6. Decision. A diamond indicates a branch or decision point. A few words within the symbol briefly describe the decision to be made. Labeled arrows lead from the decision symbol to the action the computer should take for each possible answer. For example, FIELD = 999? may appear within the symbol, and labels such as YES and NO may identify possible paths.

7. Magnetic tape. A circle with a horizontal line at the bottom is a specialized input/output symbol representing data being read from or written on magnetic tape.

8. Document. The document symbol, which looks like a torn sheet of paper, is a specialized form of the general input/out symbol that indicates that hard copy is being read or generated. The document symbol refers only to paper documents, not to microfiche or microfilm.

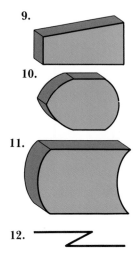

It is used where data are to be read from or output on a document such as an invoice, check, or order form.

9. Manual input. This polygon is a specialized input symbol. It represents manual input from a keyboard such as is attached to a CRT terminal or a console.

10. Display. This symbol, resembling a cathode ray tube, represents a specialized input/output operation. It shows that data will be entered from or displayed on a CRT terminal.

11. Online storage. This symbol, resembling a drum cylinder, is another generalized input/output symbol. It represents data stored on any online storage device.

12. Communications link. This jagged symbol, which looks like a bolt of lightning, indicates that data will be transmitted from one location to another via communications circuits.

ALGORITHMS

A strategy for solving a problem must be established before coding can be done. This is accomplished by working out an algorithm. An **algorithm**, as you may recall, is a list of specific steps, or a set of rules, leading to the solution of a problem.

A problem can often be solved by more than one strategy or algorithm. Suppose billing statements must be prepared and mailed to a group of customers at the end of a month. What would be the best way to do this? One way would be to process the monthly statements as a group in separate steps. First, debits and credits would be posted to all the accounts. Next, all the statements would be typed. Then all the envelopes would be prepared. Finally, the statements would be folded and inserted into the envelopes (Figure 13-8, left).

Another way would be to prepare each statement separately. The debits and credits would be posted to an account. The statement and envelope would be typed. The statement would be folded and inserted, ready for mailing. Then the statement for the next account would be prepared, and so on. (Figure 13-8, right). The strategies are different, but the end results should be the same.

To use the computer to best advantage, factors that bear on the problem, such as the amount of computer storage available, the

Figure 13-8 Algorithm for Preparing Statements. The logic on the left groups all operations together. The logic on the right completes a sequence and then goes back and repeats a sequence for the next statement.

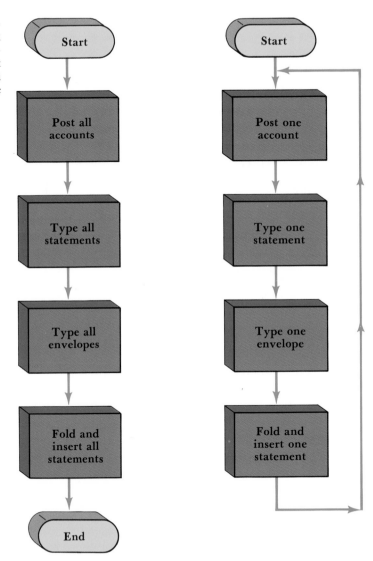

number of steps in the instructions, and access time, must be examined. The choice of algorithm is affected by factors such as available personnel and equipment, time considerations, and office layout. The algorithm that best suits all conditions is preferred.

STRUCTURED PROGRAMMING

In recent years some programmers have grown to rely heavily on structured programming techniques for planning complex programs. **Structured programming** is based on the assumption that any problem can be solved with the repeated use of three basic logic patterns or structures in a series or combined in different ways. In structured programming each step of the algorithm is designed as a self-contained group of statements in the form of one of these structures with clearly defined start and end points. Branching either into or out of the middle of a group is avoided.

The groups of statements appear on the flowchart in the order in which they are to be processed. They are executed sequentially, from the top down. Thus, there is a logical sequence beginning with the first line of a program and moving down to the last. There is no skipping about, backtracking, or executing statements out of order. The computer enters the first group at its start point, moves down through its statements, and leaves the group via the end point. Control then drops down to the start point of the next group, which the computer processes. This procedure continues until the end of the program is reached.

The advantage of a modular structured approach is that it avoids complicated, intertwined programming logic that is difficult to debug, revise, or modify.

The three basic logic structures used are the sequence structure, the selection structure, and the loop (iteration) structure (Figure 13-9). Let's look at each of these control structures and see how they apply in practical programming.

SEQUENCE STRUCTURE

The simplest structured programming algorithm is called **sequence structure**. The computer moves through a set of statements from beginning to end. The statements are executed one at a time in order, and the computer stops after completing the last statement. When several such sequences are placed in tandem, the computer executes each in turn.

Figure 13-10 illustrates a sequence structure algorithm that

Figure 13-9 Control Structures. Three basic logic structures are used as building blocks upon which to construct more complicated programming logic.

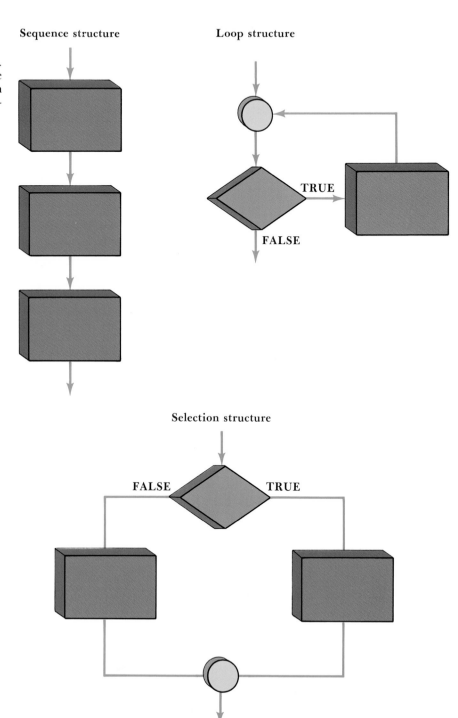

Figure 13-10 Sequence Structure Algorithm. This figure illustrates a sequence structure that computes shipping charges. First the table at the right is read in, and then the shipping weight is computed for one package.

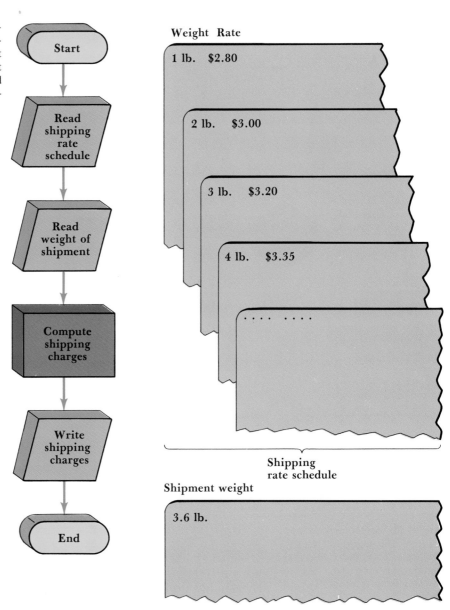

computes shipping charges. The program involves only one pass through the computations. First, a shipping rate schedule is read in and stored by the computer. Next, it reads the weight of the shipment from the shipment weight record and computes the shipping

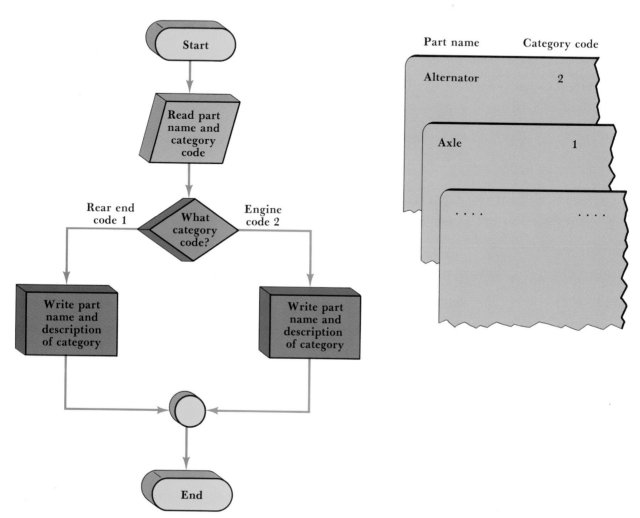

Figure 13-11 Selection Structure Algorithm. This algorithm uses a selection structure that causes the computer to branch to one of two paths after reading a record.

charges. Finally, it writes out the shipping charges. The computer moves through the sequence from START to END only once. The program has no branches or loops and is executed the same way each time it is run.

SELECTION STRUCTURE

A second structured programming algorithm is the **selection structure**. In this arrangement the computer reads in information and then branches to one of two different tracks or branches, depending on a test condition. Each branch has one entry point and one exit point.

In Figure 13-11 the computer reads a part name and category code. Depending upon the category code of the part, it will select one of two paths to follow. Each path directs the computer to write out the part name and description of the category to which it belongs. This algorithm is similar to the sequence structure in that the program reads a record, directs the computer to perform an action only once, and then directs the computer to terminate execution. The difference is the presence of a decision point. The computer must decide which branch will be taken. In this case the selection of the particular branch depends upon the category code read.

In actually writing a program to perform a selection structure, an IF-THEN-ELSE statement is used. The logic is simple. IF a particular condition exists, THEN the computer will perform an action (will follow one branch), ELSE it will not (will follow the other branch).

LOOP (ITERATION) STRUCTURE

This algorithm is based upon repeating a series of steps over and over. The computer executes the steps and loops back to a given point while a given condition is true. The sequence is repeated until the condition is no longer true and a given test condition directs it to stop. Figure 13-12 is an example of a program that directs the computer through a loop. It compares advertising expenses to total sales and computes the advertising percentage. The program reads in total sales, advertising expenses, and a trailer record with a field called LAST. A **trailer record** marks the physical end of the input file. The final record in the file has a 999 recorded in the LAST field; 999 is the signal to the computer that all records to be processed have been read in.

As the program is written, the computer reads a record and tests it for LAST. If the record is not LAST, the computer processes the record, reads another record, and then loops back. When 999 is read in, the computer directs control to end.

This logic is actually implemented with what is called a DOWHILE statement. The computer will always test a condition first

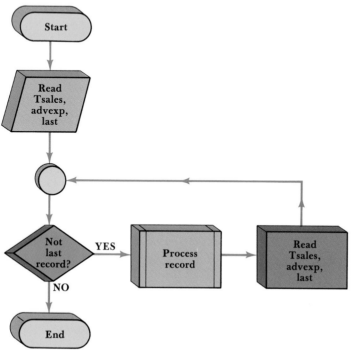

Figure 13-12   Loop Structure Algorithm. This algorithm is based on the loop structure, which causes a series of steps to be repeated until the last record is reached.

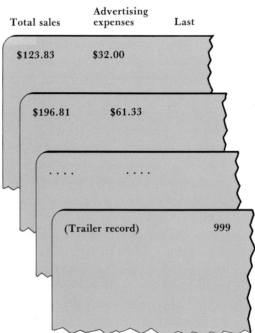

and will DO an operation over and over WHILE a particular condition exists. When the condition is no longer met, the computer will stop executing the loop.

SOME DESIGN AND LOGIC EXAMPLES

The programmer frequently combines the elementary programming logic steps illustrated in the previous section into larger working units. Some typical business data processing problems and their flowcharts will be described in the remainder of this chapter.

FRANCHISE REPORT   Figure 13-13 illustrates a typical programming situation in which individual records are processed and a summary report is prepared on reaching the last record in the file. The program uses a loop structure to print out a series of operating reports for a number of franchisees and a report for the franchisor.

The computer reads a record containing the franchisee's name, sales, and expenses. The computer determines whether the last record has been reached. If it has not, the computer processes a record by calculating gross profit and prepares a report summarizing these data for that franchisee. The computer then reads a record from another franchisee, performs the calculations, and prepares another report. The computer continues to perform the process record routine until the last record in the file is reached, at which point the computer branches to a management routine. The management routine prepares summary data for the franchisor in which operating expenses and gross profits for all units are calculated. Then a franchisor report is printed out.

PAYROLL PROGRAM   Figure 13-14 illustrates a program for calculating net pay and preparing paychecks for a group of employees. The program contains a loop structure and a selection structure. The program reads in a payroll record including hours worked, pay rate, employee name, deductions, and other data. The computer determines whether the last record in the file has been reached. Since the first record is present, the computer branches to a predefined routine called process record. This routine has a selection structure that determines whether the employee's pay code is hourly or salary. It then

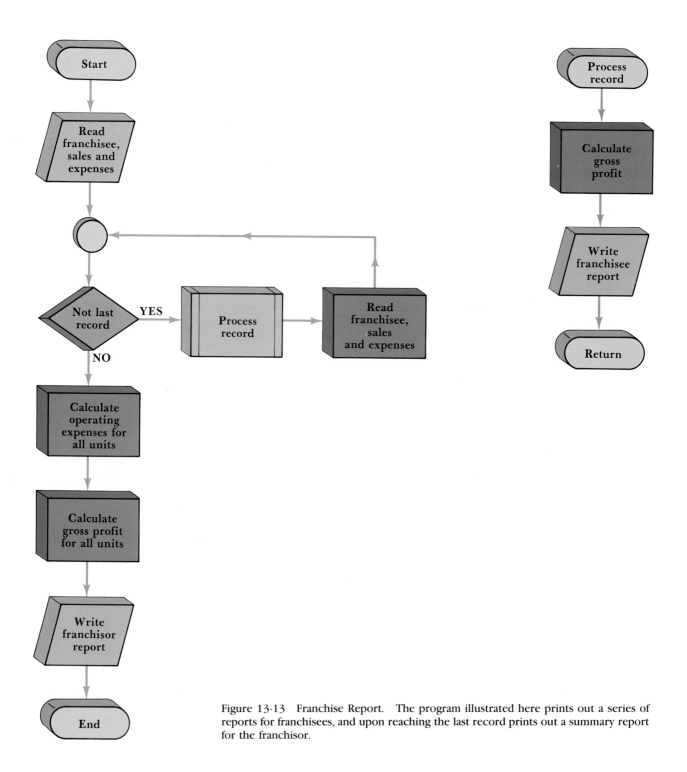

Figure 13-13   Franchise Report.   The program illustrated here prints out a series of reports for franchisees, and upon reaching the last record prints out a summary report for the franchisor.

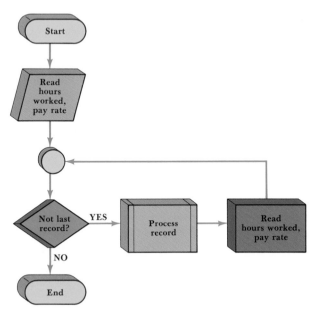

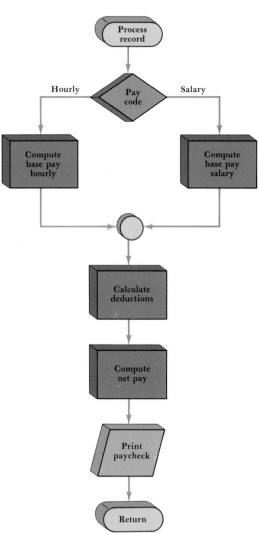

Figure 13-14   Program to Calculate Net Pay and Prepare Checks. The program illustrated here prepares paychecks for a group of employees. It contains both loop and selection structure logic.

computes the base pay accordingly. Next the program calculates the deductions and computes the net pay. Finally, it prints out a paycheck and then reads another payroll record. This process continues until the last record in the file is reached, whereupon the computer terminates execution.

FUZZY LOGIC FOR COMPUTERS

Source: Copyright © 1984 by The New York Times Company. Reprinted by permission.

When Hans Berliner first developed his backgammon-playing computer program, it had a problem. The computer played a strong game most of the time. But every so often it would make a move that was so atrocious it would blow the game.

The Carnegie-Mellon University computer scientist solved the problem in what might seem like a paradoxical fashion. He made the rules governing the computer's strategy less precise. Instead of specific instructions, he gave the computer more general guidelines. The computer went on to beat the world champion.

Computers are known for their cold precision and logic. But, as in the case of the backgammon program, some scientists are now trying to make the computers behave less precisely and logically. These scientists say that if computers are to take on more of the tasks that people do, if they are ever to have "common sense," they must think in a more approximate or "fuzzy" way, as people do.

"Fuzziness is an essential part of human thinking," said Lotfi A. Zadeh, a professor of computer science at the University of California at Berkeley. "It's not something that can be treated with benign neglect."

Professor Zadeh is a pioneer in developing what is known as fuzzy logic. For 20 years fuzzy logic has been an obscure branch of mathematics with a funny name. Now it is bursting into commercial use.

Fuzzy logic, its proponents contend, allows a computer to handle approximate concepts, like "usually," or "slightly," or "tall," or "expensive." People often find such "fuzzy quantifiers" far more useful than precise numbers. A person helping another person park a car, for instance, usually does not say to turn the wheel 10 degrees to the left. He says turn it slightly to the left, or a little more to the left.

The advantage of such fuzzy thinking is that sometimes it is impossible to be precise. In his original backgammon program, Mr. Berliner tried to draw a specific boundary line between when the computer should pursue one strategy, like blocking its opponent's moves, and another strategy, like abandoning the blockade to bring its pieces home. But that was like trying to draw a boundary between day and night. Sometimes the computer would doggedly stick to its blockade too long.

With fuzzy logic, the program was able to shift strategies gradually. As the game got closer to the end and the computer closer to winning, it became less interested in maintaining the blockade and more interested in moving its remaining pieces off the board. . . .

With fuzzy logic, computers can take over the functions using rules like "If the temperature is high and the pressure is normal, increase the intake of air slightly." The computer would have several rules like this and would value them differently. The higher the temperature, the more weight this rule would be given in determining the action the computer takes. F. L. Smidth & Company of Denmark sells a fuzzy logic controller for cement kilns. . . .

Fuzzy logicians think the next applications will be in so-called expert systems, which are programs that mimic the behavior of human experts in such tasks as diagnosing diseases or equipment failures.

But most developers of expert systems remain cool to the concept. They agree that it is important to give computers the ability to deal with uncertainty and with approximations, and to reason qualitatively as well as quantitatively. But they say that fuzzy mathematics is just one possible approach, and probably not the best. The disagreements between the fuzzy logicians and the traditional artificial intelligence community have sometimes become emotional.

"People in the fuzzy logic tradition strike me as being like a religious movement," said John McDermott, an expert systems designer at Carnegie-Mellon. "I don't think its usefulness has been clearly demonstrated." . . .

Structured programming has become so popular because the concept offers several advantages. It is much easier to follow the logic flow from the flowchart. Logic errors are minimized because data flow is from the top down, with a minimum of branching. Because program flow is so clearly defined, programs can be revised more easily, with less chance of error. The flowchart modules are relatively standardized and can be easily transferred to other programs.

SUMMARY AND KEY TERMS

- A **flowchart** is a diagram prepared by the programmer that shows the sequence of steps in solving a problem. **System flowcharts** describe the flow of data through all parts of a data processing system, while **program flowcharts** show the sequence of steps followed in executing a program.

- **Block diagrams**, sometimes called **macroflowcharts**, show major steps without detail. **Detail flowcharts**, sometimes called **microflowcharts**, show each step or calculation in the process.

- **Structured flowcharts** show each major block as an independent module. Structured flowcharting adds flexibility and simplicity to programs.

- Flowcharts are drawn using a **template** showing **standard flowchart symbols**. The most commonly used symbols are terminal, input/ output, process, predefined process, connector, decision, magnetic tape, document, manual input, display, online storage, and communications link. The symbols are connected on the chart with **flow lines.**

• An **algorithm** is a list of specific steps leading to the solution of a problem. Often several algorithms are evaluated in preparing a program.

• In **structured programming** each step of the algorithm is designed as a self-contained group of statements. Three basic control structures are used.

• In **sequence structure** the computer moves through a set of statements from beginning to end, involving only one pass through the computation. In **selection structure** the computer branches to one of several different tracks or paths, depending upon a **test condition**. In **loop (iteration) structure** the computer repeats a series of steps until a given test condition is met and then it stops repeating.

• These basic structures are frequently combined into complex programs that perform accounting, billing, and collection routines or prepare orders, reports, documents, and so forth.

EXERCISES

1. Why do programmers flowchart a problem?

2. What is the difference between a system flowchart and a program flowchart?

3. What is an algorithm? Select a problem and give several solutions to it.

4. Using the algorithms and solutions developed in Exercise 3, prepare flowcharts for each.

5. What is the difference between sequence structure and loop structure?

6. Describe structured programming.

7. What are loops? List four situations in which loops may be used.

8. Define a trailer record. How is it used?

9. What are the advantages of structured programming?

10. Extend the flowchart in Figure 13-10 to change it from a sequence structure to a loop structure.

11. Flowchart programs to perform the following functions.

   a. Read in balance, deposits, and withdrawals from a record and compute and print out the new balance. Use a sequence structure.

   b. Read a part name and code from a record and branch accordingly.

   c. Write a modular program that updates a subscription list.

   d. Read a record containing the number of items in stock and cost per unit. Multiply to find total cost and print it out. Then loop back to read another record. Include a "test for last" record.

   e. Compute simple interest due on each account in a file.

   f. Read in the number of parts left in stock. If under 100, write a "short supply" message. If 100–500, write "adequate supply" message. If more than 500, write an "oversupply" message. Use structured programming.

14

Learning Objectives

After studying this chapter, you should be able to list the advantages and limitations of the following languages:

1. BASIC
2. COBOL
3. FORTRAN
4. Pascal
5. RPG
6. PL/I
7. APL
8. Assembler

Chapter Outline

BASIC
   Advantages and Limitations
   General Characteristics
COBOL
   Advantages and Limitations
   General Characteristics
FORTRAN
   Advantages and Limitations
   General Characteristics
Pascal
   Advantages and Limitations
   General Characteristics
RPG
   Advantages and Limitations
   General Characteristics
PL/I
   Advantages and Limitations
   General Characteristics
APL
   Advantages and Limitations
   General Characteristics
Assembler Language
   Advantages and Limitations
   General Characteristics

Programming Languages

A programmer must communicate with a computer system in order to give it directions. We know that computers will not respond to directions in ordinary English. They are capable of carrying out only instructions written in the machine language of 0s and 1s. Interpreters and compilers in the computer translate human instructions into machine language, and computer designers have developed many languages in which to present these instructions to the machine.

Some languages are geared to the needs of the user rather than to the computer's limitations. These are called **problem-oriented languages (POLs)**, or high-level languages. Of these, some languages, such as COBOL, are more like spoken English, while others, such as FORTRAN or APL, are closer to mathematical notation. Still others, such as assembler, LOGO, and RPG, were designed with special characteristics for particular applications.

No one language has yet been developed that possesses all the characteristics of an "ideal" language. In evaluating a language, many factors must be considered. For instance, is the language easy to learn and easy to use? Does it possess good mathematical capabilities? Is it programmer oriented? Does it adequately serve the special purpose for which it was designed?

An ideal language is **standardized**, so that programs written in it will run on different machines without revision. It is available on many different computers. A language that resembles English is **self-documenting** and is easier to follow for people with little programming knowledge. Languages that require large amounts of primary memory are of necessity limited to computers with large memories.

In this chapter you will read about the eight principal computer languages in business use, with a discussion of their development and origins, advantages and limitations, and general characteristics (see Table 14-1). Together with C, LISP, SNOBOL, ALGOL, and Ada, these languages are used to write almost 99 percent of the programs for modern computers. Appendix A covers the BASIC language more thoroughly so students can learn to write programs in it.

TABLE 14-1
Programming
Language
Comparison

	BASIC	COBOL	PASCAL	FORTRAN	RPG	PL/I	APL	ASSEMBLER
Easy to learn	X		X		X			
Programmer oriented	X	X	X			X	X	
Good math capabilities	X		X	X		X		X
Good alphanumeric capabilities		X				X	X	X
Resembles English		X				X		
Self-documenting		X				X		
Available on many machines	X	X		X	X			X
Standardized		X		X				
Manufacturer controlled						X	X	X
Efficient on computers			X			X		X
Large primary storage capacity required		X					X	
Interactive capability		X						X
Machine dependent						X	X	X

BASIC

Figure 14-1 John G. Kemeny (*left*) and Thomas E. Kurtz (*right*). Kemeny and Kurtz developed the BASIC language while teaching at Dartmouth University. Their goal was to create a language that would be easy to learn and that would help students to understanding programming.

BASIC (Beginner's All-purpose Symbolic Instruction Code) was developed in the early 1960s by John G. Kemeny and Thomas E. Kurtz of Dartmouth College, working under a grant from the National Science Foundation (Figure 14-1). BASIC was intended to be an easy-to-learn, interactive language for students. BASIC is generally implemented as an interpretive language. An **interpretive language** allows the programmer or operator to interact directly with the computer during program execution. It resembles FORTRAN, but is a bit less complicated.

BASIC is now one of the most widely accepted languages in schools, colleges, and universities. It has also rapidly become the principal language of microcomputers. One version, **MBASIC**, developed by the Microsoft Company, is available on many home computers. BASIC is much used in commercial time-sharing applications and for business and scientific programming. It is available on both large and small computer systems.

ADVANTAGES AND LIMITATIONS

The great virtues of BASIC are that it is easy to learn, is easy to use, and does not require a special terminal or keyboard. BASIC is a real

Figure 14-2 BASIC Programming Application. People with no technical background can learn BASIC quickly, so BASIC programs make it easy to bring computer capabilities into the office.

time, interactive language. It is also flexible, with a wide range of applications (Figure 14-2). It has fair **mathematical capability**, and can manipulate arrays of numbers easily. An **array** is a group of related numbers or words stored in the computer in adjacent memory locations. An array is sometimes referred to in BASIC as a **matrix** (**matrices** plural). BASIC is **machine independent**. This means it can run on computers of many different sizes and types with little or no revision. (A program in a machine dependent language can be run only on a given make or model of computer. Running it on other machines means that all or part of the program must be rewritten.) One major advantage of the language is the relatively small amount of primary memory required.

BASIC, however, is not geared for handling large quantities of input and output data, nor is it suited to processing jobs with many files. Many different versions of BASIC exist. Unfortunately, this lack of uniformity has worked against the language. Many programs cannot be transferred from one computer to another without modification.

Figure 14-3 Sample BASIC Program. The statements in this program are either instructions to the computer or remarks. Remarks, which begin with the BASIC reserved word REM, do not direct the computer. They contain information for the user's benefit, such as the title of the program, the date it was written, or comments on symbols used.

```
10 REM PROGRAM COMPUTER INVENTORY
20 PRINT "ENTER PART NAME"
30 INPUT A$
40 PRINT "ENTER NUMBER OF UNITS IN STOCK"
50 INPUT A
60 PRINT "ENTER NUMBER OF UNITS ADDED TO STOCK"
70 INPUT B
80 PRINT "ENTER NUMBER OF UNITS REMOVED FROM STOCK"
90 INPUT C
100 PRINT "THANK YOU"
110 PRINT
120 LET E=(A+B)-C
130 PRINT "THERE ARE ";E
140 PRINT A$;" REMAINING IN STOCK"
150 END
```

GENERAL CHARACTERISTICS

The American National Standards Institute (ANSI) has published a nucleus of statements for BASIC. Although not extensive, the ANSI list represents a major step toward standardizing the language. The rules discussed below apply to one version of BASIC and may vary from system to system.

BASIC has a standard character set consisting of the alphabet, the numbers 0 through 9, and a group of special characters. Because the BASIC interpreter reads only these characters, all programming statements must be written from this group.

BASIC programs are composed of instructions called **statements** (Figure 14-3). Each statement directs the computer to perform one or more operations. BASIC statements consist of words, symbols, and numbers. Each statement is entered as a single line and is assigned its own sequential line number.

The BASIC language uses two types of words: reserved and assigned. Both kinds of words are incorporated with mathematical operators to form the programming statements.

Reserved words have a specific meaning to the computer. They direct it to perform certain actions, and they can be used only to give directions. For example, the word INPUT tells the computer to read in data from the keyboard. The PRINT statement tells it to output data, calculated by the program or stored in the computer, on the print unit or other output device.

Assigned words, or **variable names**, are selected by the programmer to represent various storage locations. For example, the name B1 may stand for a memory location holding an account balance. B2 might be assigned to hold the account balance of a second customer, and so on. In this way, assigned names serve to easily identify data stored in various locations in the computer's memory.

Names must conform to BASIC language rules. They may not be reserved words. They may contain only one or two characters—an alphabetic letter followed by a number or a dollar sign ($). See line 30 in Figure 14-3 for an example. Names that represent numbers may contain one alphabetic letter or one alphabetic letter followed by a single digit 0 through 9, for example, A, B, H, N2, B9, P7. Assigned names for alphabetic quantities consist of an alphabetic letter followed by a dollar sign, for example, A$, G$, U$.

Because the number of combinations possible using only two characters is limited, the number of variables that can be represented in a single program is limited.

BASIC is described in more detail in Appendix A.

COBOL

COBOL (Common Business Oriented Language) is used extensively in business, education, and government (Figure 14-4). The initial draft of COBOL was presented in 1960 by the Conference on Data Systems Languages (CODASYL). This group was formed by many computer users and manufacturers and the U.S. Department of Defense to develop a universal language that could be used in business and the military. Dr. Grace Murray Hopper was a major contributor to the structure and development of the COBOL language (Figure 14-5). COBOL was designed so that it could be run on different makes and models of computers. Major interest in the language appeared when the federal government required that any large computer it purchased be equipped for COBOL.

A committee of CODASYL meets regularly to evaluate changes to the language. COBOL is unique in that it is formally sup-

Figure 14-4 COBOL Programming Application. COBOL was designed specifically for processing the type of data used by businesses, and large business applications remain its primary use.

Figure 14-5 Dr. Grace Hopper. Dr. Hopper served for many years with the U.S. Navy and was a prime mover in the development of COBOL.

ported by its users, that is, large firms, government agencies, and others contribute time and money to maintain and improve the language. Other languages, such as BASIC, have no formal sponsors to plan and implement improvements. Each computer manufacturer or user is left on his or her own to modify the language, and yet thoughtful modification is essential if a language is to remain current and keep its utility.

ADVANTAGES AND LIMITATIONS

One of COBOL's major advantages is its resemblance to English. Because COBOL was designed to reflect common business usage, it incorporates terms such as ADD, SUBTRACT, MOVE TO, WRITE, and PERFORM. Complicated mathematical notation, symbols, and binary code are avoided. As a result, programs written in COBOL can be followed by programmers with little training.

Because the coding is easy to understand, programs written in COBOL generally require relatively little documentation to explain each step. COBOL program documentation does, of course, include flowcharts, descriptive narratives, and input/output specifications.

COBOL has good literal capability. **Literal capability** is a language's ability to manipulate words, sentences, or paragraphs of text material. This asset is important in business data processing because names, addresses, lists, descriptive material, and sentences are frequently used.

COBOL is machine independent. Because it can run on many different makes or models of computers with little or no revision, a firm can change its computer equipment, farm out jobs to other machines, or send programs to other users with considerable assurance that the program will run satisfactorily.

Since COBOL is a major language in business data processing, COBOL compilers are available on most large business computers.

Although COBOL has many advantages, it also has limitations. Compilers for the full range of statements require a large primary storage capacity. Because these compilers fill many thousands of bytes of primary storage, programs cannot usually be run on small machines. COBOL, therefore, is limited to computers with a sizable memory.

COBOL is also wordy. Programs require dozens of statements, each one like a complete sentence constructed from English language words. This structure makes COBOL easier to follow, but results in a long, verbose program.

It is generally more difficult to perform complex mathematical operations in COBOL than in most other languages. Because of its mathematical limitations, it is not preferred by scientific or mathematical programmers.

GENERAL CHARACTERISTICS

COBOL, like English, has rules of spelling, punctuation, and syntax. The basic unit of the COBOL language is the **sentence** which ends in a period (Figure 14-6). Sentences are composed of **words**, which are made up from the standard character set of the alphabet, numbers 0 through 9, and a group of special characters.

COBOL sentences may be imperative or conditional. Imperative sentences direct the computer to perform a given task. Condi-

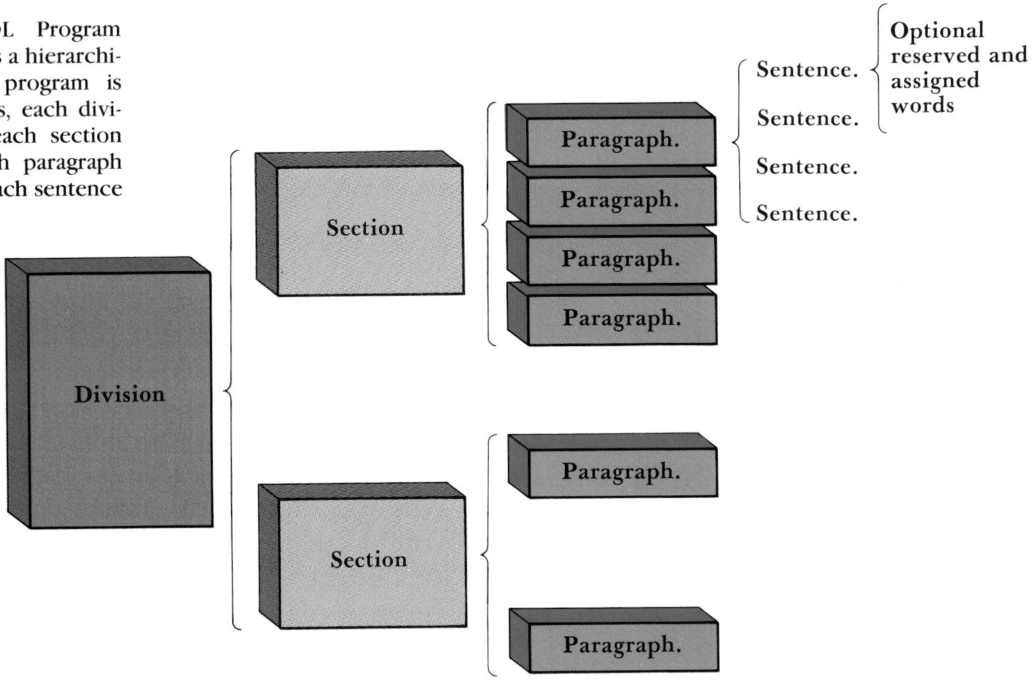

Figure 14-6 COBOL Program Structure. COBOL has a hierarchical structure. Each program is divided into divisions, each division into sections, each section into paragraphs, each paragraph into sentences, and each sentence into words.

tional sentences instruct the computer to follow one of several courses, depending on the value of a quantity in storage or the result of a calculation.

Sentences are grouped into **paragraphs**. Each paragraph is given a name by the programmer. Paragraphs usually contain one or more sentences referring to the same operation. The statements that calculate payroll deductions may make one paragraph; all the instructions needed to print out a formatted paycheck may be another. The programmer can refer to all the steps in a paragraph by calling out the paragraph name.

Paragraphs are further grouped into **sections**. Sections may be compared to chapters in a book, each concerned with a different aspect of a subject.

Finally, all sections are grouped into four **divisions**: identification, environment, data, and procedure division (Table 14-2). Each division performs a different function, but all are interrelated parts

TABLE 14-2 COBOL Program Divisions

DIVISION NAME	FUNCTION
Identification	Identify programmer, program, and company.
Environment	Assign files to input and output devices. Specify computer.
Data	Assign names to quantities and fields, allocate storage spaces, and define format of data records.
Procedure	Define actions and steps computer is to follow in solving problem.

of the same program. Figure 14-7 shows a COBOL program.

When composing a sentence in COBOL, a programmer follows set rules and conventions. The words cannot be chosen arbitrarily. There are three types of words—reserved words, assigned words, and optional words—each type with its own function.

The **reserved words** are the commands that direct the computer to perform various tasks. The COBOL compiler converts the commands into step-by-step, machine language instructions, telling the CPU how to perform a specified activity.

The reserved words have a particular meaning in the language. Their use is restricted by several conventions. They may be used only in the way the language allows. Spelling must be exact. And other words cannot be substituted for them. For example, the reserved word ADD in a COBOL sentence always tells the computer to set up the circuitry to perform addition. A programmer could not use words such as ADDED, PLUS, or AND to perform this same calculation.

Assigned words or **variable names** are selected by the programmer to represent data calculated or stored in the computer. Names represent the quantities that will be manipulated by the reserved words. In this way, a programmer can refer to and manipulate a quantity, even though its value changes during a program.

A programmer assigns names to fields in a data record, as well as to the totals, intermediate totals, paragraphs, and temporary storage areas. Words chosen as names must conform to certain language rules. They may not be more than 30 characters long; they must contain at least one alphabetic letter; a reserved word cannot be chosen as a name.

Finally, **optional words** are used in composing sentences. These words have no effect on the program flow, but they improve

Figure 14-7 Sample COBOL Program. This example, which is a simple program to read and write data in an 80-column format, shows the four major divisions.

```
IDENTIFICATION DIVISION.
PROGRAM ID. LISTING1.
ENVIRONMENT DIVISION.
CONFIGURATION SECTION.
SOURCE COMPUTER. CYBER-170-720.
OBJECT COMPUTER. CYBER-170-720.
SPECIAL-NAMES.
INPUT-OUTPUT SECTION.
FILE CONTROL.
     SELECT IN-FILE ASSIGN TO INPUT.
     SELECT OUT-FILE ASSIGN TO OUTPUT.
DATA DIVISION.
FILE SECTION.
*    DEFINE INPUT OF THE PROGRAM.
FD   IN-FILE
     LABEL RECORDS ARE OMITTED.
01   RECORD-IN              PIC X(80).
*    DEFINE OUTPUT OF THE PROGRAM.
FD   OUT-FILE
     LABEL RECORDS ARE OMITTED.
01   RECORD-OUT.
     02 FILLER             PIC X(01).
     02 DATA-OUT           PIC X(80).
PROCEDURE DIVISION.
LETS-GO.
     OPEN INPUT IN-FILE.
     OPEN OUTPUT OUT-FILE.
     MOVE SPACES TO RECORD-OUT.
     WRITE RECORD-OUT AFTER PAGE.
READ-AND-WRITE.
     READ IN-FILE AT END GO TO CLOSE-UP.
     MOVE RECORD-IN TO DATA-OUT.
     WRITE RECORD-OUT AFTER 1.
     GO TO READ-AND-WRITE.
CLOSE UP.
     CLOSE IN-FILE, OUT-FILE.
     STOP RUN.
```

Figure 14-8 FORTRAN Programming Application. As the oldest high-level programming language, FORTRAN has been widely accepted. It is particularly suited to the needs of scientists, engineers, and business statisticians who deal primarily with numerical data.

the readability of COBOL sentences. IS, THAN, and ARE are examples of optional words.

FORTRAN

Developed in the late 1950s by John Backus and a group from IBM, **FORTRAN (FORmular TRANslating system)** was intended to be a language for scientists and mathematicians to program their technical problems. Thousands of hours were spent writing a compiler that would accept statements in algebraic form and convert them into machine language instructions.

Unlike COBOL, FORTRAN is not supported by a group of users. Instead, manufacturers and users alike modify, improve, and change the language to suit their own needs. The American National Standards Institute publishes several approved versions of FORTRAN as guidelines for computer manufacturers and compiler writers. As new versions and improvements of FORTRAN are written, ANSI considers them for inclusion in their uniform standards.

Interest in FORTRAN has diminished in recent years as newer languages with strong mathematical capability have been introduced. However, it is still used for much mathematical and scientific programming (Figure 14-8).

ADVANTAGES AND LIMITATIONS

FORTRAN's primary advantage is its excellent mathematical capability. It closely resembles algebraic equations, which are familiar to most individuals working in science or math. Using FORTRAN, a programmer can read in and store alphabetic and numeric data, manipulate it, perform complex mathematical and logical operations, and write out the results.

FORTRAN is very compact. Usually only a few statements are needed to direct the computer to solve a complex problem. COBOL requires many more statements to move, process, and output data. Because some versions of FORTRAN require a compiler with only approximately 4K bytes of storage, FORTRAN compilers are available for small as well as large computers.

Improvements in FORTRAN have increased its literal capability so much that it is no longer limited only to mathematical applications, but can also manipulate words, sentences, and whole paragraphs of text. However, FORTRAN still does not have the ease of literal or alphabetic manipulation that COBOL does.

FORTRAN does away with many routine housekeeping details required in other languages. For example, in FORTRAN storage areas are set up more easily and with less detailed description than is required in COBOL. Fields in a data record are more compactly and conveniently described.

Finally, FORTRAN was the pattern followed in the development of the BASIC language. A programmer who knows the fundamentals of FORTRAN can write programs in BASIC with little difficulty.

FORTRAN bears a closer resemblance to mathematical notation than to ordinary English, because it relies on codes and symbols. It is more difficult for a nonprogrammer to understand or trace program logic in FORTRAN than in COBOL, for example. FORTRAN programs must be fully documented to explain the logic used in the program and the input/output specifications.

GENERAL CHARACTERISTICS

FORTRAN employs a standard character set of the alphabet, numbers 0 through 9, and a group of special characters. The basic unit of the language is the **statement**, not the sentence as in COBOL. The

Figure 14-9 Sample FOR-
TRAN Program. Statements
beginning with C are com-
ments that help document
the steps in the program.

```
C        AVERAGE WIND SPEED, OKLAHOMA CITY
C        WRITE HEADINGS

 10 WRITE(6,20)
 20 FORMAT('1    AVERAGE WIND SPEED')
 30 WRITE(6,40)
 40 FORMAT('0   MONTH          WIND SPEED')
 50 CT=0.0
 60 TOTAL=0.0
C        READ IN MONTH AND WIND SPEED
 70 READ(5,80)MTH1,MTH2,MTH3,WIND,LAST
 80 FORMAT(3A4,2X,F4.1,2X,I3)
C        TEST FOR END-OF-FILE
 90 IF(LAST)100,100,150
C        INCREASE COUNTER AND TOTAL
100 CT=CT+1.0
110 TOTAL=TOTAL+WIND
C        LIST MONTHS
120 WRITE(6,130)MTH1,MTH2,MTH3,WIND
130 FORMAT(' ',3A4,5X,F4.1)
140 GO TO 70
C        CALCULATE AND WRITE MEAN
150 AVRGE=TOTAL/CT
160 WRITE(6,170)AVRGE
170 FORMAT('0MONTHLY AVERAGE WIND SPEED IS ',F4.1)
180 STOP
    END
```

statement is a group of symbols, words, and punctuation formed into an expression. Each expression tells the computer to perform one or more operations.

The statement is composed of names assigned by the programmer, symbols called **arithmetic operators** ($+$, $-$, $*$, $/$, for example), and reserved words that instruct the computer to perform operations, move data, do calculations, and so on.

FORTRAN statements resemble algebraic equations. They do not look like English text, do not end with periods, and are not formed into paragraphs, as in COBOL.

A FORTRAN program has no special sections or divisions (Figure 14-9). Statements are placed in the program in the order in which they are to be carried out. The computer executes each instruction, one at a time, branching where directed, until the last statement in the program has been executed.

A programmer constructs FORTRAN statements by combining mathematical operators, reserved words, names, and so on. These instructions give certain information to the compiler. They must describe the format of the I/O data, as well as indicate whether numbers are whole numbers, decimals, or exponents.

FORTRAN contains two types of words, reserved words and assigned words. There are no optional words. Each reserved word has a particular meaning to the computer and can be used only to perform that specific task. Reserved words are incorporated into programming statements along with the names of the quantities on which they are to operate.

Assigned words are variable names chosen by the programmer to represent quantities in storage or data fields on a record. Names must conform to certain FORTRAN rules and cannot exceed six letters in length.

PASCAL

Pascal was developed by Niklaus Wirth of Zurich, Switzerland, in the late 1960s. Because it was one of the first languages developed after the advent of structured programming, Pascal reflects top-down, modular programming design. Pascal strikes a balance between wordy languages such as COBOL and terse languages such as FORTRAN. It is finding increased support from computer users in universities and some businesses who prefer a language that is easy to learn and efficient in computer usage.

ADVANTAGES AND LIMITATIONS

Pascal consists of only a small number of basic constructions and reserved words, yet it can perform a wide range of processing activities. It runs efficiently on large or small computers, and the programmer needs little training to follow the program logic.

One major limitation of Pascal, like BASIC, is its lack of standardization. The American National Standards Institute has not yet established a standard for this language, and many versions exist. A

```
PROGRAM AVERAGE (INPUT, OUTPUT);
    VAR
        NUMBER, TOTAL, AVERAGE : REAL;
        COUNT : INTEGER;
    BEGIN
        TOTAL := 0;
        COUNT := 0;
        READ(NUMBER);
        WHILE NOT EOF DO
            BEGIN
                TOTAL := TOTAL + NUMBER;
                COUNT := COUNT + 1;
                READ(NUMBER);
            END;
        IF COUNT > 0
            THEN
                BEGIN
                    AVERAGE := TOTAL / COUNT;
                    WRITELN(COUNT, 'NUMBERS WERE READ, AVERAGE IS ',AVERAGE);
                END;
            ELSE WRITELN('NO NUMBERS WERE READ');
END.
```

Figure 14-10 Sample Pascal Program. In this program, lines are indented to show levels of organization. A program module, or block of statements to do a particular task, starts with BEGIN.

program written for one computer system may well not run on another without extensive modification. Another disadvantage of Pascal is its limited file handling capabilities. Finally, Pascal does not possess the ability to manipulate large collections of numbers or words stored as an array as do some other major languages.

GENERAL CHARACTERISTICS

Pascal programs are composed of **modules**, each of which performs a particular activity. The **statements** in the modules may be organized into **levels**, indicating their relationships. The level of a statement is shown by its degree of indention from the left margin (Figure 14-10). This visual arrangement makes it easier to follow the program logic.

Statements in a Pascal program are composed of reserved words, symbols, and identifiers. **Reserved words** are terms that have special meanings to the compiler. **Symbols** used in Pascal include mathematical symbols and punctuation marks.

Identifiers are names that represent various constants, variables, procedures, or functions. Some identifiers are standard, that is, they describe standard processes to the compiler, but they can be redefined if the programmer wishes. The programmer can also select additional identifiers to represent values or procedures defined in the program.

RPG

RPG (Report Program Generator) is more a system of preparing reports than a true language. It is widely used on small computers to prepare business reports, accounts receivable, inventory listings, statements, and so on. RPG is a file-oriented language with a fixed order of execution: input, processing, output (Figure 14-11).

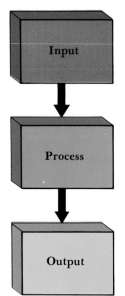

Figure 14-11 RPG File Processing. RPG programs follow a fixed order of execution. Because the programs do not deviate from this procedure, RPG is a limited-purpose language suitable for applications that do not require complex programming logic.

ADVANTAGES AND LIMITATIONS

RPG is one of the simpler languages to learn. It has few formal language rules, syntax requirements, or reserved words. It requires a minimum of programming effort and skill to prepare business reports and other documents. Because the basic pattern of execution is fixed, the programmer simply decides what will take place within each step. RPG is designed to ease the processing, updating, and maintenance of large data files. It requires a smaller compiler than most POLs and is usable on small computers.

RPG is suited to report preparation. It has restricted mathematical capability. It will perform addition, subtraction, multiplication, and division, but, compared to FORTRAN or COBOL, its facility for looping, branching, and making decisions is limited.

RPG is not standardized. It is machine dependent, with each computer having its own version. A program written in RPG for one computer may need extensive modification before it will run on another.

GENERAL CHARACTERISTICS

RPG is designed to facilitate file processing, that is, file description, file manipulation, and outputting.

CROSSWORD PUZZLE ON SOFTWARE

ACROSS

1. Toboggan
5. Slipped
9. Unthinking repetition
13. American National Standards Institute: abbr.
17. Conceal
18. _____ Nostra
19. Makes mistakes
20. Schooner's "sheet"
21. "Rub-_ _____ -dub, three men . . . "
22. Clue
23. Sausage, e.g.
24. Shiny fabric
25. User guides, manuals, and instructions
28. Invoices
29. Leg: slang
30. Perch
31. Swing dance of the 1930s
33. Ms. MacGraw
36. The center of the operating system
39. Formulators
43. "Filthy _____ " (money)
45. Clear after taxes
46. Defeat
47. Kazan
48. Gen. Robert _ _____
49. Motorists' org.
50. Goes on
51. Papas
52. A flashing pointer that moves around a CRT screen
54. Magician's word
56. Baxter and Bancroft
57. Wyatt of the Wild West
59. Office of Naval Intelligence: abbr.
60. Eternal City, to Italians
62. Blatant
65. Consolation
68. Dumbbell
72. Secluded from sight: abbr.
73. Closes up
74. Disencumber
76. Ireland of old
77. Assistant
78. Places
79. "Peter _____ "
80. Rockies ski resort
81. Highway foundations
83. Computer language named for French mathematician
85. Superman's insignia
86. Texas city
87. Sailor
88. Gangster's gun: slang
90. Computer language especially for business
93. Type fonts
100. Allege
101. A logic pattern in structured programming
102. Mend argyles
103. On the ocean
104. What "bookworms" do
105. Not working
106. Give off
107. Resounded
108. BASIC statements
109. Doe
110. Reps.' opponents
111. Lather

DOWN

1. _____ roe
2. Beach resort
3. School's purpose: abbr.
4. Detect and fix mistakes in computer program
5. Plot
6. Cut of meat
7. " _____ It Romantic?"
8. Collection of information on which a program is to operate
9. Send money
10. Famous brown-and-white cookie
11. Compiler or interpreter program
12. N.Y.'s time zone
13. In BASIC, these identify various storage locations
14. Spike
15. Window part
16. Kinds; types
26. Manufacture
27. Sesame plant
28. Prohibit
32. Bonnets
33. Mr. Guinness
34. Humdinger
35. Cake decorator
37. Relative of DNA
38. Kind of tide
39. Gnat, for one
40. Flair
41. Use a surfboard
42. Backtalk
44. In BASIC, these give directions to the computer
46. Computer language invented by Kemeny and Kurtz
49. Timetable abbr.
50. Ms. Horne and others
53. Acorn producer
55. Baker's products
56. "What Kind of Fool _____ ?"
58. A version of computer instructions written in abbreviated form
61. A type of parity check bit
62. Shadowbox
63. Pointer Sisters, for example
64. Opera heroine
66. Foods for fillies
67. Historic periods
69. Remove by rubbing
70. Makes angry
71. Small bills
73. Exceptional: abbr.
75. Letterhead abbr.
79. Marched in a procession
80. Winged
82. Balance: abbr.
83. Golf standard
84. F.B.I. men
87. Candle
89. Pre-Soviet rulers
90. Part of T.L.C.
91. Stove part
92. Necklace element
94. Doughnut feature
95. Arrived
96. Decorate a Christmas tree
97. Jacob's brother
98. Take care of
99. Droops
101. Kettle cover

The solution for this puzzle immediately precedes the index.

The language uses names, codes, numbers, and letters entered in specific columns on coding forms. The information on the forms is entered into the computer and constitutes the program. The specifications sheets used in coding RPG programs are:

File description specifications

File extension specifications

Line counter specifications

Input specifications

Calculation specifications

Output format specifications

The specifications forms are used to define files and fields to be read by the computer, the fields to be operated on, and any mathematical computations to be performed (Figure 14-12). They also specify column heads to be listed, the graphic layout to be followed, and how the data are to be output.

PL/I

PL/I (Programming Language I)—the I stands for "one"—was developed by IBM Corporation as a multipurpose language. It is both a business and a scientific language, suitable for batch processing as well as use on terminals. Designed to incorporate the best features of FORTRAN and COBOL, PL/I resembles both, but has many other features and capabilities. PL/I is used to program problems in business, education, social science, science, and other areas.

ADVANTAGES AND LIMITATIONS

One principal advantage of PL/I is its free style. Unlike other languages, it has no restrictions regarding columns, paragraphs, and statement numbers. PL/I is modular. A novice programmer can use the language after learning only a small part of it. As skills are gained, programming capabilities can be extended by learning additional features. (In many other languages the programmer needs a fairly thorough understanding of the entire language before using any part of it.)

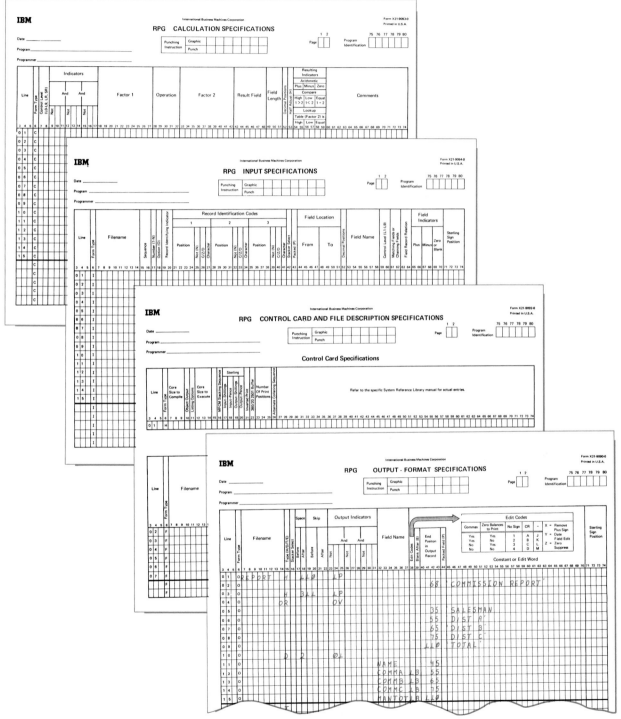

Figure 14-12 Sample RPG Program. In RPG, the information on the specification forms is entered into the computer and constitutes the program.

Figure 14-13 Sample PL/I Program. PL/I programs may be formatted as shown here with statements on separate lines and arranged in blocks, or the programs may be free-form, with statements arranged one after another.

```
PRINT: PROC OPTIONS(MAIN);
       DCL IN FILE RECORD SEQUENTIAL INPUT,
           DATA CHAR(100),
           LAB(3) LABEL INIT(A,B,C);
       DO I = 1 TO 3;
         ON ENDFILE(IN) GO TO OUT;
         GO TO LAB(I);
         A: OPEN FILE(IN) TITLE('T1');
            GO TO READ;
         B: OPEN FILE(IN) TITLE('T2');
            GO TO READ;
         C: OPEN FILE(IN) TITLE('T3');
         READ: READ FILE(IN)  INTO (DATA);
              PUT FILE(SYSPRINT) SKIP LIST(DATA);
              GO TO READ;
        OUT: CLOSE FILE(IN);
           END;
       END PRINT;
```

PL/I has a built-in feature called a **default option** that corrects common mistakes made by programmers. When it detects a minor programming error or omission, the PL/I compiler assumes it knows what the programmer's intentions were, makes a correction, and continues with the program. This feature makes programming easier and prevents minor errors or bugs from blowing up an otherwise acceptable program.

PL/I compilers require a sizable amount of primary memory so the language cannot be used on small computers.

PL/I is a proprietary language; written at the expense of IBM, it is controlled by them. As a result, it is used mostly on IBM computers.

GENERAL CHARACTERISTICS

As a free-form language, PL/I has few coding conventions. Programming statements are entered as a string of words, numbers, and symbols. Source statements are separated by semicolons. Statements are not confined to individual lines on coding sheets, do not have margin restrictions, and are not blocked into paragraphs. Figure 14-13 shows a sample program.

PL/I has a standard character set of the alphabet, numbers, and a group of special characters. Many of the special characters are code symbols, called **operators** that have specific meanings for the computer and direct it to perform various functions. They include the mathematical symbols $+$, $-$, $*$, and $/$. Additional symbols allow the programmer to call for logical and mathematical comparisons. The programmer can connect strings of characters or cause the computer to branch, depending on the value of a quantity.

Identifiers are variable names assigned to quantities in storage or to strings of characters. They can label a single quantity, alphabetic or numeric arrays, entire data files, groups of statements, or even conditions.

Identifiers are combined with operators and reserved PL/I words, called **key words**, to form statements. With them, the programmer can manipulate data, move quantities, perform calculations, and store or output results.

APL

APL (A Programming Language) was developed by Ken Iverson and IBM specifically as a conversational language. Someone with only minimum programming skills can perform many tasks. For example, a user can type in two rather large numbers separated by a plus sign ($+$) and the computer will sum the two numbers and print out the answer on the next line. Or the user can subtract, multiply, divide, find the square root, or perform other mathematical calculations by listing only the values and the operator that specifies the procedure.

ADVANTAGES AND LIMITATIONS

APL is one of the most powerful interactive languages yet developed. It is modular in structure, offering simple, easy-to-use features for the beginner and complex features for the experienced programmer.

APL deals with most of the programmer's routine housekeeping tasks. Data input and output are easily handled with no need for detailed field descriptions. The programmer can assign names to

CONTRASTING SIX
PROGRAMMING
LANGUAGES

This illustration contrasts the way programming commands are written in six different languages. All examples do the same thing. They multiply 87 by 243 and give the answer either by printing it or saving it in a specific memory location.

BASIC

```
10 LET A = 87
20 LET B = 243
30 LET C = A * B
40 PRINT A; " TIMES ";
50 PRINT B; " = "; C
60 END
```

ASSEMBLY
LANGUAGE

```
          OBJECT
ADDRESS   CODE      SOURCE STATEMENT       COMMENT

000000  016702  MULT:    MOV X,R2      ;LOAD 243 INTO REGISTER 2
        000012
000004  070267           MUL Y,R2      ;MULTIPLY BY 87
        000010
000010  010367           MOV R3,Z      ;STORE RESULT AT Z
        000006
000014  000000           HALT          ;STOP
000016  000363  X:       .WORD 243.
000020  000127  Y:       .WORD 87.
000022  000000  Z:       .BLKW 1       ;SAVE SPACE FOR ANSWER
                         .END MULT
```

PASCAL

```
PROGRAM SAMPLE(OUTPUT);
VAR
  A, B, C : INTEGER;
BEGIN
  A := 87;
  B := 243;
  C = A * B;
  WRITELN(OUTPUT, ' ', A,
    ' TIMES ', B, ' = ', C)
END.
```

```
COBOL    IDENTIFICATION DIVISION.
         PROGRAM-ID. SAMPLE.
         ENVIRONMENT DIVISION.
         CONFIGURATION SECTION.
         SOURCE COMPUTER. IDIAC-747.
         OBJECT COMPUTER. IDIAC-747.
         DATA DIVISION.
         WORKING-STORAGE SECTION.
         01  A; PICTURE IS S9(3).
         01  B; PICTURE IS S9(3).
         01  C; PICTURE IS S9(6).
         PROCEDURE DIVISION.
         000-MAIN-LINE.
             MOVE 87 TO A.
             MOVE 243 TO B.
             MULTIPLY A B GIVING C.
             DISPLAY A, " TIMES ",
                 B, " = ", C.
             STOP RUN.

FORTRAN      INTEGER A, B, C
             A = 87
             B = 243
             C = A * B
             WRITE (6,50) A, B, C
         50 FORMAT(1X, I3, ' TIMES ',
            *  I3, '=', I6)
             STOP
             END


    PL/I  XYZ: PROCEDURE OPTIONS(MAIN);
             DECLARE (A,B,C) FIXED
             BINARY;
             A = 87;
             B = 243;
             C = A * B;
             PUT LIST (' ', A, ' TIMES ',
                 B, ' = ', C);
             END XYZ;
```

Figure 14-14 APL Keyboard. The many APL symbols reduce the need for writing out the complex control operations needed in other languages. APL programs can be run only using terminals with the special keyboard and only on computers with memory capacity large enough to handle the language translator such symbols require.

stored values, manipulate data, perform calculations, and store arrays of numbers, names, and lists.

APL offers a wide variety of sophisticated mathematical and processing tools to the programmer. These are called out by striking the appropriate symbol on the keyboard (Figure 14-14).

A feature of APL is its line-by-line execution. Each instruction is executed immediately and the result printed out on the next line. Unacceptable statements are detected immediately. There are no format restrictions on data input and output. The APL language translator accepts decimal numbers, whole numbers, exponent values, and other such data. Results are printed out with the required decimal points and exponents supplied by the translator.

APL programs can be run only on large computers, because the language translator requires a sizable primary memory capacity. At the present time the American National Standards Institute has not published an APL standard. Furthermore, the sparse nature of the language and its special symbols and operators make APL a more difficult language for the nonprogrammer to follow than some others. The large number of special symbols for the variety of operations the language can handle requires a special keyboard.

GENERAL CHARACTERISTICS

APL is a free-form language with little formal structure. It is composed of special symbols, called **operators**, **variable names**, and **reserved words**. The sample APL program in Figure 14-15 shows its general form.

```
     ∇ STUCOH
[1]    H←G←0
[2]    D←0
[3]    C←0
[4]    'ENTER NUMBER OF STUDENTS IN CLASS'
[5]    A←□
[6]    'ENTER NUMBER OF HOURS PER WEEK CLASS MEETS'
[7]    B←□
[8]    'ENTER NUMBER OF OFFICE HOURS PER WEEK'
[9]    C←□
[10]   D←A×B
[11]   E←C+B
[12]   'YOUR STUDENT CONTACT HOURS ARE ';D
[13]   G←G+D
[14]   'YOUR ASSIGNED HOURS ARE ';E
[15]   H←H+E
[16]   'DO YOU WANT TO ENTER ANOTHER WORKLOAD? 0=NO, 1 = YES'
[17]   F←□
[18]   →2×⍳F=1
[19]   'THE FACULTY CONTACT HOURS ARE ';G
[20]   'THE FACULTY ASSIGNED HOURS ARE ';H
     ∇

     STUCOH
ENTER NUMBER OF STUDENTS IN CLASS
□:
     50
ENTER NUMBER OF HOURS PER WEEK CLASS MEETS
□:
     3
ENTER NUMBER OF OFFICE HOURS PER WEEK
□:
     4
YOUR STUDENT CONTACT HOURS ARE 150
YOUR ASSIGNED HOURS ARE 7
DO YOU WANT TO ENTER ANOTHER WORKLOAD? 0=NO, 1 = YES
□:
     1
ENTER NUMBER OF STUDENTS IN CLASS
□:
     75
ENTER NUMBER OF HOURS PER WEEK CLASS MEETS
□:
     5
ENTER NUMBER OF OFFICE HOURS PER WEEK
□:
     ,5
YOUR STUDENT CONTACT HOURS ARE 375
YOUR ASSIGNED HOURS ARE 10
DO YOU WANT TO ENTER ANOTHER WORKLOAD? 0=NO, 1 = YES
□:
     0
THE FACULTY CONTACT HOURS ARE 525
THE FACULTY ASSIGNED HOURS ARE 17
     ∇STUCOH[□]∇
```

Figure 14-15 Sample APL Program. APL programs use language translators that require a large amount of primary memory.

Much of the power of APL is due to its operators, 50 or more code symbols such as ρ, Γ, ε, and ⊂. With them, the programmer can make arithmetic or logical comparisons, perform functions, find square roots, determine maximum or minimum values, replace quantities, transfer control, and so on.

The APL language can process data in an execution or a definition mode. In the **execution mode** data are entered, operations are specified, and results are available instantly. In a **definition mode** interpretation and execution do not occur until after a list of instructions is entered and the programmer directs the computer to begin.

Like most interactive languages, APL has an editing feature to permit correction and revision of programming statements and data. As the statements are entered, they are stored in the CPU's memory. They can be changed or replaced by typing in the number of the line and the new information. The computer will automatically make the change. This feature permits file updating, selective replacement of values, and corrections.

An important capability of APL is its ability to operate on groups of numbers stored as arrays. For example, a string of numbers can be typed on the terminal and assigned a name:

$$B \leftarrow 2\ 4\ 6\ 8$$

If the programmer later types the letter B, the computer will respond by printing out

$$2\ 4\ 6\ 8$$

If the programmer types in the statement

$$2 \times B$$

the computer will multiply each item in the array by 2 and print out the results:

$$4\ 8\ 12\ 16$$

ASSEMBLER LANGUAGE

Assembler language is a machine-dependent coding language more closely related to machine language than the others discussed so far. It is efficient from the standpoint of the machine, because it makes the most compact use of the computer's primary storage capacity. It is used to program long, repetitive jobs and system software.

ADVANTAGES AND LIMITATIONS

Programs in assembler language are designed to utilize fully a computer's primary storage and register capacities. This can save processing time on a long production run.

Use of assembler language facilitates modular or structured programming. Programs are often written as subroutines or modules, which can later be combined to solve other, different problems. Assembler language is available on most computers and requires less primary storage than most POLs.

The efficiency of assembler language on the computer is at the cost of the programmer's time and effort. It is much more difficult to write an assembler language program than a similar program in a higher level language. Each step in processing and manipulating data must be detailed, byte by byte. Storage areas must be figured and specified.

To use assembler language, the programmer must have a thorough understanding of the computer's architecture and register system. The programmer must be familiar with many coding systems, such as hexadecimal, binary, ASCII, and EBCDIC, and be able to convert from one to the other.

Assembler language is machine dependent. A program written in assembler language for one computer will not necessarily run on a machine of another model or make.

GENERAL CHARACTERISTICS

Assembler language is symbolic. It is based on mnemonic symbols, assigned names, and storage addresses.

A **mnemonic symbol** is a letter symbol or code chosen to stand for the machine language numeric code for each operation. It is called mnemonic (meaning "assisting memory") because the letter symbols are much easier to remember and work with than the strings of binary numbers the machine reads. Each operation or procedure the computer performs, such as add, move data, or multiply, is initiated by a numeric machine language code called an **operation** or **op code**. Each op code is assigned a mnemonic symbol to identify the operation in the program. For example, addition of values in storage slots is specified by A; addition of values in registers is specified by

A MODERN TOWER OF BABEL

Source: Gerald A. and Myrna L. Silver.

Languages tend to come into and go out of fashion as computer technology and applications change. Dozens of languages have been devised for modern computers. This chapter describes the most important languages in business, education, and industry today. But there are others that are popular and gaining followers. Let's look at a few of them.

ADA

Ada was developed by the United States Department of Defense as a common language for Defense Department programming. Ada was accepted as a standard language by ANSI in 1983. It has rapidly become important for programming military and government computers. Ada was named after Ada Countess of Lovelace, a colleague of Charles Babbage (see pages 46–49). Because of its widespread military acceptance, Ada could become more important not only for defense and government use, but in education, business, and industry as well.

C

C was devised in the early 1970s by Bell Laboratories mainly to write operating system programs. It has proven to be an easy-to-use language for writing source commands for operating systems and utility programs. C is a modern form of assembler language, and was used to write the UNIX operating system. As more microcomputers come into use, there will be a greater emphasis on C, particularly by programmers modifying or expanding their operating systems.

FORTH

In the early 1980s Charles H. Moore, a radio astronomer, developed a language designed principally to control large telescopes. Forth was so efficient that it soon was used to write process control programs for microcomputers. It requires little computer memory, but does need a sophisticated and skilled programmer to write it properly.

LISP

LISP development was begun in the late 1950s by John McCarthy at MIT who was working on artificial intelligence programming. LISP, short for list processing, manipulates information not as numbers but as words, phrases, shapes, or symbols. An object such as a tree can have associated with it a list of characteristics such as branches, leaves, or color. From this list certain things can be inferred; for example, trees are green, grow outdoors, give shade, and so on. As more work is done on artificial intelligence and software that mimics the processes of the human mind, there will be a greater use of LISP.

PROLOG

A derivative of LISP is PROLOG, another language designed for artificial intelligence programming. PROLOG does not follow formal rules of structure. Instead it relies upon relationships of quantities or descriptions of objects provided by the programmer. This means that the strictly written formulas or procedures of other high-level languages are not needed.

LOGO

When children take up computer programming, they need a language suited to their thought processes and ability. LOGO, developed in the late 1960s at MIT by Seymour Papert, was designed for children. LOGO is easy to learn. It uses simple words and a vocabulary much like English. In LOGO the programmer controls a symbol called a turtle that is moved about on the screen. Using generalized commands, the programmer directs the turtle to draw illustrations. LOGO allows the user to process lists of data and move information about without the rigorous commands found in other high-level languages.

AR; comparison of algebraic values is specified by C. The assembler translates these codes into the machine language equivalent for execution.

An assembler language statement consists of the mnemonic symbol for the operation, and the **assigned name** or **storage address** and operands. An **operand** is an entity to which an operation is applied. The statement tells the computer what operation is to be performed and the quantity or location to be operated upon.

The character set used in assembler language depends on the particular computer. Generally, it includes the full alphabet, numbers, and a dozen or so special characters.

Figure 14-16 illustrates a sample program written in assembler language.

It should be evident that there is no ideal language, perfect for all programming uses. Languages vary in popularity as programming needs change. New languages are constantly being developed to simplify the programmer's task, but the goal of all languages is to allow people to direct machines in the most efficient and practical manner possible.

Figure 14-16 Sample Assembler Program. Assembler language is a symbolic language using mnemonic codes and storage addresses that make programs machine-dependent.

```
LOC      OBJECT CODE   ADDR1  ADDR2  STMT  SOURCE STATEMENT

000000                                 1  SORTPGM  START  0
000000   05A0                          2           BALR   10,0
000002                                 3           USING  *,10
                                       4           OPEN   CDFILE,PTFILE
                                       5+*  360N-CL-453 OPEN  CHANGE LEVEL 3-3

000002   0700                          6+          CNCP   0,4
000004                                 7+          DC     0F'0'
000004   4110 A206           002D8     8+          LA     1,=C'$$BOPEN '         3-3
00000B   4500 AD12           00014     9+TJ000001  BAL    0,*+4+4*(3-1)
00000C   00000310                     10+          DC     A(CDFILE)
000010   00000348                     11+          DC     A(PTFILE)
000010   0A02                         12+          SVC    2
000016   5830 A2CE           002D0    13           L      3,TABSTR              ADD. OF TABLE INTO REG3
00001A   1B22                         14           SR     2,2
00001C   5A30 A2E6           002E8    15  LOCPA    A      3,=F'80'              ADD 80 TO TABLE LOC FOR NEXT SLOT
000020   5920 A2EA           002EC    16           C      2,=F'1000'            COMPARE COUNT TO MAXIMUM
000024   4780 A044           00046    17           BE     SORTA                 IF 1000 GOTO SORTA
000028   5A20 A2EE           002F0    18           A      2,=F'1'               ADD 1 TO COUNT
                                      19           GET    CDFILE,CDWORK
                                      20+*  360-N-CL-453
00002C   5810 A2F2           002F4    21+          L      1,*A(CDFILE)          GET CHANGE LEVEL 3-0
000030   5800 A2F6           002F8    22+          L      0,=A(CDWORK)          GET DTF TABLE ADDRESS
000034   58F1 0010           00010    23+          L      15,16(1)              GET WORK AREA ADDRESS
000038   45EF 0008           0000B    24+          BAL    14,B(15)              GET LOGIC MODULE ADDRESS
                                                                               BRANCH TO GET ROUTINE
00003C   D24F 3000 A0EE  000F0 00000  25           MVC    0(80,3),CDWORK        MOVE 80 BYTES TO LOC AT REG 3
000042   47F0 A0A1           000C1    26           B      LOOPA                 READ ANOTHER CARD
000046   1852                         27  SORTA    LR     5,2                   SAVE COUNT IN REG5
000048   1842                         28           LR     4,2                   SAVE COUNT IN REG4
00004A   5830 A2CE           002D0    29  SORTB    L      3,TABSTRT             GO BACK TO BEGINNING OF TABLE
00004E   1824                         30           LR     2,4                   RESET COUNTER
000050   5A30 A2E6           002E8    31  SORTC    A      3,=F'80'              BEGIN COMPARISON, ADD 80 BYTES TAB.
000054   4620 A07A           0007C    32           BCT    2,SORTD               COUNTS COMPARISONS
000058   D504 3050 3000  00050 00000  33           CLC    0(5,3),90(3)          COMPARE 5 BYTES OF 2 LINES OF TABLE
00005E   4720 A064           00066    34           BH     SWITCH
000062   47F0 A04E           00050    35           B      SCRTC
000066   D74F 3000 3050  00000 00050  36  SWITCH   XC     0(80,3),80(3)         MAKE ANOTHER COMPARISON
00006C   D74F 3050 3000  00050 00000  37           XC     80(80,3),0(3)         TRANSPOSE 80 BYTES
```

SUMMARY AND KEY TERMS

- A variety of programming languages have been developed to facilitate communication between people and machines. There is no one ideal language, but each has its own characteristics, advantages, and limitations.

- In evaluating languages, some of the characteristics considered are: Is it easy to learn, easy to use, and programmer oriented? Does it have good **mathematical** or **literal** capabilities? Is it **self-documenting**? Is it available on many machines? Is it **standardized** and **machine independent**? How much primary memory is required?

- **BASIC**, developed by John G. Kemeny and Thomas E. Kurtz, is now widely used in schools and businesses, particularly on small computers. It is an **interpretive** language. Programs are composed of instructions called **statements**. BASIC uses **reserved words** and **assigned words**.

- **COBOL** is a major language used in business, education, and government. It was developed and is supported entirely by its users. COBOL resembles English, has good **literal capability**, and is machine independent. It is composed of **reserved**, **assigned**, and **optional words**. Words are formed into **sentences**, then grouped into **paragraphs**, which are in turn grouped into **sections** and **divisions**.

- **FORTRAN** was developed as a major language for mathematical and scientific applications. It is compact and resembles mathematical notations. FORTRAN has no special sections or divisions. It is machine independent.

- **Pascal** was developed to facilitate structured programming. It is easy to learn and efficient on computers. Pascal statements are composed of **reserved words**, **symbols**, and **identifiers**.

- **RPG** is a file-oriented language, using a fixed order of execution. Its input, processing, and output structure is suited to the preparation of reports, but has restricted mathematical capability.

- **PL/I** was designed by IBM Corporation as a multipurpose language. It has a free-style form, with built-in **default options**. The language uses **operators**, **identifiers**, and **key words**.

- **APL** is a powerful **interactive language** with excellent mathematical capability. It features an **execution** and a **definition mode**. It requires a special keyboard for its many operator symbols.

• **Assembler language** is machine dependent. It uses **mnemonic codes** that specify the operations to be carried out. The programmer must have a knowledge of the physical nature and capabilities of the machine being programmed.

EXERCISES

1. What does the name BASIC stand for and how was the language developed?

2. In which areas is BASIC widely used?

3. What are three advantages of the BASIC language?

4. List six advantages of COBOL.

5. List several disadvantages of COBOL.

6. How is a COBOL program structured?

7. List five advantages and two limitations of FORTRAN.

8. How does the structure of FORTRAN statements differ from that of COBOL?

9. What are the advantages of Pascal language?

10. For what kind of job is RPG best suited? What are its limitations?

11. What are the major advantages and limitations of PL/I?

12. What are the major advantages and limitations of APL?

13. What are operators in APL and how are they used?

14. What is the difference between the execution mode and the definition mode in APL?

15. What are the advantages and limitations of assembler language programming?

15

Learning Objectives

After studying this chapter, you should be able to
1. Define key terms related to word processing and office automation
2. Trace the history and development of the integrated office
3. List the advantages of office automation
4. Describe the basic word processing system
5. Describe the electronic mail system
6. Describe several teleconferencing techniques

Chapter Outline

History of Office Automation
Office Integration
Subsystems of the Integrated Office
    Word Processing
    Duplicating
    Filing
    Micrographics
    Electronic Mail
    Teleconferencing

Automation and the
Integrated Office

T he impact of the computer has been felt more strongly in offices than anywhere else. Thousands of offices—large and small, in business, government, and education—have undergone great changes since its introduction.

Offices are moving from the paperwork age into the electronic age. New office equipment and communication technology means that letters and memos can be prepared and revised automatically. Work stations located in many places in one building can be connected to each other with a coaxial cable to make possible the high speed flow of information between them. The traditional system of sending business correspondence through the postal system is becoming outdated. Electronic mail and facsimile systems do away with the physical movement of paper, speed up information flow, and reduce costs. Electrons are replacing paper.

In this chapter we look briefly at the historical development of office automation, describe the integrated office approach, and survey some new techniques that make this approach possible, such as word processing, teleconferencing, electronic mail, and micrographics.

HISTORY OF OFFICE AUTOMATION

The perfection of the typewriter by the Remington Company in the 1880s was the first step toward automating the office. It was followed by the appearance of mechanical calculators and unit record machines. In the same period the voice-recording experiments of Alexander Graham Bell and Thomas Edison led to the invention of the telephone and phonograph. The first office dictating machine, the Graphophone, appeared in 1886. In 1923 the Graphophone Company was sold to the Dictaphone Company, which has ever since been a leading manufacturer of office dictating machines (Figure 15-1).

The first automatic typewriter, one designed to type many copies of the same letter, was introduced about the time of World War I. Both the Hooven and Autotypist machines could store key

Figure 15-1 Early Office Machines. Edison's gramophone, the Oliver typewriter, and the Burroughs adding machine moved data processing a step out of the manual era. With only some modifications, these machines remain the basic tools of the paperwork office.

strokes and "play them back" in the form of typewritten material. The "memory" principle of these machines was similar to that of a player piano. They were operated by a long roll of tape into which holes were punched by the original keystrokes. During World War II the Robotyper Machine and the Friden Flexowriter were widely used for typing multiple copies. From that time until the 1960s and the coming of computer technology to business data processing, little further progress was made in automatic word processing.

Then, in 1962 the IBM Corporation came out with a special computer program called the Administrative Terminal System (ATS) that made it possible for a computer to assist in text editing and word processing. IBM followed the ATS in 1964 with a major breakthrough in word processing, the Magnetic Tape Selectric Typewriter (MT/ST). This machine stored keystrokes on a reel of magnetic tape that could be replayed to produce copy to be edited or revised online. After revision the machine reproduced a final, corrected, typewritten draft with virtually no retyping.

Following the lead of IBM, other manufacturers quickly brought out machines designed to produce copy suitable for reproduction. The printed material made by the Varityper, Justowriter, and IBM Selectric Composer was of such high quality that it could be reproduced by offset printing or other means of copying without being reset in type.

Office photocopiers like the familiar Xerox machines made carbon paper, mimeograph, and ditto machines obsolete. Facsimile transmission machines that send copies of printed or graphic material over telephone lines gave an alternative to the mail. Dictation machines replaced shorthand as the major form of preparing first drafts.

Computerized word processing became popular in the 1970s. Many of these word processing systems included typesetting devices that could generate documents with a wide variety of page sizes, type faces, and graphic displays. In addition, many systems had search capabilities, that is, they could scan the recorded keystrokes on a tape or disk to locate a specified word or phrase. When the word is located, the operator can make a change before the unit continues its next search.

The microcomputers of the 1980s offices have software available for word processing, spread sheet analysis, and local area network capability. The next few years will almost certainly bring an even greater reliance upon these automated techniques, local area networks (LANs), intelligent copiers, and fully integrated office systems.

All estimates seem to indicate that the number of computer-related office jobs will continue to grow. Statistics on government computer usage clearly show this trend. According to the General Services Administration, the total number of government owned or leased computers quadrupled between 1969 and 1981. The National Bureau of Standards predicts a doubling in the number of government computers and data communications facilities and a quadrupling of graphics terminals by 1985.

OFFICE INTEGRATION

A by-product of the computer age has been a move toward office integration. In an integrated office the many separate tasks required to process and communicate information are unified in an overall system of automated electronic equipment. Subsystems that form this system include copying facilities, word processing equipment, teleconferencing, data communications, and micrographics (Figure 15-2). An integrated approach means taking a systematic look at the total office environment to find the most efficient way to process the organization's data.

An integrated office approach reduces costs and increases the speed of data flow. It provides backup systems and alternate modes of communication. More and more office managers are finding that they cannot separate word processing, copying, data storage, or communications from one another. The same computer that handles the firm's data processing may also handle its word processing. Small microcomputers can serve as work stations, greatly increasing the system's flexibility. Telephone lines that carry data and voice transmission provide more options and may save money.

There are several specific benefits that come from an integrated office approach.

1. Increased speed. It is faster to prepare and distribute documents

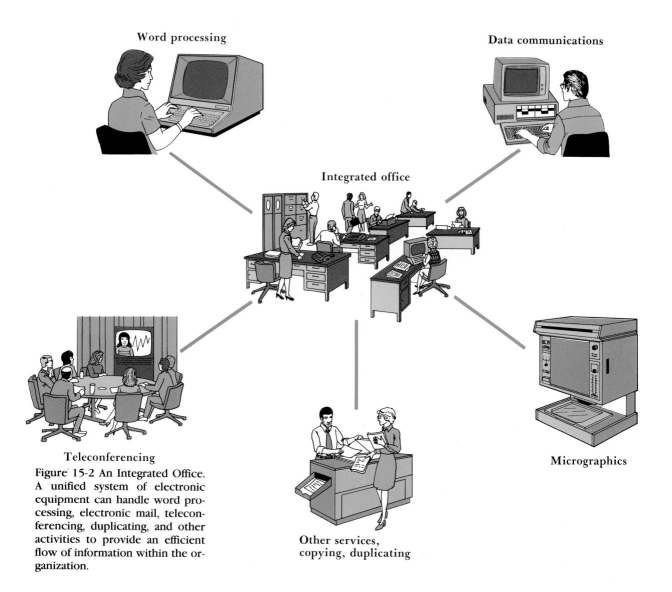

Word processing

Data communications

Integrated office

Teleconferencing

Figure 15-2 An Integrated Office. A unified system of electronic equipment can handle word processing, electronic mail, teleconferencing, duplicating, and other activities to provide an efficient flow of information within the organization.

Other services, copying, duplicating

Micrographics

using automated equipment or electronic means than to perform the same functions manually.

2. Reduction of information "float." Because less time is required to prepare and deliver documents, the time between the generation of information and its use is also reduced.

THIS LAN'S A MILLION DOLLAR BABY

Source: Modern Office Procedures, © April 1983.

Used correctly, local area networks can easily hike productivity, among other things. At Burroughs Wellcome Co., a leading pharmaceutical research firm located in Raleigh, NC, twin Xerox Ethernet local area networks link word processing equipment housed in two buildings a mile and a half apart. Part of the word processing mission is to prepare new drug documentation to be submitted to the U.S. Food and Drug Administration (FDA) for approval.

A corporate study determined that concentrating resources would cut document preparation time—dramatically, as it turned out. Recent improvements have cut preparation time by at least four weeks, which can mean thousands of dollars in sales to Burroughs Wellcome. . . .

Because the buildings are wired with Ethernet coaxial cable, documents created in remote centers can be electronically forwarded to hub centers for specialized services, such as the creation of charts, line drawings, or other graphics. Printing is done on a laser printer, which is cost-effective because it is shared by so many other devices. The printers must be very versatile . . . because most of the 2,000-3,000-page documents are peppered with scientific and mathematical terms and symbols.

Even while giving top priority to the more exotic research-related projects, the word processing department must provide good turn-around on the routine mix of work—legal papers, year-end reports, budgets, product planning, forward market plans, and massive national mailings to scientists. . . .

The first network was installed last April. The second Ethernet was installed last September, and provides backup capabilities and expanded paper options. The company is still in the process of completing the transition to Xerox equipment which began in 1980.

"We make sure that we have a communications interface between the old generation of equipment and the new," the word processing manager notes. "We have a feel for what work lends itself to an abrupt changeover and what doesn't."

Another time-saver is the Kurzweil data entry machine (KDEM) . . . which can read typed and typeset material through optical character recognition technology. For those users who use personal computers and typewriters to submit material to word processing, jobs are turned around from 6 to 12 times faster than rekeying. "By eliminating the need to rekey about 30 pages per day, we figure the KDEM unit will pay for itself in less than three years. It also will allow us to feed text directly from published sources," she states. . . .

"At the same time, we've increased productivity enormously," the office services manager says. "It's difficult to measure savings . . . but we made a stab at it four years ago. We calculated that word processing was reducing the staff time to produce 20,000 to 30,000 letter units per month by 40 or 50 percent."

"If we had remained with the one-on-one secretary concept, we figure our additional head count today combined with the cost of typing would be costing us $1 million more annually."

3. Cost reduction. Although equipment purchases may involve a substantial initial investment, in the long run integrated offices cost less to operate than do manual systems because labor costs are lower.
4. Efficient integration with other organizations. Computers and word processing systems allow firms to provide information to other organizations in a more efficient form (Figure 15-3). Because reports can be recorded onto magnetic tape or disk, or transmitted by telephone, they can be more quickly integrated into larger communications systems.
5. Improved quality. Letters, reports, and other documents are neater, are more consistent, and contain fewer errors than if produced by manual methods (Figure 15-4).

SUBSYSTEMS OF THE INTEGRATED OFFICE

The facilities of an integrated office are used to generate and duplicate written documents, transmit data, and store and retrieve information. Fully integrated offices have major subsystems such as word processing to prepare reports and correspondence; electronic mail systems to transmit and receive letters, memos, and reports; and a telephone network to provide for conference calls and teleconferencing. Rounding out the integrated office are specialized copying machines and duplicators to produce finished reports, and micrographic equipment for filing large volumes of data.

WORD PROCESSING

As we have seen, **word processing** is the application of automated methods to the preparation of letters, forms, reports, invoices, books, articles, or any material containing written words and phrases. It involves the reordering of data, and that reordering includes the editing, revising, and printing out of formatted documents. In word processing data are initially prepared as a handwritten or typed draft, or recorded on a dictating machine, or even written right on the computer keyboard. They are then transcribed on a keyboard device that stores the input on disk or tape, if it is not already in the machine. The text is then displayed on a CRT for editing or revision before it is output as a finished hard copy document.

Integrated office

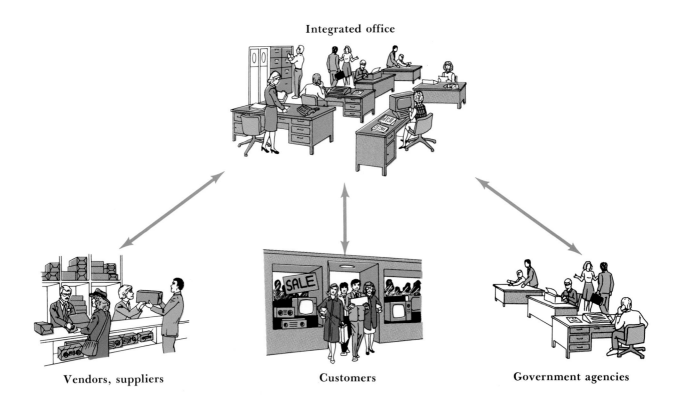

Vendors, suppliers   Customers   Government agencies

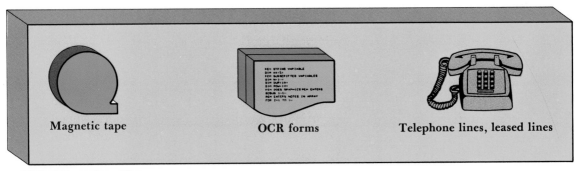

Magnetic tape   OCR forms   Telephone lines, leased lines

Figure 15-3 Information Flow. Electronic communication devices speed the movement of information into and out of an organization.

The word processing system is the hub of many automated offices. A variety of machines make it possible to readily generate reports, correspondence, and other textual documents.

A **stand alone** word processing system consists of a computer equipped with a CRT and printer (Figure 15-5). Microcomputers, to-

Figure 15-4 Spelling Error Detection. A spelling program checks each word entered against a dictionary in memory. Note that it will not recognize a typographical error or misspelling if the result is still a correctly spelled word, such as *hat* for *has* or *its* for *it's*.

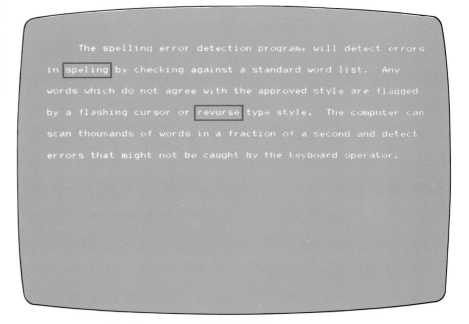

Figure 15-5 Stand-Alone Word Processing System. The stand-alone system contains all the components needed to generate textual documents—input/output devices, CPU, secondary memory, and various text and graphics software packages.

gether with disk storage and hard copy output, allow the operator to enter information, to edit it on the screen, and to store it.

Stand alone word processors store keystrokes in memory. Once the information has been keyboarded, it can be printed out in a variety of widths and formats. A small desktop system can store hundreds of pages of text (provided it has adequate secondary memory) and allow automatic indentions and other formatting options. Lines can be underscored, titles and headings centered, and corrections made by simply backspacing and retyping. Some stand alone systems consist of a general-purpose microcomputer and a word processing program such as Easywriter. This enables the computer to be used for many different applications, not just word processing.

A **shared logic system** consists of a single computer or word processing machine connected to several **work stations** (Figures 15-6 and 15-7). A work station is a terminal or device equipped with a keyboard that enables data to be entered or output from a system. The system may include a dictation tank. The **dictation tank** is a voice recording machine that provides for storage of words to be transcribed. It is much like a computer's secondary storage system. Operators at different work stations can access the information in the tank and keyboard it into magnetic storage, thus converting words and phrases into digital data to be edited and revised later.

Some word processing systems are designed to handle a high volume of dictation from many different sources. Dictation can be input through outside or inside telephones, dictation terminals, or portable cassette units. The material is then transcribed and the keystrokes stored in the system for editing and revision.

Systems may be equipped with conventional line printers or high-quality composing machines. A **composing machine** can output letter-perfect composition, such as is used in books and magazines, in hundreds of different type styles.

A **distributed data processing system** consists of a network of several stand alone word processors with their own memories. Individual letters, memos, or reports are prepared at local work stations and then transmitted throughout the network for updating or revision. Distributed systems have great capacity, since they include many word processors and computers with decentralized storage.

Figure 15-6 Shared Logic System. In this system several work stations are tied to one word processing machine.

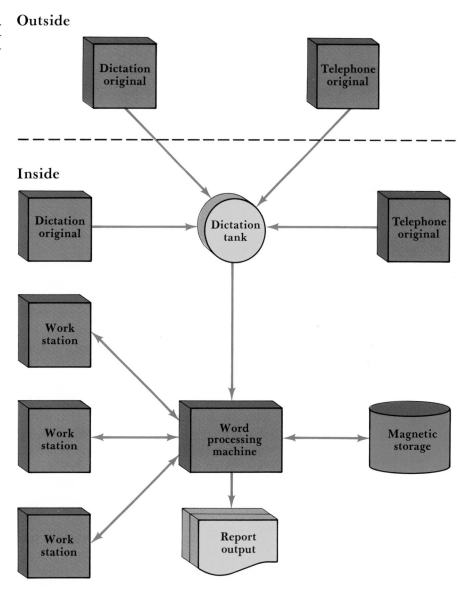

THE WORD PROCESSING CYCLE Most documents prepared on word processing machines or with word processing programs move through a cycle of four steps: idea generation and data capture, tran-

Figure 15-7 Work Station. This work station is a terminal that allows information to be sent to the word processor and can display data ready for editing or revision.

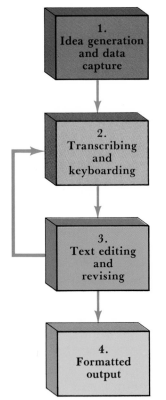

Figure 15-8 Word Processing Cycle.

scribing, text editing, and formatted output (Figure 15-8).

The first step in the word processing cycle is **idea generation and data capture**. The document is defined and designed. The necessary information is selected and gathered. The text of the document is dictated, written, or typed for transcription.

Methods by which the text can be dictated include phone dictation and portable dictation systems that record the spoken word on media such as magnetic tape or disk. **Phone dictation systems** automatically answer a telephone call and record the spoken message for later transcription. They can handle calls from phones inside or outside the office.

Dictation machines are similar to tape recorders in that they record vocal input on magnetic tape (Figure 15-9). Because they are portable, messages can be dictated whenever and wherever it is convenient. Then the completed tape is submitted for transcription.

The second step of the cycle is **transcribing** into memory. The spoken or written words are transcribed into keystrokes. If the initial draft of the report is typed or written in longhand, the operator keyboards the information into memory from the hard copy. If the initial data is a voice recording, the operator, using a **transcribing machine**, listens to the recording on earphones and types in the data (Figure 15-10).

The third step is **text editing**. In this step the information that

Figure 15-9 Dictation System. Portable dictation machines are used to collect voice input in the field for later entry into the word processing system.

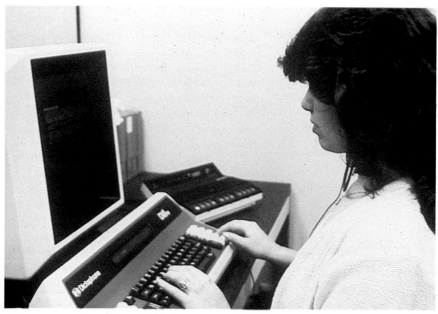

Figure 15-10 Transcribing and Keyboarding. The operator listens to the tape and transcribes the spoken words into keystrokes. Once keyboarded into memory the information can be edited or manipulated later.

has been keyboarded is output as a typewritten copy of the dictated material or as a display on a screen. The person generating the material makes changes and revisions on the draft. The originator may enter changes directly on the screen or return the hard copy to an operator who keyboards the changes into memory. The material is then rerun to produce a revised draft.

Special software capabilities make the revising process easier and more accurate. For example, search capabilities allow the unit to locate all instances of a particular word or value in a stored piece of copy. These characters can then be deleted or replaced via keyboard input. Some programs can detect spelling errors. All words entered are checked against an approved spelling list stored in memory. Misspelled words are instantly flagged and brought to the operator's attention. The editing and keyboarding step may be repeated several times until a final copy is approved.

The fourth and final step of the word processing cycle is **for-**

ARE VDTs A HAZARD TO PREGNANT WORKERS?

Source: Reprinted by permission of *The Wall Street Journal*, © Dow Jones & Company, Inc., 1984. All rights reserved.

Spurred by persistent but unproven fears about harmful radiation, pregnant women are demanding—and starting to win—transfers away from work on video display terminals.

The women's demands arise from concern that VDTs—either through the emission of low-level radiation or some other unknown factor—may cause miscarriages, premature births, birth defects and newborn deaths. Pressure to address the issue is growing: Most of the 10 million Americans operating VDTs are women, and by 1990, 40 million workers may be receiving and processing information on the terminals with televisionlike screens.

So far, eight U.S. and Canadian unions have won transfer rights, extra unpaid leave or the right to use lead aprons for pregnant VDT users. The affected employers include Time Inc., Boston University, Air Canada, Bell Canada, the Village Voice, Mother Jones magazine and the cities of San Francisco and Honolulu. Now, bills are pending in five states that would require employers to provide alternative work for pregnant VDT operators.

Computer makers are lobbying hard against the legislation. Protecting pregnant workers from VDTs is "like protecting them from light bulbs," says Charlotte LeGates, an official of the Computer Business and Equipment Manufacturers Association . . .

In reality, neither side in the controversy can point to any conclusive evidence. Since 1979, VDT operators at as many as two dozen U.S. and Canadian work sites may have experienced an abnormally high rate of pregnancy problems. But investigations at four such workplaces couldn't pinpoint terminals as the culprits.

At the National Institute for Occupational Safety and Health, epidemiologist Jane Gordon says she assures pregnant callers that "we don't have any evidence there is any imminent risk. But we don't have the facts available." The federal agency is about to start an unprecedented three-year study of the pregnancies of 3,000 workers.

Ontario Hydro, a Canadian electrical utility, plans the first animal-health study of the terminals' main suspected radiation hazard. Scientists will expose animals to very low-level radiation, which pulsates from a VDT's sides and rear.

"We feel the question is still open. The door hasn't been closed on possible damage to the fetus," says Robert Facey, an assistant health physicist for the provincial utility. Ontario Hydro's 27,000 employees use 2,000 VDTs; the number will reach 8,000 by the late 1980s. A union accord allows pregnant staff workers to seek transfers from VDT work, but their new jobs may pay less.

Concern over employee morale, rather than health risks, has prompted some companies to reassign pregnant VDT operators. . . .

The transfers don't always work out. Time's 1983 agreement with the Newspaper Guild covering 1,300 editorial and business staff members requires it to make "every reasonable effort" to reassign VDT users who are pregnant or planning pregnancies. But the company has already rejected one request because the not yet pregnant employee had little seniority and worked just six hours a week preparing page layouts.

When Jan O'Brien, a municipal affairs reporter for the Vancouver Province, became pregnant, she offered to dictate her copy over the telephone from city hall rather than use a VDT. The newspaper instead transferred her to a researcher's position, at the same pay. But she dislikes her new post. The 33-year-old reporter complains, "There hasn't been an imaginative use of my abilities."

Still, many employers refuse to consider alternative assignments. A few, such as the Philadelphia Inquirer, prefer to provide lead aprons. But some scientific experts say that the aprons don't provide adequate protection and that their weight could harm the fetus. They say that metal shielding of the machines is the best protection.

matted output. In this final step a permanent copy of the document is generated. Some word processing systems produce final copy on ordinary computer printers such as the dot matrix, thimble, and daisy wheel printers described in Chapter 7. If high quality output is desired, then a composing machine is a better choice.

The final draft may appear in a variety of formats. Word processing machines can print out text copy in many different line widths, justification styles, and type styles and sizes.

DUPLICATING

The duplicating function is an important part of the integrated office. Automated duplication allows large amounts of information to be distributed quickly and easily to those who need it.

Finished documents may be duplicated in many different ways. If under a few hundred copies are needed and the document is not too long or complex, a plain paper **office copier** will do the job. If longer or more complex reports are to be copied, an **intelligent copier** may be required (Figure 15-11). An intelligent copier can copy, collate, or sort pages. Many machines can reduce or enlarge pages, and some can copy in color.

If a large number of copies is needed, duplicating by **offset printing** is more practical in terms of time and cost. Offset presses can print upwards of 10,000 copies an hour. Some presses have automatic plate-making and collating mechanisms. These devices convert

Figure 15-11 Duplicating Machine. An intelligent copy machine can copy, collate, and sort pages in one operation.

original copy or artwork into paper or metal masters suitable for long runs, and automatically mount them on the press. The machine then prints and collates the finished job.

FILING

Filing is the classifying and storing of information, reports, letters, and documents for later retrieval. In some instances the source, or original, documents are filed; in others copies of the documents are kept. Filing may be done either by hand or by electronic means.

The immense filing capabilities of computer systems have already been described.

MICROGRAPHICS

Organizations that must use or mail large volumes of information, such as bookstore chains that need lists of books in stock or sales offices that require price lists on goods in inventory, are relying in-

Figure 15-12 Microform Examples. Microfiche is much more efficient for storing computer output. A 1-ounce microfiche record can hold the same amount of information as 10 pounds of computer printout paper. Microfilm images can also be mounted on tab cards for sorting and filing.

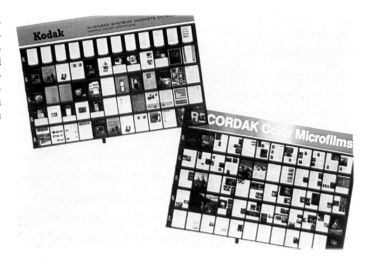

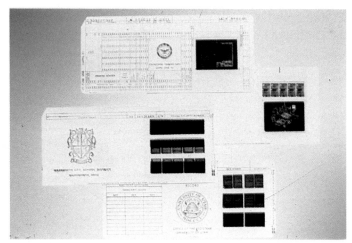

creasingly upon micrographic systems. **Micrographics** is the production of greatly reduced images on photographic film.

As we saw in Chapter 7, the common **microforms** are **microfilm**, **microfiche**, and **aperture cards** (Figure 15-12). Microform records are usually made by photographing and reducing printed pages on a microfilm camera, but they can also be generated directly by computer (Figure 15-13). Whichever method is used, the result is

Figure 15-13 Micrographics System. Information from the CPU is converted into microform images by the output device. The microform records can then be filed and later displayed on microform readers so they can be read by people.

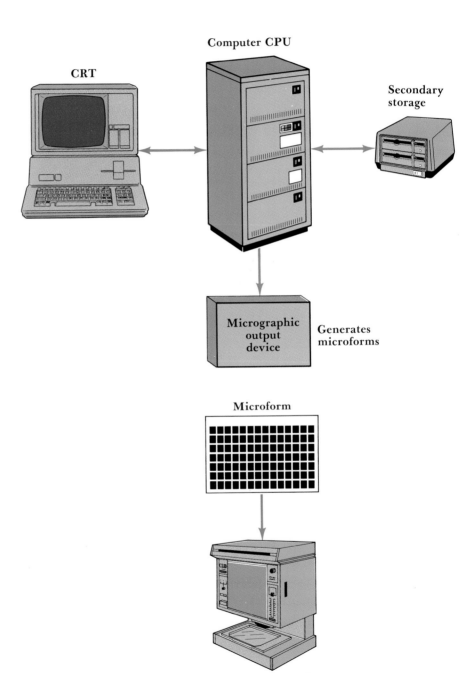

CRT

Computer CPU

Secondary storage

Micrographic output device

Generates microforms

Microform

Microform reader

that large volumes of information are reduced in size and stored on small pieces of film. Once reduced, the data can be filed or mailed without taking up a lot of space.

Microforms are viewed through readers that enlarge the small images on a big screen. Some readers are equipped to make permanent paper copies of the enlarged images.

ELECTRONIC MAIL

The high cost of postage and the time needed for the physical delivery of mail have led to an increasing use of **electronic mail**. Electronic mail facilities replace or supplement the postal service with a system of microcomputers connected by telephone, microwave, or other communications links (Figure 15-14).

In some systems messages are transmitted from one computer to another, and waiting messages are stored on disk (Figure 15-15).

Other systems use a **telecopier** or **facsimile machine** (Figure 15-16). An operator loads a document into the machine. The device scans the page and converts the data into electronic pulses that are transmitted by telephone lines to a remote location. At the receiving end the pulses are converted back into a facsimile of the original document.

In still other systems messages are sent from a keyboard attached to an ordinary telephone line. Messages are routed to other offices and displayed on a terminal. Figure 15-17 shows this system in use.

Electronic mail is faster and less expensive than ordinary mail because no physical documents are transferred. Documents can be transmitted simultaneously to many receiving stations. Original records are protected from loss, because they are not sent through the mails. However, electronic mail does involve the initial expense of specialized communications equipment and continuing charges for rental of microwave links, long distance calls, or reserved telephone lines.

TELECONFERENCING

Teleconferencing is a form of electronic communication that allows individuals at different locations to participate in a conference (Fig-

Figure 15-14 Electronic Mail System. Mail can be sent from one microcomputer to another through a system of coaxial cables.

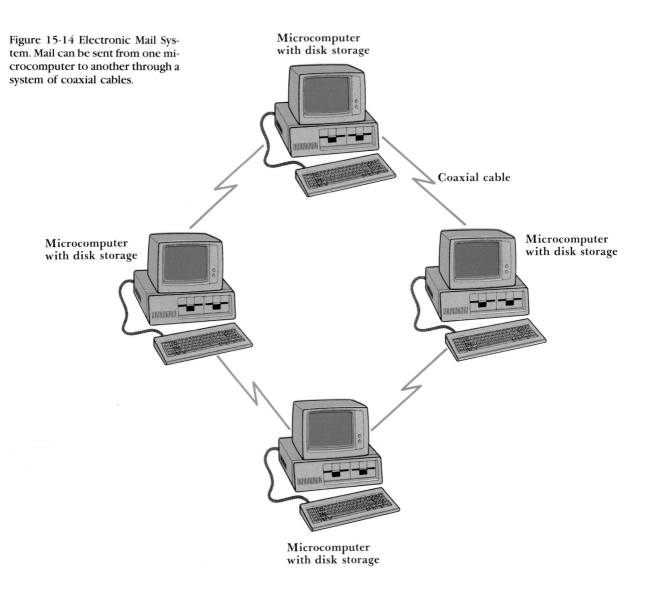

Microcomputer
with disk storage

Coaxial cable

Microcomputer
with disk storage

Microcomputer
with disk storage

Microcomputer
with disk storage

ure 15-18). Using teleconferencing procedures, managers or other personnel can share information, obtain input, and make decisions.

Hard copy printers, video terminals, and picture phones enable participants to send information to one another. **Slow-scan video equipment** can transmit still pictures or graphics. **Full video**

Figure 15-15 Electronic Mail. Electronic mail can be displayed on a CRT or printed out in the form of hard copy.

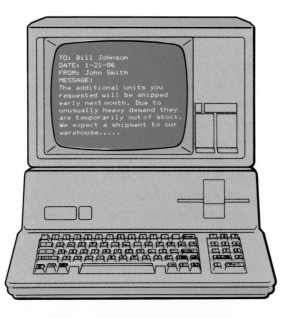

Figure 15-16 Telecopier. The telecopier machine transmits a facsimile of an original document, both text and pictures. The facsimile (or fax) machine can send a letter from coast to coast or to another country in about a minute.

equipment links participants through a television system that lets each person see and hear the others. **Computer conferencing**, tying together computer terminals, allows many users to share information by way of printers or CRT displays.

Figure 15-17 Message Center.

The commander unit allows the executive to set the priorities — who is seen, spoken to, and what is done. One–button commands respond to messages and give the secretary instructions.

REPLY MESSAGES		
REF TO WHAT 01	I'LL C/B TOMRW 11	GIVE TO SALES 21
YES 02	I'LL HANDLE IT 12	GIVE TO SVC 22
NO 03	YOU HANDLE IT 13	PLS COME IN 23
THANK YOU 04	SET APPT 1f	BE RIGHT THERE 24
TAKE MESSAGE 05	TAKE ORDER 15	SEND THEM IN 25
PLS CALL BACK 06	BRING FILE 16	PLS WAIT 26
PLS C/B IN 1 HR 07	TO CUST SVC 17	LV LIT/CARD 27
PLS C/B TOMRW 08	GIVE TO ACCTG. 18	FILL OUT APPL. 28
I'LL C/B IN 15 MIN 09	GIVE TO ENGRG. 19	IN MEETING 29
I'LL C/B IN 1 HR 10	GIVE TO PURCH. 20	IGNORE LAST MSG. ...30

OUT OF OFFICE MESSAGES	ORIGINATE MESSAGES	
OUT OF OFFICE 01	PLS COME IN 01	NEXT PLEASE.........11
OUT TO LUNCH 02	SEND CALL THROUGH ..02	INTERRUPT ME........12
OUT FOR 15 MIN 03	WHICH LINE? 03	GOING TO LUNCH 13
OUT FOR 1 HR 04	PLS CALL ME 04	GOING TO R/R........14
OUT FOR DAY 05	BRING MSG/APPTS 05	BACK IN OFFICE 15
OUT OF TOWN 06	PLS GET COFFEE 06	
IN MEETING 07	CAN WE MEET NOW? ...07	
OUT, PLS PAGE.......08	MAY I COME IN? 08	
LV MSG W/SECY 09	NEEDS SIGNATURE 09	-C- -D-
ON VACATION........10	SEND THEM IN 10	

The master unit, when not sending or receiving messages, always displays the day, date, and time. It has a built–in alarm clock for important appointments. Calls are screened silently without inter-ruption, and callers are not left on hold for long periods of time.

Teleconferencing techniques can be effective office tools because they save time and money. They cut out travel expenses, such as transportation and hotel bills, and cut down on time away from the office. Teleconferences can be held using hardware already in place in many offices, such as computer terminals and telephone systems.

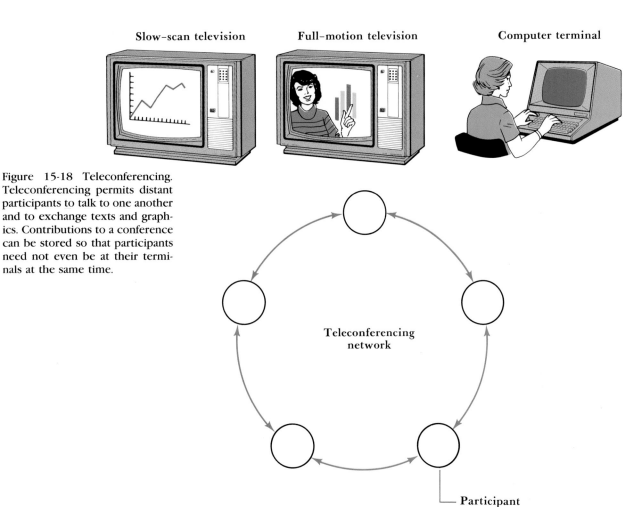

Slow–scan television   Full-motion television   Computer terminal

Figure 15-18 Teleconferencing. Teleconferencing permits distant participants to talk to one another and to exchange texts and graphics. Contributions to a conference can be stored so that participants need not even be at their terminals at the same time.

Teleconferencing network

Participant

The office of tomorrow will be very different from the office of today. Paper documents will be replaced by electronic recording and storage techniques. Working hours will become more flexible, and often employees will be able to perform office tasks at home. Travel to and between offices will be replaced by computer conferences, and the whole pace of the modern office will become faster and more responsive to the needs of customers and clients.

SUMMARY AND KEY TERMS

• **Office automation** has evolved over many years beginning in the late 1800s. Significant early inventions included the telephone, the phonograph and dictating machine, and the manual and automatic typewriter. Later inventions were the electric typewriter with memory capability, the photocopier machine, and more sophisticated dictation equipment. The introduction of the computer and **local area networks (LAN)** led to the fully **integrated office**.

• The advantages of the **integrated office** are increased speed, reduction of information float, cost savings, integration with other organizations, and improved quality of reports.

• **Word processing** is the application of automated methods to the preparation of letters, forms, and reports. In a **stand alone system** one computer is equipped with a CRT and printer. In a **shared logic system** one computer serves several **work stations**. In a **distributed data processing system** several stand alone processors are integrated into a network.

• The word processing cycle has four steps: **idea generation and data capture**, **transcribing**, **text editing**, and **formatted output**.

• **Duplicating** is performed by plain paper **office copiers**, **intelligent copiers**, and **offset presses**.

• Large volumes of information can be handled by **micrographics**, using **microfilm**, **microfiche**, **aperture cards**, or other **microforms**.

• **Electronic mail** replaces postal service with a system of microcomputers connected by telephone, microwave, or other communications links.

• **Teleconferencing** enables individuals at different locations to participate in a conference. The electronic systems that make this possible include **slow scan**, **full video**, and **computer conferencing** arrangements.

EXERCISES

1. Briefly trace the major steps in the development of office automation.

2. List the advantages of integrated office methods over manual methods.

3. Compare stand alone, shared logic, and distributed data word processing systems.

4. List the steps in the word processing cycle.

5. Describe special hardware or software used in each step of the word processing cycle.

6. List some kinds of equipment for duplicating reports.

7. Define filing.

8. Describe how micrographics are used in the integrated office.

9. Describe how the electronic mail system delivers messages.

10. List various forms of teleconferencing.

16

Learning Objectives

After studying this chapter, you should be able to
1. Define key terms related to business systems
2. Describe the evolution of the business systems department
3. List the responsibilities of the business systems department
4. List the steps in designing and implementing a business system
5. List the elements that must be considered when evaluating business systems
6. Describe the purpose of system evaluation and follow up

Chapter Outline

What are Business Systems?
   Data in Business Systems
   Need for Business Systems
   Evolution of Business Systems
Function of Business Systems Departments
Preliminary Study and Planning
Systems Analysis
   Work Measurement
   Cost
   Hardware
   Software
   Personnel
   Time
Systems Design
   Office Layout and Equipment
   Establishing Procedures and Policies
   Forms Design
   Information Retrieval and File Design
   Selecting Personnel
Systems Development
   Hardware Installation
   Software Preparation
   Communications
   Vendor Capability
Systems Implementation and Evaluation
System Control

Systems Analysis and Design

Prompt and effective decision making is vital to the success of any business enterprise. Sometimes only a few dollars rest upon making the correct business decision, but other times it involves thousands of dollars and affects hundreds of people. Systems analysis is a useful tool for solving general business problems. It can also be applied to making more specific judgments about equipment and procedures and seeing that they are used efficiently in business.

In this chapter we look at the business enterprise as a total system and review the role of the business systems department, problem solving methodology, and the means by which systems are planned, evaluated, and implemented. We also look at specific details that must be assessed when installing data processing systems.

WHAT ARE BUSINESS SYSTEMS?

A **business system** is a collection of hardware, personnel, procedures, and techniques that function as an organized whole. It is the organizational structure within a firm that enables it to achieve its goals. Business systems include policies, methods, personnel, data processing software and hardware, and communications procedures.

Systems are composed of subsystems. These smaller units have individual functions, but act in accord with the goals of the overall system. The advantage of the system is that the total is greater than the sum of the parts. Figure 16-1 diagrams a simplified business system.

DATA IN BUSINESS SYSTEMS

In all organizations, whether in business, government, or education, decisions are made by administrators. Administration in a business system usually consists of a board of directors and management. An essential function of the board of directors is to determine long- and short-range goals. Establishing objectives requires

447

Figure 16-1 Simplified Business System. A business system is composed of subsystems that function as an organized whole.

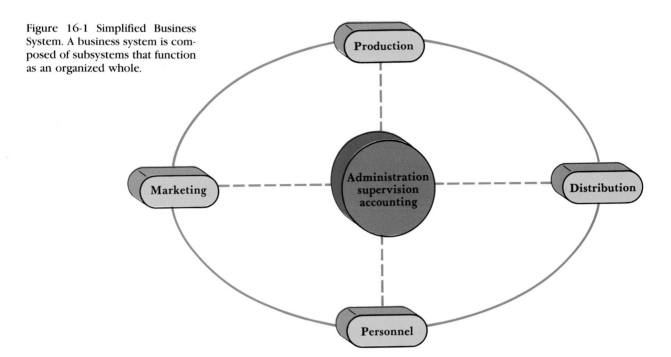

a careful analysis of business conditions, customer needs and buying patterns, production capacity, staff, and finances. To assess these elements accurately the administration must have data acquired, processed, and reported in its most useful form.

Once the organization's directors select certain objectives, it is management's job to direct the subsystems of the firm toward these goals and to measure progress toward them.

Because different levels of management need various types of information at different times from all divisions of the firm, the firm's facilities for recording, manipulating, and reporting data can be one of its major assets. Good management decisions rest upon the availability of data and many factors (Figure 16-2).

To be of most value to a firm, data should be

Ready when needed

Ready where needed

Appropriate to the problem in terms of relevance and completeness

Figure 16-2 Value of Business Data. The quality of management decisions is directly related to the quality of the data on which they are based.

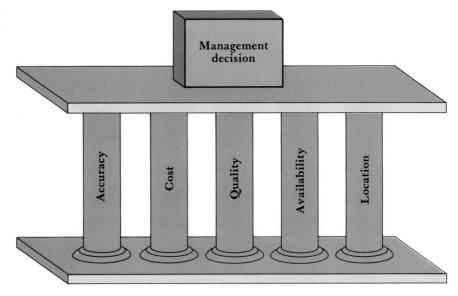

Accurate

Gathered, processed, and reported at a reasonable cost

NEED FOR BUSINESS SYSTEMS

Business firms cannot afford to solve data flow problems in an unorganized, unsystematic way. Mistakes are expensive; time is limited. A planned and organized strategy for processing information is essential to

Gain maximum cost savings in processing and handling data

Gain maximum time savings in outputting results

Establish an orderly procedure for growth

Develop a uniform method of operation

Avoid costly errors

Improve the quality of decisions

Improve organization responsiveness to customers' needs

Improve allocation of physical resources

Figure 16-3 Business Decisions. Many businesses have developed into large organizations with many branch offices that operate worldwide. Decisions affecting these firms involve many dollars, many locations, and many people, and they must be made systematically.

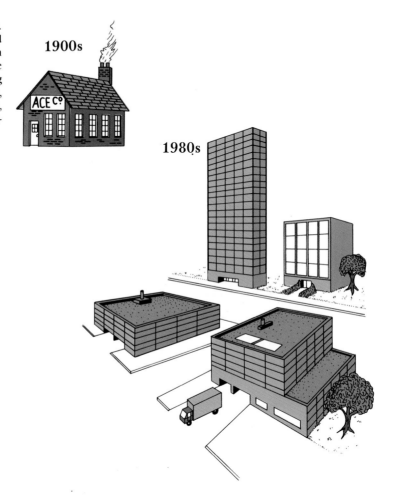

Produce the best product at the lowest cost

Eliminate duplication of effort

EVOLUTION OF BUSINESS SYSTEMS

At the beginning of this century, when most firms were small and material and labor costs were low, data processing needs were minimal (Figure 16-3). Few firms used systematic business methods to plan their activities and carry out their goals. When a problem came

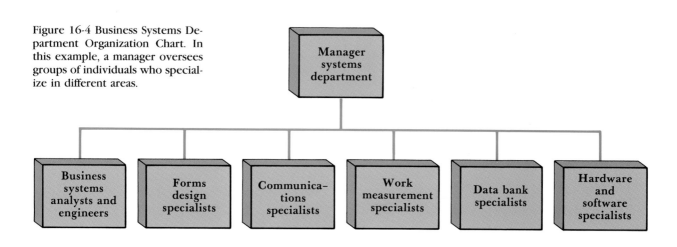

Figure 16-4 Business Systems Department Organization Chart. In this example, a manager oversees groups of individuals who specialize in different areas.

up, it was solved on the spot. The solution chosen was usually the easiest one to implement. The result was a patchwork of policies and procedures. Careful analysis of problems and attention to strategy were ignored in favor of finding immediate answers. This approach is sometimes called "brush fire" problem solving. To this day some firms use these methods.

As firms grew, capital investment increased, costs of labor and materials rose, and management turned to more orderly means of solving problems. One or two employees were assigned the task of using quantitative means to examine business procedures. They became known as **business systems engineers** or **business systems analysts**. Eventually, many firms established a separate **business systems department**. This department is responsible for applying measurable and quantifiable approaches to data flow problems.

FUNCTION OF BUSINESS SYSTEMS DEPARTMENTS

Since World War II business systems departments have continued to grow in importance. Teams of business systems engineers, analysts, and data processing specialists are indispensable to many business firms. Figure 16-4 diagrams the organization of a typical systems department. The systems experts make critical studies of the depart-

Figure 16-5 System Investigation. The system analyst reviews the forms, procedures, policies, and methods used in a system. The analyst structures his investigation around six basic questions.

ments of the firm and make recommendations regarding their operations.

A major responsibility of the business systems department is to improve the flow of data. In studying a system, analysts review its current forms, procedures, policies, and methods. The personnel, machines, space requirements, and office layout are looked at to see if and how the system could be improved or whether a new system should be developed. Analysts ask six basic questions in investigating each element in the study (Figure 16-5).

1. What is done?
2. How is it done?
3. Why is it done?
4. Who does it?
5. When is it done?
6. Where is it done?

Systems analysts conduct many types of surveys to evaluate a system. Data flow and word processing studies point out bottlenecks and problem areas. Time and motion studies further define problems and even point to solutions.

When solving business systems problems, systems analysts generally move through five basic phases (Figure 16-6): (1) preliminary study and planning, (2) systems analysis, (3) systems design, (4) systems development, and (5) systems implementation and evaluation. Let us review each of these major phases in detail.

PRELIMINARY STUDY AND PLANNING

The object of the **preliminary study** is to answer the question, "Does a new or revamped system appear to be sufficiently practical and economical to warrant further study and investigation?" The preliminary study looks at the fundamental needs of a business and reviews broad plans for making needed improvements. It defines the problem, states ultimate objectives, and offers some tentative plans.

An important part of the preliminary study is selecting the people who will conduct the study and defining of their responsibilities. In the **task force** approach management forms a committee of knowledgeable employees from various departments. After the committee has completed its study and made recommendations, it disbands.

Another approach is to appoint an **ongoing committee** with members from operating units, data processing and business systems departments, and managers (Figure 16-7). This type of committee does a preliminary investigative study, makes recommendations to management, and has the continuing responsibilities of implementing recommendations and monitoring the need for future modifications or changes.

Still another approach is to give one individual, with the title of **project director**, the necessary funds and authority to carry out the study. He or she may also be responsible for implementing changes and recommendations.

The preliminary study should provide a clear definition of the goals of the new system. The outcomes desired from a new system must be stated in measurable terms, with specific times and dates defined. The study should begin to answer such questions as: How many dollars will be saved? When? What specific problems will be solved by the new system? How much faster, more accurate, and pre-

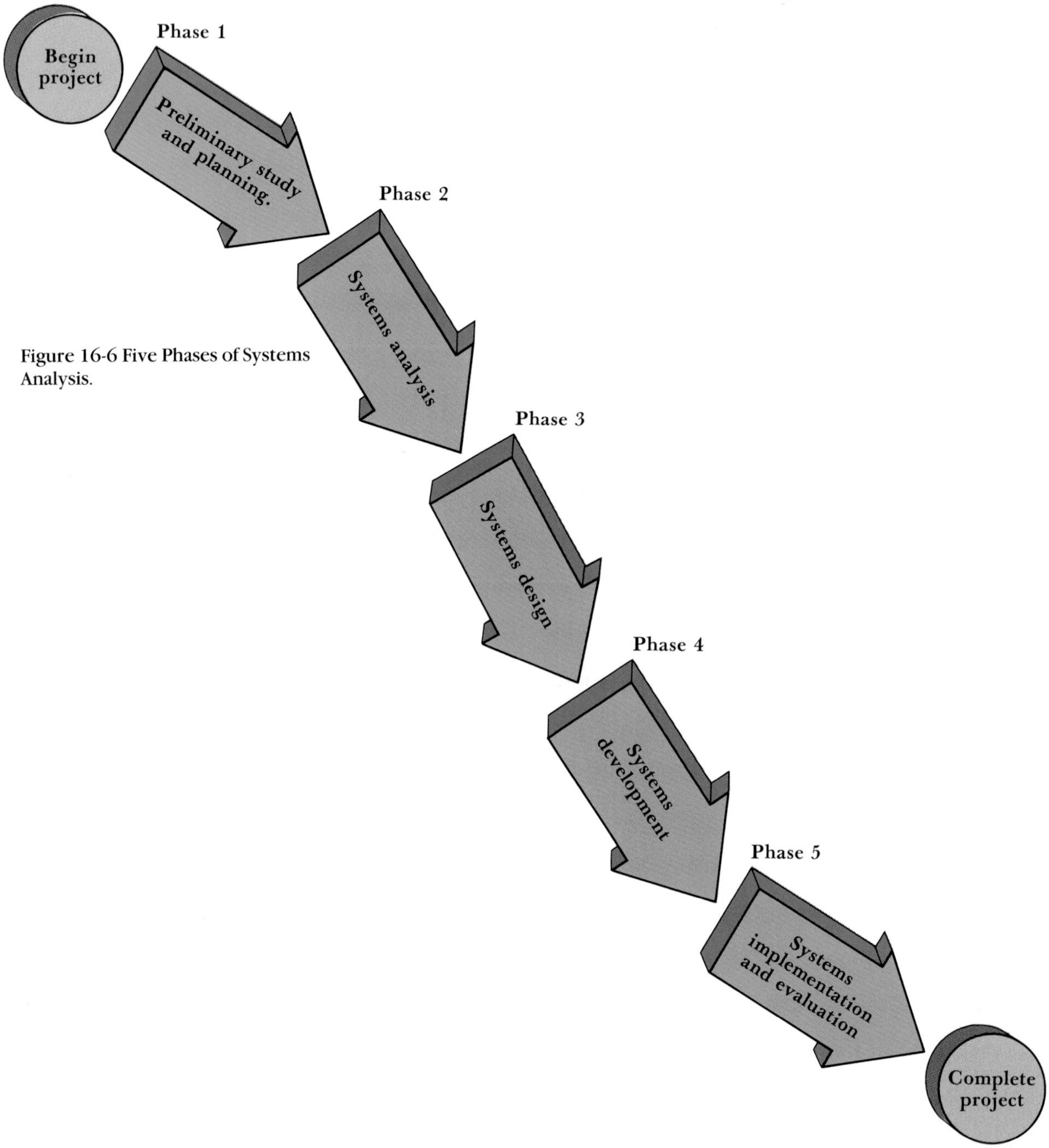

Phase 1

Begin project

Preliminary study and planning.

Phase 2

Systems analysis

Figure 16-6 Five Phases of Systems Analysis.

Phase 3

Systems design

Phase 4

Systems development

Phase 5

Systems implementation and evaluation

Complete project

Figure 16-7 Ongoing Committee. An ongoing committee can observe a system in operation over a long period and accumulate information for improving it.

cise will the results be? What existing machines can be eliminated? When? What new machines need to be purchased? When?

During this phase the business systems analyst discusses the firm's needs with people inside and outside the organization: employees, managers, division heads, customers, vendors, other firms, consultants, and so forth (Figure 16-8).

The preliminary phase of the study is essential to avoid making unnecessary changes or changes that do not justify the costs involved. It is also essential for planning because a successful new system cannot be designed until its goals are defined, and there would be no way of evaluating its success without a measure for comparison.

SYSTEMS ANALYSIS

In the second phase of solving business problems the analyst reviews the existing system in greater detail, gathers more data, and analyzes information. This step involves systematically collecting all

Figure 16-8 Preliminary Study Phase. Any piece of information can add to the understanding of a situation and may provide a critical key to a problem's solution. People inside and outside the organization are consulted to get as many views of the situation as possible.

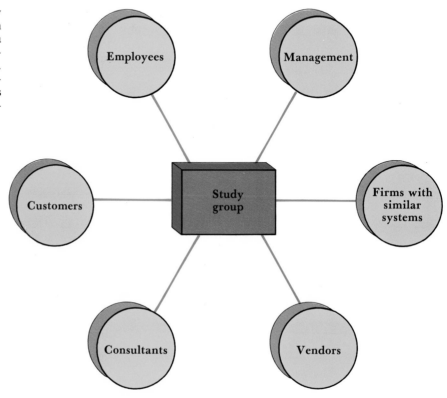

pertinent information that will later be used to design the new or improved system.

During the systems analysis phase a number of people, from inside and outside the firm, are called upon for help and cooperation (Figure 16-9). Outside consultants may be hired. Department and branch managers are interviewed to determine their data needs. Personnel, hardware, and software are evaluated in terms of their usefulness in solving the problem and their cost.

WORK MEASUREMENT

A variety of study techniques are used in the analysis phase. The systems analyst observes machines in operation and employees at work. One tool the analyst may use is a **work sampling study** to de-

Figure 16-9 Interviews and Gathering Data. Direct interviews with the people who work in the system can reveal information that observers from outside could not find. All sources are tapped by the analyst.

termine the content of each job. In work sampling a measure is made of the number and types of calculations performed, the number and types of forms handled, and so forth.

Work measurement enables the analyst to compare the output of employees before and after a new system is in place. It allows the quantity as well as the quality of clerical work to be measured.

Logs, run books, histories, and records may be reviewed to gain some idea of the quantity of data processed by the firm. Special detailed records may be kept for a short period of time to learn more about the nature of a given data processing problem.

Time studies are often used to determine how long it takes to perform a task. This is usually done by observing and timing employees as they go about their assigned responsibilities.

COST

The analyst must thoroughly examine all aspects of the proposed system to determine whether it is worth the expenditure. Some of the questions asked are:

A JOB DESCRIPTION FOR A SYSTEMS ANALYST	JOB DUTIES

A JOB DESCRIPTION FOR A SYSTEMS ANALYST

JOB DUTIES

Formulates logical statements of business problems and devises procedures for solutions of the problems through use of data processing systems or other means. Confers with users to determine and define the problem and type of data to be processed. Prepares logic flowcharts, tables, diagrams to assist in analyzing problems utilizing, if necessary, various business techniques. Devises logical procedures to solve problems, usually using data processing. Analyzes existing system logic difficulties and revises the logic and procedures involved as necessary.

Prepares definitions of problems; defines what program needs to do with regard to machine logic, flowcharting, and EDP instruction, devises data verification methods and prepares standard systems procedures and documentation. Actively involved in implementation of system and responsible for training of user personnel and preparation of user procedures and EDP procedures.

BACKGROUND REQUIRED

Degree in accounting, or computer sciences; minimum of two to three years experience in a profit oriented organization, with responsibility for systems analysis and projects implementation in accounting functions. Should be familiar with all systems documentation functions. Experience in programming (COBOL) helpful. Should be familiar with all systems documentation techniques; experience in on-line systems development and Data base techniques preferred.

Should equipment be leased or purchased?

What will maintenance costs be?

Which outside supplier will provide maintenance service at the lower cost?

What one-time costs are involved?

What recurrent costs are involved?

What would it cost to change or expand the new system at a later date?

What training and implementation costs are involved?

How much will physical plant alterations cost?

How do the costs of the new system compare to the cost of operation of the old system.

HARDWARE

The analysis of any system that requires the purchase of new equipment will entail some study of the performance, speed, and capacity of key pieces of equipment. Suppose a large computer is being evaluated. Here are some specific questions analysts ask regarding the equipment.

What size CPU and amount of primary storage are required for present needs?

What peripheral equipment should be purchased for present needs?

Can the selected equipment be expanded to meet growth needs?

Which brand of computer is best in terms of present and anticipated needs?

Should equipment be centralized or decentralized?

Should one large computer or several small ones be purchased?

How difficult is it to program the computer?

Who will be in charge of the new equipment?

SOFTWARE

The programming and software of a new system must also be studied (Figure 16-10). The following questions are often asked:

What new programs will have to be written?

Should programs be written or purchased?

Are appropriate software packages available?

How long will it take to write, test, and debug new programs?

What skills will the staff need to write the new software?

What software is available from equipment vendors at no cost?

Can existing programs be converted to the new system?

Can the new programs be run on machines that may be purchased later?

PERSONNEL

Implementing a new system affects the individual employees of a

Figure 16-10 Program Preparation. Part of the analysis of a system is an examination of existing programming and consideration of what new kinds of material might be needed.

firm as well as the organization as a whole. The analyst studies the personnel area, too.

Will new people be needed? How many?

Will people be laid off? How many?

How many jobs will be upgraded?

How many employees will have to be relocated?

Will retraining be necessary?

How will salaries be affected?

Are there people now in the firm who already have the new skills that will be needed?

What will the effect be on employee morale?

Who should supervise the changes to the new system?

TIME

A new system must be feasible from a time as well as cost standpoint.

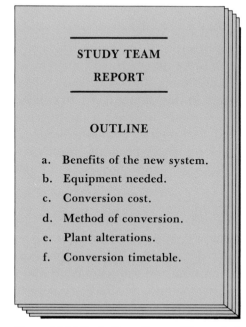

Figure 16-11 Study Team Report. The goal of a study team report is to state what must be done and how it is to be done and to give management the information it needs to accept or reject a plan. Such a report would be needed before any change is made—before a major new system is installed and before modification of the new system based on evaluation of its operation are planned.

What would be the best point in the business cycle to install the new system?

How long will the installation take?

Should the old system be operated alongside the new? For how long?

For how long should consultants be employed to monitor the new system?

How long will it be before the new system can be expected to run smoothly?

These questions are typical of those asked by analysts. There are many more questions that may be asked, depending upon the specific problem and facilities being considered. A study team report may now be prepared summarizing the progress made and describing the proposed system (Figure 16-11).

SYSTEMS DESIGN

Once the relevant information has been gathered and analyzed, a system must be designed. The analyst, working with equipment suppliers, consultants, and other knowledgeable people, actually designs the system in this phase. Plans, drawings, and layouts are prepared. Specifications are written for the purchase of equipment, forms are designed, and policies established. Specific pieces of hardware and particular computer programs or other software are selected. In this phase the analyst concentrates on the following elements.

OFFICE LAYOUT AND EQUIPMENT

The analyst recommends the most efficient office layout to facilitate data flow (Figure 16-12). He or she is concerned with shortening processing time and reducing labor and equipment costs.

The analyst may also be responsible for the purchase of any new equipment required by a system and for arranging for the most efficient use of the equipment after it has been installed.

ESTABLISHING PROCEDURES AND POLICIES

A new system must be documented to help employees learn how to use the equipment efficiently. The systems analyst often devises procedure and policy manuals for this purpose. Manuals help to ensure uniform practices and policies. They specify such things as which forms to use, when to use them, how to handle exceptions, and where forms are to be routed.

Well-written policy manuals help both the employee and the organization. They not only provide the employee with a clear statement of company policy and methods, but assure that each branch or division in the company will acquire, report, and process data in the most efficient way.

FORMS DESIGN

Data forms are essential to almost all business systems. In some cases hundreds of different forms are used within a firm. The success of a

Figure 16-12 Office Layout. Understanding day-to-day operations may make the need for simple physical changes obvious.

Original desk arrangement

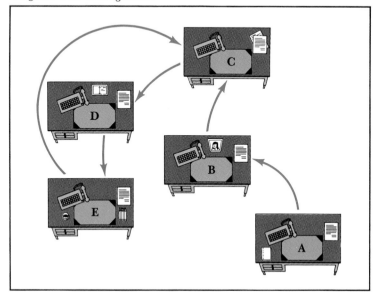

Routing schedule: A→B→C→D→E→C

Changes recommended by analyst

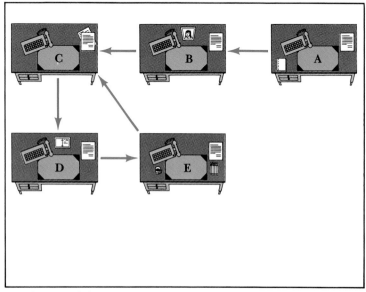

Routing schedule: A→B→C→D→E→C

new system often depends on whether adequate forms and source documents have been developed.

The systems analyst must specify content, layout, distribution, and routing of the forms. He or she is also responsible for designing source documents and reports. All documents designed must comply with existing hardware requirements.

Forms design includes the physical characteristics of the form as well as its content. Consideration must be given to size, paper, type size, number of copies required, printing process, and cost. The analyst must also determine the quantity to be ordered, the system of inventory to be used, and the methods of packing and dispensing the forms. Forms must be reviewed periodically to see that they are adequate, necessary, and up to date.

INFORMATION RETRIEVAL AND FILE DESIGN

The job of the analyst also includes designing data files for information storage and retrieval systems. Modern business depends heavily on data files to store a firm's records. The analyst should design files that will yield accurate and complete data and will be easy to correct and update. In some organizations this task is delegated to the DBMS administrator.

SELECTING PERSONNEL

The systems analyst may also write job descriptions and job orders. Job descriptions outline the duties and functions of each job. Job orders specify the number of employees needed for each job classification.

In writing a job description, the analyst indicates the level of skill and training required to perform the job. This information guides the personnel department in hiring new employees (Figure 16-13).

The duties of the systems analyst may also include planning programs for job orientation or in-service training. He or she may arrange classroom training or instruction from vendors and prepare, revise, and order training manuals, teaching aids, slide films, video cassettes, and other media.

Figure 16-13 Personnel Interview. The systems designer can list what qualifications seem necessary for a task. The personnel director must be able to recognize the person who could accomplish it.

Figure 16-14 Equipment Installation and Testing. The analyst must consider equipment's performance, reliability, capacity, compatibility with existing equipment, ease of use, and effects on personnel and procedures.

SYSTEMS DEVELOPMENT

Once a system has been designed, the next step is to build it. In the development phase the analyst begins assembling the system now on paper. Equipment is ordered, forms printed, and programs written, tested, and debugged.

The development and physical construction of a system may take months or even years. In some instances building specifications must be drawn up, bids let out, or teams of programmers assigned to write and develop software. An effort is made to schedule specific dates when new equipment is to arrive and personnel is to be shifted to the new system. Recruitment of employees may begin.

HARDWARE INSTALLATION

Sophisticated hardware, such as computers, word processing machines, copiers, or facsimile equipment, is installed and tested (Figure 16-14). It may take many weeks of on-site testing before a piece of equipment is certified ready for use. It is particularly important that hardware be thoroughly checked out and broken in. Careful attention to hardware at this stage can reduce costly breakdowns and interruption of service after the full system is in operation.

SOFTWARE PREPARATION

If a system uses a computer or involves electronic data processing, programs must be written, debugged, tested, and maintained. Often, the analyst specifies the function and purpose of a proposed program, flowcharts the preferred algorithm, and indicates the input/output requirements. These specifications are then given to a programmer who actually writes the program. When the program is running satisfactorily, documentation is prepared explaining the program logic, how data are input, program options, and so on.

An important piece of software written by programmers is the benchmark program. A **benchmark program** includes various options and functions to be run on a computer in order to test its capability and compare its performance against others. Accurate time records are kept to see which computer is able to perform the benchmark program the quickest, thus giving an indication of the overall efficiency of the equipment.

COMMUNICATIONS

The systems analyst contracts for equipment to meet the communications requirements of a system. Microwave links or coaxial cable may be installed. Data entry machines may be put in place and data concentrators and leased lines acquired.

VENDOR CAPABILITY

A **vendor** is an individual or organization that supplies goods or services to another individual or organization. The systems analyst should look at a vendor's abilities in many areas before selecting a particular make of equipment. Several key factors are evaluated: reputation and past performance, thoroughness and attitude in respond-

Figure 16-15 Checklist for Vendor Capabilities.

✓	**Reputation**
✓	**Proposal**
✓	**Experience**
	Past performance
✓	**Maintenance staff**
	Support services
✓	**Software**
	Training courses
	Manuals
	Local offices

ing to proposals, capabilities, size of maintenance staff, and extent of support services. Figure 16-15 is a sample checklist of important criteria to be considered when choosing a vendor.

Two major considerations in selecting vendors are their experience in their field and their ability to handle the specific needs of a particular firm. Some vendors specialize in computers, communications equipment, office machines, or software. A number of manufacturers have been in business for many years and employ an experienced staff of systems engineers, machinists, technicians, and consultants.

The support services provided by vendors vary greatly. Some include full installation, maintenance, and repair services in their purchase or lease fee. Some have large branches located in major cities and provide training courses, operating manuals, and extensive help in adapting to a new system.

SYSTEMS IMPLEMENTATION AND EVALUATION

Once a new system has been developed, the systems department must implement it properly. Systems implementation requires careful planning to see that the transition is made without waste, errors, or excessive costs. Employee morale is a factor in maximizing productivity. The systems analyst must have the cooperation of both employees and management. Personnel must be shown the advantages of the new system and how it will affect each individual.

A new system may be implemented in several ways (Figure 16-16). It can begin all at once or progress step by step. Sometimes a new system is set up to operate in parallel alongside the old. When the new system is running smoothly, the old system is dropped. The systems analyst must observe the new system in operation to make sure that there is no backsliding into the old, less efficient method.

The final step in the process is measuring results. Were the results expected? Did costs go down? By how much? Are results more accurate? In what way? If the benefits did not materialize, why not? How can the system be improved?

As output of the new procedure is evaluated, the systems analyst may decide to modify the plan. Then this revised plan is implemented and the output once again evaluated. This procedure is repeated until the most efficient arrangement of staff, equipment, office layout, and data processing methods is reached.

SYSTEM CONTROL

In many instances the systems analyst is involved in the analysis and design of a system, but then loses control once it is implemented. There are instances where a well-conceived business system has gone awry after it is installed. This was due to the lack of follow-up by the analyst, or in some cases the system was installed in a location distant from the analyst's office. Some cases of system failure are traced to poor system management or follow-up rather than ill-conceived plans. Ideally, the analyst tries to conceive and implement a system that will correct its own errors or bring failures or omissions to the attention of management before they create losses of data, erroneous results, or serious financial problems.

Figure 16-16 Implementation
Plans.

All-at-once change

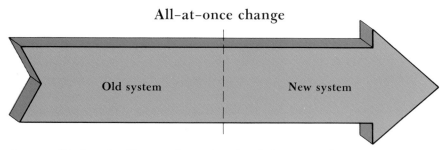

On a specific date the old system is terminated and the new one begun.

Step-by-step change

The old system is phased out piecemeal and the new one brought in gradually.

Parallel implementation

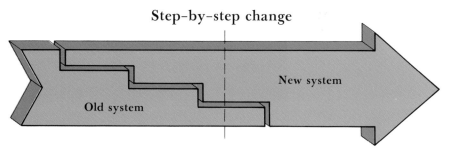

The old system is kept running alongside of the new one and then finally discontinued.

The real test of a system is its ultimate performance. Systems analysts must carefully assess whether or not the equipment that has been installed in fact meets the test benchmark standards and the needs of the enterprise. Business needs are continually changing, and a piece of equipment or system that was suitable at one time may not be at another. The challenge faced by the systems analyst is to see

FROM DATA PROCESSING TO INFORMATION PROCESSING *Source:* David Katch, *Infosystems*, Aug. 1978, p. 59.	The need to put information to use has become critical in the business world. Management needs information to serve its decision-making processes, dictating that systems must move away from *data* processing towards *information* processing. This means change—change in management thinking at all levels, in approaches, in definitions, and in responsibilities. As we move toward these changes, we would do well to keep in mind the words of James A. Michener: "What we must do, I believe, is to accept change, even embrace it and seek it out, but at the same time to control it so that it contributes to the quality of life rather than subtracts from it. The task of the educated man is to evaluate change and mold it to his ends, and the man who performs this task most intelligently will live the best life."

that the business system remains responsive and competitive in a rapidly changing world.

SUMMARY AND KEY TERMS

- A **business system** is a collection of hardware, personnel, procedures, and techniques that function as an organized whole to accomplish the goals of the firm.

- For information to be of greatest value, it must be available **when** and **where** needed, be at the right **level of accuracy**, of the necessary **kind and quality**, and be processed at a reasonable **cost**.

- Business problem solving strategies evolved from **brush fire**, nonsystematic approaches to orderly methods.

- Business systems departments involve experts who study the flow of data in organizations. They analyze **what** is done, **how** and **why** an operation is performed, and ask **who** performs it, **when**, and **where**.

- Systems analysis moves through several phases. First a **preliminary study** is done to define goals.

- In the **systems analysis** phase data is gathered and analyzed, interviews are conducted, and **time study**, **work sampling**, and other measurement techniques are used. Factors related to cost, hardware, software, personnel, and time are investigated.

- In the **systems design** phase the analyst cooperates with consultants, vendors, and others to write specifications and establish policies.

Office layout, procedures, forms design, information retrieval and file design, and personnel are considered.

• In the **systems development** phase equipment is installed; forms are printed; programs are written, tested, and debugged; communications links are installed; and vendors are evaluated and selected.

• The final phase is **systems implementation and evaluation**. Outcomes are measured and compared to anticipated goals. A system may be modified to produce the most efficient arrangement of personnel, equipment, and methods.

EXERCISES

1. Define business systems.

2. Compare the early methods of solving business problems with those of the computer age.

3. Give several examples in which the guess, hunch, or chance method is used to solve business problems.

4. Select a simple data flow problem, such as inventory in a small retail store, and trace its solution through the five steps in the analytical approach.

5. What are the major responsibilities of the modern business systems department?

6. Select a data flow problem such as registration and enrollment in your college. Using the six questions often asked by business systems analysts, investigate an improved system.

7. Write a set of policies and procedures for handling returned merchandise in a small retail store.

8. Select a data flow task such as writing up a sales slip in a shoe store. Have several students go through the steps in filling out the forms. Perform a time study and work sampling on the operation.

9. What support can a vendor provide when a firm plans a new computer system?

10. Why is it important to measure system performance?

Part 7 Computers and the Future

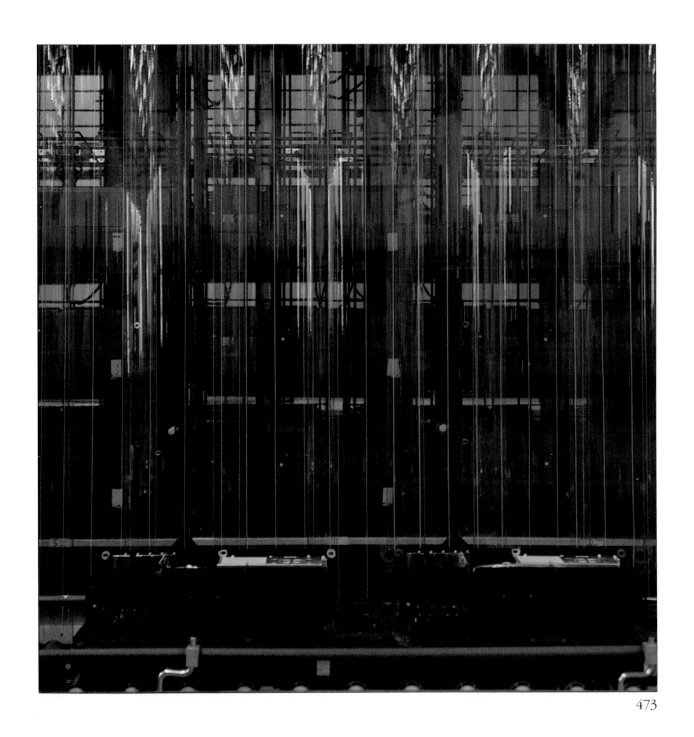

17

Learning Objectives

After studying this chapter, you should be able to
1. List the major manufacturers of computer equipment
2. Describe the structure of data processing departments
3. Describe high growth areas in data processing
4. Summarize the skills, aptitudes, and working conditions involved in data processing jobs
5. List major data processing career opportunities
6. Discuss education and training for data processing careers

Chapter Outline

The Computer Industry
Structure of Data Processing Departments
  Small Data Processing Department
  Medium Size Data Processing Department
  Large Data Center
  Personnel Requirements
Jobs in Data Processing
  Salaries
  Job Environments
  Skills and Aptitudes
Job Descriptions and Opportunities
  Data Entry Operator
  Programmer
  Systems Analyst
  Console Operator (Digital Computer Operator)
  Data Base Manager
  Communications Engineer
  Librarian
  Documentation Specialist
  Instructor
  Data Processing Director
  Salesperson
  Customer Engineer
Education and Training
  Individual Courses
  Community Colleges
  Colleges and Universities
  Home Study Courses
  Manufacturers' Training Programs
  Certificate in Data Processing

Your Career in Computers and Information Processing

If you have chosen to enter the field of computers as a career, you have selected one of the most vital and dynamic areas of industry. The computer field offers satisfying, lifelong work opportunities for men and women with the right skills, training, and experience.

We have seen that firms that manufacture computers and data processing equipment have exhibited growth rates well above other industries, and this trend is expected to continue into the future. The demand for people in all computer related fields—computer engineers, programmers, installers, and equipment designers, to name only a few—will grow equally as fast. There are entry-level positions for undergraduate students and more advanced employment for those with bachelor's, master's, or doctorate degrees in computer science or information systems.

In this chapter we will look at the makeup of the computer and data processing industry, describe various job categories and high growth areas, and discuss the education and training necessary to fill these jobs.

THE COMPUTER INDUSTRY

The computer industry consists of a diverse assortment of business organizations, ranging from industrial giants such as the IBM Corporation to small software houses employing only one or two people. Much of the computer industry revenues are generated by the large mainframe manufacturers, such as IBM, Sperry, and Burroughs, who produce the huge computers used by large corporations or for such complex tasks as air traffic control or weather forecasting.

Much of the recent growth in the computer industry is due to the sale of microcomputers. Automated business equipment manufacturers—producers of copiers, electronic typewriters, word processing and communications machines—have also experienced above average growth rates. These manufacturers include such firms as Wang Labs, Lanier, and Exxon, as well as IBM and Burroughs. IBM is the largest of these firms.

PIONEERING PEOPLE: WILLIAM HEWLETT AND DAVID PACKARD

Source: Reprinted with permission of *DATAMATION®* magazine, © Copyright by Technical Publishing Company, a Dun & Bradstreet Company, 1982—all rights reserved.

William Hewlett and David Packard are the dynamic duo of the computer and electronics business. Together they built from scratch a company that means high quality, high-technology products.

The two first crossed paths while undergraduates at Stanford University. They became friends, and later, in 1938, when Packard returned West after a two-year stint as an engineer with General Electric in Schenectady, N.Y., they decided to go into the electronics business together. Their first plant was the now-legendary garage behind a house Packard rented in Palo Alto. Their initial capital was $538. Total product line: the Model 200A audio oscillator, an electronic instrument used to test sound equipment.

The Model 200A was first shown at a meeting of the Institute of Radio Engineers (now the IEEE) in the fall of 1938. Shortly after, the two young engineers embarked on a modest advertising campaign: they mailed about 25 letters to some hot prospects. Sure enough, orders started coming in, a few of them prepaid. Then, a sales agent in Los Angeles put Hewlett and Packard together with Walt Disney Studios. Could the two engineers modify their oscillator to cover a different frequency range? Could two young, ambitious engineers do a little extra work for one of the biggest and most famous movie studios? Is the sky blue?

In a short time, the Model 200B audio oscillator was in production and being used to make the animated Disney film "Fantasia," Hewlett and Packard had themselves a business, and in 1939 they made it official. The Hewlett-Packard Co. was born.

After a year, they moved their work to a small building and began hiring their first sales reps. Among the young company's early objectives: keep the business on a pay-as-you-go basis, do not run a "hire 'em, fire 'em" operation, and concentrate on making a contribution—that means new products.

Today, of course, the company has grown, but the philosophy remains the same. HP does business around the world, business that in 1980 was worth more than $3 billion. The company that started in a tiny Palo Alto garage now makes more than 4,000 different products and has nearly 60,000 employees.

Computer usage has spawned the development of entirely new secondary industries. The software publishing business is now a major component of the computer industry. Computer users spend millions of dollars each year on software. To meet this demand, large and small firms have entered the market with products aimed at business, personal, hobby, and educational applications. This software, on floppy disks or cassette tape, is sold through computer stores, book stores, and mail order houses.

Millions of dollars are also spent each year on floppy disks, paper, ribbons, and other computer supplies. This facet of the industry is rapidly growing to meet the needs of computer users who require supplies and materials for their machines.

STRUCTURE OF DATA PROCESSING DEPARTMENTS

The size and complexity of data processing departments naturally vary with the kind and size of the business they serve. A small firm may need only a few data processing employees to operate a small computer. A medium-size organization may employ from 5 to 50 individuals. A large firm, on the other hand, might employ hundreds of people to operate a network that ties together hundreds of computers in various parts of the country and around the world.

SMALL DATA PROCESSING DEPARTMENT

In the smallest and simplest organization one or two employees are responsible for all data processing operations. They often serve as combination programmers, computer operators, systems analysts, and managers.

But data processing is a complex field. Different skills are required of the programmer and the systems analyst, for example. Because different skills are involved, there is a need for specialization. Figure 17-1 shows a typical organization chart for a small data processing department. It has four specialized employees: a data entry clerk, a programmer, a computer operator, and a manager.

The relatively low volume of work processed by a small business usually limits the need for programming languages to only a few, easily handled by one or two programmers. The availability of ready-made software, such as Lotus 1-2-3, VisiCalc, and similar software, further reduces the need for programmers. Little or no systems programming, such as modifying the operating system of a computer, is done.

MEDIUM SIZE DATA PROCESSING DEPARTMENT

Smaller insurance companies and manufacturers, sales agents and brokers, advertising agencies, and other moderately sized companies

Figure 17-1 Organization Chart of a Typical Small Data Processing Department.

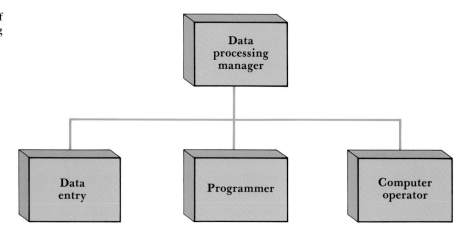

Figure 17-2 Organization Chart of a Typical Medium-Size Data Processing Department.

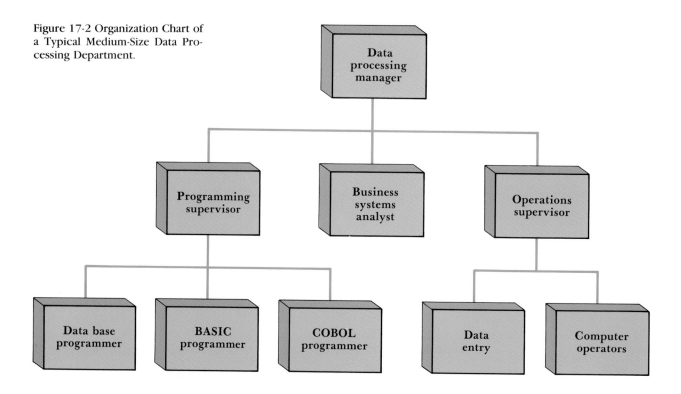

usually have about 5 to 50 employees in their data processing departments.

The needs of the companies and the larger number of employees permit more specialization within the department. Figure 17-2 is an organization chart of a medium-size department. The head of the department supervises employees and guides the operation of the department. Reporting to the manager are a programming supervisor, a business systems analyst, and an operations supervisor. There is a staff of programmers and computer operators. If the firm programs in more than one language, it may keep on staff several programmers, each proficient in a different language and assigned to different types of problems. If a large workload merits a 24-hour operation, an operations supervisor would be in charge of three shift supervisors.

LARGE DATA CENTER

A data center in a large firm may employ several hundred workers and occupy an entire floor of a large office building. Figure 17-3 is an organization chart of a data processing department in a large firm.

The larger the company, the greater the specialization in the data processing department. With specialization comes greater efficiency and output. There may be dozens of terminal operators, supervisors, systems analysts, systems engineers, programmers, business systems analysts, clerks, librarians, and documentation specialists (Figure 17-4). Because large firms process a high volume of work, the department may be on a 24-hour operating schedule, with three shifts of supervisors and operators.

Some companies organize their staff into small working groups, each handling a different problem. One project director is assigned several programmers, systems analysts, and clerks. This team approach allows a concentrated effort on a particular problem.

The more usual arrangement is to sort employees into specialized groups that concentrate on one aspect of data processing as a whole, such as systems, programming, operations, and support.

SYSTEMS GROUP   The systems group plans and expands the operating system, modifies the computer control programs, and alters

Figure 17-3 Organization Chart of a Typical Large Data Processing Department.

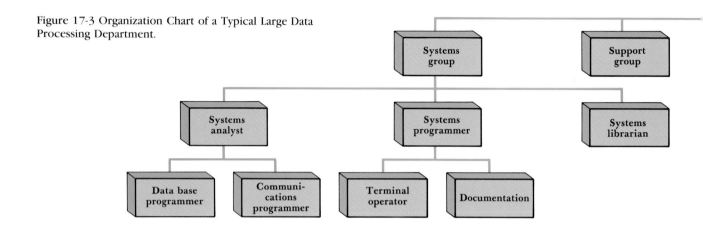

Figure 17-4 Staff Employed in Large Data Processing Organization. Large firms employ terminal operators, systems analysts, clerks, and documentation specialists.

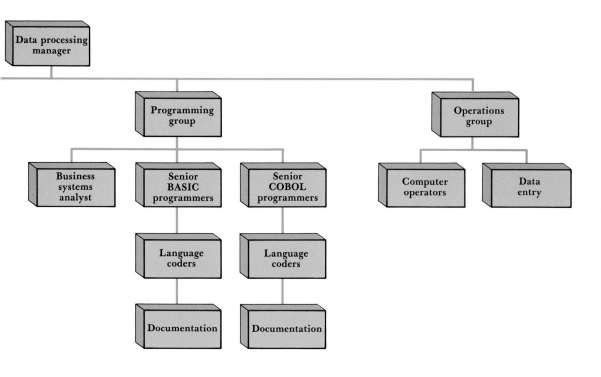

compilers. It also maintains and develops communications and data base software. The systems group employs systems analysts, systems programmers, and librarians.

PROGRAMMING GROUP   Some companies must process a wide variety of problems in business, engineering, mathematics, graphics, and research. They employ programmers with specialized abilities in languages such as COBOL, BASIC, FORTRAN, RPG, and assembler.

With more personnel available, the functions usually performed by a single programmer in a smaller setup may be further specialized and assigned to several individuals. For example the tasks of documentation, data entry, and writing programming instructions may be divided among several people. A senior programmer may lay out the overall program and give separate modules of the program to other programmers for coding. The parts are assembled into a running program, with documentation done by yet another specialist.

OPERATIONS GROUP   Computer operations is responsible for operating computers, loading tapes, and filing floppy disks and other storage media. The group operates the printers, optical scanners, and other machines in the data processing department.

The operations function may also be divided into specialized activities. Companies with several types and sizes of computers in one installation may assign staff to operate a particular computer, I/O device, or other communications equipment. A group of supervisors coordinates the operation.

SUPPORT GROUP   Large firms have a support staff for the data processing department. The greater volume of programming increases the need for tape and program librarians, mathematicians, statisticians, technicians, clerk typists, and other supporting personnel.

PERSONNEL REQUIREMENTS

Personnel needs are dictated by the volume, type, and degree of sophistication of data processing done by a firm. The number of people needed in each department is determined from a review of reports and records. A firm that does a great deal of data entry will probably hire more terminal operators and supervisors than a firm that does more systems design and programming. The latter firm will need more coders, programmers, and systems analysts than terminal operators.

To fill the positions in the data processing department, the personnel department and the data processing manager usually follow routine procedures. The data manager supplies job descriptions for the personnel department to use as a guide in recruiting employees. Applicants are interviewed and screened by the personnel department. They fill out applications which give pertinent data such as previous employment, experience, and education. The personnel department may also test applicants to evaluate mental capacity and performance. The applicants that seem to fulfill the basic requirements of the position are interviewed by the data processing manager or supervisor. The results are evaluated and a selection made.

The data processing manager or supervisor introduces the new employee to the job. Usually the employee is given a training or

TELECOMMUTERS: WORK TRAVELS TO THEM

Source: Martin Porter, *New York Post*, November 13, 1984, p. 31.

Joseph Wynn starts work each morning at a computer in his Bronx apartment.

A paraplegic, Wynn is a telecommuter—someone whose work commutes electronically while the worker stays home.

Wynn is a word processor for American Express—one of several New York-based companies, including Metropolitan Life Insurance and NYNEX, experimenting with telecommuters.

Among Wynn's duties are processing various forms American Express uses regularly, making transcriptions and taking dictation.

Intrigued by the idea of transplanting some of their work away from the office, leading New York corporations including Citibank, AT&T, IBM, and Marine Midland Bank last year funded a $200,000 study of telecommuting.

The report found that about 100,000 Americans now perform their work from home on computers. It also found that the work done by as many as 7 million people technically could be done by computer from home if their employers wanted to do it that way. Marcia M. Kelly, president of Electronic Services Unlimited, which did the study, believes as many as 18 million workers could be telecommuting in a decade.

Telecommuting got Joseph Wynn off the disability rolls. "I didn't think it was going to be too hot working from the house," he says, "but it turned out to be a great idea."

The American Express program, known as Project Homebound, began two years ago with an investment of $200,000. The homes of ten handicapped people were equipped with Wang word processors and hook-ups to the company's central dictation system.

After a nine-month trial run, nine participants joined the full-time American Express staff. They work seven hours a day and earn about $15,000 per year.

Metropolitan Life has similarly arranged for a few handicapped programmers to work at home on IBM PCs. And the company is experimenting with other employees as well. Recently it gave five managers in its computer center personal computers for after-hours home use. The company found that overtime hours worked at home were more productive than late hours at the office.

indoctrination course or is closely supervised for a period of time. Many firms use periodic employee evaluation procedures to decide which employees should be advanced in status, pay, and responsibility. In-service training is another responsibility of data processing management. As new equipment is acquired or new procedures installed, retraining programs, seminars, and courses are offered to employees.

JOBS IN DATA PROCESSING

There are now jobs in data processing in almost any field you can think of—business, industry, government, nonprofit organizations, education at all levels, medicine, and so on. Workers in business data processing are employed in manufacturing, public utilities (transportation, electric power, communications), wholesale trade, retail trade, finance (real estate, insurance, banking), and other services.

When making a career choice you should investigate those areas that show the greatest potential for future need of trained, skilled personnel. Some high-growth areas where much current research and development is going on include conversational languages, voice synthesizers and detectors, robotics, and communications. The extensive use of microcomputers will mean an enormous demand for marketing, repairing, and maintaining these devices.

Whatever the area of expertise or field of occupation there are, of course, some basic things to consider about any job.

SALARIES

Salaries vary according to job classification, years of experience, and training. They vary also with the geographic area, the demand for workers with a given specialty, and current business and economic conditions (Table 17-1). As a rule, data processing salaries are above the national average. As in any business, however, a surplus of applicants in a particular job category will mean lower salaries, other things being equal.

JOB ENVIRONMENTS

Generally, employment in data processing requires little physical effort. Because firms house their data processing equipment in modern, air-conditioned quarters, employees often work in newer, better equipped, and more comfortable quarters than many other clerical and office workers.

Some individuals work in relative isolation. Others travel thousands of miles each year and meet hundreds of people. Many data processing firms offer fringe benefits such as educational allowances.

TABLE 17-1   Average Annual
Data Processing Salaries by
Installation Size

JOB TITLE	ALL	OVER $1 MIL	UNDER $1 MIL
Vice President	47,562	67,650	44,772
Director of DP or MIS	36,264	49,158	35,155
Service Coordination/User Liaison	27,794	27,949	26,881
Manager of Systems Analysis	37,526	41,500	36,484
Senior Systems Analyst	35,671	35,100	35,456
Systems Analyst	26,420	28,278	26,265
Manager of Applications Programming	33,131	42,700	31,548
Lead Applications Programmer	29,756	38,143	27,728
Senior Applications Programmer	26,900	33,425	25,425
Applications Programmer	22,121	25,692	21,286
Junior Applications Programmer	16,907	19,530	16,536
Systems Analysis/Programming Manager	32,378	40,885	30,148
Lead Systems Analyst/Programmer	33,714	46,028	30,874
Senior Systems Analyst/Programmer	30,461	34,992	28,647
Systems Analyst/Programmer	25,123	28,478	23,842
Manager of Operating Sys. Programming	34,877	43,934	30,651
Senior Systems Programmer	33,947	35,102	32,800
Manager of Database Administration	29,850	55,000	26,706
Manager of Computer Operations	24,071	31,080	23,240
Shift Supervisor	20,237	20,864	20,241
Lead Computer Operator	17,416	19,314	17,091
Computer Operator	14,685	15,626	14,588
Control Clerk	13,867	14,518	13,595
Data Entry Supervisor	15,875	18,500	15,835
Data Entry Operator	13,012	12,740	13,054
Word Processing Supervisor	17,750	24,750	17,086
Word Processing Operator	14,435	17,537	14,230

Source: DATAMATION, September 15, 1984, p. 80.

Company health plans, profit sharing, bonus programs, and liberal
vacation benefits are common.

SKILLS AND APTITUDES
Generally, the specific job determines the skills and aptitudes required. Some jobs require a high degree of manual dexterity, others

almost none. Some call for years of study in mathematics or electronics. Others require a practical knowledge of selling and marketing principles.

You should talk to a counselor or guidance officer, and review your aptitude test scores and interest measures with them, to evaluate your capabilities.

JOB DESCRIPTIONS AND OPPORTUNITIES

Information about specific job categories is available in many places. The Dictionary of Occupational Titles (D.O.T.), found in most school and public libraries, thoroughly describes various job categories including duties and skills and aptitudes necessary.

Occupational guides published by state employment offices are another good source of job descriptions. These guides usually outline job duties, working conditions, employment opportunities, pay and hours, promotion, and training. They also tell you where to find additional information.

Many large-scale employers, such as state and local governments, school districts, and large private firms, publish job availability and employment bulletins. These cover job descriptions, requirements, salary, and how to apply.

In the preceding chapters we have already described many human functions in computer systems. The following review of jobs gives you an overview of the many opportunities in data processing.

DATA ENTRY OPERATOR
Keyboard operators enter, process, and display data through online terminals (Figure 17-5). Countless businesses that must keep large files of information up to date and available, such as banks, hotels, motels, airlines, automobile rental agencies, and stock brokerage houses, now employ many data entry operators.

PROGRAMMER
Programmers are responsible for the development of programs from planning and flowcharting to coding and debugging. Generally, pro-

Figure 17-5 Data Entry Operator. Data entry operators are employed by banks, hotels, airlines, and other organizations. They keyboard information that will later be processed by computer.

Figure 17-6 Programmer. The programmer's responsibilities include planning, coding, debugging, and documenting programs.

grammers plan the solution of a stated clerical, administrative, or statistical problem (Figure 17-6).

The programmer must determine what information should be entered in the program and in what form, the mathematical and logical operations the computer must perform, and the type of output desired. Sometimes the work is divided among several people so that one person does the research and early planning of the program, another person does the actual coding, and another the documentation.

Working conditions are good, and jobs are available in many different fields. The long-range employment outlook is good; it should parallel the total growth in jobs for skilled office employees. As new programming languages are developed, some retraining to acquire new skills may be necessary.

SYSTEMS ANALYST

Systems analysts study business problems and formulate procedures for solving them (see Chapter 16). They provide guidelines that programmers develop into computer instructions. The work involves an-

Figure 17-7 Systems Analyst. A systems analyst studies a problem and formulates a procedure for solving the problem, giving guidelines to programmers and others who will implement the solution.

Figure 17-8 Console Operator. Console operators check the status of the computer, load tapes, operate printers, and monitor communications equipment.

alyzing subject matter and identifying conditions and criteria required to automate a procedure. The analyst specifies the number and type of records, files, and documents to be used, outlines actions to be followed by personnel and computers in enough detail so that programming can be done, presents recommendations and proposed procedures to management, recommends equipment configurations, coordinates the development of test problems, and participates in trial runs of new and revised systems (Figure 17-7).

CONSOLE OPERATOR (DIGITAL COMPUTER OPERATOR)
Console operators monitor the control console of large mini or mainframe computers (Figure 17-8). They determine the procedures to be followed from the programmer's instruction sheet for the run, get the necessary equipment ready, load the computer with required tape reels, disks, or cards, and start the run. If the computer stops or signals an error, they try to locate the source of the trouble. Console operators also run a variety of auxiliary equipment, including machines that transfer data from one medium to another.

A console operator may work alone on a single computer or with several others in a computer installation. Many firms operate their computers around the clock, using three shifts.

The role of the console operator is basic to the industry and should grow in the next decade. The position is important in both batch-oriented and large real time systems such as those serving airline and ticket reservation terminals.

Improvements in computers and in programming languages have simplified, rather than complicated, machine operations, so machines are often less complex to run than they were a decade or two ago. As a result, you should find that it is now easier to qualify for openings in computer console operations.

DATA BASE MANAGER

The shift to management information systems and the growing use of data bases have created the need for data base managers. Data base managers plan, design, and implement data bases. They see that information is properly structured and added to or removed from data bases as necessary.

COMMUNICATIONS ENGINEER

Communications engineers design and install communications systems. They plan local area networks (LANs) and design microwave, fiberoptics, satellite, and telephone communications links. They are also responsible for maintaining and testing communications equipment and lines.

LIBRARIAN

Librarians support the activities of the system personnel. They catalog and file data, reports, programs, and documentation on programs. In large computer installations librarians file and catalog magnetic tape, disks, and occasionally punched cards.

DOCUMENTATION SPECIALIST

Documentation specialists, sometimes called technical writers, prepare written descriptions and instruction manuals for software and hardware. They codify the details and specifications on running a program that are supplied by the programmers or systems analysts.

AMERICA IS ALL EARS FOR RAMONA

Source: Jerry Cohen, *Los Angeles Times*, October 15, 1984.

At some time or another, half of the telephone users in the United States, pen or pencil and note pad at the ready, will listen with rapt attention to Ramona's every utterance—if only briefly. . . .

Hers is the voice that comes on the line after the caller gives a live operator the party he or she wants to telephone. It is a voice that is cheerful, clear and cordial—only thing is, it is delivered by microchips into which the digits have been burned. . . .

If all this sounds distressingly impersonal, be assured: A real live Ramona does exist. The system is not all electronic processing and voice synthesizing, although those are the high-tech functions that make it so successful.

The real Ramona lives in a Main Line suburb outside Philadelphia, has a husband and three grown children. She once wanted to be an actress but her parents warned her that the theater was a chancy way to make a living. So after graduating from New York University, she got a master of arts degree at Northwestern University, where she majored in speech pathology ("a high-class version of speech therapy").

Her professional name is Ramona Lenny and her married name is Ramona Alpert. . . .

Besides being a speech pathologist, she has for many years done radio and television commercials and narration for industrial and technical films.

Because she was born in New York City but has lived in Illinois and Mississippi as well as Pennsylvania—and is married to an Oklahoman—she has developed what is known in the trade as a "cosmopolitan voice." Which means, she said, "I have no regional dialect."

When she learned that Telesciences Inc., a New Jersey firm that is among a handful in the United States supplying audio response units to phone companies, was looking for "a voice" for its system, she applied for the job. She won out over 40 applicants because, said Bob Brewster of Telesciences, she had the "conversational tone" that his firm was looking for. Once hired, she was plunked down in a New Jersey recording studio and after reciting, "The number is," she enunciated the figures zero through nine in three different inflections: a rising one, a falling one and a neutral one—because that's the way people talk: in rising and falling timbres mixed with monotones.

She also recorded the numbers "one hundred" and "one thousand" for use when a phone listing ends in two zeros or three zeroes.

From that point the computer took over—just as it takes over now when you call information and ask for a number in one of the stations where the system is installed. In layman's terms, here's what happens after you dial 411:

An operator, after accepting the name of the firm or person desired, calls up on the screen of a computer terminal a series of listings. Once the right listing is found, the operator pushes a button that activates the automatic intercept system and the computer instantaneously puts the number together digit by digit. Then the recorded voice of Ramona takes over.

Her voice pronounces the number once, pauses, then repeats it. If a customer needs additional aid, he simply stays on the line and in a few seconds an operator returns. . . .

Ramona's widespread electronic presence is a great satisfaction to Ramona Lenny-Alpert back in Pennsylvania, who occasionally dials information and hears her own voice—although, ironically, not in the Philadelphia area, where the phone company contracts with a competitor of Telesciences.

But when she dials long-distance information and her voice responds, she said, "I love it. It's very exciting to hear my voice. I never get tired of it. I always listen to the number twice." . . .

They prepare notes, drawings, and textual statements regarding the program flow, format of input and output records, and so on. For firms that sell hardware equipment, software products, or time sharing to customers, they write manuals, operations guides, reference manuals, and installation instructions for users.

A documentation specialist needs good writing skills as well as an understanding of computers and data processing.

INSTRUCTOR

Instructors teach customers how to use software and hardware products produced by a firm. They often travel to the customer's plant or office to train the people who will operate the equipment or use the software product. In some cases they conduct classes at their firm's location to train salespeople, customer engineers, and customers.

To be successful an instructor should have a data processing background, enjoy teaching adults, and be willing to travel.

DATA PROCESSING DIRECTOR

Data processing directors or managers are responsible for the overall output and operations of the data processing department. They coordinate the activities of the computer installation with those of other departments and organizations in order to provide reliable, uninterrupted service to the firm. As administrators they supervise the employees in the data processing department and plan workloads, staffing, recruiting and training, and promotion.

Figure 17-9 Marketing. Individuals employed in computer marketing assist customers in assessing their needs and selecting the right equipment for the job.

Managers must keep up with new developments in equipment and systems. They must be able to communicate well, both orally and in writing.

SALESPERSON

There is a wide variety of positions related to the selling of computers, terminals, related hardware, software, and time sharing and similar services. Those engaged in selling, whether for manufacturers, service businesses, or retail stores, demonstrate equipment, analyze needs, and make recommendations concerning new devices and services.

Thousands of retail computer stores have opened across the country. They employ a large number of clerks, salespeople, installers, and others (Figure 17-9). The hours and working conditions vary greatly with the employer and the kind of equipment or service sold. Some travel may be involved.

To be successful a salesperson must have a good grasp of data processing fundamentals, enjoy being with people, and like selling.

CUSTOMER ENGINEER

Customer engineers are employed by computer manufacturers to visit firms that have purchased their systems. They help the customer make the most efficient use of the available equipment. Installers often travel to new installations and remain until the system is in operation and performing properly. Maintenance people visit computer installations at regular intervals to do preventive maintenance. They clean, lubricate, and adjust machines and perform routine diagnostic tests on computers, line printers, terminals, and other peripherals (Figure 17-10). They also make repair calls.

The employment outlook for this group is good and should grow as more machines go into homes and small businesses. Many firms that make computer components and supporting equipment also hire technicians, installers, maintenance people, and engineers.

To do the work you need training in technical skills and knowledge of electronics and hardware.

Figure 17-10 Maintenance and Repair. Customer engineers (CEs) maintain and repair computer equipment at the user's site.

EDUCATION AND TRAINING

Two- and four-year colleges, trade and vocational schools, and universities offer a variety of courses in data processing. Some business organizations offer training to employees through on-the-job training (OJT) programs.

INDIVIDUAL COURSES

Courses may last from six weeks to a year. They usually cover a specific, but limited, skill. A course in COBOL or BASIC programming is an example. Another typical course would train the student to be a data entry clerk. Many of these types of courses are offered by trade and vocational schools.

These individual courses allow the student to enter the industry without devoting a large amount of time and money to training and preparation. However, for advancement and greater opportunity, additional academic coursework, training, and supervised on-the-job instruction are usually required.

COMMUNITY COLLEGES

Many community colleges offer two-year programs that lead to either an Associate in Arts degree or a certificate of proficiency in data processing. Either is valuable in getting into the job market.

The emphasis in coursework varies. Some community colleges stress data processing for business and industry with a curriculum designed to train students for jobs in insurance, banking, manufacturing, and government. Other schools stress equipment and hardware and provide courses in practical operations and maintenance. The student may, for example, be given instruction in electronics and electromechanical theory and practice, computer logic, arithmetic and mechanics, including troubleshooting, testing, and repairing computer systems. Still other colleges offer mathematically oriented courses that stress numerical methods and the mathematical elements of computer programming.

Graduates of a two-year course may qualify as beginning programmers, salespersons, or maintenance or installation engineers. Or they may transfer to a four-year school and pursue a B.A. or B.S. degree.

COLLEGES AND UNIVERSITIES

As in the two-year programs, information systems curriculums in four-year schools and universities vary greatly. Some programs have even been developed to meet special needs or the employment demands of firms in a given community.

Most four-year schools give courses in programming languages and an introduction to data processing. Business schools offer undergraduate and graduate work in business management and business systems analysis. Other programs cover information systems technology, systems analysis, or computer technology.

Many universities offer graduate work, leading to a master's degree or doctorate, in information systems, computer science, and business administration. Colleges of education frequently offer undergraduate and graduate concentrations in data processing for teachers through the business education program.

HOME STUDY COURSES

Several equipment manufacturers and private schools offer comprehensive home study courses in basic computer systems, programming, and systems engineering. These programs utilize programmed instruction, film strips, audio and video tapes, self-testing, and supervised reading.

MANUFACTURERS' TRAINING PROGRAMS

Firms such as IBM maintain customer education centers offering coursework in basic systems, programming languages, and applications. They provide packaged home study courses, examinations, and advisory services and give certificates of completion.

Many firms provide customers with training programs designed primarily for in-service training of employees or for orientation to their services. Manufacturers' courses cover engineering, manufacturing, project management, and systems programming.

CERTIFICATE IN DATA PROCESSING

A certificate of proficiency is awarded by the Data Processing Management Association (DPMA) to individuals who pass a written examination. The examination is given annually at many schools and colleges throughout the country and is open to those who have had five years work and study experience in data processing.

The certificate is an asset when seeking employment in data processing. It certifies that the holder has a broad educational background as well as a practical knowledge of data processing. The DPMA recommends an educational background that provides a balanced coverage of essentials, including data processing equipment, computer programming and software, principles of management, quantitative methods, and systems analysis and design.

Only a few decades ago there were just a handful of people

working in the computer and electronic data processing field. The growth of job opportunities in the industry has been remarkable. Although thousands of clerical workers have been displaced from their jobs by computer technology, thousands of new jobs have been created for those who can operate computers, write programs, sell equipment and supplies, or design new systems.

It is almost certain that in another decade there will even more jobs, and many new job categories will open up. No one can say for sure what the specifics of these jobs will be. But we do know that the study of computers and communications will be rewarding. These fields offer career opportunities and chances for advancement and should be given serious consideration as you plan your future.

SUMMARY AND KEY TERMS

• The computer and data processing industry has experienced a growth rate well above other industries. Companies in the field range from industrial giants to small software houses.

• Small data processing departments in an organization have only 1 or 2 employees, medium-size departments have from 5 to 50 workers, and large data centers employ hundreds of people, sometimes on a 24-hour operating schedule. Employees may be classified into **systems**, **programming**, **operations**, and **support** groups.

• In assessing employment, applicants should consider salaries, job environments, fringe benefits, and their own skills and aptitudes.

• Among the major data processing job possibilities are data entry operator, programmer, systems analyst, console operator, data base manager, communications engineer, librarian, documentation specialist, instructor, data processing director, salesperson, customer engineer, installer, and maintenance technician.

• Education and training in computers and data processing can be gained through individual courses, comprehensive programs at two and four-year colleges and universities, home study courses, and courses offered by manufacturers.

• A certificate of proficiency in data processing is awarded to individuals who pass a written examination sponsored by the DPMA.

EXERCISES

1. What has been the average industry growth rate of large mainframe manufacturers?

2. List some major manufacturers engaged in the sale of office systems.

3. List some new industries that have emerged as a result of increased computer usage.

4. Describe the personnel requirements of a small data processing department.

5. Describe the personnel requirements of a medium size data processing department.

6. Describe the personnel requirements of a large data processing department.

7. What is the function of systems group employees?

8. Describe the salary range for various job titles in data processing.

9. List five major data processing job categories.

10. What organization awards the certificate of proficiency?

18

Learning Objectives

After studying this chapter, you should be able to
1. Discuss the need for industry standards
2. Describe information networks and data banks and some potential abuses
3. List some pieces of legislation to control abuses of data banks
4. Describe some legal, emotional, and psychological considerations related to the use of computers
5. Discuss the proper role of the computer in society
6. List some areas of future opportunities brought by the computer

Chapter Outline

Issues of the Future
  Need for Industry Standards
  Impact on Education
  Information Networks and Data Banks
Legislation to Control the Use of Data Banks
  Electronic Crime
  Technology and Humanistic Considerations: The Role of the Computer in Society
The Future is Here
  Conversational Languages
  Artificial Intelligence
  Voice Communication with Machines
  Microcomputers
  Robotics
  Communications
  Computer-Aided Design and Manufacturing

The Computer in Society:
Issues and Opportunities

Wе have been focused on the technical and applied aspects of computers, the practical things such as how computers are integrated into business systems. Now let us conclude by looking at some of the broader issues and new opportunities this powerful electronic tool has brought to society.

Certainly the computer has created new problems for society. But it has also brought with it many benefits and expanded opportunities, particularly for young people entering the job market today. Consider the new vistas opened by the invention of robotics, artificial intelligence, voice synthesizers, and modern communications. These technologies, and others still on the drawing boards, hold out the promise that our work will become less tedious and more challenging, shops and offices more productive, and society better educated and able to cope with its problems.

In this chapter we discuss the need for industry standards, impact of computers on education, abuses of data banks and information networks, and legal considerations. We also look at some of the philosophical, emotional, and psychological questions raised by the use of computers.

ISSUES OF THE FUTURE

The use of the computer raises questions about the nature of our schools, our legal system, and our technological society. Let us look at some of the major issues that must be dealt with in the computer age.

NEED FOR INDUSTRY STANDARDS

At present there are few **industry standards** governing the development of computer hardware, software, or systems. As a result, new computer languages, systems, and programs are being developed that are incompatible with one another. This represents an enormous loss of time and money in duplicated effort. For example, some computer peripheral equipment, such as disk storage devices and memory modules, cannot be used interchangeably from one computer to another. This may be to the advantage of certain computer manufacturers, but works to the detriment of the user.

The computer industry is in a position much like that of other industries before the turn of the century. Chaos existed because there were few national standards. For example, electric power was available in alternating and direct current and in many different voltages and frequencies. There were few agreed upon standards for wire sizes, fasteners, pipe, threads, drills, tools, and so on. The lack of standards threatened many industries and brought about the development of the National Bureau of Standards and the American Standards Association, later known as the American National Standards Institute (ANSI). These organizations and the International Standards Organization (ISO) have brought a degree of order out of this chaos.

If society is to make the most of computers, much needs to be done in establishing standards for computer hardware, software, and data bases. Efforts have already been made by ANSI, which publishes standards for certain languages, including FORTRAN and COBOL. But much more needs to be done. For example, hundreds of computer manufacturers market computers that have similar, but still different, instruction sets, physical architecture, input/output design, operating systems, data exchange rates, and data transfer circuits. Data format, file processing, data gathering, processing, and reporting techniques also need to be standardized. Even the basic element of computer construction, the integrated circuit (IC), is not standardized. Hundreds of manufacturers produce IC chips that have little in common, save their supply voltage and pin design.

Another area that greatly needs standardization is computer logic and algorithms for problem solving. Now a programmer develops a set of steps for solving a business problem, which is then programmed for the computer. He or she sets up his or her own solution to solve a problem that may be solved in an equally satisfactory way over and over in hundreds of similar installations in banks, businesses, schools, and government agencies. This duplication of effort is wasteful.

Published standards on common business programs, such as tax preparation, financial accounting, cost accounting, real estate,

Figure 18-1 Computers in the Classroom. Because of their low cost, computers are valuable instructional tools found in many schools, classrooms, and study halls.

loans, banking, and distribution, could reduce the wasted effort considerably. Once a common logic has been developed and accepted, it can be incorporated in programs by various firms with the assurance that their programs meet the standard.

Finally, there exists a need for a national clearing house of computer software and programs. Such an organization could establish documentation standards, a uniform software licensing or usage fee, standard abstracting, and indexing procedures.

IMPACT ON EDUCATION

All levels of education—elementary, secondary, college, and university—as well as instructional, curricular, and administrative processes are being affected by the computer. The computer is used for many administrative tasks, such as processing student records, counseling, and reporting grades. Classrooms, laboratories, lecture halls, admissions offices, libraries, study halls, and dormitories around the country are more and more frequently equipped with some kind of computer (Figure 18-1).

Figure 18-2 Computer-Assisted Instruction. These students are engaged in a computer-assisted learning experience in which the computer provides drill work and exercises.

The computer supplements or in some cases replaces the teacher. It provides drill work, exercises, remedial material, enrichment material, and tests. It simulates a dialogue with the student (Figure 18-2). This raises many questions. Will the teacher of the future continue to interact with students or merely become a programmer? Will the human aspect of the instructional process be affected if people are replaced, even in part, by machines? Will the teacher continue to create the material he or she presents or substitute packaged programs delivered by machine? What will the next generation of students be like if they have been trained, educated, influenced, nurtured, and stimulated by a computer?

Other questions sparked by the use of computers in education concern the future curriculum and content of course work. What kind of knowledge will students need to survive in our future society? Computer technology changes so fast that textbooks may be obsolete by the time they are printed. Learning about the computer itself may be one of the most important aspects of education. The computer-literate student will need to know how the computer works, how to program, and how to use the computer as a general-purpose problem solving tool.

INFORMATION NETWORKS AND DATA BANKS

One of the most significant attributes of the computer is its ability to store and retrieve vast amounts of data and information. Business and government institutions can gather enormous amounts of data on millions of people or organizations and assemble them into files that can be electronically accessed, searched, revised, or printed out.

Many government and private agencies maintain data banks. The National Driver Registration files, for example, contain entries on the driving records of people in every state in the union. TRW Credit Data, TransUnion, and other credit reporting agencies maintain records on over 150 million people. The Reuben H. Donnelley Corporation has mailing lists containing tens of millions of households. These lists are sold commercially. The Veterans Administration, Social Security Administration, Department of Commerce, and numerous other public and private agencies maintain millions of records on virtually everyone in the country.

Information gathering and reporting systems such as these are perhaps necessary, but they also create potential problems. The dissemination of information about a person without that person's knowledge and consent is a serious invasion of privacy. A mistake in entering data into a computer can be detrimental to a person's ability to obtain credit, to be accepted at a school, to be hired for a job. Computer errors have denied individuals loans or the right to purchase a home or automobile.

UNIVERSAL IDENTIFICATION NUMBERS   Some computer experts have proposed that the government issue a **standard universal identifier** number to every American citizen. The number would remain with that individual from birth until death. The experts propose the number be used as the basis for maintaining and preparing files, posting to accounts, and keying all vital information to each person. Some members of Congress have suggested that a secure, counterfeit-resistant identification card be required for all United States workers.

But there has been opposition to this idea, and Congress has regularly debated and resisted issuing universal identifier numbers because of the many problems such a system would create. Government agencies and businesses could access a vast variety of information on an individual using one key number. This number might be used to spy and maintain surveillance files or dossiers on people.

However, in the absence of a standard universal identifier, many business firms, schools, and government agencies have begun to use social security numbers to index files. The Social Security Administration never intended the social security number to be used as a standard universal identifier. It was designed exclusively to aid in cataloging social security files.

One of the main problems with using the social security number is it does not meet the criteria for a successful standard universal identifier. First, duplicate social security numbers have been inadvertently issued by the Social Security Administration. Second, the number does not include an error-checking digit to eliminate the transposition or loss of digits.

Unless Congress enforces the limited use of the social security number, more and more private and commercial firms and nonfederal agencies will use it, and it will become a de facto standard universal identifier.

THE IMAGE SYSTEM: COMPUTER ART

Paul Xander of the New York Institute of Technology is working with "The Image System," a prototype for painting with the computer. Using an electronic pen and a digitizing tablet (see the top left photo) to paint over a given basic image (the second photo in the left column) with a palette of some 255 colors, a virtually infinite number of versions are possible. Shown are five such images that reveal a progression of added details and some experiments with colors and textures. In the third photo in the left column the artist is adding the outline of clouds to the basic image.

LEGISLATION TO CONTROL THE USE OF DATA BANKS

Several pieces of legislation have been passed at the state and national levels to control the misuse of data banks and credit information.

FREEDOM OF INFORMATION ACT   Passed in 1970, the Freedom of Information Act gives citizens and other agencies the right of access to many kinds of data kept in government files. It was an attempt by Congress to provide for the open flow of data in government and to protect the public's right to know about government activities. The Act does allow government agencies to withhold certain data of a personal nature from the public, but with this major exception it is a formal declaration of the availability of records and information of all government agencies.

FAIR CREDIT REPORTING ACT   In 1971 Congress passed the Fair Credit Reporting Act in an attempt to eliminate abuses found in the consumer credit reporting industry. The Act requires agencies to follow reasonable procedures to safeguard credit information. It requires that a subject be informed when a credit investigation is being conducted. It gives the responsibility of enforcement to the Federal Trade Commission.

PRIVACY ACT OF 1974   The Privacy Act requires that every federal agency identify every system of records that it maintains and regularly review the contents of its files to be sure that the information in them is necessary and relevant. The Act specifically forbids maintaining data files on citizens' religious or political affiliations or activities. It also requires every federal agency to publish a list of the systems of records it maintains. This list must include the name and location of the data system and the category of individual on whom records are maintained. This information must be made accessible and available to citizens.

RIGHT TO FINANCIAL PRIVACY ACT OF 1979   By the end of the 1970s many government agencies were still collecting and misusing data. The Right to Financial Privacy Act sought to limit the government's right to obtain information from financial institutions. The law forces government agencies to seek a subpoena before they can ask a bank to turn over records. They must show that there is a bona fide law enforcement reason for requesting such data. In the event data are released, the individual is to be notified that personal information has been released.

FEDERAL REPORTS ACT.   The Federal Reports Act, revised in 1980, was designed to reduce the federal paperwork burden for individuals, small businesses, state and local governments, and others. Its goal was to minimize the cost to the federal government of collecting, maintaining, using, and disseminating information. The Act has been instrumental in coordinating and integrating federal information gathering policies and practices, and sees that confidentiality is kept, consonant with other federal laws.

ELECTRONIC CRIME

While old-fashioned acts of fraud, theft, breaking and entering, and embezzlement are still prevalent, new versions of these crimes, executed on or assisted by a computer, are occurring with increasing frequency. These crimes may be so subtle in nature that they are extremely difficult to detect. The U.S. Chamber of Commerce estimates that electronic crimes such as computer fraud or embezzlement exceed $100 million annually.

Electronic breaking and entering can be perpetrated on a computer file quickly and quietly. There are no jimmied locks or fingerprints. However, valuable information, programs, or services can be stolen. Fraudulent data can be entered to change a program to print out unauthorized checks or release funds. Records can be altered to cover up cash thefts. Computer processing time itself, a new valuable resource in our society, can be stolen.

The new criminal is not an unsophisticated clerk who sees the opportunity to pocket a few dollars from the till, but a person with skills in computer technology, programming, and communications science through which he or she can steal millions of dollars and cover up virtually every trace of the crime.

Businesses and law enforcement agencies are taking action

ROBIN HOOD AND HIS MERRY COMPUTER

Source: *Los Angeles Times*, April 30, 1983.

Stanley V. Slyngstad stole from the state and gave to the poor, armed with a computer instead of a longbow as he dispensed $17,000 taken from the government agency where he worked.

He gave an unemployed carpenter $600 for a truck; $1,200 went to a welfare mother for car repairs and children's clothing, and $400 a week went to another welfare mother who thought she was on salary for computer training.

"I used my own money until it ran out," said Slyngstad, 44, who had been a sought-after and highly praised computer programmer with the state Division of Vocational Rehabilitation. "Then I used the state's—an unlimited supply. I was blatant as hell."

Slyngstad pleaded guilty Wednesday in Thurston County Superior Court to first-degree theft. He faces up to 10 years in prison and has been ordered to keep away from state computer terminals pending sentencing.

"I'm a thief but I'm not a criminal," he said in court. "I'm just a feller who likes to help people. There's a ton out there that could still use it."

He said that he had been a farmer in the 1960s but that poor crops and a storm left him destitute. "There were times I wished somebody would give me money when I was down and out," he said.

As a state employee, Slyngstad programmed a computer to manage millions of dollars for vocational rehabilitation. He stole the $17,000 between April, 1982, and last February by telling the computer to issue at least 25 false benefit-check authorizations.

Then, according to state troopers, Slyngstad spent his evenings drinking beer and dispensing charity at Charlie's Tavern in Olympia. His good will included $100 tips on the bar.

Police caught on to the scheme late last year after they were tipped by a suspicious recipient of the bogus state checks. But Slyngstad had erased the evidence from the computer when they checked.

He finally was arrested March 11 after a fellow state worker noticed that checks were being issued to a Stanley Lyngstad at Slyngstad's address. Slyngstad lost his $30,000-a-year job.

Leslie F. James, director of the rehabilitation division, said Washington state had hired Slyngstad away from Oregon, where he also worked for the state.

"Slyngstad's probably one of the best programmers I've ever worked with," James said. "If he hadn't started drinking, I don't think this would have happened."

State Patrol Lt. Fred L. Pilon said he hopes investigators have discovered everything Slyngstad took. But "with the computer system the way it is," he said, "who knows?"

Pilon said security has been "greatly tightened" since the thefts.

against the growing number of electronic crimes. The FBI has given hundreds of its special agents courses in detecting computer crimes. Many local police departments have implemented special training programs in computer crime investigation techniques. Many states have passed laws to combat computer-related crimes, and more are considering new legislation each year.

TECHNOLOGY AND HUMANISTIC CONSIDERATIONS: THE ROLE OF THE COMPUTER IN SOCIETY

Feelings of self-worth and feelings of being needed and wanted derive in large part from our work. In years past workers felt a kinship to their work and derived deep psychological satisfaction from it. Employees could see the results of their labor and derive from them a sense of pride that could be transferred to other areas of life.

But in the computer age, many new jobs are fragmented (Figure 18-3). They are only a part of a more complex operation that is little understood by the individual employee. Workers may feel no personal relationship to this type of job; they may feel like cogs in a machine and as if their work has no beginning and no end. They often don't see the results of their efforts and rarely receive a pat on the back.

How will society provide worker acceptance when the computer takes a person's job satisfaction away? What compensating psychological rewards or status can society offer workers so that they will feel part of the system, rather than in opposition to it? The computer has brought these issues into focus.

Before the computer age all judgments about people were made by people. Judges, teachers, doctors, friends, employers, and neighbors formed opinions. Raises, promotions, loan approvals, and so on were the result of a human thought process. Consider, for example, how the computer has affected the process of granting credit. Before the computer age the client went to the bank, filled out some forms, and had a personal interview. The applicant's forms were reviewed by a loan officer, but the personal interview was critical. During the interview the client was evaluated by another human being on subtle, human attributes, not the least of which were personal appearance, attitude, and trust. In short, the loan officer "sized up" the

Figure 18-3 Keyboard Operators. Today some jobs are fragmented and employees do not see the final results of their efforts.

prospect's honesty, making judgments on character and ability to repay the loan. Many years of business and personal experience were brought into the transaction.

Today many loan and credit decisions are made not by people, but by computer. The computer analyzes factual data and provides the loan officer with a "go–no go" decision. The interaction between people is replaced by a mechanical exchange in which electronic input and machine output are substituted for human judgments.

A major social issue is to what extent society wants to turn over judgments to machines. The challenge will be to find ways to preserve human responses in an increasingly mechanized society.

There are no rules that tell us how much automation we can or should accept. We can control both the rate at which new inventions are integrated into society and the amount that will be spent on developing new technology. We can set limits on the expansion of automation to allow time for society to adjust to the shock waves.

If the balance between computers and people is allowed to be made wholly on economic considerations, we may discover an over-

MICROSCAPES: WHAT'S IN A PHOTO?

The American Telephone & Telegraph Co. (AT&T) recently sponsored an exhibit of microphotographs, and titled the show "Microscapes." These extraordinary images reveal ordinary items found in the computer world magnified thousands of times, so that they no longer look as they do in their true sizes. Magnification gives an entirely new dimension to ordinary objects, although some of the photos in this series show what many people would not think of as "ordinary" items. In the computer world, however, they are common.

It is fun to study these photos and let your imagination run free. The caption under each begins with a suggestion of what the subject of the photo might be, and is followed by an explanation of what it actually is.

Credit: Microscapes, courtesy of AT&T Technologies

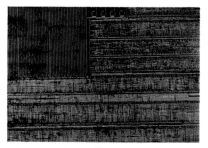

The American flag? No, a 32-bit microprocessor, sometimes called a "computer on a chip." Specifically, it's the AT&T WE32000 chip. Its true size is 4/10th of an inch square. The chip holds 150,000 separate components. (Photo by Phillip Harrington)

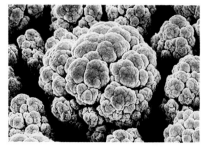

Cauliflower? It looks very much like that vegetable, but this highly magnified photo actually shows electro-deposited gold. The gold is deposited during the process of making circuit-board connectors. (Photo by Robert Woods)

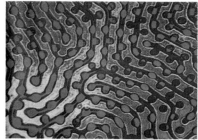

View from above of rice paddies? The neat geometry is in reality a magnified view of the tiny magnetic domains called "bubbles" in which bits of information are stored. (Photo by Leonard Stein)

An American Indian design? Far from it. This 256K random access memory chip from AT&T contains 300,000 memory cells on a piece of silicon that is approximately one-half by one-quarter inches in diameter. (Photo by Phillip Harrington)

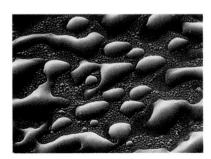

Water dripping from a ceiling? You are seeing droplets, but of silicon, the material from which chips are made. The droplet formation is caused by irradiating the silicon with a laser light beam, after which the silicon resolidifies. (Photo by Robert Woods)

A modern textile fabric? A beautiful rainbow of color is revealed in a microphoto of a compound used to polish certain layers of silicon during chip manufacture. (Photo by Phillip Harrington)

Primitive jewelry? In a way, this image looks more like its real self than most of these other magnified photos do. Pictured is a drop of solder flux on a copper mirror. (Photo by Charles Lewis)

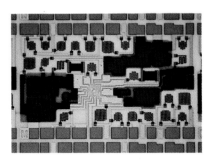

Plan for a housing project? No, but the chip designer has some of the same problems as a real estate developer, that is, how to fit the most bits of information (houses) on the least amount of chip space (land). The photo is of a thin film integrated circuit. (Photo by Charles Lewis)

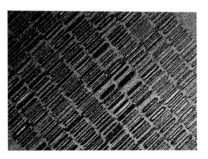

Aerial view of a parking lot? The "cars" aren't cars at all. Instead, they are the magnetic domains that contain coded information in a nine-track magnetic tape. (Photo by John Carnevale)

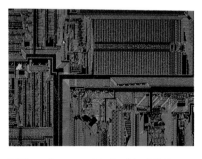

What do you think this is? In reality, it is a digital signal processor in a telephone unit. But it could be a piece of abstract art, or whatever else your imagination suggests. (Photo by Phillip Harrington)

abundance of technology in business and government and a critical shortage of social and humanistic considerations.

What could happen if computer judgments dominate in designing our machines, planning our destiny, and monitoring our progress? What could happen to our security if a computer takes over the role of decision maker and historian? What could happen to us if a machine became the primary force in society, where most judgments were made by machine, recorded by machine, and executed by machine?

Technology has brought air pollution, crowded cities, depletion of natural resources with its benefits. Yet we step into a jet airplane and are able to fly around the world in a matter of hours. We press a button and on our television screen see and hear a man at the moment he is speaking halfway around the world. A computer is programmed to search 50 million records in little more time than it takes for us to reach for a pencil and paper.

People need time to adjust and understand this new, faster way of life. They need places where they can be free of the modern computer society, where they can think, contemplate, and allow their minds to move at their own speed. The real challenge lies in defining the rightful role of the computer in society.

THE FUTURE IS HERE

Picture a factory producing color television sets. Each set begins as an electronic chassis that is stamped out and then moves down the assembly line. As each circuit board is finished, it is tested and then mounted in place. After the picture tube has been plugged in, the set is turned on and some precision adjustments are made. Then the test pattern disappears and a perfectly balanced color picture flashes on the screen, complete with sound. The set is inspected and found to be working properly. It is carefully placed in a shipping carton with packing and the box taped closed. Finally, a shipping label is typed and glued to the side of the carton. The set is then sent on its way to a retail store somewhere in the Midwest.

As you look around the factory, you become aware of a startling fact. There are no people—only machines. The entire process

Figure 18-4 Increase in Computer-Related Employment. Many new jobs have opened in the labor market due to the influx of computers.

of assembling, testing, packing, and even shipping the sets is completely automated, untouched by human hands. There are a couple of people employed in the plant. But they sit in a glassed-in control room, drinking coffee as they watch robots do all the work.

Does this picture of a computerized manufacturing plant predict a world in which people are superfluous and jobs nonexistent? A decade or two ago some experts predicted that the computer and automation would bring about mass layoffs and unemployment. In the last decade the unemployment rate has risen and fallen sharply due to many factors. The computer, however, has created more jobs than it has eliminated (Figure 18-4).

While it is true that jobs have been lost because of computers and information technology, the benefits far outweight the disadvantages. In some instances workers are required to upgrade their skills in order to remain employed. There has been an increase in clerical employment, largely due to the computer's ability to handle a large volume of work. The computer has generated entire new industries which manufacture, sell, install and repair computer and data processing equipment.

Let us look at some of the new technologies that show great promise and opportunity precisely because we now have computers at our disposal.

CONVERSATIONAL LANGUAGES

Much time and effort is being spent on developing conversational languages for computers. Languages that are more like natural communication and everyday English will allow people to communicate with computers in a comfortable style, thus greatly increasing the utility of the machines.

ARTIFICIAL INTELLIGENCE

A number of computer manufacturers are expending research funds on developing computers that mimic human intelligence. These systems are sometimes called **expert computers,** and are part of a growing field known as **artificial intelligence.** This is a rapidly growing field of research and development, and will provide many new jobs and employment opportunities in the future. This work will involve equipment and system design and developing applications in business, schools, and industry for "expert" computers.

VOICE COMMUNICATION WITH MACHINES

A great deal of research is being done on voice **synthesizers and recognition** devices. The purpose is to enable computers to accept data input by the human voice rather than through a keyboard. The computer will then output data by simulating ordinary speech, which should make output systems more flexible and greatly expand computer applications. Voice recognition will allow people to direct machines without hands on control and make possible such things as typewriters that will respond to the human voice or automobiles that will be guided and controlled by speech.

MICROCOMPUTERS

In the years ahead millions of small computer systems will be installed in homes, schools, automobiles, and small offices. This high level of use will cause an enormous demand for marketing, repair, and maintenance of these small systems. It will also stimulate software services including writing, distributing, and retailing new types of programs.

ROBOTICS

It has been said that machines should work and people should think. Business and industry are continually searching for machines to do the physical work of humans, freeing people to do more creative tasks (Figure 18-5). **Robots** are suited for use in hazardous or hostile environments or for monotonous, repetitive tasks. Robots are especially useful in operations where short runs of complicated goods are to be assembled or precision parts are handled. Many robotic devices will find their way into large and small businesses and perhaps even some homes in the next few years (Figure 18-6).

A number of American and Japanese companies are manufacturing robots. These companies specialize in machines that can assemble, sort, construct, or handle goods in manufacture. This indus-

Figure 18-5 Highly Accurate Robot. This machine is able to place a delicate disk in position with a precision of .002 inch.

Figure 18-6 Robotics Industry Growth. (*Source: Electronic Business Magazine*, June 15, 1984)

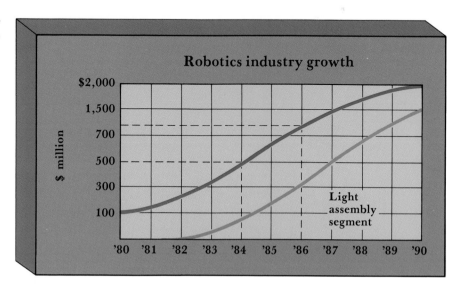

try is growing as many new applications are found for robots. The greater use of robots may well create more jobs than it eliminates. Automated production means lower manufacturing costs, and this

CENSUS BUREAU WANTS NATION'S ROBOTS TO BE HELD ACCOUNTABLE

Source: Andrea Adelson, *Daily News of Los Angeles*, December 27, 1984.

The Census Bureau has made a nose count of men, women and children in the United States every decade since 1790.

However, come January the bureau will add a new type of laborer to its list of things to count—robots.

Making a census of automatons shouldn't imply anything Orwellian, bureau spokesman Ray Bancroft said. It's only an acknowledgement of the "growing importance" of robots to the economy, said Bancroft from Suitland, Md.

The nation's pulse-takers already count the quantity and value of thousands of products in their five-year census of 450 manufacturers, he said.

New products are occasionally added to the survey, a potpourri of statistics on everything from cars to consumer buying, Bancroft said. The figures are turned over to Commerce Department number-crunchers who use them to forecast the nation's gross national product and make economic projections.

The manufacturers' census and more frequent industrial reports on major producers "are an information tool used by business and government to check on how the manufacturing community is doing," he said.

New products are occasionally added to the surveys, but Bancroft didn't know what criterion was used to put robots on the list. The government hasn't decided yet how often to order a robot roll call.

But the Census Bureau does want to learn how many industrial robots are manning the nation's assembly lines, how many homes now are staffed by robots rather than butlers and how many R2D2s are being assembled outside of Hollywood movie lots.

The information is to be used to assess robot production, evaluate automation's impact on domestic industries and monitor the influx of foreign robots, the Census Bureau said.

means more people can afford to buy goods. This in turn will boost demand and create a market for more robots. Robots must be installed, serviced, and replaced when new and better machines come along.

COMMUNICATIONS

The breakup of the American Telephone and Telegraph system into regional companies, the growth of closed circuit cable television, the expansion of satellite communications, and the development of fiberoptics all mean great changes for the communications industry.

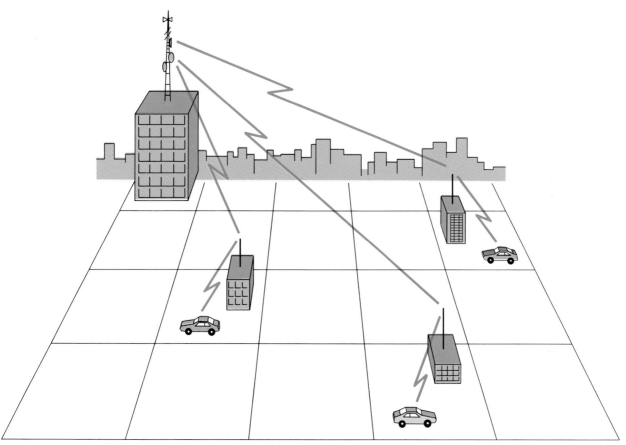

Figure 18-7 Cellular Telephone. A city may be broken down into cells, and all mobile communications between cells are controlled by a central computer.

These innovations will profoundly affect the way voice and data are transmitted and will bring communications to more people in more places than ever before.

The computer will make possible the operation of new communications devices, for example, a new type of mobile phone service using the **cellular telephone** (Figure 18-7). Cellular telephones provide better telephone service from moving vehicles and make many more channels available on one frequency. As the device is improved and its price falls, more businesses will be able to afford this computer-managed telephone service.

Figure 18-8 Computer Aided Design (CAD). In this figure, a new automobile design is being tested, using the computer to help design the vehicle.

Figure 18-9 Computer Aided Manufacturing (CAM). One form of CAM is numerical control (N/C), in which metal-working machines are directed by computers.

COMPUTER-AIDED DESIGN AND MANUFACTURING

Much research and development has gone into the use of computers to aid in the engineering and design of equipment as well as the manufacture of goods. In **computer-aided design (CAD)** the computer prepares and tests mechanical designs and makes engineering drawings (Figure 18-8). CAD eliminates the need for manual drawing and drafting and increases both the quality and quantity of designs that can be produced by an engineer.

Once a new product has been designed, **computer-aided manufacturing (CAM)** can be used to produce the goods (Figure 18-9). CAM deals with process control, inventory control, and work scheduling. One of the most important areas of CAM is **numerical control (N/C)**. In N/C a computer is connected to metalworking machines and directs equipment to grind, mill, punch, or cut metal, plastic, or other materials. Parts can be produced with greater precision and without the need for a human operator to guide each motion of the metalworking machine.

Both CAD and CAM will experience a good deal of growth in

the next decade. This will create new jobs and allow goods to be produced at lower cost with higher standards of precision and quality.

We are now just beginning to integrate many of the new technologies described in this chapter into our businesses and our lives. The future is here and the student who understands the impact of these new technologies will have an advantage in the labor market and at the same time be better able to cope with the broad social changes that the computer will inevitably bring.

SUMMARY AND KEY TERMS

- There is a need for **industry standards** in computer hardware and software.

- The way in which people are taught and the curriculum offered by schools have been affected by the computer on all levels of education.

- Both government and private agencies maintain **data banks** containing millions of records. A **standard universal identifier** number and the social security number have been proposed as means of cataloging information in data banks.

- At least five major pieces of legislation have been passed since 1970 to help control the abuses and misuse of data banks and credit information.

- Computer-related crimes, such as electronic theft, require a different approach to law enforcement and crime detection.

- Among the emotional and psychological effects of the computer are feelings of alienation and resistance and questions related to job satisfaction and self worth. Society must ultimately decide upon the proper balance between the use of computer and human activity.

- Areas of new technological development include **conversational languages, artificial intelligence** and **expert computers**, voice **communication** with machines, microcomputer expansion, **robotics**, communications, **computer-aided design (CAD)**, and **computer-aided manufacturing (CAM)**.

EXERCISES

1. List some areas that require industry standardization.

2. Describe some applications of the computer in education.

3. List some agencies that maintain large data banks.

4. Discuss the use of standard universal identifier numbers.

5. Name five pieces of legislation aimed at controlling abuses of data banks.

6. Describe some computer crimes.

7. Describe how an employee may feel when his work involves the use of computers.

8. Describe the types of jobs best suited for robots.

9. Describe some areas of communications affected by the computer.

10. Describe some ways the computer is used to aid design and manufacturing.

Appendixes

Appendix A An Introduction to BASIC Programming

Appendix A presents a brief introduction to the BASIC language. It explains how to write, enter, and edit BASIC programs and how to execute them.

The first part of Appendix A describes common BASIC commands and statements. The second part consists of three well-documented example programs. Accompanying each example is a statement of the problem the program was written to solve, a flowchart, a complete listing of the program, and a detailed description of each BASIC statement by line number. These example programs should be studied carefully in order to learn the function of the BASIC statements used.

At the end of Appendix A is a group of programming assignments. Each assignment includes programming instructions, a description of the input data, and a description of the desired output. In carrying out these assignments, study the problem carefully and prepare a flowchart before coding. After the program has been coded, it should be keyboarded, tested, debugged, and run.

THE AVAILABILITY OF BASIC

BASIC is available on computers ranging from large mainframes to small pocket computers. Most microcomputers have BASIC either permanently installed in read-only memory or provided on a disk. BASIC may be available on multiuser systems, which are made up of terminals connected by cables to a nearby minicomputer or mainframe. Timesharing systems, in which terminals are connected to large computers by telephone lines, also may use BASIC. You will need to learn how to access BASIC for the system available to you.

LANGUAGE VARIATIONS

There are many variations, or dialects, of BASIC. Specific language rules vary from computer to computer, so consult the language reference manual for the system you are using.

One of the most common dialects of BASIC is Microsoft BASIC, developed by Microsoft, Inc., and available on many microcomputers including the Apple, TRS-80, NEC, Atari, and the IBM PC. The programs and examples in this appendix are in Microsoft BASIC and were run on an IBM PC. Although the implementations of Microsoft BASIC may vary slightly from one computer to another, programs and examples in this appendix should run with no difficulty on many systems and require only minor modification on others.

CODING CONVENTIONS AND RULES

Unlike some other languages, BASIC requires no special coding forms. Programs may be written on ordinary paper. Each BASIC statement must begin with a line number. Line numbers follow in sequence, with the lowest number assigned to the first statement in the program and the highest to the last statement. On almost all systems, line numbers up to at least 9999 are permitted. If you are writing a very long program, check your manual to see how high line numbers may go.

It is standard practice to assign line numbers in increments of 10, beginning with the number 10. The sequence 10, 20, 30, 40, . . . is followed. This practice makes it easier to add a line later if needed. For example, in the sequence just mentioned, you could easily insert a line 14 between lines 10 and 20, but there would be no room if the sequence read 10, 11, 12, 13, 14, 15, 16, 17, 18, 19, 20. BASIC statements are executed in order of the statement numbers. Statement 10 is executed, then statement 20, and so on.

ELEMENTS OF BASIC

There are two types of instructions in BASIC, statements and commands. **Statements** begin with line numbers and are used to write programs. When statements are typed into the computer, they are stored in the computer's memory, and nothing will happen until a command is given. **Commands** do not have line numbers. They are executed immediately upon being typed into the computer. Commands are used to do such things as load a program from a disk, run it, and clear the computer's memory so a new program can be typed in. Statements and commands use **reserved words.** (See Table A-1.) Reserved words may be used only in the ways specified in the BASIC language manual for the particular system you are using. How reserved words are used is described in more detail later in this appendix.

Variable names are words chosen by the programmer to represent numeric or alphabetic data to be used in a program. They must conform to BASIC language rules. In some systems, variable names of only one or two characters are permitted. They must be one letter of the alphabet or one letter followed by a single numeral (0-9) or a dollar sign ($). Reserved words may not be used for variable names. (Some versions of BASIC permit variable names of any length from one to forty characters. In this appendix, variable names of one and two characters will be

STATEMENTS	SYSTEM COMMANDS
DATA	NEW (CLEAR, SCRATCH)
DEF	DIR (CAT)
DIM	LOAD "PROGRAM NAME"
END	RUN
FOR/NEXT	LIST
GOSUB	SAVE
GOTO	KILL (UNSAVE)
IF/THEN	CTRL-C key (ESC, BREAK, ATTN)
INPUT	CONT
LET	RENUM
PRINT	
READ	
REM	
RESTORE	
RETURN	
TAB	
PRINT USING	

used, since they will work on any system.)

Variable names selected to represent numbers may contain either one letter of the alphabet or one letter followed by one digit.

EXAMPLE: A, B, H, N2, B9, P7
Variable names selected to represent alphabetic data consist of one letter followed by a dollar sign. Alphabetic variables are called *strings*. Strings on some systems may be up to 255 characters long, even though the names used to refer to them in the program may be limited to two characters.

EXAMPLE: A$, G$, U$,
Variable names that are easily remembered should be chosen to avoid confusing one variable with another. In a program involving numeric data for speed, distance, and time, the variable names A1, A2, and A3 could be used, but using S for speed, D for distance, and T for time will make it much easier to remember which variable name stands for which quantity.

SYSTEM COMMANDS

System commands are used to do such things as load a program from a disk, delete lines from the program, renumber the program lines, run the program, and write it back onto the disk for future use. System commands vary from one computer to another, but almost all computers have commands to perform the following functions.

CLEAR MEMORY
The command NEW tells the computer to delete any lines in primary memory and readies the system to receive a new program. Some com-

puters use the commands CLEAR or SCRATCH to perform this operation.

EXAMPLE: NEW
      OK

DISPLAY DIRECTORY

The letters DIR instruct the computer to display a directory of available programs in secondary storage. Some systems use the letters CAT (catalog) or FILES for the same purpose.

EXAMPLE: DIR
      (The computer lists available programs in memory.)

LOAD PROGRAM INTO MEMORY

The LOAD command causes the computer to load a program in secondary storage on disk or other media into primary memory ready for running or modification. The word LOAD is followed by the name under which the program has been stored. Most versions of BASIC require the name to be enclosed in quotation marks.

EXAMPLE: LOAD ''KELLY''
      (The computer transfers the program named KELLY from secondary storage into primary memory.)

INITIATE EXECUTION

The command RUN directs the computer to begin executing the program in primary memory.

EXAMPLE: RUN
      (The computer begins running whatever program is currently in primary memory.)

LIST PROGRAM

The LIST command tells the computer to list all statements in primary memory. It provides a convenient way to output statements in sequence.

EXAMPLE: LIST
      (The computer lists all statements currently in primary memory.)

EXAMPLE: LIST 10
      (The computer lists only line 10.)

EXAMPLE: LIST 10–30
      (The computer lists line 10 through line 30.)

EXAMPLE: `LIST 10, 30`
> (The computer lists only line 10 and line 30.)

SAVE PROGRAM

The SAVE command causes the computer to retain a file of programming statements in its secondary storage system. It copies the program from primary memory onto disk or other media and saves it under the name assigned.

EXAMPLE: `SAVE "KELLY"`
> (The computer copies the program named KELLY from primary memory to secondary storage.)

REMOVE PROGRAM FROM SECONDARY STORAGE

The KILL or UNSAVE command directs the computer to delete a file or program from the secondary storage system.

EXAMPLE: `KILL "KELLY"`
> (The computer removes the file KELLY from storage. The file can no longer be recalled.)

INTERRUPT OR RESUME EXECUTION

CTRL-C key directs the computer to interrupt execution. CTRL-C is typed by pressing the key for the letter C while holding down the CONTROL key. On some systems the ESC, BREAK, or ATTN key is used. Execution can be resumed by keying CONT.

EXAMPLE: `CTRL-C`
> (The computer stops executing the program currently running.)

EXAMPLE: `CONT`
> (The computer resumes executing the program that was interrupted.)

DELETE LINE

To remove a line from memory, you key in the line number to be deleted, then press the RETURN key. A partially typed line can be deleted by striking the CTRL-X, DELETE, or ESC key.

EXAMPLE: `10 READ A, B, C` (carriage return)
> `10` (carriage return)
> (The computer deletes line 10 from memory.)

The left arrow (←) causes the computer to delete the previously typed character. Each time you strike the left arrow key, the next character to the left is deleted from the line. On keyboard printers, a left arrow will be printed, while on a screen the cursor will be repositioned to the left.

EXAMPLE: 10 PRINT ''BEGIN ←←←←← START''
        (The computer deletes the five characters BEGIN and replaces them with the characters START.)

RENUMBER LINES
The RENUM command instructs the computer to renumber all program statements by 10s, beginning with 10. It allows you to give uniform line numbers to a program after you have added a series of statements.

EXAMPLE: 2 . . .
        10 . . .
        15 . . .
        23 . . .
        30 . . .
        RENUM
        (The computer renumbers statements in program. When listed, program appears as follows.)
        10 . . .
        20 . . .
        30 . . .
        40 . . .
        50 . . .

PROGRAMMING STATEMENTS

Programming statements make up the actual BASIC program. They perform such functions as reading in data, controlling branching, making comparisons, and assigning numeric values to variables. The following are the most common statements used in BASIC language programming. The words in capital letters are reserved words listed in Table A-1.

REM
The REM statement is used to place comments or explanatory notes throughout a program. REM is short for "REMARK." REM statements are for the programmer's use. He or she includes them as a first line to

identify the program and throughout the program to explain statements. A REM statement is not an executable instruction. The REM
statement only tells the computer to read in the remark and write it out
when the program is listed.

EXAMPLE:

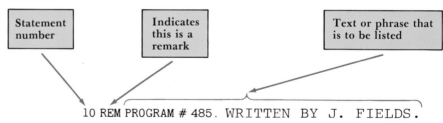

10 REM PROGRAM # 485. WRITTEN BY J. FIELDS.

EXPLANATION: The programmer uses a REM statement to include the
title, PROGRAM # 485, WRITTEN BY J. FIELDS, in the program listing.

READ AND DATA

The READ and DATA statements are used to load values, listed within a
program, to variable names. The READ statement specifies the names
under which the data will be stored. The DATA statement gives the values that are to be assigned to the names. The DATA statement is usually
placed at the end of the program, before the END statement.

EXAMPLE:

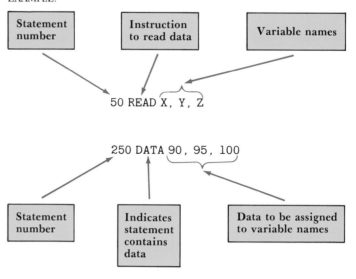

50 READ X, Y, Z

250 DATA 90, 95, 100

EXPLANATION: When it encounters the READ statement, the computer
will seek out the first DATA statement. It will load the first data item
(90) into memory under the name X, the second item (95) under Y, and
the third item (100) under the name Z.

EXPLANATION: This example reads in four pieces of alphabetic data and assigns the first one the name A$, the second B$, and so on.

RESTORE

The RESTORE statement allows the items in a DATA statement to be used over again. The RESTORE statement causes the computer to go back to the beginning of the list of items in the DATA statement and assign them to the names in the next READ statement. This is used to test different loops in a program with the same data, to assign the same values to another set of variable names, or to perform several procedures on the same set of data.

EXAMPLE: 50 READ X, Y, Z

    . . .

    90 RESTORE
    100 READ A, B, C

    . . .

    250 DATA 90, 95, 100

EXPLANATION: The example from above has been modified to include a RESTORE statement. The computer assigns the three variables listed in the DATA statement to the names X, Y, and Z. When it reaches the RESTORE statement at line 90, it returns to the beginning of the DATA statement. The READ statement at line 100 tells it to read in the three variables again and assign them to the names A, B, and C.

END

The END statement indicates that the end of the program has been reached. It tells the computer to stop executing the program. This statement is required by many language interpreters and is the last statement in the program.

EXAMPLE:

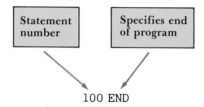

EXPLANATION: The END statement at line 100 tells the computer that there are no more instructions to be executed.

INPUT

The INPUT statement allows the operator to enter data from the keyboard while the program is executing. Each time the computer encounters an INPUT statement in the program, it prints a question mark (?) and waits for the data to be keyed in.

INPUT statements allow different data to be entered each time the program is run. The programmer can also use the input statement to direct the computer to follow several different branches while the program is running.

EXAMPLE:

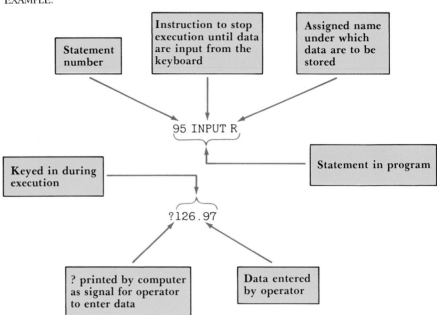

EXPLANATION: The computer executes all the statements in the program until it reaches statement 95. It prints out a ? on the terminal and waits for the operator to key in the value of R (in this case R = 126.97).

PRINT

The PRINT statement directs the computer to output data on the CRT or print unit of the computer. Some computers use an LPRINT statement to direct output to a line printer and the PRINT statement to direct it to the screen. There are two types of PRINT instructions. The first directs the computer to output stored data by giving the assigned name under which the data are stored. The second type gives the actual text to be printed. The arrangement of the data in the printout is specified by the form and punctuation marks used in the statement.

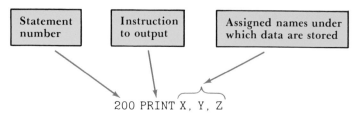

200 PRINT X, Y, Z

OUTPUT:

90   95   100

EXPLANATION: When the computer reaches statement 200, it prints out the values of X, Y, and Z. When a comma is used to separate the data names in the PRINT statement, the computer automatically sets up a five-column format. (Only three are used in this example.)

EXAMPLE:

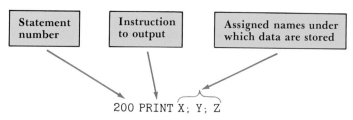

200 PRINT X; Y; Z

OUTPUT:

90 95 100

EXPLANATION: When semicolons are used to separate variable names in a PRINT statement, the computer does not insert any extra space between the items printed out. On most systems, positive numbers are preceded by a blank space. (A minus sign would be in this space if the number were negative.) Also, on many systems numbers are always followed by a blank space. So although the semicolon prevents *extra* space between the numbers, there will be some space because of the fact that numbers come accompanied by their own spaces. As will be seen in the next example, alphabetic variables (strings) do not have preceding or following spaces.

EXAMPLE:

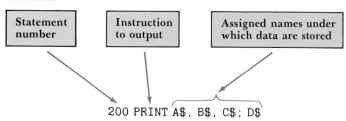

200 PRINT A$, B$, C$; D$

OUTPUT:

```
JOAN        SARA        TIMJOHN
```

EXPLANATION: Both semicolons and commas may be used in one statement. The computer prints the first three alphabetic values in column
format, as instructed by the commas, and the last value is printed with
no space preceding it.

EXAMPLE:

Statement number	Instruction to output	Literal text to be output

```
80 PRINT "THE AMOUNT OF THE PAYMENT DUE IS:"
90 PRINT X
```

Statement number	Instruction to output	Assigned names under which data are stored

OUTPUT:

```
THE AMOUNT OF THE PAYMENT DUE IS:
59
```

EXPLANATION: When it encounters statement 80, the computer prints out
the text enclosed in quotation marks exactly as it appears, including
punctuation and spacing, but without the quotation marks.

EXAMPLE:

Statement number	Instruction to output	Literal text to be output	Assigned names under which data are stored

```
80 PRINT "THE AMOUNT OF THE PAYMENT DUE IS: $"; X
```

OUTPUT:

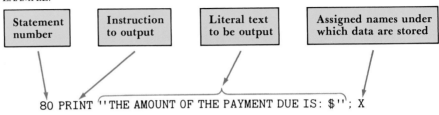

```
THE AMOUNT OF THE PAYMENT DUE IS: $ 59
```

EXPLANATION: The instruction to output literal text is combined with an instruction to output stored data.

EXAMPLE: 100 PRINT

OUTPUT: (Computer prints blank line here)

EXPLANATION: A blank PRINT statement is used as a means of printing out a blank line. This is a convenient way to cause the computer to skip a line before printing.

TAB

The TAB statement directs the computer to print out information in a specific column. It is used when the programmer wishes to line up columns of data in specific positions. Its function is similar to the TAB key on an ordinary typewriter.

EXAMPLE:

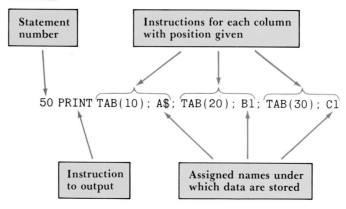

OUTPUT:

EXPLANATION: Statement 50 directs the computer to output the value stored under A\$ starting in type position 10, the value stored under B1 in type position 20, and the value stored under C1 in type position 30.

EXAMPLE:

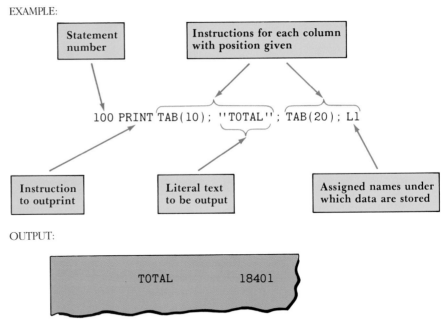

OUTPUT:

TOTAL   18401

EXPLANATION: The computer tabs to type position 10 and prints out the word TOTAL, then tabs to type position 20 and outputs the quantity stored under L1.

PRINT USING

The **PRINT USING** statement gives the programmer control over the format of output information, for example, the position of dollar signs, commas, or decimals in a number or the alignment at the right of numbers in a column. A # sign (called a pound or number sign) is used to represent the space reserved for each possible character in the format. If there are fewer characters than reserved spaces, the position is left blank. If the number being output has more decimal places than specified by the # signs in the PRINT USING statement, the number is rounded off. A semicolon separates the format description from the number being output.

EXAMPLE:

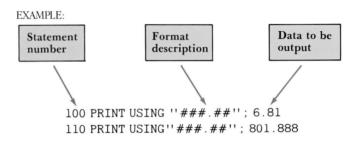

```
100 PRINT USING ''###.##''; 6.81
110 PRINT USING''###.##''; 801.888
```

OUTPUT:

```
    6.81
  801.89
```

EXPLANATION: The computer prints both numbers aligned at the right. Leading spaces precede the first number because more positions are specified than are occupied by the number. The second number is rounded off, since more decimal places are given than there are positions allotted for them.

ASSIGNMENT

The assignment statement LET assigns a value to the variable name that appears to the left of the equal sign. The statement can be used to assign numeric or alphabetic values.

EXAMPLE:

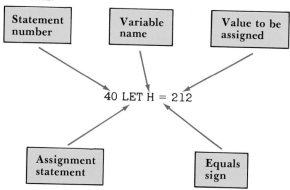

EXPLANATION: Statement 40 assigns the value 212 to the variable which has been given the assigned name H by the programmer.

EXAMPLE:

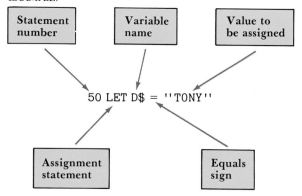

EXPLANATION: Statement 50 assigns the alphabetic quantity TONY to the name D$.

FOR-NEXT

A combination of a FOR statement and a NEXT statement is used to repeat a sequence of instructions a specified number of times. The FOR statement indicates how many times the sequence will be executed. The NEXT statement marks the end of the sequence. The FOR-NEXT statements are used to create a loop composed of the instructions appearing between them. This loop can read in records in a file, print out lines of data, or perform mathematical calculations many times.

EXAMPLE:

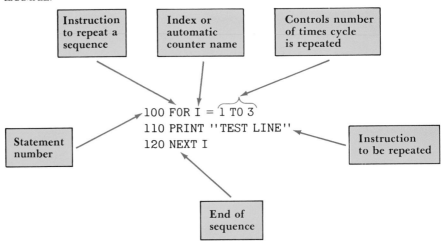

```
100 FOR I = 1 TO 3
110 PRINT "TEST LINE"
120 NEXT I
```

OUTPUT:

```
TEST LINE
TEST LINE
TEST LINE
```

EXPLANATION: Statement 100 directs the computer to execute statement 110 three times. Each time, it will print out the text TEST LINE. After the third execution the loop is terminated and the next statement in the program (130) will be executed.

EXAMPLE:
```
50 FOR I = 1 TO 5
60 PRINT "THE VALUE OF THE INDEX IS:"; I
70 NEXT I
```

OUTPUT:

```
THE VALUE OF THE INDEX IS: 1
THE VALUE OF THE INDEX IS: 2
THE VALUE OF THE INDEX IS: 3
THE VALUE OF THE INDEX IS: 4
THE VALUE OF THE INDEX IS: 5
```

EXPLANATION: This example illustrates a FOR-NEXT loop that outputs the current value of its index. The first time through the loop, I equals 1, and 1 appears on the output. When execution reaches line 70, the value of I increases to 2, and execution returns to statement 50 at the top of the loop. This time I equals 2, and this value appears on the output, I increases to 3 at line 70 and the loop repeats. This process is repeated for index values of 4 and 5. When the value of the index is more than the value given in the FOR statement (in this case, more than 5), the loop is terminated.

EXAMPLE:

```
20 LET A = 0
40 FOR I = 1 TO 6
50 LET A = A + 2
60 PRINT A
70 NEXT I
```

OUTPUT:

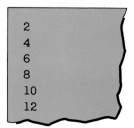

```
2
4
6
8
10
12
```

EXPLANATION: This example illustrates a LET statement within a FOR-NEXT loop. The LET statement is executed six times, and the value of A increases by 2 each time.

IF-THEN

The IF-THEN statement is a conditional branching instruction. The computer tests for a specified condition. If the condition is true, it branches to the statement indicated. The test performed is a relational comparison—to see if one value is less than, equal to, not equal to, or greater than another. The value may be a variable (A4), a constant (6.92), or an arithmetic expression (X*3−B). The branch takes place only when the test condition is true. If it is not true, the program moves to the next statement in the line number sequence:

The common **relational operators** in BASIC are:

RELATION	OPERATOR
Greater than	>
Less than	<
Equal to (or the same as)	=
Not equal to	><
Greater than or equal to	>=
Less than or equal to	<=

EXAMPLE:

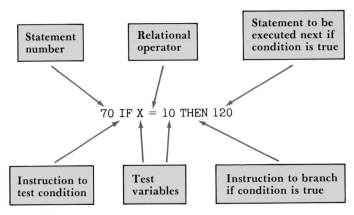

EXPLANATION: When the computer encounters statement 70, it compares the value of X to 10. If X equals 10, the program executes statement 120 next. If X has any other value, the branch is ignored and the next statement executed.

EXAMPLE:

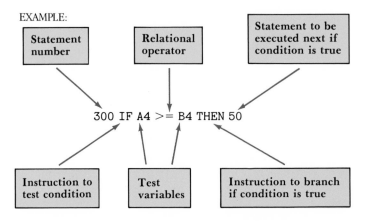

EXPLANATION: When the computer encounters statement 300, it compares the value of A4 to B4. If A4 is greater than or equal to B4, the program executes statement 50 next. If the condition is not true (A4 is less than B4), the branch is ignored and the next statement executed.

Mathematical instructions must be given to the computer in a specialized form, because it cannot understand formulas written in conventional algebraic notation. The programmer must convert the steps in the formula into a form recognized by the computer.

A group of symbols called arithmetic or **mathematical operators** are used in LET or PRINT statements to direct the computer to perform computations. The operators used on most BASIC systems are:

OPERATION	OPERATOR
Exponentiation (raising to a power)	$\wedge$ or **
Multiplication	*
Division	/
Addition	+
Subtraction	−

If more than one mathematical operation is included in a LET or PRINT statement, the computer performs the operations in a specific order, called the **hierarchy of operations.**
The order is:

1. Clear parentheses
2. Perform exponentiation
3. Perform multiplication and division
4. Perform addition and subtraction

When a mathematical calculation is performed in a LET statement, the mathematical expression to the right of the equals sign is evaluated and the result placed in storage under the assigned name on the left. These results can be printed out, shown on the terminal, or used later in the program for further calculations.

EXAMPLE: 20 LET Z = 2.5 + 302.6
       30 PRINT Z

OUTPUT:

305.1

EXPLANATION: When the computer encounters statement 20, it adds 2.5 and 302.6 and places the result (305.1) in the storage location named Z. By referencing the name Z, the programmer can print out these results later or use them in other calculations.

EXAMPLE: 10 LET K = 3.5
       20 PRINT "THE ANSWER IS"; 120 + K$\wedge$2

OUTPUT:

THE ANSWER IS 132.25

EXPLANATION: Only one statement is necessary to instruct the computer to perform calculations and print out the answer. Following the hierarchy of operations, the computer performs exponentiation before addition. H raises K (3.5) to the 2nd power and then adds the result (12.25) and 120. The results are printed out after the literal message. Note that the results are not assigned to a storage location.

Suppose we want to translate the algebraic formula equation

$$A = G + J + K - \frac{100}{L}$$

into computer terms and perform the calculation.

EXAMPLE: 30 LET G = 2
        40 LET J = 30
        50 LET K = 3.5
        60 LET L = 5
        70 LET A = G + J + K − 100/L
        80 PRINT ''A =''; A

OUTPUT:

A =   15.5

EXPLANATION: The computer scans statement 70 moving from left to right. According to the hierarchy of operations, division is performed first. First, 100 is divided by L (100/5 = 20). Then the computer again scans from left to right, and G (2), J (30), and K (3.5) are added. Finally, 20 (from 100/L) is subtracted to give the final results.

Now look at this equation.

$$A = G + J + \frac{K - 100}{L}$$

Although the terms are the same in this and the previous example, the presence of the parentheses makes them two different equations.

EXAMPLE: 70 LET A = G + J + (K − 100)/L
        80 PRINT ''THE ANSWER IS''; A

OUTPUT:

THE ANSWER IS 12.7

EXPLANATION: Following the hierarchy of operations, the parentheses are cleared first (K − 100= −96.5). Then, this intermediate answer is divided by L (−96.5/5 = −19.3). Finally, this value is added to G (2) and J (30) to give the final answer of 12.7.

DIM

The DIM statement is used to assign storage locations automatically for data that will be read in by the program. When the programmer assigns a name to a piece of data being read in with the READ or INPUT statements, the computer automatically reserves the storage location under that name to hold the data as they are read in. The programmer can reference each piece of data later by using the name (or address) of the location in which it is stored. This arrangement is sufficient when only a few pieces of data are to be read into storage.

If many pieces of data are involved, it is more convenient to have the computer assign the names automatically. In BASIC, this is done by telling the computer to reserve a sufficient number of adjacent storage locations to hold all the data. This block of locations, called an **array**, is assigned one name by the programmer. In BASIC an array is sometimes referred to as a **matrix** (plural **matrices**). The computer automatically assigns a number, called a **subscript**, to each location in the array, depending on its position. In this way, each location has a unique name—the array name and a subscript. The data stored in that location can be referenced by using its unique name.

A DIM statement is used to reserve the storage slots for the data to be read in. Loops containing READ or INPUT statements, and controlled by FOR-NEXT statements, are used to read in the data and assign them to the proper locations in the array.

EXAMPLE:

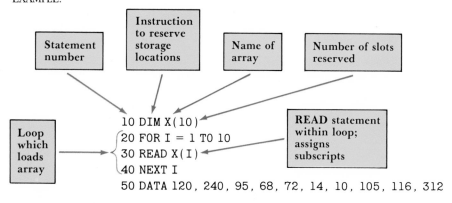

EXPLANATION: Statement 10 names an array X and reserves 10 adjacent storage locations. The FOR-NEXT loop directs the computer to read in 10 pieces of data and assign each to a unique storage location. In the first pass, I equals 1, and the computer reads in the first piece of data (120). It substitutes the value of I in statement 30 and assigns the data to that storage location X(1). In the second pass, I equals 2 and data item

240 is stored in X(2). This process continues until all items are stored in the array. The data in storage looks like this:

Array X

Storage Location	Data
X(1)	120
X(2)	240
X(3)	95
X(4)	68
X(5)	72
X(6)	14
X(7)	10
X(8)	105
X(9)	116
X(10)	312

The DIM statement must always appear in the program before the arrays listed in it are loaded. It is often placed first in the program, after the REM statement.

Any single element in the array may be printed out or used elsewhere in the program by reference to its name and subscript. For example, LET C = X(5) would assign the value of X(5) or 72 to C.

Arrays are usually printed out using PRINT statements within FOR-NEXT loops.

More than one array can be set up in a DIM statement:

EXAMPLE: 10 DIM A(6), B(10)

EXPLANATION: This statement sets up six storage locations for array A and ten for array B.

One array can be loaded before the other by using separate FOR-NEXT loops. Alternately, they can be loaded by reading in one value of A and one value of B with the same READ statement in a FOR-NEXT loop. In this case, both arrays must have the same number of rows and columns.

EXAMPLE: 30 READ A(I), B(I)

Array X in the above examples is a one-dimensional array and has only one column. Each item has only one subscript in its name. Two-dimensional arrays, with rows and columns, can also be set up to hold data. The DIM statement must tell the computer how many rows and columns are needed in the array. Several FOR-NEXT loops are used to load these arrays. Data in two-dimensional arrays can be printed out with a PRINT statement in the FOR-NEXT loops. Each item in the array can be referenced by using its assigned name and subscripts to identify column and row. For example, Y(3,2) refers to column 3, row 2 or array Y.

Suppose we wanted to load the same data as Array X into a two-dimensional array, named Y, with two rows and five columns.

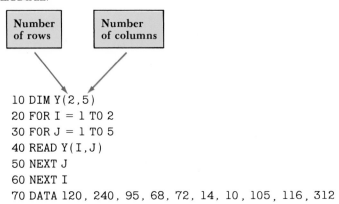

```
10 DIM Y(2,5)
20 FOR I = 1 TO 2
30 FOR J = 1 TO 5
40 READ Y(I,J)
50 NEXT J
60 NEXT I
70 DATA 120, 240, 95, 68, 72, 14, 10, 105, 116, 312
```

EXPLANATION: The first pass through the outer loop, the I index, which loads the rows, is set at 1. The J index of the inner loop will load the columns. The first pass through the outer loop, J equals 1 and data item 120 is stored in location Y(1,1). The inner loop is repeated: J equals 2 and the next data item, 240, is placed in location Y(1,2)—the first row of the second column. Then J becomes 3 and 95 goes into Y(1,3). This continues for two more repetitions. Then control returns to statement 20 and I will be set to 2. J will be reset to 1 and the second row of the columns will be loaded. The data in storage will look like this:

ARRAY Y

Rows	COLUMNS				
	J = 1	J = 2	J = 3	J = 4	J = 5
I = 1	120	240	95	68	72
I = 2	14	10	105	116	312

STANDARD FUNCTIONS

BASIC offers a variety of built-in mathematical functions that the programmer can use to perform various arithmetic procedures, such as generating random numbers, finding absolute values, square roots, cosines, and so on. Functions are used in LET or PRINT statements.

Each function has a name consisting of three letters, and a term enclosed in parentheses. The term within the parentheses, called the **argument,** is the quantity to be operated upon. An X in the parentheses represents the quantity and is called a **dummy argument.** The programmer replaces it with the **argument quantity** when the function is written into a statement.

The commonly available functions are:

FUNCTION	PURPOSE
ABS(X)	Absolute value of X
ATN(X)	Angle (in radians) whose tangent is X

COS(X)	Cosine of X radians
EXP(X)	Natural exponent of X (*e* to the power X)
INT(X)	Integral part of X
LOG(X)	Logarithm of X to the base *e* (in x)
RND(X)	A random number between 0 and 1
SGN(X)	Sign of X, defined as: If X < 0 SGN(X) = −1 If X = 0 SGN(X) = 0 If X > 0 SGN(X) = +1
SIN(X)	Sine of X radians
SQR(X)	Positive square root of X
TAN(X)	Tangent of X radians

The values found by these procedures may be printed out or used for further calculations during the program run. The argument may be a constant, a variable, or an arithmetic expression.

EXAMPLE:

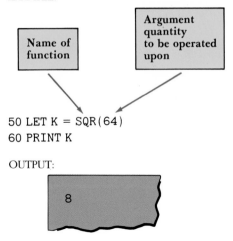

```
50 LET K = SQR(64)
60 PRINT K
```

OUTPUT:

```
8
```

EXPLANATION: Statement 50 calls out the standard function SQR, which computes the square root of 64. The value of K becomes 8.

EXAMPLE: 80 LET X = 68
         90 PRINT SQR(X + 32)

OUTPUT:

```
10
```

EXPLANATION: The computer first evaluates the expression (X + 32) to arrive at 68 + 32 = 100. Then, it extracts the square root from 100, and prints out the final value.

DEF statements allow the user to add his or her own user-defined functions to the standard built-in functions.

A user-defined function is named, described, and coded in a DEF statement. Like standard functions, each user-defined function has a name consisting of three letters and followed by X in parentheses as the argument.

EXPLANATION: The first two letters of the name must be F and N. The last letter is an alphabetic letter assigned by the programmer. Valid names would be FNA, FNK, FNT, and so on. There may be up to 26 user-defined functions in a program. The function is described by a mathematical expression to the right of an equals sign that follows the name. The function can be called out in the program whenever needed by the name assigned in the DEF statement. It operates on an argument as though it were a standard function, outputting results or placing them in storage under an assigned name.

EXAMPLE:

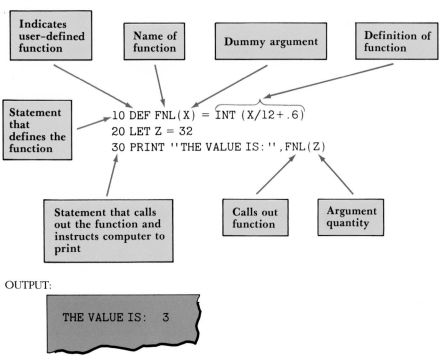

OUTPUT:

```
THE VALUE IS:   3
```

EXPLANATION: The user-defined function in statement 10 is a formula that converts inches into feet, rounding off the answer to the nearest foot. Statement 20 assigns a value of 32 to Z. The PRINT statement at line 30 calls out the function FNL and directs it to operate on Z. The computer substitutes the value of Z for the dummy argument X in the DEF statement and then evaluates the steps in the expression. It divides 32 by 12, giving 2.6666, and adds 6, giving 3.2666. Then it retains the integer part of the number and drops the fraction. The answer 3 is printed out as directed. FNL will probably be used several more times during the program run, operating on different variables each time.

GOSUB AND RETURN

GOSUB and RETURN statements are used in writing subroutines in BASIC. They are a fundamental tool of structured programming and are preferred to the GOTO statement. Subroutines are written as independent blocks or modules. They are sequences of instructions or even previously written functioning programs that may be used several times in a program to perform sorts, merges, arithmetic calculations, heading routines, and so on.

The GOSUB instruction directs control to the subroutine and the RETURN statement directs control back to the statement following GOSUB.

EXAMPLE:

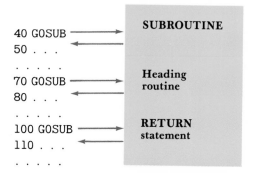

```
40 GOSUB               SUBROUTINE
50 . . .

. . . . .
70 GOSUB               Heading
                       routine
80 . . .

. . . . .
100 GOSUB              RETURN
                       statement
110 . . .

. . . . .
```

EXPLANATION: When the computer reaches the first GOSUB statement at line 40, it branches control to the subroutine. A RETURN statement at the end of the subroutine directs control back to statement 50. When the computer reaches the second GOSUB statement at line 70, control is again transferred to the subroutine. When the subroutine is executed, the RETURN statement sends control back to statement 80 in the main program. The last transfer takes place at lines 100 and 110.

EXAMPLE:
```
10 REM GOSUB EXAMPLE
20 READ A, B, C
30 LET A = A∧3 + B * C
40 GOSUB 120
50 LET A = A + 2
60 LET X = A∧2 * B − 4
70 GOSUB 120
80 LET B = B + A
90 LET X = B + 100
100 GOSUB 120
110 GOTO 230
120 PRINT ''      CALCULATIONS''
130 PRINT
```

```
140 PRINT
150 PRINT " A"; "          B"; "          C"; "          X"
160 REM SUBROUTINE
170 PRINT
180 PRINT A; B; C; X
190 PRINT
200 PRINT
210 RETURN
220 DATA 2, 3, 4
230 END
```

OUTPUT:

```
CALCULATIONS

A     B     C     X

20    3     4     0


CALCULATIONS

A     B     C     X

22    3     4     1448


CALCULATIONS

A     B     C     X

22    25    4     125
```

EXPLANATION: In this example the same subroutine is called in three times. The GOSUB statement at line 40 sends control to the subroutine beginning at line 120. The RETURN statement at line 210 sends control back to line 50. A GOSUB statement at line 70 sends control to the same subroutine, and the RETURN statement sends it back to line 80. Line 100 directs control to execute the subroutine a third time, and then control returns to line 110. Line 110 sends control to the END statement to terminate program execution.

Whenever possible you should use the GOSUB statement to perform a loop structure. This causes control to return to the same module in the program where the loop started. However, there may be occasional instances where you may wish to use a GOTO statement to generate a loop or branch control. As a general rule, the use of the GOTO should be avoided.

GOTO

The GOTO statement is an unconditional branch statement. It instructs the computer to interrupt the sequence of the program and to execute next the statement specified.

EXAMPLE:

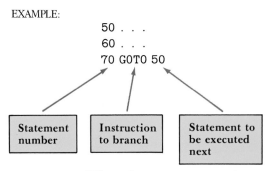

```
50 . . .
60 . . .
70 GOTO 50
```

| Statement number | Instruction to branch | Statement to be executed next |

EXPLANATION: When the computer reaches statement 70, it branches back to line 50, thus setting up a loop.

BASIC DEMONSTRATION PROGRAMS

Here are three sample programs to show you how the BASIC statements just described might be used. Each example includes a statement of the program's purpose, a flowchart showing its logic, the program listing and run, and a program analysis that explains each statement.

You should study each of these examples carefully. Compare the flowchart and the program analysis to the program listing. Reread the first part of this appendix if you want to review or clarify the type of statements used in the programs.

SAMPLE PROGRAM 1

This program calculates the number of student contact hours and assigned hours a professor has per class and the total number for all classes. The variables are input on the keyboard during execution. Figure A-1 shows the program listing and run. The flowchart appears in Figure A-2.

The algorithm is a simple loop that inputs the variables, calculates the contact and assigned hours for a class, prints them out, then adds them to accumulating totals. The last step in the loop is to ask the user whether the loop should be repeated. The two accumulating totals are assigned an initial value (usually zero) before the loop is entered and their values are printed out after the loop is completed. Assigning an initial value to a variable is called **initializing**.

PROGRAM ANALYSIS

STATEMENT NUMBER	EXPLANATION
10	Program description
20	Initializes one accumulating total G, to zero
30	Initializes one accumulating total H, to zero

```
LIST
10 REM CALCULATE STUDENT CONTACT HOURS
20 LET G=0
30 LET H=0
40 PRINT ''ENTER NUMBER OF STUDENTS IN CLASS''
50 INPUT A
60 PRINT ''ENTER HOURS PER WEEK CLASS MEETS''
70 INPUT B
80 PRINT ''ENTER NUMBER OF OFFICE HOURS PER WEEK''
90 INPUT C
100 LET D=A*B
110 LET E=C+B
120 PRINT ''YOUR STUDENT CONTACT HOURS ARE '';D
130 PRINT ''YOUR ASSIGNED HOURS ARE '';E
140 LET G=G+D
150 PRINT
160 LET H=H+E
170 PRINT ''DO YOU WANT TO ENTER ANOTHER WORK LOAD? 0=NO,1=YES''
180 INPUT F
190 IF F=1 THEN 40
200 PRINT ''THE FACULTY CONTACT HOURS ARE '';G
210 PRINT ''THE FACULTY ASSIGNED HOURS ARE '';H
220 END

RUN
ENTER NUMBER OF STUDENTS IN CLASS
? 50
ENTER HOURS PER WEEK CLASS MEETS
? 3
ENTER NUMBER OF OFFICE HOURS PER WEEK
? 4
YOUR STUDENT CONTACT HOURS ARE   150
YOUR ASSIGNED HOURS ARE   7
DO YOU WANT TO ENTER ANOTHER WORK LOAD? 0=NO,1=YES
? 1
ENTER NUMBER OF STUDENTS IN CLASS
? 45
ENTER HOURS PER WEEK CLASS MEETS
? 3
ENTER NUMBER OF OFFICE HOURS PER WEEK
? 5
YOUR STUDENT CONTACT HOURS ARE   135
YOUR ASSIGNED HOURS ARE   8
DO YOU WANT TO ENTER ANOTHER WORK LOAD? 0=NO,1=YES
? 0
THE FACULTY CONTACT HOURS ARE   285
THE FACULTY ASSIGNED HOURS ARE   15
```

Figure A-2 Program Flowchart for
Program One

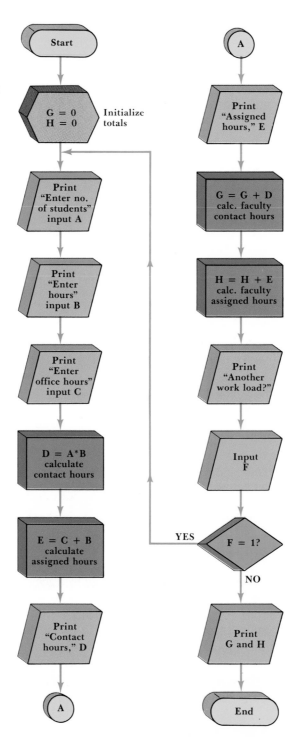

40–50	Asks user to enter A (A is input)
60–70	Asks user to enter B (B is input)
80–90	Asks user to enter C (C is input)
100	Calculates student contact hours (D)
110	Calculates assigned hours (E)
120–130	Prints out D and E
140	Adds D to the accumulating total G
150	Skips a line in printout
160	Adds E to the accumulating total H
170	Asks user to enter F (1 if loop is to be repeated, 0 if not)
180	Inputs F
190	Tests to see if F is 1; if it is, branches to statement 40
200–210	If F is 0, prints out values of G and H
220	Terminates program

SAMPLE PROGRAM 2

The program listed in Figure A-3 calculates the true annual interest rate of a loan when the purchase price, interest rate, down payment, and a fixed number of installments are given. The following formula is used:

$$r=\frac{2Mi}{B(N + 1)}$$

The meaning of the symbols in the formula and the names assigned to them in the program are as follows.

FORMULA SYMBOL	PROGRAM ASSIGNED NAME	MEANING
r	R	True annual interest rate
M	12	Number of payments in one year
i	I	Total interest paid
B	B	Initial unpaid balance
N	N	Annual rate of interest

Substituting the assigned variable names for the original symbols, we have

$$R=\frac{2*12*I}{B(N + 1)}$$

The program begins by initializing certain variables to zero. It asks the user to input the purchase price, down payment, interest rate, and number of installments. It calculates the true annual interest rate and prints out this amount, along with the amount of the loan, actual interest charges, and total amount repaid. Then it gives the user the option of repeating the calculations for another set of data. These steps are flowcharted in Figure A-4.

FIGURE A-3   Program Two

```
LIST
10 REM TRUE ANNUAL INTEREST RATE
20 LET B = 0
30 LET N1 = 0
40 LET I = 0
50 LET R1 = 0
60 LET R2 = 0
70 LET R = 0
80 PRINT
90 PRINT ''PLEASE ENTER THE TOTAL PURCHASE PRICE, ''
100 PRINT ''AND THE AMOUNT OF THE DOWN PAYMENT: ''
110 INPUT P, D
120 PRINT
130 PRINT ''ENTER THE INTEREST RATE, ''
140 PRINT ''AND THE NUMBER OF INSTALLMENTS: ''
150 INPUT N, S
160 PRINT
170 PRINT ''THANK YOU.''
180 PRINT
190 LET B = P−D
200 LET N1 = N/100
210 LET I = B * N1 * S/12
220 LET R1 = 2*12*I
230 LET R2 = R1/(B * (S+1))
240 LET R = R2 * 100
250 PRINT
260 PRINT ''THE TRUE ANNUAL INTEREST RATE FOR THIS LOAN IS '';
270 PRINT R; '' PERCENT.''
280 PRINT ''THE TOTAL AMOUNT OF THIS LOAN IS: $''; B
290 PRINT ''THE ACTUAL INTEREST CHARGES ARE: $''; I
300 PRINT ''THE TOTAL AMOUNT REPAID IS $''; B+I
310 PRINT
320 PRINT ''TO COMPUTE INTEREST RATE AND CHARGES ON ANOTHER LOAN, ''
330 PRINT ''PLEASE ENTER 1. OTHERWISE, ENTER 0.''
340 INPUT X
350 IF X = 1 THEN 20
360 PRINT
370 PRINT ''THANK YOU, GOODBYE.''
380 PRINT
390 END

RUN
PLEASE ENTER THE TOTAL PURCHASE PRICE,
AND THE AMOUNT OF THE DOWN PAYMENT:
?   6300,300

ENTER THE INTEREST RATE,
AND THE NUMBER OF INSTALLMENTS:
?   15,36
```

THANK YOU.

THE TRUE ANNUAL INTEREST RATE FOR THIS LOAN IS   29.1892   PERCENT.
THE TOTAL AMOUNT OF THIS LOAN IS: $ 6000
THE ACTUAL INTEREST CHARGES ARE: $ 2700
THE TOTAL AMOUNT REPAID IS $ 8700

TO COMPUTE INTEREST RATE AND CHARGES ON ANOTHER LOAN,
PLEASE ENTER 1. OTHERWISE, ENTER 0.
?   1

PLEASE ENTER THE TOTAL PURCHASE PRICE,
AND THE AMOUNT OF THE DOWN PAYMENT:
?   8027, 1000

ENTER THE INTEREST RATE,
AND THE NUMBER OF INSTALLMENTS:
?   18,48

THANK YOU.

THE TRUE ANNUAL INTEREST RATE FOR THIS LOAN IS   35.2653   PERCENT.
THE TOTAL AMOUNT OF THIS LOAN IS: $ 7027
THE ACTUAL INTEREST CHARGES ARE: $ 5059.44
THE TOTAL AMOUNT REPAID IS $ 12086.4

TO COMPUTE INTEREST RATE AND CHARGES ON ANOTHER LOAN,
PLEASE ENTER 1. OTHERWISE, ENTER 0.
?   0

THANK YOU, GOODBYE.

The variable names used in the program are:

P = Loan
D = Down payment
N = Interest rate
S = Number of installments
B = Unpaid balance $(B=P-D)$
N1 = Interest rate changed to decimal $(N/100)$
I = Total interest $(B*N1*S/12)$
R1 = Intermediate value $(2*12*I)$
R2 = Intermediate value $(R1/(B(N+1)))$
R = True annual interest rate $(R2*100)$ in percent
X = Test for repeat cycle; 1 = yes

Figure A-4 Flowchart for Program
Two

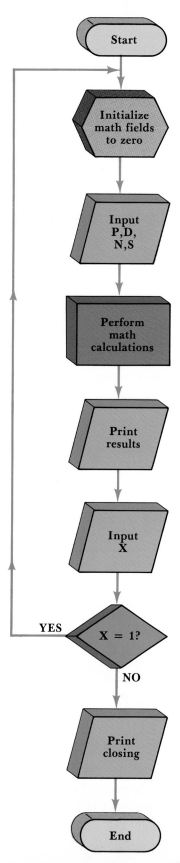

SAMPLE PROGRAM 3

The program in Figure A-5 sequences a list of names input by the user into alphabetic order and prints out the stored list. Four FOR-NEXT loops control the data manipulation. The first loop reads in the data. It can terminate in one of two ways—by reaching its maximum of 100 or by reading in a value of XXXX. The next two FOR-NEXT loops sort the data. The last loop prints out the sorted data.

The BASIC interpreter assigns consecutive numeric values to each character in the standard character set so that each alphabetic letter has a numeric equivalent. The computer can compare these numeric values to see if one is greater than, equal to, or less than the other, and then rearrange alphabetic strings depending on the result.

The sort program operates by comparing one value to the other values in the list, one at a time. As long as the first value is smaller or equal to the other value, no movement takes place. As soon as the computer reaches a value that is greater than the first one, it transposes the two values and the smaller one becomes the new test value. By the end of the first pass through the list, the smallest value in the list has been found and will be placed in location one. Now the computer repeats the search, looking for the next smallest value for location two, and so on, until the list has been alphabetized. Figure A-6 is the program flowchart.

In this example, N$ is the name of the array holding the names input from the keyboard. X$ is the name of the temporary storage location used in the transposition process. N represents the number of items read in.

FIGURE A-5 Program Three

```
LIST
10 REM SORTING DATA INTO ALPHABETICAL ORDER
20 DIM N$(100)
30 LET N=0
40 PRINT ''LIST THE NAMES TO BE SORTED''
50 PRINT ''PLEASE TYPE IN XXXX AS YOUR LAST ITEM''
60 PRINT
70 FOR I = 1 TO 100
80    INPUT N$(I)
90    IF N$(I) = ''XXXX'' THEN 120
100 LET N = N+1
110 NEXT I
120 FOR I = 1 TO N-1
130    FOR J = I+1 TO N
140       IF N$(I) <= N$(J) THEN 180
150       LET X$ = N$(I)
160       LET N$(I) = N$(J)
170       LET N$(J) = X$
180    NEXT J
190 NEXT I
200 PRINT
210 PRINT
220 PRINT ''HERE IS THE SORTED LIST OF NAMES''
230 PRINT
240 FOR I = 1 TO N
250    PRINT N$(I)
260 NEXT I
270 END

RUN
LIST THE NAMES TO BE SORTED
PLEASE TYPE IN XXXX AS YOUR LAST ITEM

? ROBBINS
? DIAZ
? NORTON
? GLENN
? GREEN
? SMITH
? CHAN
? HOLMES
? KENT
? RICE
? BIRCH
? XXXX

HERE IS THE SORTED LIST OF NAMES
BIRCH
```

```
CHAN
DIAZ
GLENN
GREEN
HOLMES
KENT
NORTON
RICE
ROBBINS
SMITH
```

PROGRAM ANALYSIS

STATEMENT NUMBER	EXPLANATION
10	Program description
20	Reserves storage for N$
30	Initializes the counter N to zero
40–60	Requests data to be entered
70–110	Loop reads in data
70	Directs computer to perform the following steps up to a maximum of 100 times. After 100 repetitions control goes to next step at statement 120
80	Inputs one value of N$ and assigns it the current value of I (from the FOR statement) as subscript
90	Tests data item to see if it is "XXXX"; if so, goes to next step; if not, continues reading
100	Increases N, which counts items input from keyboard
110	End of range of loop; returns control to statement 70
120–190	Loops perform sort
120	Begins outer loop. Indicates which position in sorted list is being searched for. Executes N-1 times. Each pass fills one position. When I is greater than N-1, all positions are filled and control passes to the next step
130–180	Inner loop pinpoints the other value being compared and performs transposition when the second value is smaller than the first
130	Limits inner loop to N repetitions; sets value of J to I + 1 to read in other value for comparison

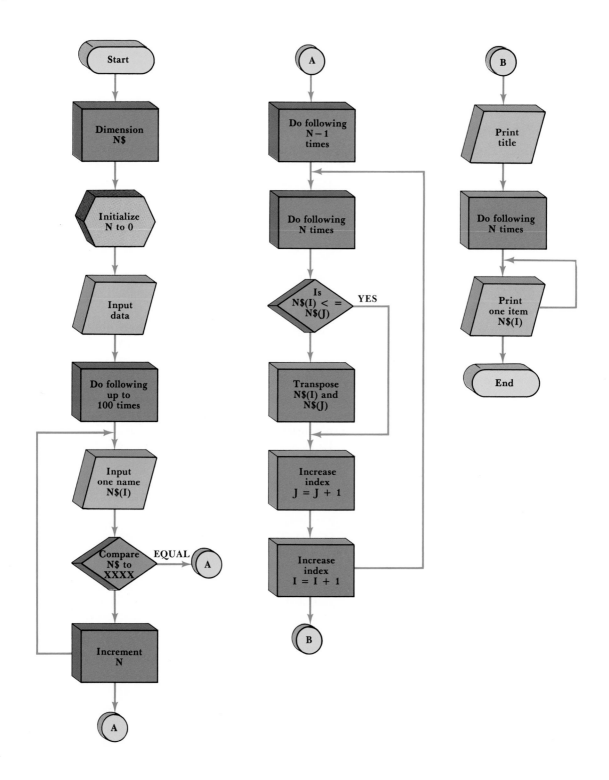

140	Compares first and second values. If first is smaller or equal to second, control goes to end of loop to increment J to compare first value to next value in list. When the first value is larger than the other value, control drops to statement 150 to perform transposition
150–170	Transposes two values; executed only when first value is larger than the second value
150	Moves first value to temporary location
160	Moves second value to first location
170	Moves value from temporary location to second location
180	End of range of inner loop; returns control to statement 130 and compares new smaller value to remaining values in list
190	End of range of outer loop; returns control to statement 120
200–230	Prints out title
240–260	Loop prints out sorted list
270	Terminates execution

PROGRAM ASSIGNMENTS

The rest of this appendix consists of six program assignments. They range from relatively short, easy programs to more difficult ones that require loops and branches. Each assignment includes a set of directions, input data, and output format.

Analyze each problem carefully. You should prepare a flowchart before doing any coding. Once you have worked out the algorithm and logic, you can code, run, and debug the program. Several different algorithms can be used to solve these problems. As a rule, the simplest and most direct approach is the best.

In coding the problem, use good programming style. Each program should begin with a REM statement giving the program title, name, and perhaps the date. Be sure to include adequate REM statements to document each step. Most students find it easier to get their programs running properly before adding graphics or more elaborate formatting.

Prepare a documentation file for each program. The file should include a description of the problem, a flowchart, the program listing, sample data input, and the formatted output.

PROGRAM ASSIGNMENT 1

DIRECTIONS   You are to write a program in BASIC which will read in your name, address, and other data and then print out the data. The purpose of this assignment is to introduce you to your computer system and to teach you how to log on your computer. The program will not need any computations or branches. Include a REM statement at the beginning of the program. Begin each line of output in column 1 and single statements spaced down the page. Prepare both a listing and a run of your program.

INPUT DATA

Student name

Address

City

State zip

Phone number

OUTPUT FORMAT

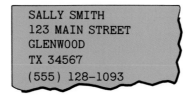

```
SALLY SMITH
123 MAIN STREET
GLENWOOD
TX 34567
(555) 128-1093
```

PROGRAM ASSIGNMENT 2

DIRECTIONS   This assignment requires you to use arithmetic operators and READ and DATA statements. Write a program to read in two whole numbers and two decimal numbers; to add the two whole numbers and print out the result; and to multiply the two decimals and print out the result on a separate line. No formatting is required, and the output is to begin in column 1. Include REM statements. Prepare both a listing and run.

INPUT DATA

1000, 2000

36.18, 9.30

OUTPUT FORMAT

```
3000
336.474
```

PROGRAM ASSIGNMENT 3

DIRECTIONS   Prepare a program to compute the total cost of an item in inventory and print out a formatted report giving the quantity of goods in stock and their total wholesale value. The total value of goods is computed by multiplying the number of items in stock by the wholesale cost per item. Include REM statements at the beginning of the program and at other appropriate points. Use READ and DATA statements to input information.

INPUT DATA

Artist brush #2

116 in stock

$1.29 per item

OUTPUT FORMAT

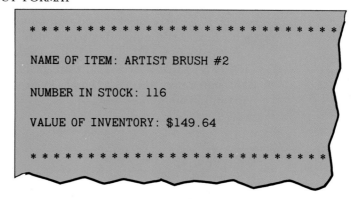

```
* * * * * * * * * * * * * * * * * * * * * * * * * *

  NAME OF ITEM: ARTIST BRUSH #2

  NUMBER IN STOCK: 116

  VALUE OF INVENTORY: $149.64


* * * * * * * * * * * * * * * * * * * * * * * * * *
```

PROGRAM ASSIGNMENT 4

DIRECTIONS   Prepare a program to read in the names of students in a class and their scores on a test; to compute the average score for the class; and to print out each student's name and test score and the class average. The data is to be read in from the keyboard using the INPUT statement. Include a test for last. The last record in the file should be ZZZZ, which will cause the computer to branch to the calculation. The average is found by adding all the scores and dividing that total by the number of scores read in. Use an IF-THEN statement and a FOR-NEXT loop.

In this problem the student is to supply data for a class of up to 20 students. Different scores may be used and of course the average will be computed accordingly.

INPUT DATA

Alice Kramer, 93
Ralph Holden, 61
Susan Chan, 83
. . .
. . .
ZZZZ, 99

OUTPUT FORMAT

```
ALICE KRAMER  93
RALPH HOLDEN  61
SUSAN CHAN    83
 . . .
 . . .
CLASS AVERAGE 82.3
```

PROGRAM ASSIGNMENT 5

DIRECTIONS   Write a program to report the status of payments on accounts. Read in a list of names of account holders and monthly payments made. If the monthly payment is below $25, write out the message PAYMENT TOO LOW. If it is exactly $25, write out ACCOUNT CURRENT. If it is over $25, write ACCOUNT OVERPAID. Include REM statements, use READ and DATA statements to input the information, and include a test for last.

INPUT DATA

Randolph, $21.30
Wilson, $65.21
Jones, $25.00
. . .
. . .
ZZZZ, 99.99

OUTPUT FORMAT

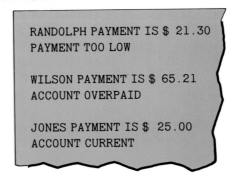

```
RANDOLPH PAYMENT IS $ 21.30
PAYMENT TOO LOW

WILSON PAYMENT IS $ 65.21
ACCOUNT OVERPAID

JONES PAYMENT IS $ 25.00
ACCOUNT CURRENT
```
. . .

PROGRAM ASSIGNMENT 6

DIRECTIONS   This assignment involves an algorithm to alphabetize a list of goods in inventory. (An alphabetizing algorithm was illustrated in Sample Program 3.) Write a program to read in exactly 20 stationery items, alphabetize them, and print out the list. The data should be input to the program using a FOR-NEXT loop and READ and DATA statements. Include REM statements to document each step in the program. Use an IF-THEN statement to branch where necessary.

INPUT DATA

Pencils

Erasers

Paper clips

Gum tape

. . .

. . .

OUTPUT FORMAT

```
ERASERS
GUM TAPE
 . . .
PAPER CLIPS
PENCILS
 . . .
```

Appendix B   Data Representation and Computer Arithmetic

The decimal numbering system, which uses 10 digits—0, 1, 2, 3, 4, 5, 6, 7, 8, and 9—has been in use in Western civilization for many centuries. However, other numbering systems, such as binary and hexadecimal, have been increasingly popular since the advent of computers.

This appendix describes the fundamentals of data representation and reviews the decimal, binary, and hexadecimal systems. It also discusses how the computer performs its arithmetic operations.

EARLY DATA REPRESENTATION

The first attempt to represent data probably involved using fingers, rocks, or sticks. Each finger, rock, or stick stood for one object being counted. This early numbering system is based on two principles. First, each unit represents only one object. Second, only two states can be represented—an object exists or it does not.

As society became more complex, this crude system of data representation became inadequate. A shorthand method of dealing with larger numbers was needed. Numbering systems were developed that use different symbols to represent quantities of more than one. For example, in the Roman numeral system, shown in Figure B-1, I is a unit that represents 1 object, II is still only a repetition of that unit to represent more than 1 object, but X (for 10 objects) is a new symbol that represents more than 1. The next step was to devise a system in which the position of the symbol gave it a different value. This led to the development of number systems that use bases and place values

The **base** of a numbering system is the number of states it recognizes. For example, a system with 10 states (0, 1, 2, 3, 4, 5, 6, 7, 8, 9) is called base 10. A system with 8 states (0, 1, 2, 3, 4, 5, 6, 7) is called base 8.

Place value is the value assigned to a symbol according to its position in the number (Figure B-2). Place value is a power of the base of a numbering system. In base 10, the rightmost position, or the symbol before the decimal (or reference) point, is equal to the symbol times 10^0 or 1. (Any number to the zero power (n^0) equals 1.) The position to its left is equal to the symbol times 10^1 or 10. The next position is the symbol times 10^2 or 100 (10×10); the next position, the symbol times 10^3 or 1,000 ($10 \times 10 \times 10$); and so on.

FIGURE B-1 Use of Symbols to Represent Objects.

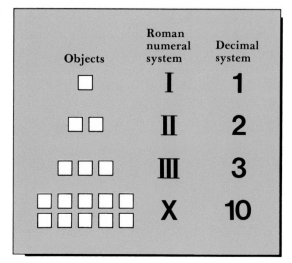

FIGURE B-2 Place Value.

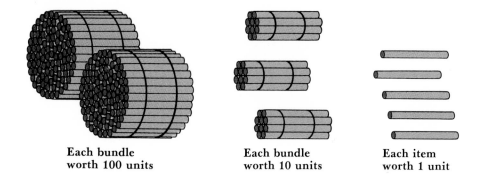

Each bundle worth 100 units

Each bundle worth 10 units

Each item worth 1 unit

DECIMAL REPRESENTATION

Our common numbering system is the **base 10** or **decimal system**. Ten different **symbols** represent the states:
0, 1, 2, 3, 4, 5, 6, 7, 8, 9.
The decimal system also uses **place values**. In the following example, each digit in the number 345 has a different place value.

Power	10^2	10^1	10^0
Place value	100	10	1
Digit	3	4	5 = 300 + 40 + 5

The value of each digit depends on its position with respect to the other digits. The number in the right-hand column (5) represents five units because it is in the units, or ones, column. The number in the tens column (4) represents 10 × 4, or 40 units. The number in the left column (3) is in the hundreds column and represents not 3 units, but 3 × 100, or 300 units. It is the place value that determines the actual quantity a numeral represents.

Looking at it in another way, we see that the number 345 is the same as

$$
\begin{array}{rr}
3 \times 100 & 100 \\
& 100 \\
& 100 \\
4 \times 10 & 10 \\
& 10 \\
& 10 \\
& 10 \\
5 \times 1 & 1 \\
& 1 \\
& 1 \\
& 1 \\
& \underline{1} \\
& 345
\end{array}
$$

In the decimal system of representation, the following place values are used.

10^5	10^4	10^3	10^2	10^1	10^0
Hundred thousands	Ten thousands	Thousands	Hundreds	Tens	Ones
100,000	10,000	1,000	100	10	1

BINARY REPRESENTATION

Early computer engineers designed machines that used the decimal system. But since these computers had to be able to represent and store 10 states, they proved to be complicated and inaccurate. There was a need to represent data in a form compatible with computer hardware capabilities. Computers, in fact most electronic devices, are inherently two-state machines. Switches, relays, lamps, diodes, transistors, and so forth are either off or on, charged or not charged, conducting or not conducting. Therefore, a number system with only two states is the most efficient for the machine. The **base 2** or **binary system** is such a two-state system. The two symbols that represent these states are 1 and 0.

PLACE VALUES The binary numbering system uses place values to represent numbers larger than its base, just as the decimal system does. Each place value is a power of 2 (the base) and increases in magnitude as it moves to the left. The first eight binary place values (given here in familiar decimal system terms) are

Place value	2^7	2^6	2^5	2^4	2^3	2^2	2^1	2^0
Decimal equivalent	128	64	32	16	8	4	2	1

The following table gives some examples of binary numbers and their decimal equivalents.

| BINARY NUMBER | | | | | | | | DECIMAL EQUIVALENT | | |
128	64	32	16	8	4	2	1	100	10	1
0	0	0	0	0	0	0	1			1
0	0	0	0	0	0	1	1			3
0	0	0	0	0	1	0	1			5
0	1	0	0	0	0	0	1		6	5
1	0	0	0	0	1	1	0	1	3	4
1	1	1	1	1	1	1	1	2	5	5

With eight place-value positions (each capable of only two conditions), any number from 0 to 255 can be represented. Larger numbers can be represented by adding more place values. The number of numerals that can be represented is doubled each time a place value is added.

To a human, the binary system appears inconvenient and awkward. It requires many more place-value positions to represent a number than does the decimal system. But an electronic device can manipulate long strings of binary numbers both efficiently and rapidly.

BINARY MATHEMATICS   In an electronic device the two states are represented electronically as a pulse train (see Figure B-3). An electrical voltage of 0 lasting a given length of time represents a binary 0. A positive electrical voltage lasting a given length of time represents a binary 1. Each storage unit of the computer is capable of representing only one of two possible states, 1 or 0. By connecting storage units in series, positions for place value are created, and larger numbers can be represented. Thus, any decimal number can be represented as a binary number, and all mathematical operations, such as addition, subtraction, and multiplication, can be performed upon it. The principles involved are similar to those used in manipulating decimal numbers. Although it is unnecessary for you to become proficient in binary mathematics, you should have some understanding of the process. Here are some fundamental rules for binary mathematical operations.

FIGURE   B-3 Pulse Train.

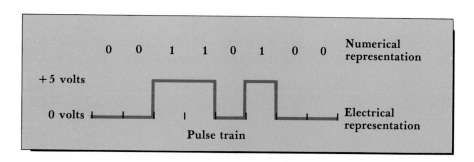

Addition of binary numbers is performed in a manner similar to adding decimal numbers.

Zero plus zero equals zero $(0 + 0 = 0)$

Zero plus one equals one $(0 + 1 = 1)$

One plus zero equals one $(1 + 0 = 1)$

One plus one equals zero with one to carry $(1 + 1 = 10)$

The following are examples of binary addition. Decimal equivalents are given.

8421		168421		8421	
0101	5	0101	5	0110	6
+1010	10	+1111	15	+0111	7
1111 = 15		10100 = 20		1101 = 13	

The basic mathematical operation performed by the computer is addition. It can also perform subtraction, multiplication, and division using the same facilities. Subtraction is performed by a process known as **subtraction by the twos complement**, while multiplication is performed by **serial addition** and division by **serial subtraction**. The mechanics of the actual processes are performed internally by the computer without operator intervention. The programmer has only to specify the values to be operated on and the mathematical operation to be carried out.

HEXADECIMAL REPRESENTATION

For some computer applications, the binary system is not suitable as a means of representing data. The **hexadecimal system**, using **base 16**, is sometimes used to represent information in storage. This system uses 16 different characters:

0, 1, 2, 3, 4, 5, 6, 7, 8, 9, A, B, C, D, E, F

The first 10 states have the same values and symbols as the decimal system. The last 6 are represented by the first 6 letters of the alphabet.

Table B-1 lists the symbols required to represent the first 16 values in the decimal, hexadecimal, and binary systems.

Each hexadecimal place value is expressed in binary by one group of four digits. Therefore, a hexadecimal number with two place values requires eight binary digits and one with three place values requires 12 binary digits. For example

HEXADECIMAL	BINARY	DECIMAL
A5	1010 0101	165
2E7	0010 1110 0111	743
F00	1111 0000 0000	3,840

TABLE B-1 Various Numbering Systems

DECIMAL	HEXADECIMAL	BINARY
0	0	0000
1	1	0001
2	2	0010
3	3	0011
4	4	0100
5	5	0101
6	6	0110
7	7	0111
8	8	1000
9	9	1001
10	A	1010
11	B	1011
12	C	1100
13	D	1101
14	E	1110
15	F	1111

With only 16 combinations to remember, programmers can easily refer to large binary numbers by their hexadecimal names, such as

0010	1111	0001	1110	1100 = 2F1EC = 193,004
2	F	1	E	C

and

1110	0010	1110	0000	1101	1010	1011 = E2E0DAB = 237,899,179
E	2	E	0	D	A	B

Conversion of large binary numbers to the decimal system is not difficult. First the hexadecimal name for the binary number is determined. Then the hexadecimal number is converted to the decimal number. Conversion from decimal to binary is also simplified by first converting the number to hexadecimal and then to binary. The computer, of course, makes this conversion automatically.

Hexadecimal printouts are often used when dumping and displaying the contents of primary memory. This is a valuable debugging aid for some kinds of programming. To understand them requires a knowledge of hexadecimal and the ability to convert data between the decimal and the hexadecimal systems. A knowledge of hexadecimal conversion is also necessary for writing programs in assembler language.

HEXADECIMAL TO DECIMAL CONVERSION   Conversion between the two systems is most easily accomplished by using a table such as Table B-2. This table will convert hexadecimal numbers up to 8 place values or positions. The place values are numbered from 1 to 8, right to left, along

HEX	DEC	HEX	DEC	HEX	DEC	HEX	DEC
0	0	0	0	0	0	0	0
1	268,435,456	1	16,777,216	1	1,048,576	1	65,536
2	536,870,912	2	33,554,432	2	2,097,152	2	131,072
3	805,306,368	3	50,331,648	3	3,145,728	3	196,608
4	1,073,741,824	4	67,108,864	4	4,194,304	4	262,144
5	1,342,177,280	5	83,886,080	5	5,242,880	5	327,680
6	1,610,612,736	6	100,663,296	6	6,291,456	6	393,216
7	1,879,048,192	7	117,440,512	7	7,340,032	7	458,752
8	2,147,483,648	8	134,217,728	8	8,388,608	8	524,288
9	2,415,919,104	9	150,994,944	9	9,437,184	9	589,824
A	2,684,354,560	A	167,772,160	A	10,485,760	A	655,360
B	2,952,790,016	B	184,549,376	B	11,534,336	B	720,896
C	3,221,225,472	C	201,326,592	C	12,582,912	C	786,432
D	3,489,660,928	D	218,103,808	D	13,631,488	D	851,968
E	3,758,096,384	E	234,881,024	E	14,680,064	E	917,504
F	4,026,531,840	F	251,658,240	F	15,728,640	F	983,040
8		**7**		**6**		**5**	

TABLE B-2 Hexadecimal to Decimal Conversion

the bottom of the table. Each place value is a power of 16, the base, and represents these units:

8	7	6	5	4	3	2	1
268,435,456	16,777,216	1,048,576	65,536	4,096	256	16	1

A hexadecimal 1 in position 3 means there is 1 group of 256 units in a number. An A in that position means there are 10 groups of 256 units in the number, or 2,560 decimal units. A hexadecimal B in position 2 means there are 11 groups of 16 units, or 176 (11 × 16) decimal units, and so forth.

The table provides a convenient method of simplifying the conversion of hexadecimal and decimal numbers. The decimal value of each hexadecimal position is found and added to give the equivalent decimal number.

Here is an example of hexadecimal conversion, using the place values listed above.

```
HEXADECIMAL 1CB3 = DECIMAL 7,347
hexadecimal 3 in position 1 =  3 × 1     =     3 in decimal
hexadecimal B in position 2 = 11 × 16    =   176 in decimal
hexadecimal C in position 3 = 12 × 256   = 3,072 in decimal
hexadecimal 1 in position 4 =  1 × 4,096 = 4,096 in decimal
                                           7,347
```

DECIMAL TO HEXADECIMAL CONVERSION A reverse procedure will convert decimal numbers to hexadecimal values, also by using Table B-2. It is basically the process of rearranging the units represented by a number into new groups corresponding to the place values of the hexadecimal system.

For example, look at the steps involved in converting the decimal value 32,184 to its hexadecimal equivalent:

HEX	DEC	HEX	DEC	HEX	DEC	HEX	DEC
0	0	0	0	0	0	0	0
1	4,096	1	256	1	16	1	1
2	8,192	2	512	2	32	2	2
3	12,288	3	768	3	48	3	3
4	16,384	4	1,024	4	64	4	4
5	20,480	5	1,280	5	80	5	5
6	24,576	6	1,536	6	96	6	6
7	28,672	7	1,792	7	112	7	7
8	32,768	8	2,048	8	128	8	8
9	36,864	9	2,304	9	144	9	9
A	40,960	A	2,560	A	160	A	10
B	45,056	B	2,816	B	176	B	11
C	49,152	C	3,072	C	192	C	12
D	53,248	D	3,328	D	208	D	13
E	57,344	E	3,584	E	224	E	14
F	61,440	F	3,840	F	240	F	15
	4		3		2		1

1. Find the decimal number on the table equal to or almost as large as the number being converted. In this case, it is 28,672 in position 4. The hexadecimal equivalent is 7___. This number will contain four place values, and the leftmost digit is a hexadecimal 7. This means the decimal number contains 7 groups of 4,096 units (7 × 4,096 = 28,672).

2. Now subtract 28,672 from 32,184 since these units have been regrouped. This leaves 3,512 units.

$$\begin{array}{r} 32{,}184 \\ -28{,}672 \\ \hline 3{,}512 \end{array} \qquad 7\text{\_\_\_}$$

3. The closest decimal value to 3,512 is 3,328 in position 3. Its hexadecimal equivalent is D__. 3,512 contains 13 groups of 256 units, with 184 units still left to be regrouped. The hexadecimal number now looks like this:

$$\begin{array}{r} 3{,}512 \\ -3{,}328 \\ \hline 184 \end{array} \qquad 7D\text{\_\_}$$

4. Decimal 176 is the closest value to 184 and its hexadecimal is B_, with 8 units left. The number is now

$$\begin{array}{r} 184 \\ -176 \\ \hline 8 \end{array} \qquad 7DB\text{\_}$$

5. Eight decimal units are equal to 8 hexadecimal units, and these are added to give the final answer. The decimal number 32,184 is equal to hexadecimal 7DB8.

Here is another example:

DECIMAL   12,431 = HEXADECIMAL 308F

$$
\begin{array}{rr}
12{,}431 & \\
-12{,}288 = & 3\_\_\_ \\
\hline
143 & \\
-128 = & 08\_ \\
\hline
15 & \\
-15 = & \underline{F} \\
\hline
0 & 308F
\end{array}
$$

Glossary

ABSTRACT A summary of a program, briefly describing its purpose, major features, options, and procedures.

ACCESS TIME The time required to locate and retrieve a given piece of data from memory.

ADA A new programming language sponsored by the Department of Defense, designed for use in military and business systems.

AI (ARTIFICIAL INTELLIGENCE) The field of computer work involving hardware and software that simulate human intelligence, thought, and reasoning.

ALGORITHM A list of specific steps or a set of rules leading to the solution of a problem.

ALPHANUMERIC Referring to a set of characters that includes letters, digits, special characters, and punctuation marks.

ALU (ARITHMETIC AND LOGIC UNIT) The section of the central processing unit of a computer that performs arithmetic and logic operations.

ANALOG COMPUTER A computer that processes data input in a continuous form or data represented as an unbroken flow of information.

ANALOG DATA Data represented in a continuous form, as contrasted with digital data represented in a discrete (discontinuous) form. Examples of analog data are physical variables measured along a continuous scale, such as voltage, resistance, and rotation.

ANSI American National Standards Institute.

APL (A PROGRAMMING LANGUAGE) A mathematically oriented programming language.

APPLICATIONS PROGRAM Software written to solve a specific problem.

ARCHITECTURE The design and organization of the components of a computer system. The structure of a data base.

ARRAY A group of related numbers or words stored in the computer in adjacent memory locations.

ASCII (AMERICAN STANDARD CODE FOR INFORMATION INTERCHANGE) A standard system that can represent 128 different characters.

ASSEMBLER LANGUAGE A low-level programming language that uses symbolic operation codes and addresses.

ASSEMBLY PROGRAM A service program, also called an assembler, that translates assembly language into machine language.

ASYNCHRONOUS TRANSMISSION A system of transmitting characters without reference to a clock or timed intervals.

ATM (AUTOMATED TELLER MACHINE) A remote terminal that allows automated transfer of funds in bank accounts.

AUDIO RESPONSE UNIT An output device that generates audible signals and tones and can synthesize the human voice.

BASE The number of states a numbering system recognizes and the number of symbols used to represent the states.

BASIC (BEGINNER'S ALL-PURPOSE SYMBOLIC INSTRUCTION CODE) A high-level programming language used on many microcomputers.

BATCH PROCESSING The processing of data at some time after a transaction has occurred. Also called offline processing.

BINARY NOTATION A fixed-base notation in which the base is 2.

BIT The smallest unit of information that can be held in memory. Abbreviated form of the term binary digit, a 0 or a 1.

BLOCK A group of records, words, or characters, that for technical or logical reasons are treated as a unit in input or output. A section of a program treated as a unit.

BLOCK DIAGRAM A flowchart that shows the major steps or modules in the solution of a problem.

BLOCKING Combining two or more records into one block.

BPI (BITS PER INCH) A measure of capacity, or density, of storage media.

BPS (BITS PER SECOND) A measure of line capacity, of data transmission speed.

BUBBLE MEMORY A system in which data are stored as magnetized areas on thin film semiconductor.

BUFFER A device or routine that stores up characters and transmits them once sufficient data have been accumulated.

BUG A logical or clerical error, or a malfunction.

BYTE A group of adjacent bits that form a character.

CAD (COMPUTER-AIDED DESIGN) The use of the computer to prepare and test mechanical designs and make engineering drawings.

CAM (COMPUTER-AIDED MANUFACTURING) The application of the computer to such manufacturing tasks as process control, inventory control, and scheduling of work.

CARD PUNCH A device that records information in cards by punching holes to represent letters, numerals, or special characters.

CARD READER A device that senses holes in punched cards and converts them to pulses sent to the CPU for processing.

CELLULAR STORAGE A secondary storage system in which data are stored in cartridges that are housed in a honeycomb pattern of cells.

CHAIN PRINTER An impact printer that uses type slugs carried by the links of a revolving chain.

CHANNEL A path along which signals can be sent. A track on paper or magnetic tape.

CHECK BIT An extra bit added to a byte to detect an inaccuracy in transmission.

CHIP See **integrated circuit**.

574

CLOCK See **cycle clock**.

COBOL (COMMON BUSINESS ORIENTED LANGUAGE) A high-level programming language used in business.

CODASYL (CONFERENCE ON DATA SYSTEMS LANGUAGES) The group of users and manufacturers of data processing systems that developed and maintain the COBOL language.

CODING The operation of converting instructions into language commands that can be processed by a computer.

COM (COMPUTER OUTPUT MICROFORM) A form of output that uses miniature photographic images to store or output information.

COMMUNICATIONS LINK The hardware and circuitry used to connect elements of a system in order to transmit and receive information.

COMPILER A computer program that converts a program written in a high-level language into machine language.

COMPUTER An electronic device capable of receiving input, processing data, and generating output according to stored instructions with high speed and accuracy.

COMPUTER WORD A group of bytes stored in one memory location and treated as a unit.

CONTROL PROGRAM The portion of the operating system that manages overall operations, schedules work, logs jobs, and monitors status.

CONTROL UNIT The part of the computer that guides the overall operation and timing of the CPU.

COUNTER A component of the control unit of the central processing unit that counts and records the number of pulses sent to it.

COUPLER See **modem**.

CPU (CENTRAL PROCESSING UNIT) The portion of the computer that performs calculations, controls its operation, and contains primary memory.

CRT (CATHODE RAY TUBE) An output device that converts electric signals into visual form by means of a controlled electron beam.

CURSOR A flashing pointer that can be moved about on the face of a CRT.

CYCLE CLOCK A component of the control unit of the central processing unit that sends out pulses that regulate the opening and closing of electronic circuits within the CPU.

CYLINDER The group of tracks accessed simultaneously by a set of read/write heads on a disk storage device.

DAISY WHEEL A printing device consisting of a flat wheel of spokes with a different letter or character on each spoke.

DASD (DIRECT ACCESS STORAGE DEVICE) A memory system that can locate or retrieve data by reference to the data's address or location.

DATA Factual information of value to an individual or organization, suitable for communication, interpretation, or processing by humans or machines.

DATA BASE A collection of all the data used by an individual or organization, structured in a systematic way to eliminate duplication and to facilitate retrieval and processing for many applications.

DATA CAPTURE The first step in the word processing cycle wherein information is dictated, written, or typed for later processing.

DATA COMMUNICATIONS The transmission of information between processing sites over telephone, telegraph, satellite relay, microwave, or other circuits.

DATA CONCENTRATOR A device that stores characters and then transmits them over a line in a high-speed burst.

DATA CYCLE The fundamental sequence of data processing operations, composed of input, processing, and output.

DATA DICTIONARY A comprehensive list of elements in a data base, usually arranged alphabetically, giving the form, function, meaning, and syntax of data.

DATA INPUT The conversion of data from source documents into a form acceptable for processing by computer or other means.

DATA MODEL The part of a data base that defines the information contained in a field, its format including the type and number of characters, and reference method.

DATA OUTPUT The reporting of information processed by computer in a form suitable for use by people.

DATA PROCESSING The restructuring, manipulation, or reordering of data by people or machines to increase the data's usefulness for a particular purpose.

DATA SET The collection of information on which a program is to operate; data to be processed.

DATA TRANSMISSION The sending of data from one part of a system to another.

DBMS (DATA BASE MANAGEMENT SYSTEM) A comprehensive set of computer programs that constructs, maintains, manipulates, and provides access to a data base.

DDP (DISTRIBUTED DATA PROCESSING) A system in which a network of geographically separate, stand alone computers replaces large central computers for the processing of information.

DEBUG To detect, trace, and eliminate mistakes in computer programs or other software.

DECISION TABLE A tabular form used in preparing programs showing conditions that may occur and actions to be taken in response.

DECODER An electronic device in the central processing unit that sets up an electrical pathway in response to an instruction.

DEFAULT OPTION A built-in feature of the programming language PL/I that corrects certain errors made by the programmer.

DETAIL FILE A transaction file containing records that will be used to update a master file.

DETAIL FLOWCHART A flowchart that shows every step and operation involved in solving a problem.

DIAGNOSTIC MESSAGE A message printed out by the computer during compilation or execution of a program, pertaining to the diagnosis or isolation of errors in the program.

DIGITAL COMPUTER A computer that processes data in a discrete or discontinuous form.

DIGITAL DATA Data represented in discrete, discontinuous form, as contrasted with analog data represented in continuous form. Digital data are usually represented by means of coded characters, such as numbers, letters, and symbols.

DIGITIZER An input device that converts pictures, lines, or drawings into x-y coordinates.

DISK A metal or plastic plate coated with ferromagnetic material on which data may be recorded. A form of secondary storage. See **diskette, rigid disk**.

DISK PACK A collection of two or more disks mounted on a common shaft.

DISKETTE A thin, flexible, plastic disk coated with ferromagnetic material on which data may be recorded. Also called flexible disk, floppy disk.

DOCUMENT A medium and the data recorded on it for human use, for example, a report sheet or an invoice. By extension, any record that has permanence and that can be read by a person or machine.

DOCUMENTATION A written record of the logic, details, and input and output specifications related to a program. User guides, manuals, and instructions available for a computer.

DOS (DISK OPERATING SYSTEM) An operating system that stores the bulk of its instructions on magnetic disk.

DOT MATRIX PRINTER An impact printout device that forms characters by striking the ends of a group of wires or rods arranged in a pattern.

DRUM PRINTER An impact printout device that makes images by striking raised characters arranged around a cylinder in as many bands as there are print positions.

DUMB TERMINAL A computer terminal that does not contain a microcomputer or independent processing capability.

EAM (ELECTRICAL ACCOUNTING MACHINE) Any piece of data processing equipment that is predominantly electromechanical, such as card punch, mechanical sorter, collator, and tabulator.

EBCDIC (EXTENDED BINARY CODED DECIMAL INTERCHANGE CODE) A coding system that can represent 256 different characters.

EDIT To prepare input data for a later operation or to change the form of output data by such operations as the rearrangement or the addition of data, the deletion of unwanted data, format control, code conversion, and so forth.

EDP (ELECTRONIC DATA PROCESSING) Data processing largely performed by computers.

EFT (ELECTRONIC FUNDS TRANSFER) The transfer of funds by the electronic adjustment of records.

ELECTRONIC MAIL The sending of messages by the transmission of electronic pulses rather than by the transfer of physical documents.

END-OF-REEL MARK A reflective foil indicator that marks the end of the usable tape on a reel.

EPROM (ERASABLE PROGRAMMABLE READ ONLY MEMORY) A solid state storage device capable of read only memory that can be removed from the computer and exposed to ultraviolet light in order to be reprogrammed.

EVEN PARITY A system for checking accuracy when transmitting digital data in which a bit is added to an array of bits (a byte) to make the sum of the bits even.

EXECUTE To carry out an instruction or perform a routine.

EXECUTION CYCLE The phase in the operating cycle of the central processing unit during which an instruction is performed or carried out.

FACSIMILE MACHINE See **telecopier**

FERRITE CORE MEMORY A form of primary storage using a network of doughnut-shaped rings pressed from iron ferrite and strung on wires.

FIBEROPTICS A cable consisting of bundles of glass or plastic fibers that are able to transmit data in the form of light.

FIELD A group of related characters, or bytes, treated as a unit. One or more columns of related information on a punched card.

FILE A collection of related records treated as a unit.

FILE LABEL A magnetically recorded label before each file on a tape to give the file name and the date after which it may be destroyed. Also called header label.

FILE MAINTENANCE The activity of keeping a file up to date by adding, changing, or deleting data.

FILE PROTECTION RING A plastic ring that is placed on the hub of a reel of magnetic tape in order to record or erase data from the tape.

FILING The classifying and storing of information and documents for later retrieval.

FLEXIBLE DISK See **diskette**.

FLIP-FLOP CIRCUIT An electronic circuit that can be used as a binary counter because it reverses its electrical state each time it receives a pulse.

FLOPPY DISK See **diskette**.

FLOWCHART A graphic representation of the definition, analysis, or method of solution of a problem, in which standardized symbols are used to represent operations, data flow, equipment, and so forth.

FONT A set of characters molded on a printing element.

FORTRAN (FORMULA TRANSLATING SYS-TEM) A programming language that resembles mathematical notation and is used primarily for scientific applications.

FULL-DUPLEX CIRCUIT A circuit in which data can flow in two directions at the same time.

GATE An electronic circuit that performs a mathematical or logical operation.

GIGO (GARBAGE IN—GARBAGE OUT) A term to express the fact that the quality of a computer result can be no better than the quality of the input data and processing instructions.

GRAPHICS Output in the form of black and white or color images, such as lines, plots, charts, and drawings.

HALF-DUPLEX CIRCUIT A circuit in which data flow can be shifted from one direction to the other, that is, a circuit that can receive or transmit data in one direction at a time.

HARD COPY Output in a permanent physical form that can be read or viewed by people, such as a paper printout.

HARDWARE The electronic and mechanical machines and devices—the physical equipment—used to input, process, and output data.

HEADER LABEL See **file label**.

HOLLERITH CARD A punched card containing 80 columns and 12 rows of punch positions.

IC (INTEGRATED CIRCUIT) A solid state device containing a complex group of transistors and electronic circuits etched on a small piece of silicon, about $\frac{1}{16}$ inch square.

IDENTIFIER See **variable**.

IMPACT PRINTER An output device that forms characters by striking a raised letter against a ribbon, imprinting it on a sheet.

INFORMATION See **data**.

INITIALIZE To set a counter, switch, address, or other contents of storage to zero or other starting value at the beginning of or at prescribed points in the operation of a computer routine.

INK JET PRINTER An output device that forms letters from a continuous stream of ink droplets.

INPUT See **data input**.

INSTRUCTION CYCLE The phase in the operating cycle of the central processing unit during which an instruction is called from storage and the required circuitry to perform that instruction is set up.

INTELLIGENCE CHANNEL A track on paper or magnetic tape that transmits information such as a letter or number.

INTELLIGENT COPIER An office copy machine that can copy, collate, and sort pages.

INTELLIGENT TERMINAL A computer terminal equipped with an independent microprocessor, capable of performing logic, decisions, and local processing.

INTERACTIVE LANGUAGE A language designed to allow the programmer to communicate with the computer during the execution of the program.

INTERACTIVE PROGRAM A computer program that permits data to be entered or the course of programming flow to be changed during its execution.

INTERBLOCK GAP (IBG) An area on magnetic tape between blocks of records.

INTERNALLY STORED PROGRAM A set of instructions read into computer memory that directs the computer.

INTERPRETER A computer program that translates statements in a programming language into machine instructions line by line.

I/O (INPUT/OUTPUT) A general term referring to the equipment used to communicate with a computer, the data involved in such communication, or the media carrying the data.

IRG (INTERRECORD GAP) An area on magnetic tape between records.

K An abbreviation for the prefix kilo, meaning 1,000, in decimal notation. In computer terminology an abbreviation for a value equal to 2^{10}, or 1,024.

KERNEL The center of the operating system containing routines that call in and out other software.

KILOBYTE (KB) 1,024 bytes.

LAN (LOCAL AREA NETWORK) A communications system that links work stations within a geographically limited area, usually by coaxial cable, to enable users to share computer resources.

LANGUAGE TRANSLATOR See **compiler**.

LASER TRANSMISSION Transmission of data in the form of flashes of a coherent beam of light.

LCD (LIQUID CRYSTAL DISPLAY) Visual display in which the output images are formed by a liquid suspended in an electrical field.

LED (LIGHT EMITTING DIODE) A semiconductor device that glows and is used in displaying binary or alphanumeric information.

LIBRARY A collection of related files.

LINE PRINTER An output device that converts electronic pulses into readable characters on a page.

LIST STRUCTURE A data base schema that allows out-of-sequence records to be processed through the use of a system of pointers or linkage addresses to direct the computer.

LISTING Loosely, a printout of all cards or records in a file or all statements in a program.

LOAD-POINT MARK A reflective foil indicator that marks the beginning of the usable tape on a reel.

LONGITUDINAL PARITY CHECK An accuracy-checking system in which all bits in a track are tallied at the end of its length, and a check bit added to generate an even or odd number of bits.

LOOP STRUCTURE A logic pattern in structured programming in which the computer repeats a sequence until a certain test condition prevails. Also called iteration structure.

LSI (LARGE-SCALE INTEGRATED CIRCUIT) A solid state device containing thousands of electronic components manufactured on a single chip of silicon.

MACHINE LANGUAGE A language that is used directly by a machine.

MACROFLOWCHART See **block diagram**.

MAGNETIC DISK See **disk, diskette, rigid disk**.

MAINFRAME In a large computer, the central processing unit. Sometimes refers to a large computer, including its I/O devices.

MANUAL DATA PROCESSING Data processing done mentally or with paper and pencil, adding machine, or desk calculator.

MARK SENSE To mark a position on a punched card with an electrically conductive pencil, for later conversion to machine punching.

MASS STORAGE A secondary storage system capable of storing hundreds of millions of records.

MASTER FILE A file that is used as an authority in a given job and that is relatively permanent, even though its contents may change.

MATHEMATICAL MODEL A planning tool in which business conditions are analyzed and solved by mathematical techniques.

MATRIX See **array**.

MB (MEGABYTE) About 1 million bytes, or 1024K bytes.

MENU A list of options and choices of programs available or processing modules within a program from which a user selects.

MICR (MAGNETIC INK CHARACTER REC-OGNITION) Recognition of characters printed with ink that contains particles of a magnetic material.

MICROCOMPUTER A miniature computer manufactured on a small chip, using solid state integrated circuitry, that possesses characteristics of larger systems.

MICROELECTRONICS The design and construction of miniature electronic components using integrated circuits and solid state technology.

MICROFORM A photographic film on which reduced images of data are stored, such as microfilm or microfiche.

MICROFLOWCHART See **detail flowchart**.

MICROGRAPHICS The production of greatly reduced images on photographic film.

MICROPROCESSOR The central processing unit of a computer, manufactured on a small silicon chip.

MICROSECOND (μs) One-millionth of a second.

MILLISECOND (ms) One-thousandth of a second.

MINICOMPUTER A small, desktop digital computer with at least one I/O device and memory between 32K and 64K bytes or over.

MIPS (MILLIONS OF INSTRUCTIONS PER SECOND) A unit for measuring the speed of a computer.

MODEM (MODULATOR/DEMODULATOR) A device used to connect a terminal or a computer to a transmission line. Also called a **coupler**.

MONITOR See **operating system**.

MOUSE An input device that is moved about on a tabletop and directs a pointer on a CRT.

MULTIPLEXER A device that interleaves data from several sources and sends them over a single transmission line.

MULTIPROCESSING A system in which two or more central processing units are wired together to share processing.

MULTIPROGRAMMING A mode of operation in which two or more programs are processed by one computer concurrently.

NANOSECOND (ns) One-billionth of a second.

NETWORK A system of computers or terminals interconnected by communications circuits.

NETWORK STRUCTURE A data base schema using master records, which may be linked to several subordinate records, which may be linked to several masters.

NODE A central point around which are clustered a group of local terminals or work stations in a telecommunications network.

OBJECT PROGRAM A fully compiled or assembled program that is ready to be loaded into the computer.

OCR (OPTICAL CHARACTER RECOGNI-TION) The ability of certain light-sensitive machines to recognize printed letters, numbers, and special characters.

ODD PARITY A system for checking accuracy in transmitting digital data in which a bit is added to an array of bits (a byte) to make the sum of the bits odd.

OFFLINE PROCESSING See **batch processing**.

ONLINE PROCESSING See **transaction-oriented processing**.

OP CODE (OPERATION CODE) The part of a computer instruction that directs the machine to carry out a specific operation such as to add or to compare data.

OPERAND A part of a computer instruction that describes the location where data will be found and where the results will be sent.

OPTICAL CHARACTER READER An input device that can recognize certain handwritten, typed, or printed characters and convert them into electronic pulses.

OPTICAL SENSE READER An input device that can interpret certain handwritten marks and convert them into electronic pulses.

OS (OPERATING SYSTEM) Software that controls the execution of computer programs and that may provide scheduling, debugging, input/output control, accounting, compilation, storage assignment, data management, and related services.

OUTPUT See **data output**.

PAGING A procedure for expanding the memory capacity of a computer by moving data between primary memory and a secondary storage device.

PARALLEL OUTPUT A form of output in which all characters on a line are printed at the same instant.

PARITY CHECK A system for detecting the loss or gain of a bit during transmission by checking whether the number of bits (0s or 1s) is odd or even.

PASCAL A high-level programming language designed for structured programming.

PERIPHERAL EQUIPMENT Any hardware device distinct from the central processing unit that provides communications, input/output, secondary storage, or other facilities.

PIXEL A spot or point that makes up the image of a picture, drawing, or line on a CRT.

PL/I (Programming Language I) A high-level programming language used for both scientific and business applications.

PLOTTER An output device that converts electronic signals into figures, lines, or curves by connecting point-by-point coordinate values.

POINTER A number that directs the computer to the next record in a data base even though it is not in sequence.

POL (PROBLEM-ORIENTED LANGUAGE) Any high-level programming language that stresses problem-solving features and eliminates programming details.

PORT A terminal that serves as an entry point into a telecommunications network.

PRIMARY MEMORY The section of the central processing unit that during processing holds program instructions, input data, calculation results, and data to be output. Also called internal storage, main memory, primary memory.

PROCESS CONTROL A technique by which the output of a system is fed back into the system as input in order to monitor, measure, or control a manufacturing process.

PROGRAM A schedule or plan that specifies the actions a computer is to take in solving a prob-

lem; a series of instructions or statements recorded in a form that can be understood by a computer.

PROGRAMMER An individual who lays out the steps in solving a problem and writes instructions for the computer.

PROM (PROGRAMMABLE READ ONLY MEMORY) A solid state storage device capable of read only memory that can be programmed by the user.

PSEUDOCODE An abbreviated, nonexecutable version of program statements, written in ordinary language, as a step in program development and analysis.

PULSE An electronic signal or voltage, the presence or absence of which can be used in a computer to represent data as 1 (presence) or 0 (absence).

PULSE TRAIN A string of electronic pulses that transmit data.

RAM (RANDOM ACCESS MEMORY) A solid state storage device that enables data to be written in, changed, or read out repeatedly.

RANDOM ACCESS STORAGE An access mode in which records are searched for and retrieved from a secondary storage file in a nonsequential manner, usually by location. Also called direct access storage.

READ/WRITE HEAD That part of a magnetic tape drive that records data (in the form of electronic pulses) on or reads data from tape.

REAL TIME PROCESSING See **transaction-oriented processing**.

RECORD A collection of related fields treated as a unit. One whole punched card.

REGISTER A storage device that holds information being processed.

RELATIONAL STRUCTURE A data base schema that uses a group of tables to show relationships used to search out data.

RIGID DISK A round metal plate with a thin coating of ferromagnetic material on which data may be recorded. Also called disk or hard disk.

RJE (REMOTE JOB ENTRY) A system of hardware and software that enables jobs to be input, processed, and output via remote terminals.

ROM (READ ONLY MEMORY) A permanently programmed semiconductor memory device that can read out data repeatedly and whose contents cannot be changed.

RPG (REPORT PROGRAM GENERATOR) A high-level computer language used for processing large data files.

SCANNER An input device that reads symbols or codes by passing a light or laser beam over them.

SCHEMA The logical structure, plan, or method by which data are organized in a data base system.

SCROLL To move output displayed on a cathode ray tube up or down on the screen.

SECONDARY STORAGE Auxiliary memory that can be accessed by the central processing unit.

SELECTION STRUCTURE A form of program logic in which the computer branches to one of two different tracks depending upon a test condition.

SELF-DIRECTION The ability of the computer to follow sets of instructions without human intervention.

SEMICONDUCTOR A solid state electronic switching device that performs functions similar to an electronic tube.

SEMICONDUCTOR MEMORY A memory system containing thousands of microscopic transistors manufactured on a chip of silicon.

SEQUENCE STRUCTURE A form of program logic in which the computer moves through a set of statements one time without branching.

SEQUENTIAL ACCESS STORAGE An access mode in which a storage medium is searched in sequence for a desired record.

SERIAL OUTPUT A form of output in which characters are printed letter by letter usually from left to right.

SERVICE PROGRAM The part of the operating system that contains frequently used routines and functions such as language translators.

SHARED LOGIC SYSTEM A computer or word processing machine connected to several work stations that share its resources.

SHELL The software containing control and service programs surrounding the kernel in an operating system.

SIMPLEX CIRCUIT A circuit in which data can flow in only one direction.

SMART TERMINAL See **intelligent terminal**.

SOFT COPY Output in a temporary or nonpermanent form, such as a display on a cathode ray tube.

SOFTWARE Programs, procedures, rules, and documentation that direct or relate to the operation of a computer system.

SOLID STATE CIRCUIT See **semiconductor**.

SOURCE DOCUMENT A record prepared at the time or location a transaction takes place that serves as a source for data to be input to a computer system.

SPLIT SCREEN A form of cathode ray tube display in which the screen is divided into sections for simultaneous display of different information.

SPREAD SHEET SOFTWARE A program that manipulates information and displays it in the form of an electronic ledger sheet and related graphs and charts.

STAND ALONE SYSTEM An independent computer system not sharing the memory or resources of another computer.

STANDARD CHARACTER SET The limited collection of characters (letters, numbers, and special symbols) used to encode a program in a given language.

STANDARD UNIVERSAL IDENTIFIER A number used to catalog information in a data bank.

STRUCTURED PROGRAMMING A programming technique in which steps are designed as separate, independent modules linked together by control programs.

SUBROUTINE A sequence of statements that may be used as a whole in one or more computer programs and at one or more points in a computer program.

SUPERVISOR PROGRAM See **operating system**.

SYNCHRONOUS TRANSMISSION A system of sending and receiving characters at timed intervals.

SYSTEM A collection of objects, procedures, and techniques that interact in a regulated manner to form an organized whole.

SYSTEM FLOWCHART A diagram that shows the data flow in an entire organization or system, specifying work stations, operations to be performed, communications links and so forth.

SYSTEMS ANALYSIS The analysis of an activity to determine precisely what must be accomplished and how to accomplish it.

TELECOMMUNICATIONS The transmission of data in digital, audio, or video form over long distances.

TELECONFERENCING An electronic communications system that allows individuals at different physical locations to participate in a conference.

TELECOPIER A device that scans a page, converts the data into electronic pulses, and transmits the pulses to a remote location.

TELEPROCESSING The transmission of information in digital form through a network of computer terminals, and transmission lines.

TEMPLATE A pattern or guide. A plastic cutout used to draw standard flowchart symbols.

TERMINAL A remotely located input or output device connected to a computer.

TEXT EDITING The process of changing, adding, or deleting material to improve a text's usefulness, accuracy, or appearance.

THERMAL PRINTER An output device that forms characters by using heat and heat-sensitive paper.

THIMBLE A molded plastic printing element containing curved spokes, each with a different letter or character on it.

THROUGHPUT A measure of system efficiency; the rate at which work can be handled by a system.

TIME SHARING The use of a computer system by two or more users whose programs are executed concurrently.

TOPOLOGY The study of the structure, design, and layout of a network and transmission facility.

TOS (TAPE OPERATING SYSTEM) An operating system that stores the bulk of its instructions on magnetic tape.

TRACK The portion of a moving data medium, such as a drum, tape, or disk, that is accessible to a given reading head position.

TRAILER LABEL A magnetically recorded label that marks the end of a file on a tape and gives the file name, the date on which it may be destroyed, and the number of blocks or records in the file.

TRAILER RECORD A record that marks the physical end of an input file.

TRANSACTION FILE See **detail file**.

TRANSACTION-ORIENTED PROCESSING The processing of information at the time a transaction takes place and under direct control of the CPU. Also called online processing, real time processing.

TRANSCRIBING Converting spoken or written information into keystrokes for input into a computer system; converting source data into machine-readable form.

TRANSISTOR A small, solid state device that performs nearly all the functions of an electronic tube, especially amplification and switching.

TREE STRUCTURE A data base schema using master records, known as parents, which may be linked to several subordinate records, known as children, each of which is linked to only one master record.

TYPE ELEMENT An object used in printing that contains a font of molded characters.

TYPE WHEEL A wheel with letters and numbers molded around it, used to print characters.

UNIT RECORD A punched card containing information on one transaction.

UNIT RECORD PROCESSING Processing data by using a combination of human activity and electromechanical devices.

UPC (UNIVERSAL PRODUCT CODE) A machine-readable code using parallel bars to represent digits, for labeling consumer products.

VARIABLE In a computer program, a character or group of characters that refers to a value and, in the execution of the program, corresponds to an address. A named quantity that can assume different alphabetic or numeric values.

VDT (VIDEO DISPLAY TERMINAL) An output device that converts electronic pulses into visual images.

VERIFY To determine whether an operation, such as transcription of data, has been accomplished accurately. To check the results of keypunching.

VIRTUAL STORAGE Computer memory expanded beyond primary memory capacity by the use of secondary storage devices and paging.

VLSI (VERY LARGE-SCALE INTEGRATED CIRCUIT) A solid state device containing hundreds of thousands of complex electronic circuits manufactured on one chip of silicon.

VOICE RECOGNITION The conversion of tones of human speech into analog wave forms and then into a digital form that can be processed by a computer system.

VOICE SYNTHESIZER A device that converts electronic pulses into audible tones that simulate the human voice.

VOLUME LABEL A magnetically recorded label at the beginning of a reel of tape to indicate the volume number of that reel.

WINCHESTER DISK A system in which data are recorded on metal disks enclosed in sealed containers that are permanently mounted on the disk drive.

WIRING BOARD A panel with terminals and groups of jumper wires used to program unit record machines.

WORD PROCESSING The recording and revising of words or phrases by machines to produce reports or documents.

WORK STATION A microcomputer terminal, usually equipped with secondary storage, that is part of a distributed data processing system.

Photo Credits

585

3-16   Courtesy of International Business Machines Corporation

3-17   Photograph Courtesy of Gould, Inc.

4-6   Photo Courtesy of Digital Equipment Corporation

4-7   Photo Courtesy of Hewlett-Packard Company

4-8   Voice Recognition Equipment by Interstate Voice Products

4-11   Voice Recognition Equipment by Interstate Voice Products

4-12   Harold W. Hoffman/Photo Researchers

4-13   Courtesy of Apple Computer, Inc.

4-14   Courtesy of Houston Instrument

4-15   Chuck O'Rear/West Light

4-16   Courtesy of International Business Machines Corporation

4-17   National Semiconductor Corporation

4-18   National Semiconductor Corporation

4-20   Caere Corporation

4-21   Caere Corporation

4-24   Courtesy Lundy Electronics & Systems, Inc.

4-27   Photo Courtesy of Sperry Corporation

4-28   Chuck O'Rear/West Light

4-29   Courtesy of International Business Machines Corporation

5-1   Courtesy of Motorola, Inc.

5-2   Hank Morgan/Rainbow

5-3   Courtesy Storage Technology Corporation

5-6   Courtesy Intel Corporation

6-10   Dan McCoy/Rainbow

6-16   Courtesy Storage Technology Corporation

6-18   Courtesy Maxell Corporation of America

6-19   ©Michael Melford/Wheeler Pictures

6-20   Jeff Smith, 1982

6-21   Courtesy of Amcodyne, Inc.

6-24   Courtesy of Apple Computer, Inc.

6-25   Courtesy of Apple Computer, Inc.

6-26   Courtesy of International Business Machines Corporation

6-28   *(left and right)* Courtesy Storage Technology Corporation

7-3   ©Joel Gordon, 1982

7-4   Courtesy of ECZEL, Supplies for Intelligent Machines

7-5   Courtesy of ECZEL, Supplies for Intelligent Machines

7-7   *(left and right)* Photographs Courtesy of Epson America, Inc.

7-9   Courtesy of Dataproducts Corporation

7-12   Courtesy of International Business Machines Corporation

7-13   Used with permission from the Association for Information and Image Management. ©1980 AIIM. All rights reserved.

7-14   *(left and right)* Photographs courtesy of Epson America, Inc.

7-15   Brent Bear/West Light

7-16   ©Joe McNally/Wheeler Pictures

7-17   *(top left and right)* Chuck O'Rear/West Light; *(bottom left)* R. Feldmann/Rainbow; *(bottom right)* ©Laurence M. Gartel, Photo Researchers

8-2   Courtesy Intel Corporation

8-3   Dan McCoy/Rainbow

8-4   Courtesy of Radio Shack, A Division of Tandy Corporation

8-5   Photo Courtesy of Hewlett-Packard Company

8-6   Courtesy of Honeywell, Inc.

8-8   Photo Courtesy of Digital Equipment Corporation

8-9   Courtesy of Commodore Electronics Limited

8-10   Courtesy of COMPAQ® Computer Corporation

8-11   Courtesy of Radio Shack, A Division of Tandy Corporation

8-12   Courtesy of Apple Computer, Inc.

8-13   Courtesy of Apple Computer, Inc.

8-14   Courtesy of Apple Computer, Inc.

8-15   Courtesy of International Business Machines Corporation

Solutions to Crossword Puzzles

CROSSWORD PUZZLE ON HARDWARE

```
L A G S  ·  P A T  ·  P U S H  ·  O V E R
C H A T  ·  A P A R  ·  O N E A  ·  L I R A
D A T A P R O C E S S I N G  ·  G R I N
S T E R O I D  ·  S U E T  ·  G O A T E E
   ·  S E T  ·  F I B S  ·  L A W  ·  U S E
R A M  ·  S Y N O D S  ·  C O R N E A  ·
I R I S  ·  C O N E  ·  H I N D  ·  S L I M
M I C A  ·  H I T  ·  B Y T E  ·  C A S T E
   ·  R A V E S  ·  F L E E  ·  P O U T E R
T K O  ·  I C E  ·  R O N  ·  M U D  ·  O M E
R E P A C K  ·  R I T A  ·  I N A I R  ·
A E R I E  ·  P I E S  ·  T L C  ·  D A S D
P L O D  ·  F I N S  ·  S H A H  ·  A G E D
   ·  C E D I N G  ·  S H I N E R  ·  E W E
T I E  ·  O A T  ·  A I R S  ·  D A M  ·
O N S E T S  ·  A B L E  ·  A C C U S E R
N A S A  ·  C A T H O D E R A Y T U B E
E N O S  ·  O L E O  ·  S T I R  ·  E R O S
S E R E  ·  S E E R  ·  ·  A D D  ·  S E N T
```

CROSSWORD PUZZLE ON SOFTWARE

```
S L E D  ·  S L I D  ·  R O T E  ·  A N S I
H I D E  ·  C O S A  ·  E R R S  ·  S A I L
A D U B  ·  H I N T  ·  M E A T  ·  S I L K
D O C U M E N T A T I O N  ·  B I L L S
   ·  G A M  ·  S I T  ·  S H A G  ·
A L I  ·  K E R N E L  ·  P L A N N E R S
L U C R E  ·  N E T  ·  B E A T  ·  E L I A
E L E E  ·  A A A  ·  L A S T S  ·  D A D S
C U R S O R  ·  P R E S T O  ·  A N N E S
   ·  E A R P  ·  O N I  ·  R O M A  ·
S T A R K  ·  S O L A C E  ·  D I M W I T
P R I V  ·  S E A L S  ·  R I D  ·  E I R E
A I D E  ·  P U T S  ·  P A N  ·  A S P E N
R O A D B E D S  ·  P A S C A L  ·  E S S
   ·  W A C O  ·  T A R  ·  G A T  ·
C O B O L  ·  C H A R A C T E R S E T S
A V E R  ·  L O O P  ·  D A R N  ·  A S E A
R E A D  ·  I D L E  ·  E M I T  ·  R A N G
E N D S  ·  D E E R  ·  D E M S  ·  S U D S
```

Index